The Masorah of the Former Prophets in the Leningrad Codex

Texts and Studies

14

Series Editor

H. A. G. Houghton

Texts and Studies is a series of monographs devoted to the study of Biblical and Patristic texts. Maintaining the highest scholarly standards, the series includes critical editions, studies of primary sources, and analyses of textual traditions.

The Masorah of the Former Prophets in the Leningrad Codex

Volume 2
Judges

David Marcus

2018

Gorgias Press LLC, 954 River Road, Piscataway, NJ, 08854, USA

www.gorgiaspress.com

2018

ISBN 978-1-4632-0599-7   ISSN 1935-6927

Library of Congress Cataloging-in-Publication Data

A Cataloging-in-Publication Record is available from the Library of Congress.

Printed in the United States of America

PREFACE

This volume on *Judges* is the second of a projected six-volume set on the Masorah of the Former Prophets in the Leningrad Codex. An explanation of how the entries are arranged, works cited and abbreviations may be found in the *Introduction* to the volume on *Joshua* (Gorgias Press, 2017).

JUDGES

JUDGES 1:1

וַיְהִ֗י אַחֲרֵי֙ מ֣וֹת יְהוֹשֻׁ֔עַ וַֽיִּשְׁאֲלוּ֙ בְּנֵ֣י יִשְׂרָאֵ֔ל בַּיהוָ֖ה לֵאמֹ֑ר מִ֣י יַעֲלֶה־לָּ֧נוּ אֶל־הַֽכְּנַעֲנִ֛י בַּתְּחִלָּ֖ה לְהִלָּ֥חֶם בּֽוֹ׃

1:1   וַיְהִ֗י אַחֲרֵי֙ מ֣וֹת

Four times   ד֗   Mp

Com.: See **Josh 1:1**.

1:1   וַֽיִּשְׁאֲלוּ֙...בַּיהוָ֖ה לֵאמֹ֑ר

שָׁאֲלָ֖ה לֵאמֹ֑ר *twice*   שא} שאלה לאמר ב֗   Mm

<u>Judg 1:1</u>   מי יעלה לנו
Judg 20:23   האוסיף

Com.: The Masorah notes the *two* occurrences of the phrase וַֽיִּשְׁאֲלוּ֙...בַּיהוָ֖ה followed by לֵאמֹ֑ר, to distinguish them from its *two* occurrences not followed by לֵאמֹ֑ר at Judg 20:27 and 1 Sam 10:22.

JUDGES 1:2

וַיֹּ֣אמֶר יְהוָ֔ה יְהוּדָ֖ה יַעֲלֶ֑ה הִנֵּ֛ה נָתַ֥תִּי אֶת־הָאָ֖רֶץ בְּיָדֽוֹ׃

1:2   יְהוּדָ֖ה יַעֲלֶ֑ה

Unique   ל֗   Mp

Com.: The Masorah notes the *sole* occurrence of יְהוּדָ֖ה with יַעֲלֶ֑ה, to distinguish it from its occurrence without יַעֲלֶ֑ה in the parallel passage at Judg 20:18.

JUDGES 1:3

וַיֹּ֨אמֶר יְהוּדָ֜ה לְשִׁמְע֣וֹן אָחִ֗יו עֲלֵ֤ה אִתִּי֙ בְגֽוֹרָלִ֔י וְנִֽלָּחֲמָה֙ בַּֽכְּנַעֲנִ֔י וְהָלַכְתִּ֧י גַם־אֲנִ֛י אִתְּךָ֖ בְּגוֹרָלֶ֑ךָ וַיֵּ֥לֶךְ אִתּ֖וֹ שִׁמְעֽוֹן׃

1:3   לְשִׁמְע֣וֹן אָחִ֗יו

Unique   ל֗   Mp

Com.: The Masorah notes the *sole* occurrence of this lemma with the prep. ל, to distinguish it from its occurrence without this prep. in v. 17.

1:3   בְּגוֹרָלִי

Unique   ל   Mp

Com.: The Masorah notes the *sole* occurrence of this lemma with the prep. בְּ, to distinguish it from its occurrence without this prep. at Ps 16:5.

Mᴸ, contrary to M (בְּגֹרָלִי), writes the lemma here plene ו (see Breuer, *The Biblical Text*, 55).

Both Mᶜ and Mᴬ read בְּגֹרָלִי, and both have a Mp note here reading *unique and defective* (ו).

This lemma is featured in a Masoretic list of words that occur *once* with a prep. בְּ (here), and *once* without (Ps 16:5); see Frensdorff, *Ochlah*, §6, and Díaz-Esteban, *Sefer Oklah we-Oklah*, §6.

1:3   וְנִלָּחֲמָה

Four times   ד   Mp

Judg 1:3; **11:6**; **1 Sam 17:10**; 1 Kgs 20:25

וְנִלָּחֲמָה *four times*, and their references   ונלחמה ד וסימנהון   Mm

Judg 1:3	ונלחמה בכנעני
Judg 11:6	בבני עמון
1 Sam 17:10	ונלחמה יחד
1 Kgs 20:25	ונלחמה אותם במישור

Com.: The Masorah notes the *four* occurrences of this lemma in the cohortative, to distinguish them from its *five* occurrences in the perf. consec. (וְנִלְחַם); see **1 Sam 8:20**.

1:3   בְּגוֹרָלֶךָ

Unique   ל   Mp

Com.: The Masorah notes the *sole* occurrence of this lemma with the prep. בְּ, to distinguish it from its occurrence without this prep. at Prov 1:14.

JUDGES 1:4

וַיַּעַל יְהוּדָה וַיִּתֵּן יְהוָה אֶת־הַכְּנַעֲנִי וְהַפְּרִזִּי בְּיָדָם וַיַּכּוּם בְּבֶזֶק עֲשֶׂרֶת אֲלָפִים אִישׁ׃

1:4   הַכְּנַעֲנִי וְהַפְּרִזִּי

Unique   לֹ   Mp

1–2   Deut 20:17; **Judg 1:4**

Com.: The Mp heading here, and in M[A], of *unique* is inexact since there are *two* occurrences of this lemma. The note more precisely should have read *unique in the book*. M[C] has no note here.

The Masorah notes the *two* occurrences of this lemma written with a וּ cj. on הַפְּרִזִּי, to distinguish them from its *three* occurrences with a וּ cj. on both words (וְהַכְּנַעֲנִי וְהַפְּרִזִּי), and from its *sole* occurrence without a cj. on either word (הַכְּנַעֲנִי הַפְּרִזִּי) at Josh 9:1.

Dotan/Reich (*Masora Thesaurus, ad loc.*) suggest that the meaning of *unique* here is that the phrase הַכְּנַעֲנִי וְהַפְּרִזִּי in this verse does not occur along with other nations as it does in Deut 20:17.

1:4   וַיַּכּוּם

Eleven times   יֹא   Mp

Com.: See **Josh 7.5**.

JUDGES 1:6

וַיָּנָס אֲדֹנִי בֶזֶק וַיִּרְדְּפוּ אַחֲרָיו וַיֹּאחֲזוּ אֹתוֹ וַיְקַצְּצוּ אֶת־בְּהֹנוֹת יָדָיו וְרַגְלָיו׃

1:6   וַיְקַצְּצוּ

Twice   בֹ   Mp

Judg 1:6; 2 Sam 4:12

Com.: The Masorah notes the *two* occurrences of this lemma in the pl., possibly to distinguish them from its *three* occurrences in the sg. (וַיְקַצֵּץ).

1:6 בְּהֹנוֹת

Twice בֹּ Mp

Judg 1:6; 1:7

> ### JUDGES 1:7
> וַיֹּ֣אמֶר אֲדֹנִי־בֶ֗זֶק שִׁבְעִ֣ים ׀ מְלָכִ֡ים בְּהֹנוֹת֩ יְדֵיהֶ֨ם וְרַגְלֵיהֶ֜ם מְקֻצָּצִ֗ים הָי֤וּ מְלַקְּטִים֙ תַּ֣חַת שֻׁלְחָנִ֔י
> כַּאֲשֶׁ֤ר עָשִׂ֙יתִי֙ כֵּ֣ן שִׁלַּם־לִ֣י אֱלֹהִ֔ים וַיְבִיאֻ֥הוּ יְרוּשָׁלַ֖͏ִם וַיָּ֥מׇת שָֽׁם׃ פ

1:7 בְּהֹנוֹת

Twice בֹּ Mp

Judg 1:6; 1:7

1:7 מְקֻצָּצִים

Unique לֹ Mp

1:7 מְלַקְּטִים

Twice בֹּ Mp

Judg 1:7; Jer 7:18

מְלַקְּטִים *twice*, and their references   מלקטים בֹ וסימנהון   Mm

Judg 1:7	היו מלקטים תחת
Jer 7:18	הבנים מלקטים עצים

1:7 שִׁלַּם

Unique לֹ Mp

Com.: The Masorah notes the *sole* occurrence of this lemma in the perf., to distinguish it from its more numerous occurrences (6x) in the infin. (שַׁלֵּם).

1:7   לִי אֱלֹהִים

Eleven times   יֹֽא   Mp

1–5	Gen 4:25; 21:6; 48:9; **Judg 1:7; 1 Sam 22:3**
6–10	**2 Sam 3:35**; 19:14; **1 Kgs 2:23; 20:10; 2 Kgs 6:31**
11	<u>**Ps 51:12**</u>

Com.: The Masorah notes the *eleven* occurrences of לִי with אֱלֹהִים, to distinguish them from its *six* occurrences with the Tetragrammaton (לִי יְהוָה).

1:7   וַיְבִאֻהוּ

Seven times   זֿ   Mp

1–5	<u>**Judg 1:7**</u>; **1 Sam 5:1** (וַיְבִאֻהוּ); 2 Kgs 23:30 (וַיְבִאֻהוּ); **Jer 26:23** (וַיְבִאֻהוּ); **Ezek 19:4** (וַיְבִאֻהוּ)
6–7	**Ezek 19:9** (וַיְבִאֻהוּ); 2 Chr 22:9 (וַיְבִאֻהוּ)

וַיְבִאֻהוּ   *seven times*   זֿ [ויביאהו] (ויבאהו)   Mm

1–5	<u>Judg 1:7</u>	אדני בזק
	1 Sam 5:1	ופלשתים
	<Ezek 19:4>	
	Ezek 19:9	בסוגר
	{Ezek 19:8}	{ממדינות}
	2 Kgs 23:30	וירכבהו
6–7	2 Chr 22:9	אחזיהו
	Jer 26:23	אוריהו

Com.: The Masorah notes the *seven* occurrences of this lemma, written plene and defective second י (וַיְבִיאֻהוּ/וַיְבִאֻהוּ), in the pl., to distinguish them from its more numerous occurrences (13x), written plene and defective second י, in the sg. (וַיְבִיאֵהוּ/וַיְבִאֵהוּ); see Ognibeni, *'Oklah*, §1K.

All the highlighted Mp notes read *seven times* except for the one at **1 Sam 5:1**, which reads *six times defective* (second י) because it does not include the form here at Judg 1:7 that is written plene second י (וַיְבִיאֻהוּ).

In the Mm, in place of a catchword for the Ezek 19:4 reference, a catchword מְמְדִינוֹת from Ezek 19:8 has mistakenly been written.

JUDGES 1:8

וַיִּלָּחֲמ֤וּ בְנֵֽי־יְהוּדָה֙ בִּירֽוּשָׁלִַ֔ם וַיִּלְכְּד֣וּ אוֹתָ֔הּ וַיַּכּ֖וּהָ לְפִי־חָ֑רֶב וְאֶת־הָעִ֖יר שִׁלְּח֥וּ בָאֵֽשׁ׃

1:8   וַיַּכּ֖וּהָ

Four times   ד   Mp

Josh 10:35; 10:37; **Judg 1:8**; 2 Kgs 3:25

Com.: The Masorah notes the *four* occurrences of this lemma with this sfx., possibly to distinguish them from its more numerous occurrences (50x) without this sfx. (וַיַּכּוּ).

1:8   וְאֶת־הָעִ֖יר

Eight times   ח   Mp

1–5   **Judg 1:8**; 18:27; <u>**2 Kgs 20:6**</u>; <u>**Isa 38:6**</u>; **Jer 19:11**
6–8   **Jer 23:39**; 26:6; 38:23

וְאֶת הָעִיר *eight times*   ואת העיר ח   Mm

1–5	<u>Judg 1:8</u>	וילחמו בני יהודה
	Judg 18:27	והמה לקחו
	וְהֹסַפְתִּ֥י עַל־יָמֶ֖יךָ *of Kings* (<u>2 Kgs 20:6</u>)	(והוספתי) [והספתי] על ימיך דמלכים
	וּמִכַּ֥ף מֶֽלֶךְ־אַשּׁ֖וּר *of Isaiah* (<u>Isa 38:6</u>)	ומכף מלך אשור דישעיהו
	Jer 26:6	ונתתי את הבית
6–8	Jer 19:11	ככה
	Jer 23:39	ונטשתי
	Jer 38:23	ואת כל נשיך

Com.: The Masorah notes the *eight* occurrences of this lemma with a ו cj., to distinguish them from its more numerous occurrences (46x) without a cj.

The addition *of Kings* to the catchwords of the 2 Kgs 20:6 reference is to distinguish that verse from its parallel in Isa 38:6. Similarly, the addition *of Isaiah* to the catchwords of the Isa 38:6 reference is to distinguish that verse from its parallel in 2 Kgs 20:6.

1:8   שִׁלְּח֥וּ

Four times   ד   Mp

Judg 1:8; 20:48; Jer 34:11; **2 Chr 24:23**

Com.: The Masorah notes the *four* occurrences of this lemma with a *dageš* in the ל (*piel* perf.), to distinguish them from its more numerous occurrences (8x) without a *dageš* (שִׁלְחוּ), and from its *three* occurrences in the pausal form שִׁלֵּחוּ; see directly below at **Judg 1:25**.

JUDGES 1:9

וְאַחַ֗ר יָֽרְדוּ֙ בְּנֵ֣י יְהוּדָ֔ה לְהִלָּחֵ֖ם בַּֽכְּנַעֲנִ֑י יוֹשֵׁ֣ב הָהָ֔ר וְהַנֶּ֖גֶב וְהַשְּׁפֵלָֽה׃

1:9   יוֹשֵׁ֣ב

Fourteen times plene in the book   יד מל בסיפֿ   Mp

1–4   **Judg 1:9**; 1:17; 4:2; **11:21**

Com.: The Mp heading here of *fourteen times* is incorrect since there are only *four* occurrences of this lemma in the book. It is most probable that the addition of the י in the numeral of the note (יד) is erroneous; see Dotan/Reich, *Masora Thesaurus*, *ad loc.*

The Masorah notes the *four* occurrences of this lemma in the book written plene ו, to distinguish them from its *six* occurrences in the book written defective ו (יֹשֵׁב).

The Mp heading to **Judg 11:21** correctly reads *four times plene in the book* as do both M[C] and M[A] here.

JUDGES 1:11

וַיֵּ֣לֶךְ מִשָּׁ֔ם אֶל־יוֹשְׁבֵ֖י דְּבִ֑יר וְשֵׁם־דְּבִ֥יר לְפָנִ֖ים קִרְיַת־סֵֽפֶר׃

1:11   יוֹשְׁבֵ֖י

Thirty-four times plene   לד מל   Mp

Com.: See **Josh 15:63**.

JUDGES 1:14

וַיְהִ֣י בְּבוֹאָ֗הּ וַתְּסִיתֵ֙הוּ֙ לִשְׁא֤וֹל מֵֽאֵת־אָבִ֙יהָ֙ הַשָּׂדֶ֔ה וַתִּצְנַ֖ח מֵעַ֣ל הַחֲמ֑וֹר וַיֹּֽאמֶר־לָ֥הּ כָּלֵ֖ב מַה־לָּֽךְ׃

1:14   וַתְּסִיתֵ֙הוּ֙

Twice   בׄ   Mp

Com.: See **Josh 15:18**.

1:14   לִשְׁאוֹל

לִשְׁאֹל *six times* defective*   לשאול וּ חס   Mm

1–5	וַתְּסִיתֵהוּ *of Judges* (Judg 1:14)	ותסיתהו דשפ
	1 Sam 12:19	כי יספנו על (כן) [כל]
	לְשָׁלוֹם *of Samuel* (2 Sam 8:10)	לשלום דשמוֹא
	Jer 15:5	ומי יסור לשאל
	Ps 78:18	וינסו אל בלבבם
6	Job 31:30	לשאל באלה

Com.: The Masorah notes the *six* occurrences of this lemma written defective וֹ, to distinguish them from its more numerous occurrences (12x) written plene וּ (לִשְׁאוֹל).

This distinction is implied in the Mm in the additional notation *of Judges* to the Judg 1:14 reference, which distinguishes it from the parallel passage in Josh 15:8, where the lemma occurs written plene וּ as לִשְׁאוֹל. It is also implied in the additional notation *of Samuel* to the 2 Sam 8:10 reference, which distinguishes it from the parallel passage in 1 Chr 18:10, where the lemma occurs in the *kǝtîb* written plene וּ as לשאול.

* M^L, contrary to M (לִשְׁאֹל), only has *five* occurrences of this lemma since it writes the form here plene וּ (לִשְׁאוֹל); see Breuer, *The Biblical Text*, 56. However, the Mp headings at 1 Sam 12:19, 2 Sam 8:10, Jer 15:5, and the Mm heading and listings here, and at 2 Sam 8:10 and Ps 78:18, of *six times* support the enumeration inherent in the text of M.

Both M^C and M^A read לִשְׁאֹל, and both have a Mp note here reading *six times defective*.

1:14   אָבִיהָ הַשָּׂדֶה

Unique   לֹ   Mp

Com.: This lemma is featured in a Masoretic list of two-word phrases that occur *once* with the def. article within the phrase (here), and *once* without this def. article (Josh 15:18); see Frensdorff, *Ochlah*, §3, and Díaz-Esteban, *Sefer Oklah we-Oklah*, §3.

1:14   וַתִּצְנַח

Three times   גֹ   Mp

Josh 15:18; Judg 1:14; 4:21

JUDGES 1:15

וַתֹּאמֶר לוֹ הָבָה־לִּי בְרָכָה כִּי אֶרֶץ הַנֶּגֶב נְתַתָּנִי וְנָתַתָּה לִי גֻּלֹּת מָיִם וַיִּתֶּן־לָהּ כָּלֵב אֵת גֻּלֹּת עִלִּית
וְאֵת גֻּלֹּת תַּחְתִּית: פ

1:15   נְתַתָּנִי

Twice   ב֗   Mp

Josh 15:19; Judg 1:15

1:15   גֻּלֹּת[2]

Seven times defective   ז֗ חס֗   Mp

Com.: See **Josh 15:19**[a].

JUDGES 1:16

וּבְנֵי קֵינִי חֹתֵן מֹשֶׁה עָלוּ מֵעִיר הַתְּמָרִים אֶת־בְּנֵי יְהוּדָה מִדְבַּר יְהוּדָה אֲשֶׁר בְּנֶגֶב עֲרָד וַיֵּלֶךְ
וַיֵּשֶׁב אֶת־הָעָם:

1:16   וּבְנֵי קֵינִי

Unique   ל   Mp

Com.: This lemma is featured in a Masoretic list of words that occurs only *once* with a preceding וּבְנֵי; see Frensdorff, *Ochlah*, §366.

1:16   בְּנֶגֶב עֲרָד

Unique   ל   Mp

1:16   וַיֵּלֶךְ וַיֵּשֶׁב אֶת

Unique   ל   Mp

Com.: The Masorah notes the *sole* occurrence of this lemma with אֶת, to distinguish it from its occurrence without אֶת at 1 Kgs 17:5.

Com.: In M[L] two circelli have been placed on this phrase, but in M[C] these are placed on וַיֵּשֶׁב אֶת־הָעָם. *BHS* has extended the lemma to include the following word (וַיֵּלֶךְ
וַיֵּשֶׁב אֶת־הָעָם).

JUDGES 1:17

וַיֵּ֤לֶךְ יְהוּדָה֙ אֶת־שִׁמְע֣וֹן אָחִ֔יו וַיַּכּ֕וּ אֶת־הַֽכְּנַעֲנִ֖י יוֹשֵׁ֣ב צְפַ֑ת וַיַּחֲרִ֣ימוּ אוֹתָ֔הּ וַיִּקְרָ֥א אֶת־שֵׁם־הָעִ֖יר
חׇרְמָֽה׃

1:17	צְפַת
Unique	ל Mp

1:17	וַיִּקְרָ֥א אֶת־שֵׁם־הָעִ֖יר
Twice	ב֞ Mp

Judg 1:17; 1 Kgs 16:24

Com.: The Masorah notes the *two* occurrences of this phrase with the accusative
particle אֶת, to distinguish them from the sole occurrence of this phrase without אֶת
at Gen 4:17.

In M^L there are only two circelli on this four-word phrase, one on וַיִּקְרָ֥א אֶת and one
on שֵׁם־הָעִיר. With *four- or five-word* phrases it is not unusual for only *two* circelli to be
given; see **Josh 1:6** and *passim*.

JUDGES 1:19

וַיְהִ֤י יְהוָה֙ אֶת־יְהוּדָ֔ה וַיֹּ֖רֶשׁ אֶת־הָהָ֑ר כִּ֣י לֹ֤א לְהוֹרִישׁ֙ אֶת־יֹשְׁבֵ֣י הָעֵ֔מֶק כִּי־רֶ֥כֶב בַּרְזֶ֖ל לָהֶֽם׃

1:19	וַיְהִי יְהוָה
Six times	ו Mp

1–5	Gen 39:2; 39:21; Josh 6:27; **Judg 1:19**; 2 Sam 22:19
6–8	Ps 18:19; 94:22; **2 Chr 17:3**

The Mp heading here and at 2 Chr 17:3 of *six times* is inexact since there are *eight*
occurrences of this lemma.

The note more precisely should have read, as it does in M^C, either *six times at the
beginning of a verse* (all the above references except 2 Sam 22:19 and Ps 18:19), or *six
times in the Prophets and Writings* (all the above references except Gen 39:2 and 39:21).
M^A has no note here.

The Masorah notes the *eight* occurrences of this lemma with a ו consec., to distinguish
them from its *five* occurrences without this ו (יְהִי יְהוָה).

1:19   וַיֹּרֶשׁ

Twice defective   ב֗ חס   Mp

Com.: See **Josh 15:14**.

JUDGES 1:21

וְאֶת־הַיְבוּסִי יֹשֵׁב יְרוּשָׁלִַם לֹא הוֹרִישׁוּ בְּנֵי בִנְיָמִן וַיֵּשֶׁב הַיְבוּסִי אֶת־בְּנֵי בִנְיָמִן בִּירוּשָׁלַם עַד הַיּוֹם הַזֶּה׃ ס

1:21   יֹשֵׁב יְרוּשָׁלִַם

Seven times   ז֗   Mp

1–5   **Judg 1:21**; **Isa 5:3** (יוֹשֵׁב); 8:14 (לְיוֹשֵׁב); 22:21 (לְיוֹשֵׁב); Zech 12:7
6–7   Zech 12:8 (יוֹשֵׁב); 12:10 (יוֹשֵׁב)

Com.: The Masorah notes the *seven* occurrences of יֹשֵׁב in various forms with יְרוּשָׁלַם, to distinguish them from its *four* occurrences in various forms with בִּירוּשָׁלַם (יוֹשֵׁב/יֹשֵׁב בִּירוּשָׁלַם).

JUDGES 1:22

וַיַּעֲלוּ בֵית־יוֹסֵף גַּם־הֵם בֵּית־אֵל וַיהוָה עִמָּם׃

1:22   גַּם־הֵם

Three times in the Prophets   ג֗ בנב   Mp

Judg 1:22; **Ezek 10:16**; 31:17

Com.: The Masorah notes the *three* occurrences of this lemma in the Prophets, to distinguish them from its more numerous occurrences (8x) in the Torah and Writings.

JUDGES 1:23

וַיָּתִירוּ בֵית־יוֹסֵף בְּבֵית־אֵל וְשֵׁם־הָעִיר לְפָנִים לוּז׃

1:23   וַיָּתִירוּ

Unique   ל֗   Mp

JUDGES 1:24

וַיִּרְאוּ֙ הַשֹּׁ֣מְרִ֔ים אִ֖ישׁ יוֹצֵ֣א מִן־הָעִ֑יר וַיֹּ֣אמְרוּ ל֗וֹ הַרְאֵ֤נוּ נָא֙ אֶת־מְב֣וֹא הָעִ֔יר וְעָשִׂ֥ינוּ עִמְּךָ֖ חָֽסֶד׃

1:24   יוֹצֵ֣א

Nine times plene   ט מל֓   Mp

Com.: See **Josh 6:1**.

1:24   הַרְאֵ֤נוּ

Twice   בֿ   Mp

Judg 1:24; Ps 85:8

Com.: The Masorah notes the *two* occurrences of this lemma with the pl. sfx., possibly to distinguish them from its *single* occurrence with the sg. sfx. (הַרְאֵ֫נִי) at Exod 33:18

JUDGES 1:25

וַיַּרְאֵ֕ם אֶת־מְב֣וֹא הָעִ֔יר וַיַּכּ֥וּ אֶת־הָעִ֖יר לְפִי־חָ֑רֶב וְאֶת־הָאִ֥ישׁ וְאֶת־כָּל־מִשְׁפַּחְתּ֖וֹ שִׁלֵּֽחוּ׃

1:25   וְאֶת־כָּל־מִשְׁפַּחְתּ֖וֹ

Twice   בֿ   Mp

Com.: The Mp heading here of *twice* is incorrect since this is the *only* occurrence of this lemma.

Neither M^C nor M^A has a note on this lemma here.

1:25   שִׁלֵּֽחוּ

Three times   גֿ   Mp

Judg 1:25; **Job 30:11**; 30:12

שְׁלֵחוּ *three times*, and their references   שלחו גׄ וסימנהון   Mm

<u>Judg 1:25</u>	ואת כל משפחתו שלחו
Job 30:11	ורסן (מתעה) [מפני]
Job 30:12	רגלי

Com.: The Masorah notes the *three* occurrences of this lemma in pause with a *ṣerê* under the ל, to distinguish them from its *four* occurrences with a *šəwâ* under the ל (שְׁלְחוּ), *one* of which occurs in v. 8; see Ognibeni, *'Oklah*, §300, and **Judg 1:8**.

In the Mm, at the Job 30:11 reference, the catchwords וְרֶסֶן מִפְּנֵי were mistakenly written as וְרֶסֶן מַתְעֶה, a phrase that occurs in Isa 30:28.

JUDGES 1:26

וַיֵּלֶךְ הָאִישׁ אֶרֶץ הַחִתִּים וַיִּבֶן עִיר וַיִּקְרָא שְׁמָהּ לוּז הוּא שְׁמָהּ עַד הַיּוֹם הַזֶּה: פ

1:26   וַיֵּלֶךְ הָאִישׁ

Twice   בׄ   Mp

Judg 1:26; 17:8

Com.: The Masorah notes the *two* occurrences of וַיֵּלֶךְ with הָאִישׁ, to distinguish them from its *two* occurrences with אִישׁ (וַיֵּלֶךְ אִישׁ) at <u>Exod 2:1</u> and Ruth 1:1.

1:26   הַחִתִּים

Five times   הׄ   Mp

1–5   Josh 1:4; **Judg 1:26; 1 Kgs 10:29; 2 Kgs 7:6; 2 Chr 1:17**

Com.: The Masorah notes the *five* occurrences of the pl. form הַחִתִּים referring to the Hittites, to distinguish them from its more numerous occurrences (31x) in the sing. (הַחִתִּי).

1:26   וַיִּקְרָא שְׁמָהּ

Three times   גׄ   Mp

<u>Gen 26:21</u>; 26:22; Judg 1:26

Com.: The Masorah notes the *three* occurrences of this phrase without אֶת, to distinguish them from its *two* occurrences with אֶת at **1 Sam 7:12** and **2 Kgs 14:7**.

JUDGES 1:27

וְלֹא־הוֹרִישׁ מְנַשֶּׁה אֶת־בֵּית־שְׁאָן וְאֶת־בְּנוֹתֶיהָ וְאֶת־תַּעְנַךְ וְאֶת־בְּנֹתֶיהָ וְאֶת־יֹשֵׁב דוֹר וְאֶת־בְּנוֹתֶיהָ וְאֶת־יוֹשְׁבֵי יִבְלְעָם וְאֶת־בְּנֹתֶיהָ וְאֶת־יוֹשְׁבֵי מְגִדּוֹ וְאֶת־בְּנוֹתֶיהָ וַיּוֹאֶל הַכְּנַעֲנִי לָשֶׁבֶת בָּאָרֶץ הַזֹּאת:

1:27   וְלֹא־הוֹרִישׁ

Unique   ל   Mp

Com.: The Masorah notes the *sole* occurrence of this lemma with a ו cj., to distinguish it from its *four* occurrences without a cj., all *four* of which occur in this chapter in vv. 29, 30, 31, and 33.

1:27   בְּנֹתֶיהָ[1]

Twice in the book   ב בסיפֿ   Mp

Judg 1:27[a]; 1:27[b]

Com.: The Masorah notes the *two* occurrences of this lemma with defective ו that occur in this book, to distinguish them from its more numerous occurrences (5x) in other books (Numbers and Chronicles).

1:27   יֹשֵׁב

Read   יֹשְׁבֵי   יושבי ק   Mp

Com.: The *kəṯîḇ* (ישב), and the *qərê* (יוֹשְׁבֵי) are examples of *kəṯîḇ/qərê* variations, where a word ending in a י is read even though it is not written; see Frensdorff, *Ochlah*, §126, Díaz-Esteban, *Sefer Oklah we-Oklah*, §110, and Gordis, *The Biblical Text*, 97.

1:27   וְאֶת־יוֹשְׁבֵי[2]

Nine times   ט   Mp

1–5   **Josh 17:11** (יֹשְׁבֵי); **Judg 1:27[a]** (יוֹשְׁבֵי, *qərê*); **1:27[b]**; 1:27[c]; 1:30
6–9   **Judg 1:31; 1:33** (יֹשְׁבֵי); 2 Chr 21:13 (יֹשְׁבֵי); 2 Chr 32:22 (יֹשְׁבֵי)

וְאֶת־יוֹשְׁבֵי *nine times*, and their references		ואת יושבי ט וסימנהון	Mm

1–5	Josh 17:11	ויהי למנשה
	Judg 1:27[a] *three times* in it	ולא הוריש מנשה ג בו
	(Judg 1:27[b]; Judg 1:27[c])	
	Judg 1:30	זבולן
6–9	Judg 1:31	אשר
	Judg 1:33	נפתלי
	2 Chr 32:22	ויושע יהוה
	2 Chr 21:13	ותזנה את יהודה

Com.: The Masorah notes the *nine* occurrences of this lemma, written plene and defective וֹ, with אֶת, to distinguish them from its more numerous occurrences (29x), written plene and defective וֹ, without אֶת (וְיוֹשְׁבֵי/וְיֹשְׁבֵי).

This distinction is implied in the Mm of 2 Chr 32:22, where there is an addition *of the first time in the verse* to the catchword of the Josh 17:11 reference, to distinguish the occurrence of the lemma וְאֶת־יוֹשְׁבֵי from the *three* occurrences later on in the verse of וְיֹשְׁבֵי.

1:27 וַיֹּאֶל

Seven times וֹ Mp

Com.: See **Josh 17:12**.

JUDGES 1:28

וַיְהִי כִּי־חָזַק יִשְׂרָאֵל וַיָּשֶׂם אֶת־הַכְּנַעֲנִי לָמַס וְהוֹרֵישׁ לֹא הוֹרִישׁוֹ׃ ס

1:28 חָזַק

Five times הֹ Mp

1–5 **Gen 41:57**; **47:20**; **Judg 1:28**; **2 Kgs 3:26**; **1 Chr 21:4**

Com.: The Masorah notes the *five* occurrences of this lemma with a *pataḥ* under the זֹ, to distinguish them from its more numerous occurrences (15x) with a *qameṣ* under the זֹ (חָזָק).

This distinction is implied in the headings of the Mp at Gen 41:57, 47:20 and 1 Chr 21:4 (הֹ), and in the headings of the Mm at Gen 41:57 and 1 Chr 21:4 (ה פתח), where the form occurring *five times* with a *pataḥ* under the זֹ is contrasted with forms with another vowel under the זֹ, which can only be a *qameṣ*, see also Dotan/Reich, *Masora Thesaurus, ad loc.*

1:28 וְהוֹרִישׁ

Unique plene   ל מלֹ   ל   Mp

Com.: The Masorah notes the *sole* occurrence of this lemma written plene ׳, to distinguish it from its *two* occurrences written defective ׳ (וְהוֹרִשׁ) at Josh 3:10 and **17:13**.

JUDGES 1:29

וְאֶפְרַ֗יִם לֹ֤א הוֹרִישׁ֙ אֶת־הַֽכְּנַעֲנִ֔י הַיּוֹשֵׁ֣ב בְּגָ֑זֶר וַיֵּ֧שֶׁב הַֽכְּנַעֲנִ֛י בְּקִרְבּ֖וֹ בְּגָֽזֶר׃ פ

1:29 וְאֶפְרַיִם

Five times   ה   Mp

1–5   **Judg 1:29**; **Jer 31:9**; Hos 5:5; **9:13**; 10:11

וְאֶפְרַיִם *five times*, and their references   ואפרים ה וסימנהון   Mm

1–5   Judg 1:29   (ולא) [לא] הוריש
      Jer 31:9   בכרי
      Hos 9:13   להוציא
      Hos 5:5   וישראל
      Hos 10:11   מלמדה

Com.: The Masorah notes the *five* occurrences of this lemma standing alone, to distinguish them from its more numerous occurrences (8x) when it is preceded by מְנַשֶּׁה (מְנַשֶּׁה וְאֶפְרַיִם).

This distinction is implied in the Mp heading at Hos 5:5 and the Mm at Jer 31:9, which reads *five times and similarly all* מְנַשֶּׁה וְאֶפְרַיִם, that is, וְאֶפְרַיִם occurs *five times* as well as *all times* with a preceding מְנַשֶּׁה.

The Mm at Hos 9:13 notes that *two* of these *five* occurrences of וְאֶפְרַיִם (here and Hos 10:11) are at the beginning of a verse.

JUDGES 1:30

זְבוּלֻן לֹא הוֹרִישׁ אֶת־יוֹשְׁבֵי קִטְרֹון וְאֶת־יוֹשְׁבֵי נַהֲלֹל וַיֵּשֶׁב הַכְּנַעֲנִי בְּקִרְבֹּו וַיִּהְיוּ לָמַס׃ ס

1:30   קִטְרֹון

Unique   ל   Mp

1:30   נַהֲלֹל

Unique   ל   Mp

Com.: The Masorah notes the *sole* occurrence of this lemma with a *ḥolem*, to distinguish it from its *sole* occurrence with a *qameṣ* (נַהֲלָל) at **Josh 21:35**.

JUDGES 1:31

אָשֵׁר לֹא הוֹרִישׁ אֶת־יֹשְׁבֵי עַכֹּו וְאֶת־יוֹשְׁבֵי צִידֹון וְאֶת־אַחְלָב וְאֶת־אַכְזִיב וְאֶת־חֶלְבָּה וְאֶת־אֲפִיק וְאֶת־רְחֹב׃

1:31   עַכֹּו

Unique   ל   Mp

1:31   וְאֶת־יוֹשְׁבֵי

Nine times   ט׳   Mp

Com.: See directly above at **Judg 1:27**.

1:31   אַחְלָב

Unique   ל   Mp

1:31   חֶלְבָּה

Unique   ל   Mp

1–2   Lev 4:35; **Judg 1:31**

Com.: The Mp heading here, and in M^C and M^A, of *unique* is inexact since there are *two* occurrences of this lemma. The note more precisely should have read *unique in the book*.

Some other mss. and printed editions, such as *Miqra'ot Gedolot*, read the form at Lev. 4:35 with a *mappîq* (חֶלְבָּהּ); see *BHS, ad loc.*, and the lemma here is featured in a Masoretic list of *hapax legomena* that do not end in a *mappîq* (which assumes that, in contrast, the form in Lev. 4:35 does have a *mappîq*); see Frensdorff, *Ochlah*, §43, and Díaz-Esteban, *Sefer Oklah we-Oklah*, §44.

1:31	אֲפִיק

Unique	ל	Mp

	JUDGES 1:32
	וַיֵּשֶׁב הָאָשֵׁרִי בְּקֶרֶב הַכְּנַעֲנִי יֹשְׁבֵי הָאָרֶץ כִּי לֹא הוֹרִישׁוֹ׃ ס

1:32	הָאָשֵׁרִי

Unique	ל	Mp

	JUDGES 1:33
	נַפְתָּלִי לֹא־הוֹרִישׁ אֶת־יֹשְׁבֵי בֵית־שֶׁמֶשׁ וְאֶת־יֹשְׁבֵי בֵית־עֲנָת וַיֵּשֶׁב בְּקֶרֶב הַכְּנַעֲנִי יֹשְׁבֵי הָאָרֶץ וְיֹשְׁבֵי בֵית־שֶׁמֶשׁ וּבֵית עֲנָת הָיוּ לָהֶם לָמַס׃ ס

1:33	וְאֶת־יֹשְׁבֵי

Nine times	ט	Mp

Com.: See directly above at **Judg 1:27**.

	JUDGES 1:34
	וַיִּלְחֲצוּ הָאֱמֹרִי אֶת־בְּנֵי־דָן הָהָרָה כִּי־לֹא נְתָנוֹ לָרֶדֶת לָעֵמֶק׃

1:34	וַיִּלְחֲצוּ

Unique	ל	Mp

1:34	הָהָרָה

Thirteen times	יג	Mp

Com.: See **Josh 2:16**.

1:34   נָתְנוּ

Five times   הֹ   Mp

1–5   **Gen 31:7; <u>Judg 1:34</u>; 15:1**; 1 Sam 18:2; **23:14**

———————————

נָתְנוּ *five times*   נתנו ה   Mm

1–5   Gen 31:7   ואביכן
       <u>Judg 1:34</u>   וילחצו
       Judg 15:1   (מימיהם) [מימים]
       1 Sam 18:2   (ויקהו) [ויקחהו]
       1 Sam 23:14   במצדות

And *once* (וְנָתְנוּ): Deut 21:10   וחד ונתנו יהוה אלהיך בידך

Com.: The Masorah notes the *five* occurrences of this lemma with a masc. sfx., to distinguish them from its more numerous occurrences (53x) as a 3rd pers. pl. (נָתְנוּ).

This lemma occurs in the ms. in folio 136v, but the Mm note appears on the bottom of the following folio 137r.

JUDGES 1:35

וַיּוֹאֶל הָאֱמֹרִי לָשֶׁבֶת בְּהַר־חֶרֶס בְּאַיָּלוֹן וּבְשַׁעַלְבִים וַתִּכְבַּד יַד בֵּית־יוֹסֵף וַיִּהְיוּ לָמַס:

1:35   וַיּוֹאֶל

Seven times   זֹ   Mp

Com.: See **Josh 17:12.**

1:35   בְּאַיָּלוֹן

Nine times   טֹ   Mp

Com.: See **Josh 10:12.**

1:35   וּבְשַׁעַלְבִים

Twice   בֹ   Mp

Judg 1:35; <u>1 Kgs 4:9</u>

Com.: This lemma is featured in a Masoretic list of doublets that start with בו; see Frensdorff, *Ochlah*, §62, and Díaz-Esteban, *Sefer Oklah we-Oklah*, §63.

JUDGES 1:36

וּגְבוּל הָאֱמֹרִי מִמַּעֲלֵה עַקְרַבִּים מֵהַסֶּלַע וָמָעְלָה: פ

1:36   מֵהַסֶּלַע

Unique   ל   Mp

Com.: This lemma is featured in a Masoretic list of words occurring only *once* with the inseparable prep. מ, whereas normally it is with the separable prep. מִן as in מִן הַסֶּלַע (Num 20:8 and Judg 15:13); see Frensdorff, *Ochlah*, §195, and Ognibeni, *'Oklah*, §150.

JUDGES 2:1

וַיַּעַל מַלְאַךְ־יְהוָה מִן־הַגִּלְגָּל אֶל־הַבֹּכִים פ וַיֹּאמֶר אַעֲלֶה אֶתְכֶם מִמִּצְרַיִם וָאָבִיא אֶתְכֶם אֶל־
הָאָרֶץ אֲשֶׁר נִשְׁבַּעְתִּי לַאֲבֹתֵיכֶם וָאֹמַר לֹא־אָפֵר בְּרִיתִי אִתְּכֶם לְעוֹלָם:

2:1   אַעֲלֶה

Eight times   ח   Mp

1–5   **Exod 3:17; Judg 2:1; 1 Sam 28:11; 2 Sam 24:24**; Jer 30:17
6–8   **Jer 46:8; Ps 66:15; 137:6**

אַעֲלֶה *eight times*, and their references   אעלה ח וסימנהון   Mm

1–5	Exod 3:17	(וָאֹמַר =)	אמר
	Judg 2:1	(מַלְאַךְ =)	מלאכה
	1 Sam 28:11	(הָאִשָּׁה =)	לאתתה
	2 Sam 24:24	(אֲרַוְנָה =)	דארונה
	Jer 30:17	(אֲרֻכָה =)	אריך
6–8	Jer 46:8	(אֲכַסֶּה =)	למכסויה
	Ps 66:15	(קְטֹרֶת =)	קוטרתה
	Ps 137:6	(יְרוּשָׁלִַם =)	דירושלם

Com.: The Masorah notes the *eight* occurrences of this lemma in the *hiphil*, to distinguish them from its more numerous occurrences (15x) in the *qal* (אֶעֱלֶה); see Ognibeni, *'Oklah*, §8B.

This distinction is implied in the headings of the Mp at Ps 137:6 (חֲ), and of the Mm at Exod 3:17, which reads *eight times with pataḥ*, thereby assuming a contrast with a form with a different vowel under the א or ע, which can only be a *sĕḡôl*.

The catchwords in the Mm are given in the form of an Aramaic mnemonic: "The angel said to his wife that the ark is long enough to cover the incense of Jerusalem"; see Marcus, *Scribal Wit*, 54–56.

This lemma occurs in the ms. in folio 136v, but the Mm note appears on the bottom of the following folio 137r.

2:1 לַאֲבֹתֵיכֶם

Unique defective in the book   ל חס בסיפֿ   Mp

Com.: The Mp heading here, and in M[A], of *unique defective in the book* is correct, but there are no occurrences of this lemma in the book written plene וֹ. The note more precisely should have read *unique in the book and defective*; see Breuer, *The Aleppo Codex*, 212.

M[C] has no note here.

2:1 לֹא־אָפֵר

Unique ל Mp

JUDGES 2:2

וְאַתֶּם לֹא־תִכְרְת֨וּ בְרִית֙ לְיֽוֹשְׁבֵי֙ הָאָ֣רֶץ הַזֹּ֔את מִזְבְּחוֹתֵיהֶ֖ם תִּתֹּצ֑וּן וְלֹֽא־שְׁמַעְתֶּ֖ם בְּקֹלִ֑י מַה־זֹּ֥את עֲשִׂיתֶֽם׃

2:2 לֹא־תִכְרְתוּ

Unique ל Mp

Com.: The Masorah notes the *sole* occurrence of this lemma in the pl., possibly to distinguish it from its *three* occurrences in the sg. (לֹא־תִכְרֹת).

2:2 לְיוֹשְׁבֵי הָאָרֶץ הַזֹּאת

Three times גִ Mp

Judg 2:2; Jer 13:13 (יֹשְׁבֵי); **2 Chr 20:7** (יֹשְׁבֵי)

Com.: The Masorah notes the *three* occurrences of לְיוֹשְׁבֵי הָאָרֶץ in various forms with the adj. הַזֹּאת, to distinguish them from its more numerous occurrences (27x) in various forms without this adjective.

2:2   מִזְבְּחוֹתֵיהֶם

Thirteen times   יֹּג   Mp

1–3   **Deut 7:5** (מִזְבְּחֹתֵיהֶם)**; Judg 2:2; Ezek 6:13**

Com.: The Mp heading here of *thirteen times* is incorrect since there are only *three* occurrences of this lemma.

The Masorah notes the *three* occurrences of this lemma with the 3rd pl. sfx., possibly to distinguish them from its *four* occurrences with the 2nd pl. sfx. (מִזְבְּחֹתֵיכֶם).

The Mp heading at Deut 7:5 incorrectly reads *three times, twice defective and once plene*. It should have read, as does the Mm of Mᴬ here, *three times, twice plene and once defective*.

Both Mᶜ and Mᴬ correctly read here *three times*.

2:2   תִּתֹּצוּן

Twice   בֹּ   Mp

Exod 34:13; Judg 2:2

Com.: The Masorah notes the *two* occurrences of this lemma with a paragogic נ, to distinguish them from its occurrence without this נ (תִּתֹּצוּ) at Deut 7:5.

┌───┐

JUDGES 2:3

וְגַם אָמַרְתִּי לֹא־אֲגָרֵשׁ אוֹתָם מִפְּנֵיכֶם וְהָיוּ לָכֶם לְצִדִּים וֵאלֹהֵיהֶם יִהְיוּ לָכֶם לְמוֹקֵשׁ׃

└───┘

2:3   לְצִדִּים

Unique   לֹ   Mp

JUDGES 2:4

וַיְהִ֗י כְּדַבֵּ֞ר מַלְאַ֤ךְ יְהוָה֙ אֶת־הַדְּבָרִ֣ים הָאֵ֔לֶּה אֶל־כָּל־בְּנֵ֖י יִשְׂרָאֵ֑ל וַיִּשְׂא֥וּ הָעָ֛ם אֶת־קוֹלָ֖ם וַיִּבְכּֽוּ׃

2:4   אֶל־כָּל

Twice in the book   ב בסיפֿ   Mp

(וְאֶל־כָּל) **Judg 2:4**; **9:1**

אֶל־כָּל *twice* in the book   אל כל ב בסיפֿ   Mm

Judg 2:4   ויהי כדבר מלאך
<Judg 9:1>

Com.: The Masorah notes the *two* occurrences in the book of כָּל with אֶל/וְאֶל, to distinguish them from its more numerous occurrences (5x) in the book with עַל/וְעַל (עַל כָּל/וְעַל כָּל); see Díaz-Esteban, *Sefer Oklah we-Oklah*, §161E.

In Mᴸ two circelli have been placed on the phrase אֶל־כָּל־בְּנֵי but, since this phrase only occurs once in the book, it is most likely that, as in the Mm here and in the Mp at Judg 9:1, the note belongs only to the first two words.

JUDGES 2:6

וַיְשַׁלַּ֤ח יְהוֹשֻׁ֙עַ֙ אֶת־הָעָ֔ם וַיֵּלְכ֥וּ בְנֵֽי־יִשְׂרָאֵ֖ל אִ֣ישׁ לְנַחֲלָת֑וֹ לָרֶ֖שֶׁת אֶת־הָאָֽרֶץ׃

2:6   וַיְשַׁלַּח

Twenty-two times   כֿב   Mp

1–5   **Gen 8:7**; 8:8; 8:12; **19:29**; **45:24**
6–10   Exod 18:27; **Num 21:6**; 22:40; Josh 24:28; **Judg 2:6**
11–15   **Judg 3:18**; 15:5; **1 Sam 10:25**; **11:7**; **30:26**
16–20   **2 Sam 3:21**; 18:2; **2 Kgs 5:24**; **17:25**; **17:26**
21–22   **2 Kgs 24:2**; **Ps 106:15**

וַיְשַׁלַּח *twenty-two times*, and their references   וישלח כ״ב וסימנהון   Mm

1–5	<u>Gen 8:7</u>	(הערב) [העורב]
	Gen 8:8	היונה
	Gen 8:12	היונה
	Gen 19:29	לוט
	Gen 45:24	את אחיו
6–10	Exod 18:27	חתנו
	Num 21:6	בעם
	Num 22:40	ויזבח
	Josh 24:28	יהושע
	<u>Judg 2:6</u>	יהושע
11–15	Judg 3:18	המנחה
	Judg 15:5	בקמות
	1 Sam 10:25	משפט
	1 Sam 11:7	צמד
	1 Sam 30:26	(ציקלג) [צקלג]
16–20	2 Sam 3:21	ואקבצה
	2 Sam 18:2	(השלישית) [השלשית]
	2 Kgs 5:24	העפל
	2 Kgs 17:25	האריות
	<2 Kgs 17:26>	
21–22	2 Kgs 24:2	גדודי
	Ps 106:15	רזון

Com.: The Masorah notes the *twenty-two* occurrences of this lemma in the *piel*, to distinguish them from its more numerous occurrences (100+) in the *qal* (וַיִּשְׁלַח); see Ognibeni, *’Oklah*, §20A.

This lemma occurs in the ms. in folio 136v, but the Mm note appears on the bottom of the following folio 137r.

JUDGES 2:7

וַיַּעַבְד֤וּ הָעָם֙ אֶת־יְהוָ֔ה כֹּ֖ל יְמֵ֣י יְהוֹשֻׁ֑עַ וְכֹ֣ל ׀ יְמֵ֣י הַזְּקֵנִ֗ים אֲשֶׁ֨ר הֶאֱרִ֤יכוּ יָמִים֙ אַחֲרֵ֣י יְהוֹשׁ֔וּעַ אֲשֶׁ֣ר רָא֗וּ אֵ֣ת כָּל־מַעֲשֵׂ֤ה יְהוָה֙ הַגָּד֔וֹל אֲשֶׁ֥ר עָשָׂ֖ה לְיִשְׂרָאֵֽל׃

2:7   כֹּ֖ל

Five verses with the sequence כֹּל...וְכֹל...כָּל   ה פסוק כל וכל כל   Mp

Lev 11:42; Josh 24:31; **Judg 2:7; Jer 48:37;** Ezek 21:3

Com.: The Masorah notes the *five* verses with the sequence כֹּל...וְכֹל...כָּל; see Frensdorff, *Ochlah*, §309, and Jobin, *Concordance*, 119–20.

In M^L this lemma has no circellus.

2:7   וְכֹל | יְמֵי

Three times   גֿ   Mp

Com.: See **Josh 24:31**.

There is a Mm note for this lemma which occurs on the top center of folio 136r. This note could go with Josh 24:31, which is found on the preceding folio 135v or with Judg 2:7 which is found on the following folio 136v. We have followed M^C, which places the Mm at Josh 24:31, not here at Judg 2:7.

2:7   יְהוֹשֻׁוּעַ

Twice plene   בֿ מלֿ   Mp

Deut 3:21; Judg 2:7

Com.: The Masorah notes the *two* occurrences of this lemma written plene second וֹ, to distinguish them from its more numerous occurrences (100+) written defective second וֹ (יְהוֹשֻׁעַ).

2:7   אֵת כָּל־מַעֲשֵׂה יְהוָה הַגָּדוֹל

אֵת כָּל־מַעֲשֵׂה יְהוָה הַגָּדוֹל   *twice*   בֿ   את כל מעשה יהוה הגדול   Mm

Deut 11:7   עיניכם (הראות) [הראת] את כל מעשה יהוה

Judg 2:7   אשר ראו את כל מעשה יהוה

Com.: The Masorah notes the *two* occurrences of the phrase אֵת כָּל־מַעֲשֵׂה יְהוָה with הַגָּדוֹל, to distinguish them from its *sole* occurrence without הַגָּדוֹל at Josh 24:31.

JUDGES 2:8

וַיָּמָת יְהוֹשֻׁעַ בִּן־נ֖וּן עֶבֶד יְהוָה בֶּן־מֵאָה וָעֶשֶׂר שָׁנִים׃

2:8   יְהוֹשֻׁעַ בִּן־נוּן עֶבֶד יְהוָה

Twice   בֿ   Mp

Com.: See **Josh 24:29**.

In M[L] there are only two circelli on this five-word phrase, one between יְהוֹשֻׁעַ and בֶּן, and the other between עֶבֶד and יְהוָה. With *four- or five-word* phrases it is not unusual for only *two* circelli to be given; see **Josh 1:6** and *passim*.

JUDGES 2:10

וְגַם כָּל־הַדּוֹר הַהוּא נֶאֶסְפוּ אֶל־אֲבוֹתָיו וַיָּקָם דּוֹר אַחֵר אַחֲרֵיהֶם אֲשֶׁר לֹא־יָדְעוּ אֶת־יְהוָה וְגַם
אֶת־הַמַּעֲשֶׂה אֲשֶׁר עָשָׂה לְיִשְׂרָאֵל: ס

2:10   אֲבוֹתָיו

Three times plene   ג̇ מל̇   Mp

Judg 2:10; Ps 49:20; 2 Chr 30:19

Com.: The Masorah notes the *three* occurrences of this lemma written plene וֹ, to distinguish them from its more numerous occurrences (73x) written defective וֹ (אֲבֹתָיו).

JUDGES 2:12

וַיַּעַזְבוּ אֶת־יְהוָה | אֱלֹהֵי אֲבוֹתָם הַמּוֹצִיא אוֹתָם מֵאֶרֶץ מִצְרַיִם וַיֵּלְכוּ אַחֲרֵי | אֱלֹהִים אֲחֵרִים
מֵאֱלֹהֵי הָעַמִּים אֲשֶׁר סְבִיבוֹתֵיהֶם וַיִּשְׁתַּחֲווּ לָהֶם וַיַּכְעִסוּ אֶת־יְהוָה:

2:12   אֱלֹהֵי אֲבוֹתָם

Four times   ד̇   Mp

Exod 4:5 (אֲבֹתָם); **Deut 29:24** (אֲבֹתָם); **Judg 2:12**; 2 Chr 28:6

אֱלֹהֵי אֲבוֹתָם *four times*	אלהי אבותם ד̇	Mm

Exod 4:5	למען יאמינו
וְאָמְרוּ עַל אֲשֶׁר *of Deuteronomy* (Deut 29:24)	ואמרו על אשר דמשנה תורה
Judg 2:12	ויעזבו <את> יהוה
2 Chr 28:6	בעזבם את יהוה

Com.: The Masorah notes the *four* occurrences of אֱלֹהֵי with אֲבוֹתָם/אֲבֹתָם, to distinguish them from its more numerous occurrences (14x) with אֱלֹהֵי אֲבוֹתֵיהֶם (אֲבוֹתֵיהֶם).

This distinction is implied in the additional notation in the Mm *of Deuteronomy* to the Deut 29:24 reference, which distinguishes it from the parallel passage in 2 Chr 7:22, where the lemma occurs as אֱלֹהֵי אֲבוֹתֵיהֶם.

This lemma occurs in the ms. in folio 137r but the Mm note appears on the top of the preceding folio 136v.

2:12   סְבִיבוֹתֵיהֶם

Twice plene   ב מל   Mp

Gen 35:5*; Judg 2:12

Com.: The Masorah notes the *two* occurrences of this lemma written plene וֹ, to distinguish them from its *three* occurrences written defective וֹ (סְבִיבֹתֵיהֶם).

* M^L, contrary to M (סְבִיבוֹתֵיהֶם), writes the form at Gen 35:5 defective וֹ (סְבִיבֹתֵיהֶם); see Breuer, *The Biblical Text*, 6. However, both the Mp headings highlighted above, and the Mm heading at <u>Gen 35:5</u>, read *twice plene*, thus supporting the enumeration inherent in the text of M.

2:12   וַיַּכְעִסוּ

Five times defective   ה חס   Mp

1–5   **<u>Judg 2:12</u>**; 1 Sam 1:7 (תַּכְעִסֶנָּה); Jer 7:18 (הַכְעִסֵנִי); Jer 8:19 (הִכְעִסוּנִי);
        25:7 (הכעסוני, *katib*)
6   **Jer 32:29** (הַכְעִסֵנִי)

וַיַּכְעִסוּ *five times* defective in various forms   ויכעסו ה חס בליש   Mm

1–5   <u>Judg 2:12</u>   ויכעסו את יהוה
        1 Sam 1:7   כן תכעסנה ותבכה
        Jer 8:19   מדוע הכעסוני
        (*qarê*) לְרַע of לְמַעַן הַכְעִסֵנִי (Jer 25:7)   למען הכעסוני דלרע
        <Jer 7:18>
6   <Jer 32:29>

And similarly *every* form of מַכְעִסִים   וכל מכעסים דכות ב מֹ אֹ והכה יֹי
apart from *one*: 1 Kgs 14:15

Com.: Both the Mp and Mm headings of *five times defective* are incorrect since there are *six* occurrences of this lemma.

The Masorah notes the *six* occurrences of *hiphil* forms of כָּעַס written defective י, to distinguish them from the more numerous occurrences (27x) written plene י (הִכְעִיס, יַכְעִיסֵהוּ, etc.).

This distinction is implied in the additional notation of לְרַע *of* לְמַעַן הַכְעִסֵנִי in the Jer 25:7 reference, which serves to contrast that reference with the *two* other occurrences of לְמַעַן הַכְעִסֵנִי at 2 Kgs 22:17 and 2 Chr 34:25, where the lemma is written plene י (לְמַעַן הַכְעִיסֵנִי).

The Mm has an additional note that the ptcp. form מַכְעִסִים is also written defective י (3x), apart from *one* case when it is written plene י (מַכְעִיסִים) at **1 Kgs 14:15**.

This note does not deal with the *four* forms of the infin with ל (לְהַכְעִסֵנִי) at Jer 11:17, 32:32, 44:3, and 44:8; see Dotan/Reich *Masora Thesaurus, ad loc.*

The catchword in the Jer 25:7 reference is given in its *katîb* form (הכעסוני, defective י); its *qarê* form is written plene י (הַכְעִיסֵנִי).

The Mp heading for Jer 32:29 (הַכְעִסֵנִי) mistakenly reads *unique defective* (י) *in the Prophets*. But this same form occurs also in Jer 7:18.

M^A (and probably also M^C, see Castro, *El codice*, 1:132) reads here *unique defective* noting the uniqueness of this particular form וַיַּכְעִסוּ.

This lemma occurs in the ms. in folio 137r but the Mm note appears on the top of the preceding folio 136v.

JUDGES 2:13

וַיַּעַזְבוּ אֶת־יְהוָה וַיַּעַבְדוּ לַבַּעַל וְלָעַשְׁתָּרוֹת׃

2:13   וְלָעַשְׁתָּרוֹת

Unique   ל   Mp

Com.: The Masorah notes the *sole* occurrence of this lemma with the prep. ל, possibly to distinguish it from its occurrence without this preposition (וְעַשְׁתָּרוֹת) at Josh 13:31.

JUDGES 2:14

וַיִּֽחַר־אַ֤ף יְהוָה֙ בְּיִשְׂרָאֵ֔ל וַֽיִּתְּנֵם֙ בְּיַד־שֹׁסִ֔ים וַיָּשֹׁ֖סּוּ אוֹתָ֑ם וַֽיִּמְכְּרֵ֞ם בְּיַ֤ד אֽוֹיְבֵיהֶם֙ מִסָּבִ֔יב וְלֹא־יָ֣כְל֔וּ
ע֖וֹד לַעֲמֹ֥ד לִפְנֵ֥י אוֹיְבֵיהֶֽם׃

2:14   אֽוֹיְבֵיהֶם[1]

Six times plene   מל֫ ו   Mp

1–5   **Judg 2:14[a]; 2:14[b]; Ps 78:53; 81:15; 106:42**
6   **2 Chr 20:27** (מֵאֹויְבֵיהֶם)

Com.: The Masorah notes the *six* occurrences of this lemma written plene ו, to distinguish them from its more numerous occurrences (30x) written defective ו
(אֹיְבֵיהֶם/מֵאֹיְבֵיהֶם).

2:14   אֽוֹיְבֵיהֶם[2]

Six times plene   מל֫ ו   Mp

Com.: See directly above.

JUDGES 2:15

בְּכֹ֣ל ׀ אֲשֶׁ֣ר יָצְא֗וּ יַד־יְהוָה֙ הָיְתָה־בָּ֣ם לְרָעָ֔ה כַּֽאֲשֶׁר֙ דִּבֶּ֣ר יְהוָ֔ה וְכַאֲשֶׁ֛ר נִשְׁבַּ֥ע יְהוָ֖ה לָהֶ֑ם וַיֵּ֥צֶר
לָהֶ֖ם מְאֹֽד׃

2:15   וַיֵּ֥צֶר

Three times   ג֫   Mp

Gen 32:8; Judg 2:15; 2 Sam 13:2

Com.: The Masorah notes the *three* occurrences of this lemma pointed this way, to distinguish them from forms with different vocalizations, such as וַיֵּ֫צֶר (10x), וְיֵצֶר
(3x), or וַיִּ֫צֶר (1x); see Ognibeni, *'Oklah*, §301.

The Mm for this lemma at 2 Sam 13:2 is given in the form of an Aramaic mnemonic
"Jacob swore to Amnon"; see Marcus, *Scribal Wit*, 74.

JUDGES 2:16

וַיָּ֣קֶם יְהוָה֙ שֹֽׁפְטִ֔ים וַיּ֣וֹשִׁיע֔וּם מִיַּ֖ד שֹׁסֵיהֶֽם׃

2:16 וַיָּ֣קֶם

Twenty times כ Mp

1–5 Exod 40:18[a]; **40:18[b]**; **40:33**; **Judg 2:16**; **3:9**
6–10 **Judg 3:15**; 1 Kgs 7:21[a]; 7:21[b]; **7:21[c]**; **8:20**
11–15 1 Kgs 11:14; 11:23; <u>16:32</u>; 2 Kgs 21:3; **Ps 40:3**
16–20 **Ps 78:5**; Dan 9:12; 2 Chr 3:17; **6:10**; **33:3**

Com.: The Masorah notes the *twenty* occurrences of this lemma in the *hiphil*, to distinguish them from its more numerous occurrences (100+) in the *qal* (וַיָּ֫קָם); see Ognibeni, *'Oklah*, §4A.

2:16 וַיּ֣וֹשִׁיעֻם

Unique ל Mp

Com.: This lemma is featured in a Masoretic list of doublets that occur *once* with ו cj. (Neh 9:27), and *once* with ו consec. (here); see Frensdorff, *Ochlah*, §46, and Díaz-Esteban, *Sefer Oklah we-Oklah*, §47.

JUDGES 2:17

וְגַ֤ם אֶל־שֹֽׁפְטֵיהֶם֙ לֹ֣א שָׁמֵ֔עוּ כִּ֣י זָנ֗וּ אַחֲרֵי֙ אֱלֹהִ֣ים אֲחֵרִ֔ים וַיִּֽשְׁתַּחֲו֖וּ לָהֶ֑ם סָ֣רוּ מַהֵ֗ר מִן־הַדֶּ֙רֶךְ֙
אֲשֶׁ֤ר הָֽלְכוּ֙ אֲבוֹתָ֔ם לִשְׁמֹ֖עַ מִצְוֺת־יְהוָ֑ה לֹא־עָ֥שׂוּ כֵֽן׃

2:17 לֹ֣א שָׁמֵ֔עוּ

Twice ב Mp

Judg 2:17; Mic 5:14

Com.: The Masorah notes the *two* occurrences of this lemma with a *ṣerê* under the מ, to distinguish them from its more numerous occurrences (13x) with a *šəwâ* (לֹא שָׁמְעוּ).

In M[L] the circellus has been placed only on שָׁמֵעוּ, but since there are more than two occurrences of this word, the note must refer to the phrase לֹ֣א שָׁמֵעוּ, which only occurs *twice*. The circellus has been correctly placed on both words here in M[A], and in M[L] at Mic 5:14. M[C] has no note here.

JUDGES 2:18

וְכִי־הֵקִים יְהוָה ׀ לָהֶם֮ שֹׁפְטִים֒ וְהָיָ֣ה יְהוָה֮ עִם־הַשֹּׁפֵט֒ וְהוֹשִׁיעָם֙ מִיַּ֣ד אֹֽיְבֵיהֶ֔ם כֹּ֖ל יְמֵ֣י הַשּׁוֹפֵ֑ט כִּֽי־
יִנָּחֵ֤ם יְהוָה֙ מִנַּֽאֲקָתָ֔ם מִפְּנֵ֥י לֹחֲצֵיהֶ֖ם וְדֹחֲקֵיהֶֽם׃

2:18   וְכִי־הֵקִים

Unique   לֹ   Mp

Com.: The Masorah notes the *sole* occurrence of this lemma with a ו cj., to distinguish it from its occurrence without a cj. at 1 Sam 22:8.

2:18   וְהָיָה יְהוָה

Six times   ו   Mp

1–5   **Gen 28:21; Judg 2:18; 1 Sam 24:16;** 2 Kgs 18:7; Jer 17:7
6   **Zech 14:9**

Com.: The Masorah notes the *six* occurrences of this lemma with a ו cj., to distinguish them from its *three* occurrences without a cj.

2:18   וְהוֹשִׁיעָם

Twice   בֿ   Mp

Judg 2:18; Zech 9:16

וְהוֹשִׁיעָם *twice* and plene, and (their) references   והושיעם בֿ ומל וסימ   Mm

Judg 2:18   והושיעם מיד איביהם
Zech 9:16   והושיעם (יי) [יהוה] אלהיהם

Com.: The Masorah notes the *two* occurrences of this lemma with a ו cj., to distinguish them from its *sole* occurrence without a cj. (הוֹשִׁיעָם) at Isa 63:9.

By noting that this lemma occurs *twice* and written plene י, the Masorah is also implying (correctly) that this lemma does not occur elsewhere written defective י.

This lemma is featured in a Masoretic list of doublets that commence with וה; see Frensdorff, *Ochlah*, §63, and Díaz-Esteban, *Sefer Oklah we-Oklah*, §64.

2:18 יִנָּחֵם

Four times דֿ Mp

Exod 13:17; Judg 2:18; 1 Sam 15:29; Ps 110:4

יִנָּחֵם *four times* ינחם דֿ Mm

Exod 13:17 כי אמר
Judg 2:18 מנאקתם
1 Sam 15:29 וגם נצח ישראל לא
Ps 110:4 נשבע יהוה ולא ינחם

\<and *once*\> (וְיִנָּחֵם): Jer 26:13 \<וחד\> וינחם יהוה (על) [אל] הרעה

Com.: The Masorah notes the *four* occurrences of this lemma in the *niphal*, to distinguish them from its *sole* occurrence in the *hiphil* (יַנְחֵם) at Ps 78:72, and it *sole* occurrence in the *piel* (יְנַחֵם) at Job 29:25.

The Mm has an additional note that this lemma also occurs with a ו cj. (וְיִנָּחֵם) at Jer 26:13

This form is featured in a Masoretic list of words that occur *five times*, *four times* without a ו cj. and *once* with a cj. (Jer 26:13); see Frensdorff, *Ochlah*, §17.

2:18 מִנַּאֲקָתָם

Unique לֿ Mp

Com.: The Masorah notes the *sole* occurrence of this lemma with the inseparable prep. מִ, to distinguish it from its occurrence without this prep. at Exod 2:24.

2:18 וְדֹחֲקֵיהֶם

Unique לֿ Mp

JUDGES 2:19

וְהָיָה ׀ בְּמוֹת הַשּׁוֹפֵט יָשֻׁבוּ וְהִשְׁחִיתוּ מֵאֲבוֹתָם לָלֶכֶת אַחֲרֵי אֱלֹהִים אֲחֵרִים לְעָבְדָם
וּלְהִשְׁתַּחֲוֺת לָהֶם לֹא הִפִּילוּ מִמַּעַלְלֵיהֶם וּמִדַּרְכָּם הַקָּשָׁה:

2:19   הַשּׁוֹפֵט

Twice plene   ב מל   Mp

Judg 2:18; **2:19**

Com.: The Masorah notes the *two* occurrences of this lemma written plene ו, to distinguish them from its more numerous occurrences (6x) written defective ו (הַשֹּׁפֵט).

2:19   יָשֻׁבוּ

Seven times defective   ז חס   Mp

1–5   **Judg 2:19; 2 Sam 23:10; Jer 15:19; 24:7; Hos 3:5**
6–7   **Hos 14:8; Ps 6:11**

Com.: The Masorah notes the *seven* occurrences of this lemma written defective first ו, to distinguish them from its more numerous occurrences (18x) written plene first ו (יָשׁוּבוּ).

All the Mp headings highlighted above read *seven times* except for Jer 24:7, which mistakenly reads *three times*.

2:19   וְהִשְׁחִיתוּ מֵאֲבוֹתָם

Unique   ל   Mp

2:19   וּמִדַּרְכָּם הַקָּשָׁה

Unique   ל   Mp

JUDGES 2:21

גַּם־אֲנִי לֹא אוֹסִיף לְהוֹרִישׁ אִישׁ מִפְּנֵיהֶם מִן־הַגּוֹיִם אֲשֶׁר־עָזַב יְהוֹשֻׁעַ וַיָּמֹת:

2:21   גַּם־אֲנִי

Six times at the beginning of a verse   ו ראש פס   Mp

1–5   **Judg 2:21**; <u>Isa 66:4</u>; **Ezek 20:23**; Ps 71:22; Prov 1:26
6   Job 7:11

Com.: The Masorah notes the *six* occurrences of this lemma at the beginning of a verse without a ו cj., to distinguish them from its more numerous occurrences (13x) at the beginning of a verse with a cj. (וְגַם אֲנִי).

JUDGES 2:22

לְמַעַן נַסּוֹת בָּם אֶת־יִשְׂרָאֵל הֲשֹׁמְרִים הֵם אֶת־דֶּרֶךְ יְהֹוָה לָלֶכֶת בָּם כַּאֲשֶׁר שָׁמְרוּ אֲבוֹתָם אִם־לֹא:

2:22   הֲשֹׁמְרִים

Unique   ל   Mp

This lemma is featured in a Masoretic list of *hapax legomena* starting with הֲ or הַ; see Frensdorff, *Ochlah*, §65, and Díaz-Esteban, *Sefer Oklah we-Oklah*, §66.

2:22   בָּם²

Eight times where one might err   ח׳ דמט   Mp

1–5   **Judg 2:22**[b]; Isa 6:13; **30:32** (*qərê*); 63:19; Jer 6:18
6–8   Hos 14:10[a]; 14:10[b]; **Prov 28:4**

בָּם *eight times* where one might err	בם ח׳ דמטעין	Mm
1–5 Judg 2:22	ללכת בם	
Isa 6:13	אשר בשלכת	
Isa 63:19	משלת	
Isa 30:32	ובמלחמות	
Hos 14:10[a]	מי חכם ויבן	
6–8 *Twice* in the verse (Hos 14:10[b])	שנים בפסוק	
Jer 6:18	ודעי עדה	
Prov 28:4	יתגרו	

And *six* reverse cases	וחלופיהן שיתה

1–5	Hos 9:2	ותירוש יכחש (בם) [בה]
	2 Kgs 3:24	ויכו בה והכות
	2 Kgs 7:13[a]	הנשארים
	Twice in the verse (2 Kgs 7:13[b])	שנים בפסוקה
	Ezek 28:22[a]	ונכבדתי
6	*Twice* in the verse (Ezek 28:22[b])	שנים בפסוקה

Com.: The Masorah notes the *eight* cases where there is a possibility of error in reading בָּה instead of בָּם, and *six* cases of the reverse, where there is a possibility of error in reading בָּם instead of בָּה.

Curiously in the Mp of Isa 30:32 there is a *kǝṯîb* and *qǝrê* with just this possibility: the *kǝṯîb* reads בה, whereas the *qǝrê*, the preferred reading, reads בָּם.

This lemma also occurs in a Masoretic list of verses in which בָּם occurs *twice*: see Frensdorff, *Ochlah*, §334.

2:22	אִם־לֹא

Seven times at the end (of a verse)	ז סוֹף	Mp

1–5	**Gen 24:21; 27:21; 37:32; Exod 16:4; Num 11:23**
6–7	**Deut 8:2; Judg 2:22**

Com.: The Masorah notes the *seven* occurrences of this lemma at the end of a verse, to distinguish them from its more numerous occurrences (73x) at the beginning or middle of a verse.

The Mp heading at Gen 27:21 of *six times* no doubt represents a graphic error of ו *six* for ז *seven*.

> ### JUDGES 3:1
>
> וְאֵ֣לֶּה הַגּוֹיִ֔ם אֲשֶׁ֥ר הִנִּ֖יחַ יְהוָ֑ה לְנַסּ֤וֹת בָּם֙ אֶת־יִשְׂרָאֵ֔ל אֵ֚ת כָּל־אֲשֶׁ֣ר לֹֽא־יָדְע֔וּ אֵ֖ת כָּל־מִלְחֲמ֥וֹת כְּנָֽעַן׃

3:1	וְאֵלֶּה הַגּוֹיִם

Unique	ל	Mp

Com.: The Masorah notes the *sole* occurrence of this lemma, to distinguish it from its more numerous occurrences (17x) with the words reversed (הַגּוֹיִם הָאֵלֶּה); see Ognibeni, *'Oklah*, §280, no. 64.

This lemma is featured in a Masoretic list of words that occur only *once* with a preceding אֵלֶּה; see Frensdorff, *Ochlah*, §260.

3:1 לְנַסּוֹת

Three times ג Mp

Judg 3:1; 3:4; 2 Chr 9:1

Com.: The Masorah notes the *three* occurrences of this lemma without a sfx., possibly to distinguish them from its *sole* occurrence with a sfx. (לְנַסּוֹתוֹ) at 2 Chr 32:31.

JUDGES 3:2
רַ֣ק לְמַ֗עַן דַּ֚עַת דֹּרֹ֣ות בְּנֵֽי־יִשְׂרָאֵ֔ל לְלַמְּדָ֖ם מִלְחָמָ֑ה רַ֥ק אֲשֶׁר־לְפָנִ֖ים לֹ֥א יְדָעֽוּם׃

3:2 דַּעַת דֹּרוֹת

Unique ל Mp

Com.: In M[L] the circellus has been placed only on דֹּרוֹת, but since this word occurs three times it is most likely that the note refers to the phrase דַּעַת דֹּרוֹת, which only occurs this one time.

3:2 לְלַמְּדָם

Unique ל Mp

Com.: The Masorah notes the *sole* occurrence of this lemma without a ו cj., to distinguish them from its *sole* occurrence with a cj. (וּלְלַמְּדָם) at Dan 1:4.

JUDGES 3:4
וַֽיִּהְי֗וּ לְנַסֹּ֤ות בָּם֙ אֶת־יִשְׂרָאֵ֔ל לָדַ֗עַת הֲיִשְׁמְעוּ֙ אֶת־מִצְוֹ֣ת יְהוָ֔ה אֲשֶׁר־צִוָּ֥ה אֶת־אֲבוֹתָ֖ם בְּיַד־מֹשֶֽׁה׃

3:4 לְנַסּוֹת

Three times ג Mp

See directly above at **Judg 3:1**.

3:4   הֲיִשְׁמְע֖וּ

Unique   ל   Mp

Com.: The Masorah notes the *sole* occurrence of this lemma with the interrog. ה, to distinguish it from its more numerous occurrences (30x) without this interrogative.

JUDGES 3:5

וּבְנֵ֣י יִשְׂרָאֵ֔ל יָשְׁב֖וּ בְּקֶ֣רֶב הַֽכְּנַעֲנִ֑י הַחִתִּ֣י וְהָאֱמֹרִי֙ וְהַפְּרִזִּ֔י וְהַחִוִּ֖י וְהַיְבוּסִֽי׃

3:5   הַכְּנַעֲנִי הַחִתִּי וְהָאֱמֹרִי וְהַפְּרִזִי וְהַחִוִּי וְהַיְבוּסִי

עֵ ת מ פ ו ס סִמ֥   Mp

Com.: The Masorah note is in the form of a mnemonic indicating the order of the peoples in Canaan; see Frensdorff, *Ochlah*, §274, and Ognibeni, *'Oklah*, §114. Each letter represents one people; see also at **Josh 3:10, 9:1, 24:11**, Frensdorff, *Ochlah*, §274, and Ognibeni, *'Oklah*, §114.

In M^L the circellus is only on the first word הַכְּנַעֲנִי.

JUDGES 3:6

וַיִּקְח֨וּ אֶת־בְּנוֹתֵיהֶ֥ם לָהֶם֙ לְנָשִׁ֔ים וְאֶת־בְּנ֣וֹתֵיהֶ֗ם נָתְנ֣וּ לִבְנֵיהֶ֑ם וַיַּעַבְד֖וּ אֶת־אֱלֹהֵיהֶֽם׃ פ

3:6   לְנָשִׁים

Fourteen times   יד   Mp

1–5	Gen 34:21; Num 36:3; 36:6ᵃ; 36:6ᵇ; 36:11
6–10	Num 36:12; **Judg 3:6**; 21:7ᵃ; 21:7ᵇ; 21:16
11–14	1 Sam 25:43; Jer 50:37; 51:30; Ezek 44:22

Com.: The Masorah notes the *fourteen* occurrences of this lemma with the indef. prep. לְ, to distinguish them from its *two* occurrences with the def. prep. לַ (לַנָּשִׁים) at Ezek 23:10 and Prov 31:3.

JUDGES 3:7

וַיַּעֲשׂוּ בְנֵי־יִשְׂרָאֵל אֶת־הָרַע בְּעֵינֵי יְהֹוָה וַיִּשְׁכְּחוּ אֶת־יְהוָה אֱלֹהֵיהֶם וַיַּעַבְדוּ אֶת־הַבְּעָלִים וְאֶת־הָאֲשֵׁרוֹת:

3:7   וַיַּעֲשׂוּ בְנֵי־יִשְׂרָאֵל אֶת־הָרַע

Seven times   ז   Mp

1–5   **Deut 17:2**; 31:29; Judg 2:11; **3:7**; **3:12**
6–7   **2 Kgs 21:9**; **21:15**

Com.: The Masorah notes the *seven* occurrences of עֲשִׂיָּה אֶת־הָרַע *the doing of evil,* which contain the accusative particle אֶת.

The Mp heading at Judg 3:12 reads *unique* for the *sole* occurrence of its specific formulation (עַל כִּי־עָשׂוּ אֶת־הָרַע).

The Mp heading of *three times* at 2 Kgs 21:9 relates to the fact that the word הָרָע in that verse is pointed with a *qames* under the ר; see **2 Kgs 21:9**.

In M[L] the circellus has been placed only on the first two words but the note refers to the entire phrase.

3:7   הָאֲשֵׁרוֹת

Twice   ב   Mp

Judg 3:7; 2 Chr 19:3

Com.: The Masorah notes the *two* occurrences of this lemma with the def. article, to distinguish them from its *sole* occurrence without this article at 2 Chr 33:3.

JUDGES 3:8

וַיִּחַר־אַף יְהוָה בְּיִשְׂרָאֵל וַיִּמְכְּרֵם בְּיַד כּוּשַׁן רִשְׁעָתַיִם מֶלֶךְ אֲרַם נַהֲרָיִם וַיַּעַבְדוּ בְנֵי־יִשְׂרָאֵל אֶת־כּוּשַׁן רִשְׁעָתַיִם שְׁמֹנֶה שָׁנִים:

3:8   וְרִשְׁעָתַיִם[1]

Four times   ד   Mp

Judg 3:8[a]; 3:8[b]; 3:10[a]; 3:10[b]

3:8   רִשְׁעָתַ֫יִם²

Four times   דֿ   Mp

Com.: See directly above.

3:8   שְׁמֹנֶה שָׁנִים

Three times   גֿ   Mp

1–4   **Judg 3:8**; 12:14; 2 Chr 34:1 (שְׁמוֹנֶה); 36:9 (שְׁמוֹנֶה)

Com.: The Mp heading here of *three times* is incorrect since there are *four* occurrences of this lemma with שְׁמֹנֶה, written plene and defective ו.

Dotan/Reich (*Masora Thesaurus, ad loc.*) suggest that the *two* Chronicles references may have been taken as *one* since they both contain the phrase בֶּן שְׁמֹנֶה שָׁנִים.

The Masorah notes the *four* occurrences of this lemma with the sg. שְׁמֹנֶה signifying *eight years*, to distinguish them from its more numerous occurrences (6x) with the pl. שְׁמֹנִים, written plene and defective ו, signifying *eighty years* (שְׁמֹנִים שָׁנִים).

Neither M^C nor M^A has a note on this lemma here.

JUDGES 3:9

וַיִּזְעֲק֤וּ בְנֵֽי־יִשְׂרָאֵל֙ אֶל־יְהוָ֔ה וַיָּ֨קֶם יְהוָ֥ה מוֹשִׁ֛יעַ לִבְנֵ֥י יִשְׂרָאֵ֖ל וַיּֽוֹשִׁיעֵ֑ם אֵ֚ת עָתְנִיאֵ֣ל בֶּן־קְנַ֔ז אֲחִ֥י כָלֵ֖ב הַקָּטֹ֥ן מִמֶּֽנּוּ׃

3:9   וַיָּ֫קֶם

Twenty times   כֿ   Mp

Com.: See **Judg 2:16.**

3:9   וַיּֽוֹשִׁיעֵ֑ם

Four times   דֿ   Mp

Judg 3:9 (וַיּֽוֹשִׁיעֵ֑ם*); <u>**2 Kgs 14:27**</u>; **Ps 106:8**; 106:10

Com.: The Masorah notes the *four* occurrences of this lemma, written plene and defective second ו, with a ו consec., to distinguish these occurrences from its *two* occurrences with a ו cj. (וְיוֹשִׁיעֵם) at Ps 37:40 and 145:19.

* M[L], contrary to M (וַיּשִׁיעֵם), writes the form here plene second ו (וַיּוֹשִׁיעֵם); see Breuer, *The Biblical Text*, 56.

JUDGES 3:10

וַתְּהִי עָלָיו רֽוּחַ־יְהוָה וַיִּשְׁפֹּט אֶת־יִשְׂרָאֵל וַיֵּצֵא לַמִּלְחָמָה וַיִּתֵּן יְהוָה בְּיָדוֹ אֶת־כּוּשַׁן רִשְׁעָתַיִם מֶלֶךְ אֲרָם וַתָּעָז יָדוֹ עַל כּוּשַׁן רִשְׁעָתָיִם:

3:10 רִשְׁעָתַיִם[1]

Four times ד Mp

Com.: See directly above at **Judg 3:8**.

3:10 רִשְׁעָתַיִם[2]

Four times ד Mp

Com.: See directly above at **Judg 3:8**.

JUDGES 3:12

וַיֹּסִפוּ בְּנֵי יִשְׂרָאֵל לַעֲשׂוֹת הָרַע בְּעֵינֵי יְהוָה וַיְחַזֵּק יְהוָה אֶת־עֶגְלוֹן מֶלֶךְ־מוֹאָב עַל־יִשְׂרָאֵל עַל כִּי־עָשׂוּ אֶת־הָרַע בְּעֵינֵי יְהוָה:

3:12 עַל כִּי־עָשׂוּ אֶת־הָרַע

Unique ל Mp

Com.: See directly above at **Judg 3:7**.

JUDGES 3:14

וַיַּעַבְדוּ בְנֵי־יִשְׂרָאֵל אֶת־עֶגְלוֹן מֶלֶךְ־מוֹאָב שְׁמוֹנֶה עֶשְׂרֵה שָׁנָה: ס

3:14 שְׁמוֹנֶה

Three times plene ג מל Mp

Judg 3:14; **Jer 52:29**; **Ezek 40:31**

שְׁמוֹנֶה *three times* plene	שמונה ג̇ מל	Mm

<Judg 3:14>
The *second* occurrence in Jeremiah of
בִּשְׁנַת שְׁמוֹנֶה עֶשְׂרֵה *of Nebuchadnezzar*
(Jer 52:29)
Ezek 40:31
And similarly *all* Chronicles

בשנת שמונה עשרה ד(לבוכדנאר)
[לבנוכדראצר] בתר̇ דירמיה

ומעלות שמונה מעלו
וכל דברי הימ̇ דכות

Com.: The Masorah notes the *three* occurrences of this lemma written plene וֹ, to distinguish them from its more numerous occurrences (11x) written defective וֹ (שְׁמֹנֶה).

This distinction is implied in the Mm in the additional notation of the *second* occurrence in Jeremiah of *the eighteenth year of Nebuchadnezzar* to the Jer 52:29 reference, which distinguishes it from its *first* occurrence in Jeremiah (32:1), where the lemma is written defective וֹ.

The Mm also notes that this lemma written plene יֹ occurs (5x) in Chronicles.

In the Ezek 40:31 reference, the *katîb* form מעלו is written, though normally the Masorah cites the *qərê* form, which is מַעֲלָיו.

This note also occurs in the Mm of Gen 5:4 *sub* שְׁמֹנֶה.

JUDGES 3:15

וַיִּזְעֲק֤וּ בְנֵֽי־יִשְׂרָאֵל֙ אֶל־יְהוָ֔ה וַיָּ֨קֶם יְהוָ֤ה לָהֶם֙ מוֹשִׁ֔יעַ אֶת־אֵה֗וּד בֶּן־גֵּרָא֙ בֶּן־הַיְמִינִ֔י אִ֖ישׁ אִטֵּ֣ר יַד־יְמִינ֑וֹ וַיִּשְׁלְח֨וּ בְנֵֽי־יִשְׂרָאֵ֤ל בְּיָדוֹ֙ מִנְחָ֔ה לְעֶגְל֖וֹן מֶ֥לֶךְ מוֹאָֽב׃

3:15   וַיָּ֖קֶם

Twenty times   כ̇   Mp

Com.: See **Judg 2:16**.

3:15   גֵּרָ֖א

Exod 30:13 etc.	עשרים גרה השקל	Mm
Lev 11:3 etc.	(מעלה) [מעלת] גרה בבהמה	
Lev 11:6 etc.	מעלת גרה	
Judg 3:15	אהוד בן גרא	
2 Sam 16:5 etc.	שמעי בן גרא	

Weights and animals are written with ה   מתקלא ובעירה הי כתֹ

Personal names (are written) with an א   גוברא א

Com.: The Masorah notes that in all cases of weights and animals the word גֵּרָה is written with a ה, but in personal names this word is written with an א (גֵּרָא).

3:15   אִטֵּר

Twice   בֹ   Mp

Judg 3:15; 20:16

Com.: The Masorah notes the *two* occurrences of this lemma pointed this way, to distinguish them from its more numerous occurrences (5x) pointed as אִטֵּר.

JUDGES 3:16
וַיַּעַשׂ לוֹ אֵהוּד חֶרֶב וְלָהּ שְׁנֵי פֵיוֹת גֹּמֶד אָרְכָּהּ וַיַּחְגֹּר אוֹתָהּ מִתַּחַת לְמַדָּיו עַל יֶרֶךְ יְמִינוֹ:

3:16   וְלָהּ

Three times   גֹ   Mp

Gen 16:1; Judg 3:16; 1 Sam 25:35

וְלָהּ *three times*   ולה גֹ   Mm

Gen 16:1	ולה שפחה מצרית
Judg 3:16	ולה שני פיות
1 Sam 25:35	עלי לשלום

And *once* with *paṭaḥ* (וְלַהּ): Dan 7:6   וחד פתח ולה גפין ארבע

Com.: The Masorah notes the *three* occurrences of this lemma with a ו cj., to distinguish them from its more numerous occurrences (200+) without a cj.

The Mm has an additional note that this lemma also occurs written with a *paṭaḥ* at Dan 7:6.

The heading of the Mp at Dan 7:6 reads *four times, and three times with qameṣ* (ד וּגֹ), to which the Mm there adds *and one with paṭaḥ.*

3:16　　פֵּיּוֹת

Unique　ל　　Mp

Com.: The Masorah notes the *sole* occurrence of this lemma with a *ṣerê*, to distinguish it from its occurrence with a *ḥireq* and a *dageš* in the י (פִּיּוֹת) at Prov 5:4.

3:16　　גֹּמֶד

Unique　ל　　Mp

3:16　　לְמַדָּיו

Twice　ב　　Mp

Judg 3:16; 1 Sam 17:39

Com.: The Masorah notes the *two* occurrences of this lemma with the prep. ל, to distinguish them from its *two* occurrences with a ו cj (וּמַדָּיו) at **1 Sam 4:12** and 1 Sam 18:4, and from its *sole* occurrence without a ו cj. (מַדָּיו) at 1 Sam 17:38.

> ## JUDGES 3:17
> וַיַּקְרֵב֙ אֶת־הַמִּנְחָ֔ה לְעֶגְל֖וֹן מֶ֣לֶךְ מוֹאָ֑ב וְעֶגְל֕וֹן אִ֥ישׁ בָּרִ֖יא מְאֹֽד׃

3:17　　בָּרִיא

Twice plene　ב מל　　Mp

Judg 3:17; Ps 73:4 (וּבָרִיא)

Com.: The Mp heading here and in M^A reads *twice plene*, noting the *two* occurrences of this lemma, with and without a ו cj., written plene י. Since there is no defective form of this lemma, the note should more precisely have read *twice and plene*.

M^C correctly reads here *unique and plene* (for this lemma without a ו cj.).

The Mp heading at Ps 73:4 correctly reads *unique and plene*, and adds catchwords וחד ועגלון איש בריא (וְעֶגְל֕וֹן אִ֥ישׁ בָּרִ֖יא "and once") that refer the reader to this verse.

JUDGES 3:18

וַיְהִי֙ כַּאֲשֶׁ֣ר כִּלָּ֔ה לְהַקְרִ֖יב אֶת־הַמִּנְחָ֑ה וַיְשַׁלַּח֙ אֶת־הָעָ֔ם נֹשְׂאֵ֖י הַמִּנְחָֽה׃

3:18   וַיְשַׁלַּח

Twenty-two times   כֹּב   Mp

Com.: See **Judg 2:6.**

JUDGES 3:19

וְה֣וּא שָׁ֗ב מִן־הַפְּסִילִים֮ אֲשֶׁ֣ר אֶת־הַגִּלְגָּל֒ וַיֹּ֕אמֶר דְּבַר־סֵ֥תֶר לִ֛י אֵלֶ֖יךָ הַמֶּ֑לֶךְ וַיֹּ֣אמֶר הָ֔ס וַיֵּֽצְאוּ֙ מֵֽעָלָ֔יו כָּל־הָעֹמְדִ֖ים עָלָֽיו׃

3:19   הַפְּסִילִים

Four times plene   ד מל   Mp

Judg 3:19; 3:26; Isa 42:8 (לַפְּסִילִֽים); **2 Chr 33:22**

Com.: The Masorah notes the *four* occurrences of this lemma, *three* of them with the def. article and *one* with the prep. ל, written plene first י, to distinguish them from its more numerous occurrences (6x) written defective first י in various forms such as וְהַפְּסִלִים and פְּסִלִים.

The Mp heading at 2 Chr 33:22 reads *three times plene*, counting only occurrences of this lemma with the def. article.

3:19   דְּבַר־סֵ֥תֶר

Unique   ל   Mp

3:19   הָס

Twice ẓaqep qameṣ   ב זק קמֹ   Mp

Judg 3:19; Amos 6:10

| Mm | הס ב֞ זק קמ֞ | *twice zaqep qames* | הָס |

| Judg 3:19 | ויאמר |
| Amos 6:10 | ואמר הס |

Com.: The Masorah notes the *two* occurrences of this lemma in pause with a *qames* under a *zaqep*, to distinguish them from its *sole* occurrence in pause with a *qames* alongside a *sôp pasûq* in Amos 8:3.

JUDGES 3:20

וְאֵה֣וּד ׀ בָּ֣א אֵלָ֗יו וְהֽוּא־יֹשֵׁ֞ב בַּעֲלִיַּ֤ת הַמְּקֵרָה֙ אֲשֶׁר־ל֣וֹ לְבַדּ֔וֹ וַיֹּ֤אמֶר אֵהוּד֙ דְּבַר־אֱלֹהִ֥ים לִ֣י אֵלֶ֔יךָ וַיָּ֖קָם מֵעַ֥ל הַכִּסֵּֽא:

| 3:20 | הַמְּקֵרָה |

| Mp | ב֞ | *Twice* |

Judg 3:20; 3:24

| 3:20 | דְּבַר־אֱלֹהִים |

| Mp | ג֞ | *Three times* |

Judg 3:20; 1 Sam 9:27; 1 Chr 17:3

Com.: The Masorah notes the *three* occurrences of this lemma with אֱלֹהִים, to distinguish them from its more numerous occurrences (200+) with the Tetragrammaton (דְּבַר־יְהוָה).

This distinction is implied in the Mm to 1 Chr 17:3 in the additional notation *of Chronicles* to the 1 Chr 17:3 reference, which distinguishes it from the parallel passage in 2 Sam 7:4, where the lemma occurs as דְּבַר־יְהוָה.

JUDGES 3:21

וַיִּשְׁלַ֤ח אֵהוּד֙ אֶת־יַ֣ד שְׂמֹאל֔וֹ וַיִּקַּח֙ אֶת־הַחֶ֔רֶב מֵעַ֖ל יֶ֣רֶךְ יְמִינ֑וֹ וַיִּתְקָעֶ֖הָ בְּבִטְנֽוֹ:

| 3:21 | אֶת־יַד שְׂמֹאלוֹ |

| Mp | ל֞ | *Unique* |

3:21   וַיִּתְקָעֶהָ

Unique   ל   Mp

Com.: The Masorah notes the *sole* occurrence of this lemma with a fem. sfx., to distinguish it from its occurrence with a masc. sfx. (וַיִּתְקָעֵהוּ) at Exod 10:19, and from its occurrence with a pl. sfx. (וַיִּתְקָעֵם) at 2 Sam 18:14.

JUDGES 3:22

וַיָּבֹא גַם־הַנִּצָּב אַחַר הַלַּהַב וַיִּסְגֹּר הַחֵלֶב בְּעַד הַלַּהַב כִּי לֹא שָׁלַף הַחֶרֶב מִבִּטְנוֹ וַיֵּצֵא הַפַּרְשְׁדֹנָה׃

3:22   גַם־הַנִּצָּב

Unique   ל   Mp

Com.: The Masorah notes the *sole* occurrence of הַנִּצָּב lemma with גַם, to distinguish it from its *two* occurrences without גַם at Ruth 2:5 and 2:6.

3:22   לֹא שָׁלַף

Unique   ל   Mp

Com.: The Masorah notes the *sole* occurrence of this lemma without a ו cj., to distinguish it from its occurrence with a cj. (וְלֹא שָׁלַף) at Judg 8:20.

3:22   הַפַּרְשְׁדֹנָה

Unique and defective   ל וחס   Mp

Com.: By noting that this lemma is *unique* and written defective (וֹ), the Masorah is also implying (correctly) that this lemma does not occur elsewhere written plene וֹ .

JUDGES 3:23

וַיֵּצֵא אֵהוּד הַמִּסְדְּרוֹנָה וַיִּסְגֹּר דַּלְתוֹת הָעֲלִיָּה בַּעֲדוֹ וְנָעָל׃

3:23   הַמִּסְדְּרוֹנָה

Unique and plene   ל ומל   Mp

Com.: By noting that this lemma is *unique* and written plene (וֹ), the Masorah is also implying (correctly) that this lemma does not occur elsewhere written defective וֹ.

3:23   וְנָעַל֙

Twice   בֿ   Mp

Judg 3:23; 2 Sam 13:18 (וְנָעַל)

Com.: The Masorah notes the *two* occurrences of this lemma, *once* with a *qameṣ* under the ע, and *once* with a *paṭaḥ* under the ע.

The Mp at 2 Sam 13:18 correctly describes the situation in its heading of *twice, once with paṭaḥ and one with qameṣ.*

JUDGES 3:24

וְה֤וּא יָצָא֙ וַעֲבָדָ֣יו בָּ֔אוּ וַיִּרְא֕וּ וְהִנֵּ֛ה דַּלְת֥וֹת הָעֲלִיָּ֖ה נְעֻל֑וֹת וַיֹּ֣אמְר֔וּ אַ֣ךְ מֵסִ֥יךְ ה֛וּא אֶת־רַגְלָ֖יו בַּחֲדַ֥ר הַמְּקֵרָֽה׃

3:24   נְעֻל֑וֹת

Unique   לֿ   Mp

3:24   מֵסִ֥יךְ

Unique   לֿ   Mp

3:24   הַמְּקֵרָה

Twice   בֿ   Mp

Judg 3:20; 3:24

JUDGES 3:25

וַיָּחִ֣ילוּ עַד־בּ֔וֹשׁ וְהִנֵּ֥ה אֵינֶ֖נּוּ פֹּתֵ֣חַ דַּלְת֣וֹת הָעֲלִיָּ֑ה וַיִּקְח֤וּ אֶת־הַמַּפְתֵּ֙חַ֙ וַיִּפְתָּ֔חוּ וְהִנֵּ֤ה אֲדֹֽנֵיהֶם֙ נֹפֵ֣ל אַ֔רְצָה מֵֽת׃

3:25   וַיָּחִ֣ילוּ

Unique   לֿ   Mp

3:25   וְהִנֵּה אֵינֶנּוּ

Three times   גֿ   Mp

Gen 31:2; Judg 3:25; Ps 37:36

וְהִנֵּה אֵינֶנּוּ *three times*   והנה איננו גֿ   Mm

Gen 31:2	כתמול שלשום
Judg 3:25	והנה <איננו> פתח
Ps 37:36	ויעבר והנה

Com.: The Masorah notes the *three* occurrences of אֵינֶנּוּ with וְהִנֵּה, to distinguish them from its more numerous occurrences (32x) without וְהִנֵּה.

3:25   הַמַּפְתֵּחַ

Unique   לֿ   Mp

Judg 3:25; 1 Chr 9:27

Com.: The Mp heading here of *unique* is incorrect since there are *two* occurrences of this lemma. Both M^C and M^A correctly read *twice*, and add catchwords referring the reader to 1 Chr 9:27. M^A adds וְהֶם עַל והם על (וְהֶם עַל), and M^C adds והם על המפתח (הַמַּפְתֵּחַ).

It is possible that the note more precisely should have read *unique in the book*, but it seems more likely that this note has mistakenly been confused with the following one.

3:25   וַיִּפְתָּחוּ

Twice   בֿ   Mp

Com.: The Mp heading here of *twice* is incorrect since there this is the *only* occurrence of this lemma. It would seem that this note has mistakenly been confused with the preceding one.

M^A correctly reads here *unique*, but M^C has no note.

JUDGES 3:26

וְאֵהוּד נִמְלַט עַד הִתְמַהְמְהָם וְהוּא עָבַר אֶת־הַפְּסִילִים וַיִּמָּלֵט הַשְּׂעִירָתָה׃

3:26   הִתְמַהְמְהָם

Unique   ל   Mp

Com.: The Masorah notes the *sole* occurrence of this quadriliteral verb, possibly to distinguish it from the occurrences of other forms of this quadriliteral such as וַיִּתְמַהְמָהּ at Gen 19:16, הִתְמַהְמָהְנוּ at Gen 43:10, and וְהִתְמַהְמָהּ at **Judg 19:8**.

3:26   הַפְּסִילִים

Four times plene   ד מל   Mp

Com.: See directly above at **Judg 3:19**.

3:26   הַשְּׂעִירָתָה

Unique   ל   Mp

JUDGES 3:27

וַיְהִי בְּבוֹאוֹ וַיִּתְקַע בַּשּׁוֹפָר בְּהַר אֶפְרָיִם וַיֵּרְדוּ עִמּוֹ בְנֵי־יִשְׂרָאֵל מִן־הָהָר וְהוּא לִפְנֵיהֶם׃

3:27   בְּבוֹאוֹ

Unique plene   ל מל   Mp

Com.: The Masorah notes the *single* occurrence of this lemma written plene first ו, to distinguish it from its more numerous occurrences (15x) written defective first ו (בְּבֹאוֹ).

JUDGES 3:28

וַיֹּאמֶר אֲלֵהֶם רִדְפוּ אַחֲרַי כִּי־נָתַן יְהוָה אֶת־אֹיְבֵיכֶם אֶת־מוֹאָב בְּיֶדְכֶם וַיֵּרְדוּ אַחֲרָיו וַיִּלְכְּדוּ אֶת־מַעְבְּרוֹת הַיַּרְדֵּן לְמוֹאָב וְלֹא־נָתְנוּ אִישׁ לַעֲבֹר׃

3:28   אֲלֵהֶם

Six times defective in the book   ו חס בסיפ   Mp

1–5   **Judg 3:28**; **8:23**; 8:24; 18:2; 18:4
6   **Judg 19:23**[b]

Com.: The Masorah notes the *six* occurrences of this lemma in the book written defective י, to distinguish them from its more numerous occurrences (10x) in the book written plene י (אֲלֵיהֶם).

The Mp heading at Judg 8:23 enumerates the *twenty-nine* occurrences of this lemma in the Prophets, for which there is a Mm at 1 Kgs 12:16 and Ezek 33:25.

3:28   הַיַּרְדֵּן לְמוֹאָב

Unique   ל   Mp

JUDGES 3:29

וַיַּכּוּ אֶת־מוֹאָב בָּעֵת הַהִיא כַּעֲשֶׂרֶת אֲלָפִים אִישׁ כָּל־שָׁמֵן וְכָל־אִישׁ חָיִל וְלֹא נִמְלַט אִישׁ׃

3:29   שָׁמֵן

Four times   ד   Mp

Judg 3:29; **Ezek 34:14**; Hab 1:16; 1 Chr 4:40

שָׁמֵן *four times*   שמן ד   Mm

Judg 3:29	כל שמן וכל איש חיל
Ezek 34:14	ומרעה שמן תרעינה
Hab 1:16	כי בהמה שמן חלקו
1 Chr 4:40	וימצאו מרעה שמן וטוב

Com.: The Masorah notes the *four* occurrences of this lemma with a *ṣerê* under the מ, to distinguish them from its more numerous occurrences (14x) with a *səḡôl* under the מ (שָׁמֶן).

3:29   וְכָל־אִישׁ

Seventeen times   יז   Mp

1–5	Exod 35:22; 35:23; 36:1; **Judg 3:29**; **20:33**
6–10	**1 Sam 14:22; 17:19; 17:24**; 22:2ᵃ; 22:2ᵇ
11–15	**2 Sam 16:18; 17:14**; 17:24; 2 Kgs 23:2; **Ezek 39:20**
16	**2 Chr 34:30**

Com.: The Mp heading here of *seventeen* is incorrect since there are only *sixteen* occurrences of this lemma. The error is probably a graphic one confusing ז *seven* with ו *six*.

The Masorah notes the *sixteen* occurrences of this lemma with a ו cj., to distinguish them from its more numerous occurrences (39x) without a cj.

Six of the Mp headings highlighted above read *seventeen times* (Judg 3:29, 20:33, 1 Sam 14:22, 17:19, 17:24 and 2 Sam 16:18), whereas only *three* Mp headings, and the Mm heading at 2 Chr 34:30, read *sixteen times* (2 Sam 17:14, Ezek 39:20, and 2 Chr 34:30).

M[A] correctly reads here *sixteen*, but M[C] has no note.

JUDGES 3:30

וַתִּכָּנַע מוֹאָב בַּיּוֹם הַהוּא תַּחַת יַד יִשְׂרָאֵל וַתִּשְׁקֹט הָאָרֶץ שְׁמוֹנִים שָׁנָה: ס

3:30   שְׁמוֹנִים

Six times plene   ו מל   Mp

1–5   **Gen 5:26** (וּשְׁמוֹנִים); **Judg 3:30**; **1 Kgs 6:1** (בִּשְׁמוֹנִים); **2 Kgs 19:35**; **Ps 90:10**
6   Esth 1:4

שְׁמוֹנִים *six times* plene   שמונים ו מל   Mm

1–5	The middle occurrence *of Methuselah* (Gen 5:26)	מציעייא דמתושלח
	וַתִּשְׁקֹט *of Ehud* (Judg 3:30)	ותשקט דאהוד
	1 Kgs 6:1	ויהי בשמונים שנה
	בְּמַחֲנֵה אַשּׁוּר *of Kings* (2 Kgs 19:35)	במחנה אשור דמלכים
	Ps 90:10	ואם (בגברות) [בגבורת]
6	Esth 1:4	בהראתו את עשר

And *all* Chronicles   וכל דברי הימ׳ כות׳
Apart from *one* (וּשְׁמוֹנִים): 2 Chr 2:17   ב׳ מ׳ א׳ ויעש מהם

Com.: The Masorah notes the *six* occurrences of this lemma in various forms written plene ו, to distinguish them from its more numerous occurrences (23x) in various forms written defective ו (שְׁמֹנִים).

This distinction is implied in *two* of the additional notations in the Mm. The first additional notation is the *middle* (that is, the *second*) occurrence *of Methuselah* to the Gen 5:26 reference, which distinguishes it from the *first* occurrence of Methuselah in that passage (Gen 5:25), where the lemma occurs written defective as (וּשְׁמֹנִים).

The second additional notation is *of Kings* to the 2 Kgs 19:35 reference, which distinguishes it from the parallel passage in Isa 37:36, where the lemma occurs as וּשְׁמֹנִים.

The third additional notation *of Ehud* to the Judg 3:30 reference simply distinguishes it from the *three* other occurrences of the catchword in Judges (Judg 3:11, 5:31, and 8:28), that do not contain the lemma.

The Mm has an additional note that this lemma is also the norm (9x) in Chronicles, apart from *one* case when it is written defective ו (וּשְׁמֹנִים) at 2 Chr 2:17.

Two of the Mp headings highlighted above (at Gen 5:26 and 2 Kgs 19:35) read *six times*, and similarly all Chronicles apart from one.

Judges 3:31

וְאַחֲרָיו הָיָה שַׁמְגַּר בֶּן־עֲנָת וַיַּךְ אֶת־פְּלִשְׁתִּים שֵׁשׁ־מֵאוֹת אִישׁ בְּמַלְמַד הַבָּקָר וַיֹּשַׁע גַּם־הוּא אֶת־יִשְׂרָאֵל: ס

3:31   בְּמַלְמַד

Unique   ל   Mp

Judges 4:2

וַיִּמְכְּרֵם יְהוָה בְּיַד יָבִין מֶלֶךְ־כְּנַעַן אֲשֶׁר מָלַךְ בְּחָצוֹר וְשַׂר־צְבָאוֹ סִיסְרָא וְהוּא יוֹשֵׁב בַּחֲרֹשֶׁת הַגּוֹיִם:

4:2   מָלַךְ בְּחָצוֹר

Twice   בׄ   Mp

Com.: The Mp heading here of *twice* is incorrect since this is the *only* occurrence of this lemma.

Neither M[C] nor M[A] has a note on this lemma here.

JUDGES 4:3

וַיִּצְעֲק֤וּ בְנֵֽי־יִשְׂרָאֵל֙ אֶל־יְהוָ֔ה כִּ֠י תְּשַׁ֨ע מֵא֤וֹת רֶֽכֶב־בַּרְזֶל֙ ל֔וֹ וְה֗וּא לָחַ֞ץ אֶת־בְּנֵ֧י יִשְׂרָאֵ֛ל בְּחָזְקָ֖ה עֶשְׂרִ֥ים שָׁנָֽה׃ ס

4:3   וַיִּצְעֲק֤וּ

Seven times   ז   Mp

Com.: See **Josh 24:7**.

4:3   בְּחָזְקָ֖ה

Four times   ד   Mp

Judg 4:3; 8:1; 1 Sam 2:16; Jonah 3:8

Com.: The Masorah notes the *four* occurrences of this lemma, written without a ו cj., to distinguish them from the *sole* occurrence of its parallel form בְּחָזַק at Isa 40:10.

JUDGES 4:4

וּדְבוֹרָה֙ אִשָּׁ֣ה נְבִיאָ֔ה אֵ֖שֶׁת לַפִּיד֑וֹת הִ֛יא שֹׁפְטָ֥ה אֶת־יִשְׂרָאֵ֖ל בָּעֵ֥ת הַהִֽיא׃

4:4   וּדְבוֹרָה֙

Unique   ל   Mp

Com.: The Masorah notes the *sole* occurrence of this lemma with a ו cj., to distinguish it from its more numerous occurrences (6x) without a cj., *three* of which occur in this chapter in vv. 5, 9, and 10.

4:4   לַפִּיד֑וֹת

Unique   ל   Mp

Com.: The Masorah notes the *sole* occurrence of this lemma with the fem. pl. ending, possibly to distinguish it from its occurrence with the masc. pl. ending (לַפִּידִים) at Job 41:11.

4:4 שֹׁפְטָה

Unique ל Mp

Com.: This lemma is featured in a Masoretic list of *three* forms of the verb שָׁפַט, *two* containing the imper. with a paragogic ה (שָׁפְטָה) at Ps 82:8 and Lam 3:59, and *one* (here) containing the partic. fem. (שֹׁפְטָה); see Ognibeni, *'Oklah*, §16H.

JUDGES 4:5

וְהִיא יוֹשֶׁבֶת תַּחַת־תֹּמֶר דְּבוֹרָה בֵּין הָרָמָה וּבֵין בֵּית־אֵל בְּהַר אֶפְרָיִם וַיַּעֲלוּ אֵלֶיהָ בְּנֵי יִשְׂרָאֵל לַמִּשְׁפָּט:

4:5 תֹּמֶר

Unique ל Mp

Com.: The Masorah notes the *sole* occurrence of this lemma pointed this way, to distinguish it from its more numerous occurrences (22x) pointed as תָּמָר.

4:5 לַמִּשְׁפָּט

Five times ה̇ Mp

The Mp heading here of *five times* is a mistake for the correct number *fifteen*; see **Josh 20:6**.

JUDGES 4:6

וַתִּשְׁלַח וַתִּקְרָא לְבָרָק בֶּן־אֲבִינֹעַם מִקֶּדֶשׁ נַפְתָּלִי וַתֹּאמֶר אֵלָיו הֲלֹא צִוָּה | יְהוָה אֱלֹהֵי־יִשְׂרָאֵל לֵךְ וּמָשַׁכְתָּ בְּהַר תָּבוֹר וְלָקַחְתָּ עִמְּךָ עֲשֶׂרֶת אֲלָפִים אִישׁ מִבְּנֵי נַפְתָּלִי וּמִבְּנֵי זְבֻלוּן:

4:6 צִוָּה יְהוָה אֱלֹהֵי יִשְׂרָאֵל

Three times ג̇ Mp

Josh 10:40; **Judg 4:6**; 1 Chr 24:19 (צִוָּהוּ)

Mm   צוה יהוה אלהי ישראל גֿ וסימנהון   *three times,* צִוָּה יְהוָה אֱלֹהֵי יִשְׂרָאֵל
and their references

Josh 10:40	ויכה (יהושׁ) [יהושע]
Judg 4:6	ותשלח ותקרא לברק {ותקרא}
1 Chr 24:19	אלה פקדתם (לעֿ) [לעבדתם]

Com.: The Masorah notes the *three* occurrences of the phrase צִוָּה/צִוָּהוּ יְהוָה, with אֱלֹהֵי יִשְׂרָאֵל, to distinguish them from its occurrences with suffixed forms of אֱלֹהִים, such as אֱלֹהֶיךָ, אֱלֹהֵיכֶם, and אֱלֹהֵינוּ, e.g., צִוָּה יְהוָה אֱלֹהֵינוּ.

In M^L circelli have been placed on the words הֲלֹא צִוָּה יְהוָה אֱלֹהֵי but, as the Mm shows here and at Josh 10:40, the note ought to include the following word (יִשְׂרָאֵל), not the preceding one (הֲלֹא).

4:6   וּמָשַׁכְתָּ

Unique   לֿ   Mp

4:6   זְבֻלוּן

Nine times written this way, and similarly   טֿ כֿתֿ כן וכל כתיֿב דכות בֿ מֿ אֿ   Mp
all the Writings apart from *one*

Com.: See **Josh 19:27**.

> ## JUDGES 4:7
>
> וּמָשַׁכְתִּי אֵלֶיךָ אֶל־נַחַל קִישׁוֹן אֶת־סִיסְרָא שַׂר־צְבָא יָבִין וְאֶת־רִכְבּוֹ וְאֶת־הֲמוֹנוֹ וּנְתַתִּיהוּ בְּיָדֶךָ:

4:7   וּנְתַתִּיהוּ

Twice   בֿ   Mp

Judg 4:7; **Ezek 16:19**

Com.: The Masorah notes the *two* occurrences of this lemma with the 3rd masc. sfx., to distinguish it from more numerous occurrences (5x) of its alternate form וּנְתַתִּיו.

The Mp heading at Ezek 16:19 *of unique* is inexact, and that note more precisely should have read *unique in the book*. However, the heading of the Mm note there reads *twice* and lists the above *two* occurrences.

JUDGES 4:8

וַיֹּ֤אמֶר אֵלֶ֨יהָ֙ בָּרָ֔ק אִם־תֵּלְכִ֥י עִמִּ֖י וְהָלָ֑כְתִּי וְאִם־לֹ֧א תֵלְכִ֛י עִמִּ֖י לֹ֥א אֵלֵֽךְ׃

4:8   וְאִם־לֹא

Seventeen times in the middle of a verse   יֵ֗ בְּאֶמְצַ פָּסוּק   Mp

1–5   Gen 4:7; 18:21; 24:41; 24:49; 42:16
6–10   Exod 13:13; 34:20; Lev 27:27; Num 5:19; 19:12
11–15   **Judg 4:8**; 1 Sam 2:16; **6:9**; Zech 11:12; Mal 2:2
16–17   Ruth 3:13; 4:4

Com.: The Masorah notes the *seventeen* occurrences of this lemma in the middle of a verse, to distinguish them from its more numerous occurrences (29x) at the beginning of a verse.

JUDGES 4:9

וַתֹּ֜אמֶר הָלֹ֧ךְ אֵלֵ֣ךְ עִמָּ֗ךְ אֶ֚פֶס כִּי֩ לֹ֨א תִֽהְיֶ֜ה תִּֽפְאַרְתְּךָ֗ עַל־הַדֶּ֙רֶךְ֙ אֲשֶׁ֣ר אַתָּ֣ה הוֹלֵ֔ךְ כִּ֣י בְֽיַד־אִשָּׁ֔ה יִמְכֹּ֥ר יְהוָ֖ה אֶת־סִֽיסְרָ֑א וַתָּ֧קָם דְּבוֹרָ֛ה וַתֵּ֥לֶךְ עִם־בָּרָ֖ק קֶֽדְשָׁה׃

4:9   הָלֹךְ

הָלֹךְ *four times* defective   הלך דֹ חסֹ   Mm

Judg 4:9   ותאמר הלך אלך
Gen 31:30   ועתה הלך הלכת
1 Sam 6:12   במסלה אחת הלכו (הלוך) [הלך] {וילך}
Isa 20:2   ויעש כן (הלוך) [הלך] ערום ויחף

And similarly *all* Jeremiah apart from *six*   וכל ירמיה דכות בֹ מֹ וֹ

1–5   Jer 13:1   וקנית לך אזור
Jer 19:1   וקנית בקבק
Jer 31:2   (הלך) [הלוך] להרגיעו
Jer 35:2   אל בית הרכבים
Jer 39:16   לעבד מלך הכושי
6   Jer 50:4   הלוך (ובכה) [ובכו]

Com.: The Masorah notes the *four* occurrences, apart from Jeremiah, of this lemma, written defective וֹ, to distinguish them from its more numerous occurrences (32x) written plene ו (הָלוֹךְ).

The Masorah also notes that this lemma written defective וֹ (הָלֹךְ/וְהָלֹךְ) occurs (10x) in Jeremiah, apart from *six* listed cases when it is written plene וֹ (הָלוֹךְ).

It should be noted that *one* of these exceptional forms (Jer 19:1) is written defective וֹ in M (הָלֹךְ). On the other hand M^L, contrary to M (הָלֹךְ), writes Jer 28:13 plene וֹ so that, in total, M^L is in agreement with the Mm note that there are *six* plene forms in Jeremiah; see Breuer, *The Biblical Text*, 163, 177 and 392.

After the catchwords for the 1 Sam 6:12 reference, the form וַיֵּלֶךְ has mistakenly been added.

4:9   תִּפְאַרְתְּךָ

Unique   ל   Mp

Com.: The Masorah notes the *sole* occurrence of this lemma with a *šəwâ* under the second ת, to distinguish it from its *two* occurrences with a *səḡôl* (תִּפְאַרְתֶּךָ, pausal form) at Ps 71:8 and 1 Chr 29:13.

4:9   הוֹלֵךְ

Twice plene in the book   ב מל בסיפֿ   Mp

Judg 4:9; 14:3

הוֹלֵךְ *twice* plene in the book   הולך ב מל בסיפֿ   Mm

Judg 4:9	על הדרך אשר
Judg 14:3	לקחת

Com.: The Masorah notes the *two* occurrences of this lemma written plene וֹ in the book.

The Mp heading at Judg 14:3 reads *twenty-nine times plene* (וֹ) enumerating all occurrences, apart from Proverbs and Qoheleth, but the correct number should be *twenty-seven* as indicated in the Mm at 2 Sam 15:20.

4:9   קְדֵשָׁה

Twice   בֿ   Mp

Judg 4:9; 4:10

Com.: The Masorah notes the *two* occurrences of this lemma pointed this way, to distinguish them from its *sole* occurrence pointed as קֶדֵשָׁה at Judg 11:16.

JUDGES 4:10

וַיִּזְעַק בָּרָק אֶת־זְבוּלֻן וְאֶת־נַפְתָּלִי קֶדְשָׁה וַיַּעַל בְּרַגְלָיו עֲשֶׂרֶת אַלְפֵי אִישׁ וַתַּעַל עִמּוֹ דְּבוֹרָה׃

4:10   וַיִּזְעַק

Four times   דֿ   Mp

Judg 4:10; 4:13; Jonah 3:7; Zech 6:8

Com.: The Masorah notes the *four* occurrences of this lemma written with a ז, to distinguish them from its *sole* occurrence written with a צ (וַיִּצְעַק) at 1 Sam 10:17.

4:10   קֶדְשָׁה

Twice   בֿ   Mp

Com.: See directly above at **Judg 4:9**.

4:10   וַיַּעַל בְּרַגְלָיו

Unique   לֿ   Mp

4:10   עֲשֶׂרֶת אַלְפֵי

Unique   לֿ   Mp

Com.: The Masorah notes the *sole* occurrence of עֲשֶׂרֶת with אַלְפֵי (cstr.), to distinguish it from its more numerous occurrences (17x) with אֲלָפִים (absol., עֲשֶׂרֶת אֲלָפִים), *one* of which occurs in v. 6.

JUDGES 4:11

וְחֶ֤בֶר הַקֵּינִי֙ נִפְרָ֣ד מִקַּ֔יִן מִבְּנֵ֥י חֹבָ֖ב חֹתֵ֣ן מֹשֶׁ֑ה וַיֵּ֣ט אָהֳל֗וֹ עַד־אֵל֥וֹן בְּצַעֲנַנִּ֖ים אֲשֶׁ֥ר אֶת־קֶֽדֶשׁ׃

4:11   נִפְרָ֣ד

Twice   בֿ   Mp

Judg 4:11; Prov 18:1

4:11   מִקַּ֔יִן

Unique   ל   Mp

The Masorah notes the *sole* occurrence of this lemma with the prep. מ, to distinguish it from its *two* occurrences with the prep. ל (לְקַיִן) at Gen 4:5 and 4:15.

4:11   בְּצַעֲנַנִּ֖ים

Read בְּצַעֲנַנִּים   בצענים קרי   Mp

Com.: The *kǝṯîḇ* (בצענים), and the *qǝrê* (בְּצַעֲנַנִּים) represent variations in proper names; see Gordis, *The Biblical Text*, 156.

This lemma is featured in a Masoretic list of words that are read with a second נ which has not been written; see Frensdorff, *Ochlah*, §158, Díaz-Esteban, *Sefer Oklah we-Oklah*, §144, and **Josh 19:33**.

In M^L this lemma has no circellus.

JUDGES 4:13

וַיַּזְעֵ֨ק סִֽיסְרָ֜א אֶת־כָּל־רִכְבּ֗וֹ תְּשַׁ֤ע מֵאוֹת֙ רֶ֣כֶב בַּרְזֶ֔ל וְאֶת־כָּל־הָעָ֖ם אֲשֶׁ֣ר אִתּ֑וֹ מֵחֲרֹ֥שֶׁת הַגּוֹיִ֖ם אֶל־נַ֥חַל קִישֽׁוֹן׃

4:13   וַיַּזְעֵ֨ק

Four times   דֿ   Mp

Com.: See directly above at **Judg 4:10**.

4:13   וְאֶת־כָּל־הָעָם

Three times   גֿ   Mp

Judg 4:13; 1 Sam 15:8; Jer 41:10

Com.: The Masorah notes the *three* occurrences of this lemma with a וֹ cj., to distinguish them from its more numerous occurrences (14x) without a cj.

JUDGES 4:14

וַתֹּאמֶר דְּבֹרָה אֶל־בָּרָק קוּם כִּי זֶה הַיּוֹם אֲשֶׁר נָתַן יְהוָה אֶת־סִיסְרָא בְּיָדֶךָ הֲלֹא יְהוָה יָצָא לְפָנֶיךָ וַיֵּרֶד בָּרָק מֵהַר תָּבוֹר וַעֲשֶׂרֶת אֲלָפִים אִישׁ אַחֲרָיו׃

4:14   דְּבֹרָה

Three times defective   גֿ חסֿ   Mp

Gen 35:8; Judg 4:14; 5:15

Com.: The Masorah notes the *three* occurrences of this lemma written defective וֹ, to distinguish them from its more numerous occurrences (6x) written plene וֹ (דְּבוֹרָה).

JUDGES 4:15

וַיָּהָם יְהוָה אֶת־סִיסְרָא וְאֶת־כָּל־הָרֶכֶב וְאֶת־כָּל־הַמַּחֲנֶה לְפִי־חֶרֶב לִפְנֵי בָרָק וַיֵּרֶד סִיסְרָא מֵעַל הַמֶּרְכָּבָה וַיָּנָס בְּרַגְלָיו׃

4:15   וַיָּהָם

Twice   בֿ   Mp

Exod 14:24; Judg 4:15

Com.: The Mp heading at Exod 14:24 adds catchwords את סיסרא (אֶת־סִיסְרָא) to refer the reader to this verse.

This lemma is featured in a Masoretic list of doublets that start with a וי; see Frensdorff, *Ochlah*, §68, and Díaz-Esteban, *Sefer Oklah we-Oklah*, §69.

4:15   וְאֶת־כָּל־הַמַּחֲנֶ֑ה

Twice   בֿ   Mp

Judg 4:15; 7:14

Com.: The Masorah notes the *sole* occurrence of this lemma with a ו cj., to distinguish it from its occurrence without a cj. at Josh 8:13.

JUDGES 4:16

וּבָרָ֗ק רָדַ֞ף אַחֲרֵ֤י הָרֶ֙כֶב֙ וְאַחֲרֵ֣י הַֽמַּחֲנֶ֔ה עַ֖ד חֲרֹ֣שֶׁת הַגּוֹיִ֑ם וַיִּפֹּ֞ל כָּל־מַחֲנֵ֤ה סִֽיסְרָא֙ לְפִי־חֶ֔רֶב לֹ֥א נִשְׁאַ֖ר עַד־אֶחָֽד׃

4:16   וּבָרָק

Three times   גֿ   Mp

Judg 4:16; 5:1; Job 20:25

Com.: The Masorah notes the *three* occurrences of this lemma with a ו cj., to distinguish them from its more numerous occurrences (16x) without a cj.

4:16   עַד־אֶחָד

Twice at the end of a verse   בֿ סוֹף פסוק   Mp

Exod 14:28; **Judg 4:16**

Com.: The Masorah notes the *two* occurrences of this lemma at the end of a verse, to distinguish them from its *single* occurrence in the middle of a verse at Exod 9:7.

JUDGES 4:18

וַתֵּצֵ֣א יָעֵל֮ לִקְרַ֣את סִֽיסְרָא֒ וַתֹּ֣אמֶר אֵלָ֗יו סוּרָ֧ה אֲדֹנִ֛י סוּרָ֥ה אֵלַ֖י אַל־תִּירָ֑א וַיָּ֤סַר אֵלֶ֙יהָ֙ הָאֹ֔הֱלָה וַתְּכַסֵּ֖הוּ בַּשְּׂמִיכָֽה׃

4:18   סוּרָה¹

Twice accented (*milraʿ*)   בֿ בטע   Mp

Judg 4:18ᵃ; 4:18ᵇ; Isa 49:21 (וְסוּרָה)

Mm   סורה ג̇ מלרע וסימנהון   סוּרָה *three times milra*ʿ, and their references

Judg 4:18[a]   יעל

Twice in it (Judg 4:18[b])   ב̇ בו

Isa 49:21   (גולה) [גלה]

Com.: The Masorah notes the *three* occurrences of this lemma accented *milra*ʿ, to distinguish them from its *sole* occurrence accented *mil*ʿ*êl* at Ruth 4:1 (סוּרָה).

The Mp heading here *of twice accented* (*milra*ʿ) is inexact since there are *three* occurrences of this lemma. The note more precisely should have read *twice accented* (*milra*ʿ) *in the book.*

M[A] correctly reads *three times milra*ʿ, whereas M[C] has no note here.

This lemma is featured in two Masoretic lists. One is in a list of words occurring *three times*, *twice* without a ו cj., and *once* with it; see Frensdorff, *Ochlah*, §13, and Díaz-Esteban, *Sefer Oklah we-Oklah*, §14.

The other in a list of doublets that occur in the same verse; see Frensdorff, *Ochlah*, §58, and Díaz-Esteban, *Sefer Oklah we-Oklah*, §59.

4:18   בַּשְׂמִיכָה

Mp   ל̇ וכת̇ שׂ   *Unique*, and written with a שׂ

Mm   בשמיכה י̇ כת̇ שׂ וקרין ס וסימנהון   בַּשְׂמִיכָה *ten* (words) written with a שׂ but read with a ס, and their references

1–5	Judg 4:18	בשמיכה
	Isa 3:17	ושפח
	Isa 5:5	משוכתו
	Hos 9:12	בשורי
	Hos 8:4	השירו
6–10	Lam 3:8	שתם
	Qoh 12:11	וכמשמרות
	Ezek 41:16	שחיף
	Lam 2:6	שכו
	Job 40:31	בשכות

Com.: The Masorah notes the *ten* words, of which this lemma is one, when the letter ש, is read as ס; see Frensdorff, *Ochlah*, §191, and Ognibeni, *'Oklah*, §327.

By noting that this lemma is *unique* and written with ש, the Mp is also implying (correctly) that this lemma does not occur elsewhere written with a ס.

JUDGES 4:19

וַיֹּ֨אמֶר אֵלֶ֤יהָ הַשְׁקִינִי־נָ֣א מְעַט־מַ֨יִם֙ כִּ֣י צָמֵ֔אתִי וַתִּפְתַּ֞ח אֶת־נֹ֥אוד הֶחָלָ֛ב וַתַּשְׁקֵ֖הוּ וַתְּכַסֵּֽהוּ׃

4:19 **צָמֵ֔אתִי**

Unique ל Mp

JUDGES 4:20

וַיֹּ֣אמֶר אֵלֶ֗יהָ עֲמֹ֛ד פֶּ֥תַח הָאֹ֖הֶל וְהָיָה֩ אִם־אִ֨ישׁ יָב֜וֹא וּשְׁאֵלֵ֗ךְ וְאָמַ֛ר הֲיֵשׁ־פֹּ֥ה אִ֖ישׁ וְאָמַ֥רְתְּ אָֽיִן׃

4:20 **וְאָמַ֥רְתְּ**

Three times ג Mp

Judg 4:20; 1 Kgs 1:13; Isa 49:21

Com.: The Masorah notes the *three* occurrences of this lemma with a ו cj., to distinguish them, as indicated in the Mm to 2 Sam 6:22 *sub* אָמַ֥רְתְּ, from its more numerous occurrences (7x) without a cj.

JUDGES 4:21

וַתִּקַּ֣ח יָעֵ֣ל אֵֽשֶׁת־חֶ֠בֶר אֶת־יְתַ֨ד הָאֹ֜הֶל וַתָּ֧שֶׂם אֶת־הַמַּקֶּ֣בֶת בְּיָדָ֗הּ וַתָּב֤וֹא אֵלָיו֙ בַּלָּ֔אט וַתִּתְקַ֤ע אֶת־הַיָּתֵד֙ בְּרַקָּת֔וֹ וַתִּצְנַ֖ח בָּאָ֑רֶץ וְהֽוּא־נִרְדָּ֥ם וַיָּ֖עַף וַיָּמֹֽת׃

4:21 **בַּלָּ֔אט**

Four times ד Mp

Judg 4:21; 1 Sam 18:22 (בְּלָ֑ט); 24:5 (בַּלָּ֑ט); **Ruth 3:7** (בַּלָּ֑ט)

בְּלָאט   *four times*, *once* plene and *three times* defective   בלאט ד חד מל וג חס   Mm

<u>Judg 4:21</u>	ותבוא אליו בלאט
1 Sam 18:22	ויצו שאול את
1 Sam 24:5	(ויכו) [ויכרת] את כנף המעיל אשר
<u>Ruth 3:7</u>	ותבא בלט ותגל

Com.: The Masorah notes the *four* occurrences of this lemma, *once* written plene with א here, and *three times* written defective א.

The Mp heading at Ruth 3:7 mistakenly reads *twice in the Writings*. The note, however, belongs on the preceding word וַתָּבֹא, and the Mm heading at <u>Ruth 3:7</u> correctly reads *four times, once superfluous* א.

This lemma is featured in a Masoretic list of words where an א is written but not read: see the Mm to <u>Num 11:4</u> *sub* וְהָאסַפְסֻף, Frensdorff, *Ochlah*, §103, and Díaz-Esteban, *Sefer Oklah we-Oklah*, §86.

4:21   וַתִּצְנַח

Three times   ‎ג̇   Mp

Josh 15:18; Judg 1:14; 4:21

4:21   נִרְדָּם

Five times   ‎ה̇   Mp

1–5   **Judg 4:21**; Jonah 1:6; **Ps 76:7; Prov 10:5; Dan 10:9**

Com.: Since there are *five* occurrences of this lemma, the Mp heading at Ps 76:7 *of unique* is inexact, and that note more precisely should have read *unique in the book*.

JUDGES 4:22

וְהִנֵּה בָרָק רֹדֵף אֶת־סִיסְרָא וַתֵּצֵא יָעֵל לִקְרָאתוֹ וַתֹּאמֶר לוֹ לֵךְ וְאַרְאֶךָּ אֶת־הָאִישׁ אֲשֶׁר־אַתָּה מְבַקֵּשׁ וַיָּבֹא אֵלֶיהָ וְהִנֵּה סִיסְרָא נֹפֵל מֵת וְהַיָּתֵד בְּרַקָּתוֹ:

4:22   וְהִנֵּה

Twice at the beginning of a verse   ב̇ ראש פסוק   Mp

<u>Judg 4:22</u>; 19:16

וְהִנֵּה *twice* at the beginning of a verse in the book   והנה בֿ ראש פסוק בסיפֿ   Mm

Judg 4:22   ברק רדף את סיסרא
Judg 19:16   איש זקן

Com.: The Mp heading here *of twice at the beginning of a verse* is inexact since there are many more occurrences (60x) of this lemma elsewhere. The note more precisely should have read, as it does in M^C and M^A, in the Mm heading here and in the Mp heading at Judg 19:16, *twice at the beginning of a verse in the book.*

The Masorah notes the *two* occurrences of this lemma at the beginning of a verse in the book with a וֹ cj., to distinguish it from its *three* occurrences at the beginning of a verse in the book without a וֹ cj.

4:22   בְּרָקָתוֹ

Twice   בֿ   Mp

Judg 4:21: **4:22**

Com.: The Masorah notes the *two* occurrences of this lemma with the prep. בֿ, to distinguish it from its *sole* occurrence without this prep. at Judg 5:26.

JUDGES 4:23

וַיַּכְנַע אֱלֹהִים בַּיּוֹם הַהוּא אֵת יָבִין מֶלֶךְ־כְּנָעַן לִפְנֵי בְּנֵי יִשְׂרָאֵל׃

4:23   וַיַּכְנַע

Twice   בֿ   Mp

Judg 4:23; Ps 107:12

Com.: The Masorah notes the *two* occurrences of this lemma in the *hiphil*, to distinguish them from its *three* occurrences in the *niphal* (וַיִּכָּנַע); see **Judg 8:28.**

This lemma is featured in a Masoretic list of doublets that start with וי; see Frensdorff, *Ochlah,* §68, and Díaz-Esteban, *Sefer Oklah we-Oklah,* §69.

JUDGES 4:24

וַתֵּ֜לֶךְ יַ֤ד בְּנֵֽי־יִשְׂרָאֵל֙ הָל֣וֹךְ וְקָשָׁ֔ה עַ֖ל יָבִ֣ין מֶֽלֶךְ־כְּנָ֑עַן עַ֚ד אֲשֶׁ֣ר הִכְרִ֔יתוּ אֵ֖ת יָבִ֥ין מֶֽלֶךְ־כְּנָֽעַן׃ פ

4:24　　וְקָשָׁ֔ה

Unique　　ל　　Mp

Com.: The Masorah notes the *sole* occurrence of this lemma with a ‍ cj., to distinguish it from its more numerous occurrences (11x) without a cj.

4:24　　עַ֖ל יָבִ֣ין

Unique　　ל　　Mp

Com.: This lemma is featured in a Masoretic list of words that only occur *once* preceded by the prep. עַל; see Frensdorff, *Ochlah*, §76, and Díaz-Esteban, *Sefer Oklah we-Oklah*, §155.

JUDGES 5:1

וַתָּ֣שַׁר דְּבוֹרָ֔ה וּבָרָ֖ק בֶּן־אֲבִינֹ֑עַם בַּיּ֥וֹם הַה֖וּא לֵאמֹֽר׃

5:1　　וַתָּ֣שַׁר

Unique　　ל　　Mp

5:1　　וּבָרָ֖ק

Three times　　ג　　Mp

Com.: See **Judg 4:16**.

JUDGES 5:2

בִּפְרֹ֤עַ פְּרָעוֹת֙ בְּיִשְׂרָאֵ֔ל בְּהִתְנַדֵּ֖ב עָ֑ם בָּרֲכ֖וּ יְהוָֽה׃

5:2　　בִּפְרֹ֤עַ

Unique　　ל　　Mp

5:2　　פְּרָעוֹת֙

Unique　　ל　　Mp

5:2   בְּהִתְנַדֵּב

Unique   לֹ   Mp

Com.: The Masorah notes the *sole* occurrence of this lemma with the prep. בּ to distinguish it from its *two* occurrences with the prep. ל (לְהִתְנַדֵּב) at 1 Chr 29:14 and 29:17.

5:2   בָּרֲכוּ יְהוָה

Five times   הֹ   Mp

1–5   **Judg 5:2**; **5:9**; Ps 103:20; 103:21; 103:22

בָּרֲכוּ יְהוָה *five times*, and their references   ברכו יהוה ה וסימנהון   Mm

1–5   Judg 5:2   בפרע פרעות בישראל
             Judg 5:9   ושל אחריו
             Ps 103:20   מלאכיו (גבורי) [גברי] כח
             And the *one after it* (Ps 103:21)   ושל אחריו
             And the *one after it* (Ps 103:22)   ושל אחריו

Com.: The Masorah notes the *five* occurrences of this lemma without אֶת, to distinguish them from its *six* occurrences with אֶת (בָּרֲכוּ אֶת יְהוָה); see Ginsburg, 4, בּ, §495.

JUDGES 5:3
שִׁמְעוּ מְלָכִים הַאֲזִינוּ רֹזְנִים אָנֹכִי לַיהוָה אָנֹכִי אָשִׁירָה אֲזַמֵּר לַיהוָה אֱלֹהֵי יִשְׂרָאֵל:

5:3   הַאֲזִינוּ

Eight times   חֹ   Mp

1–5   **Deut 32:1**; **Judg 5:3**; Isa 1:10; 28:23; 51:4
6–8   Hos 5:1; Ps 49:2; Job 34:2

Com.: The Masorah notes the *three* occurrences of this lemma in the imper., to distinguish them from the *three* occurrences in the perf. (הֶאֱזִינוּ).

The Mp heading at Deut 32:1 reads *twice at the beginning of a verse* to include that reference and Isa 28:23, which are both at the beginning of verses.

5:3   אָנֹכִי לַיהוָה

Unique   ל   Mp

Com.: The Masorah notes the *sole* occurrence of this lemma with the prep. ל, to distinguish it from its more numerous occurrences (8x) without this preposition (אָנֹכִי יְהוָה).

5:3   אָשִׁירָה

Twice in the Prophets   ב בנביא   Mp

Judg 5:3; Isa 5:1

Com.: The Masorah notes the *two* occurrences of this lemma in the Prophets, to distinguish them from its more numerous occurrences (9x) in the Torah and Writings.

> **JUDGES 5:4**
>
> יְהוָה בְּצֵאתְךָ מִשֵּׂעִיר בְּצַעְדְּךָ מִשְּׂדֵה אֱדוֹם אֶרֶץ רָעָשָׁה גַּם־שָׁמַיִם נָטָפוּ גַּם־עָבִים נָטְפוּ מָיִם׃

5:4   בְּצֵאתְךָ מִשֵּׂעִיר

Unique   ל   Mp

5:4   בְּצַעְדְּךָ

Twice   בֿ   Mp

Judg 5:2; Ps 68:8

5:4   נָטָפוּ

Unique   ל   Mp

Com.: The Masorah notes the *sole* occurrence of this lemma with a *qameṣ* under the ט, to distinguish it from its *three* occurrences with a *šwâ* (נָטְפוּ); see directly below.

5:4   נָטְפוּ

Twice   בֿ   Mp

1–3   **Judg 5:4;** Ps 68:9; Cant 5:5

Com.: The Mp heading here of *twice* is incorrect since there are *three* occurrences of this lemma.

The Masorah notes the *three* occurrences of this lemma with a *šəwâ* under the ט, to distinguish it from its *sole* occurrence with a *qameṣ* (נָטְפוּ, pausal form), which occurs in this very verse, see directly above.

Dotan/Reich (*Masora Thesaurus, ad loc.*) suggest that the references covered by this note are only Judg 5:4 and Cant 5:5, because the forms in these passages are accented *mil‘êl* whereas the form in Ps 68:9 is accented *milra‘*.

Neither M^C nor M^A has a note on this lemma here.

JUDGES 5:6

בִּימֵי שַׁמְגַּר בֶּן־עֲנָת בִּימֵי יָעֵל חָדְלוּ אֳרָחוֹת וְהֹלְכֵי נְתִיבוֹת יֵלְכוּ אֳרָחוֹת עֲקַלְקַלּוֹת׃

5:6 אֳרָחוֹת²

Twice בֵּ Mp

Judg 5:4ᵃ; **5:4**ᵇ

Com.: This lemma is featured in a Masoretic list of doublets that occur in the same verse; see Frensdorff, *Ochlah*, §58, and Díaz-Esteban, *Sefer Oklah we-Oklah*, §59.

5:6 עֲקַלְקַלּוֹת

Unique לֵ Mp

Com.: The Masorah notes the *sole* occurrence of this lemma without a sfx., possibly to distinguish it from its occurrence with a sfx. (עֲקַלְקַלּוֹתָם) at Ps 125:5.

JUDGES 5:7

חָדְלוּ פְרָזוֹן בְּיִשְׂרָאֵל חָדֵלּוּ עַד שַׁקַּמְתִּי דְּבוֹרָה שַׁקַּמְתִּי אֵם בְּיִשְׂרָאֵל׃

5:7 פְרָזוֹן

Unique and plene ל וּמל Mp

Com.: By noting that this lemma is *unique* and written plene ו, the Masorah is also implying (correctly) that this lemma does not occur elsewhere written defective ו.

5:7   חָדֵלוּ

Twice   בֿ   Mp

Judg 5:7; 1 Sam 2:5

Com.: The Masorah notes the *two* occurrences of this lemma with a *ṣerê* under the ד, to distinguish them from its more numerous occurrences (5x) with a *šəwâ* (חָדְלוּ).

5:7   שַׁקַּמְתִּי¹

Twice   בֿ   Mp

Judg 5:7ᵃ; 5:7ᵇ

Com.: This lemma is featured in a Masoretic list of doublets that occur in the same verse; see Frensdorff, *Ochlah*, §58, and Díaz-Esteban, *Sefer Oklah we-Oklah*, §59.

JUDGES 5:8

יִבְחַר אֱלֹהִים חֲדָשִׁים אָז לָחֶם שְׁעָרִים מָגֵן אִס־יֵרָאֶה וָרֹמַח בְּאַרְבָּעִים אֶלֶף בְּיִשְׂרָאֵל:

5:8   לָחֶם

Unique   לֿ   Mp

Com.: The Mp heading here, and in Mᶜ and Mᴬ, *of unique* is inexact since there are many other occurrences (58x) of this lemma, but only *one* (here) accented *milraʿ*. The note more precisely should have read *unique milraʿ*.

This form is found in two Masoretic lists. One is in a list of words that occur only *once* written with a ח, but which otherwise are found written with a ה; see Frensdorff, *Ochlah*, §212, and Ognibeni, *'Oklah*, §148.

The other is in a list of words which only *once* occur accented *milraʿ* but which otherwise occur accented *milʿêl*; see Frensdorff, *Ochlah*, §373

5:8 יֵרָאֶה

Thirteen times יג Mp

1–5 **Gen 22:14**; Exod 13:7ª; **13:7ᵇ**; 23:17; 34:23
6–10 **Deut 16:4; 16:16ª; 16:16ᵇ; Judg 5:8**; Isa 60:2
11–13 **Zech 9:14**; Ps 84:8; 90:16

יֵרָאֶה *thirteen times* יראה יג Mm

1–5 <u>Gen 22:14</u>   יאמר היום
       Exod 13:7ª   מצות יאכל
       Twice in the verse (Exod 13:7ᵇ)   שנים בפסוק
       Exod 23:17   פעמים
       Exod 34:23   שלש
6–10 Deut 16:16ª   (שלש) [שלוש] פעמים
       Twice in the verse (Deut 16:16ᵇ)   שנים בפסוק
       Deut 16:4   שאר
       <u>Judg 5:8</u>   מגן אם יראה
       <u>Zech 9:14</u>   ויהוה עליהם
11–13 Isa 60:2   וכבודו
       Ps 84:8   אל אלהים
       Ps 90:16   אל עבדיך

Com.: The Masorah notes the *thirteen* occurrences of this lemma in the *niphal*, to distinguish them from its more numerous occurrences (52x) in the *qal* (יִרְאֶה).

5:8 בְּאַרְבָּעִים

Twice ב Mp

Deut 1:3; Judg 5:8

בְּאַרְבָּעִים *twice* בארבעים ב Mm

Deut 1:3   ויהי בארבעים שנה
<u>Judg 5:8</u>   בארבעים אלף (בישראׄ) [בישראל]

And *once* (כְּאַרְבָּעִים): Josh 4:13   וחד כארבעים אלף חלוצי (צבא) [הצבא]

Com.: The Mp notes the *two* occurrences of this lemma written with the prep. בְּ at Deut 1:3 and here, and the Mm has an additional note that this lemma occurs written with the prep. כ (כְּאַרְבָּעִים) at **Josh 4:13**.

JUDGES 5:9

לִבִּי֙ לְחֽוֹקְקֵ֣י יִשְׂרָאֵ֔ל הַמִּֽתְנַדְּבִ֖ים בָּעָ֑ם בָּרֲכ֖וּ יְהוָֽה׃

5:9   לְחֽוֹקְקֵ֣י

Unique and plene   ל וּמל   Mp

Com.: By noting that this lemma is *unique* and written plene וֹ, the Masorah is also implying (correctly) that this lemma does not occur elsewhere written defective וֹ.

5:9   הַמִּֽתְנַדְּבִ֖ים

Twice   בֿ   Mp

Judg 5:9; Neh 11:2

הַמִּֽתְנַדְּבִים *twice*, and their references   בֿ וסימנהון   Mm

<Judg 5:9>
Neh 11:2   ויברכו העם לכל האנשים

5:9   בָּרֲכ֖וּ יְהוָֽה

Five times   הֿ   Mp

Com.: See directly above at **Judg 5:2**.

JUDGES 5:10

רֹכְבֵי֩ אֲתֹנ֨וֹת צְחֹר֜וֹת יֹשְׁבֵ֧י עַל־מִדִּ֛ין וְהֹלְכֵ֥י עַל־דֶּ֖רֶךְ שִֽׂיחוּ׃

5:10   צְחֹר֜וֹת

Unique   ל   Mp

5:10   מִדִין

Three times   גׄ   Mp

Josh 15:61; Judg 5:10; Isa 10:2

מְדִין *three times*, and their references   מדין גׄ וסימנהון   Mm

Judg 5:10   ישבי על מדין והלכי
Isa 10:2   להטות מדין דלים (ולשפט) [ולגזל משפט]
Josh 15:61   במדבר בית הערבה

Com.: The Masorah notes the *three* occurrences of this lemma which, as mentioned in the Mm of Isa 10:2, have *three* different meanings, *once* as the name of a town *Middin* (Josh 15:61), *once* as *saddle rugs* (here), and *once* as the prep. מִן joined to דִין *a legal claim* (Isa 10:2).

5:10   עַל־דֶּרֶךְ

Five times   הׄ   Mp

1–5   **Gen 38:14; Judg 5:10; 1 Sam 6:12; Hos 13:7; Ps 36:5**

Com.: The Masorah notes the *five* occurrences of דֶּרֶךְ with עַל, to distinguish them from its *four* occurrences with אֶל (אֶל דֶּרֶךְ).

The Mp headings at 1 Sam 6:12 and Hos 13:7 mistakenly read *four times*, but the correct number is given in the other Mp headings highlighted above, and in the Mm headings and enumerations at Hos 13:7 and Ps 36:5.

The Mp heading at Ps 36:5 and the Mm there adds information about עַל־הַדֶּרֶךְ (with the def. article). The Mp reads *five times and similarly all* עַל־הַדֶּרֶךְ, whereas the Mm adds *and similarly all* עַל־הַדֶּרֶךְ, *apart from two*. That is, the norm for עַל־הַדֶּרֶךְ is with the prep. עַל (6x), apart from *two times* when it is with the prep. אֶל (אֶל הַדֶּרֶךְ) at Gen 38:16 and 2 Chr 6:27.

JUDGES 5:11

מִקּוֹל מְחַצְצִים בֵּין מַשְׁאַבִּים שָׁם יְתַנּוּ צִדְקוֹת יְהוָה צִדְקֹת פִּרְזֹנוֹ בְּיִשְׂרָאֵל אָז יָרְדוּ לַשְּׁעָרִים עַם־יְהוָה:

5:11	מְחַצְצִים		
Unique	ל	Mp	

5:11	מַשְׁאַבִּים		
Unique	ל	Mp	

5:11	יְתַנּוּ		
Unique	ל	Mp	

5:11	צִדְקוֹת		
Four times	ד	Mp	

Judg 5:11ᵃ;5:11ᵇ (צִדְקֹת); 1 Sam 12:7; **Mic 6:5**

Com.: The Masorah notes the *four* occurrences of this lemma, *three times* written plene ו and *once* written defective ֹ, possibly to distinguish them from the *four* occurrences pointed differently (צְדָקוֹת).

5:11	פִּרְזֹנוֹ		
Unique	ל	Mp	

Com.: Mᴸ, contrary to M (פִּרְזוֹנוֹ), writes the lemma here defective ֹ (see Breuer, *The Biblical Text*, 57).

Both Mᶜ and Mᴬ read פִּרְזוֹנוֹ. The Mp note in Mᴬ reads *unique*, whereas that in Mᶜ reads *unique and plene* (ו).

5:11	לַשְּׁעָרִים		
Unique	ל	Mp	

Com.: The Masorah notes the *sole* occurrence of this lemma with the prep. ל, to distinguish it from its more numerous occurrences (8x) with the prep. ב (בַּשְּׁעָרִים).

JUDGES 5:12

עוּרִי עוּרִי֙ דְּבוֹרָ֔ה עוּרִי עוּרִי֙ דַּבְּרִי־שִׁ֔יר ק֥וּם בָּרָ֖ק וּֽשֲׁבֵ֥ה שֶׁבְיְךָ֖ בֶּן־אֲבִינֹֽעַם׃

5:12   דַּבְּרִי

Three times   גֵ   Mp

Judg 5:12; **Jer 31:20**; Job 21:3

דַּבְּרִי *three times*, and (their) references   דברי גֵ וסימנ   Mm

Judg 5:12	עורי עורי דבורה
Jer 31:20	כי מדי דברי בו
Job 21:3	ואחר דברי תלעיג

Com.: The Masorah notes the *three* occurrences of this lemma with a *šəwâ* under the ב, possibly to distinguish them from its *sole* occurrence with a *ṣerê* (דַּבֵּרִי) at 2 Sam 14:12, or from its more common form דִּבְרֵי (13x); so Ginsburg, 4, ד, §51.

5:12   וּֽשֲׁבֵה

Unique   ל   Mp

5:12   שֶׁבְיְךָ

Unique   ל   Mp

Com.: This lemma is featured in a Masoretic list of *hapax legomena* that start with a *səgôl*; see Frensdorff, *Ochlah*, §370.

JUDGES 5:13

אָ֚ז יְרַ֣ד שָׂרִ֔יד לְאַדִּירִ֖ים עָ֑ם יְהֹוָ֕ה יְרַד־לִ֖י בַּגִּבּוֹרִֽים׃

5:13   יְרַד¹

Twice   בֵ   Mp

Judg 5:13ᵃ; 5:13ᵇ

Com.: This lemma is featured in two Masoretic lists. One is in a list of doublets that occur in the same verse; see Frensdorff, *Ochlah*, §58, and Díaz-Esteban, *Sefer Oklah we-Oklah*, §59.

The other is in a list of doublets that start with a י; see Frensdorff, *Ochlah*, §66.

JUDGES 5:14

מִנִּי אֶפְרַיִם שָׁרְשָׁם בַּעֲמָלֵק אַחֲרֶיךָ בִנְיָמִין בַּעֲמָמֶיךָ מִנִּי מָכִיר יָרְדוּ מְחֹקְקִים וּמִזְּבוּלֻן מֹשְׁכִים בְּשֵׁבֶט סֹפֵר:

5:14   מִנִּי

Twice at the beginning of a verse   ב ראש פסו   Mp

Judg 5:14; **Ezra 7:13**

מִנִּי *twice* at the beginning of a verse   מני ב ראש פסוק   Mm

Judg 5:14   מני אפרים שרשם
Ezra 7:13   מני שים טעם

Com.: The Masorah notes the *two* occurrences of this lemma at the beginning of a verse without a cj., to distinguish them from its more numerous occurrences (6x) that occur at the beginning of a verse with a cj.; see Frensdorff, *Ochlah*, §171, and Ognibeni, *'Oklah*, §95.

This lemma occurs in the ms. on folio 139r, but the Mm note appears on the bottom left of the preceding folio 138v.

5:14   בִנְיָמִין

Seventeen times plene   יז מל   Mp

1–5   **Gen 35:18**; **42:4**; **43:14**; 43:16; **43:29**
6–10   **Gen 45:12**; **49:27**; Josh 21:17*; **Judg 5:14**; 10:9 (וּבְנְיָמִין)
11–15   **1 Sam 9:1** (מִבְּן־יָמִין); **13:2**; **2 Sam 3:19**; **1 Kgs 12:23** (וּבְנְיָמִין); **Jer 32:8**
16–17   **Hos 5:8**; **Neh 11:36** (לְבִנְיָמִין)

Com.: The Masorah notes the *seventeen* occurrences of this lemma in various forms written plene second י, to distinguish them from its more numerous occurrences (100+) in various forms written defective second י.

* M^L, contrary to M (בִּנְיָמִן), writes the lemma at Josh 21:17 defective second י; see Breuer, *Biblical Text*, 53. Nevertheless, the Mm note there assumes that this reference is plene, because it not only writes it as such in the heading of the note and in the catchwords for the Josh 21:17 reference but, by adding *of Joshua* to these catchwords, it distinguishes it from its parallel in 1 Chr 6:45, where בִּנְיָמִן is written defective second י.

Similarly in that Mm note, the addition *of Kings* to the 1 Kgs 12:23 reference is to distinguish that reference from its parallel in 2 Chr 11:3, where the lemma is written defective second י.

All the Mp headings highlighted above read *seventeen times* except the one at Judg 10:9, which reads *twice, once plene and once defective* (second י), and relates only to its specific form (וּבְנְיָמִן), which occurs in its defective form at 2 Chr 11:10 (וּבִבְנְיָמִן).

5:14 בַּעֲמָמֶיךָ

Unique   ל   Mp

Com.: The Masorah notes the *sole* occurrence of this lemma with a duplicated מ, to distinguish it from its more numerous occurrences (4x) (בְּעַמֶּךָ) in its non-duplicated form.

5:14 מְחֹקְקִים

Unique   ל   Mp

Com.: The Masorah notes the *sole* occurrence of this lemma in the pl., possibly to distinguish it from its occurrence in the sg. at Deut 33:21.

5:14 וּמִזְבוּלֻן

Twice   ב   Mp

Judg 5:14; 2 Chr 30:11 (וּמִזְבֻלוּן)

וּמִזְבוּלֻן *twice*   ומזבולן ב   Mm

2 Chr 30:11   אך אנשים מאשר ומנשה
Judg 5:14   ומזבולן משכים

Com.: The Masorah notes the *two* occurrences of this lemma with a ו cj., to distinguish them from its *sole* occurrence without a cj. at 1 Chr 12:34. .

5:14   בְּשֵׁבֶט

Six times   ו   Mp

1–5   **Judg 5:14**; **2 Sam 7:14**; **Isa 11:4**; **Ps 2:9; 89:33**
6   **Lam 3:1**

———————————

בְּשֵׁבֶט *six times*   בשבט ו   Mm

1–5   Judg 5:14   ומזבולן משכים
        2 Sam 7:14   (והכחתיו) [והכחתיו] בשבט אנשים
        Isa 11:4   והכה ארץ
        Ps 2:9   תרעם בשבט ברזל
        Ps 89:33   ופקדתי בשבט פשעם
6   Lam 3:1   אני הגבר ראה עני

Com.: The Masorah notes the *six* occurrences of this lemma with the indef. prep. בְּ to distinguish them from its more numerous occurrences (10x) with the def. prep. בַּ (בַּשֵׁבֶט).

> ## JUDGES 5:15
>
> וְשָׂרַי בְּיִשָּׂשכָר עִם־דְּבֹרָה וְיִשָּׂשכָר כֵּן בָּרָק בָּעֵמֶק שֻׁלַּח בְּרַגְלָיו בִּפְלַגּוֹת רְאוּבֵן גְּדֹלִים חִקְקֵי־לֵב:

5:15   וְשָׂרַי

Twice   בֹ   Mp

Gen 16:1; **Judg 5:15**

———————————

וְשָׂרַי *twice* at the beginning of a verse   ושרי ב ראש פסוק   Mm

Gen 16:1   ושרי אשת אברם
Judg 5:15   ושרי ביששכר

Com.: The Mm heading here and at <u>Gen 16:1</u>, and the Mp headings at Gen 16:1 and in M^C and M^A here, read *twice at the beginning of a verse.* But, since there are no other examples of this lemma in the middle or end of a verse, these headings more precisely should have read *twice, and at the beginning of a verse.*

Normally such a note indicates the presence or absence of a וֹ cj. at the beginning of a verse, but there are no examples of שָׂרִי without a וֹ cj. at the beginning of a verse.

5:15   דְּבֹרָה

Three times defective   גׄ חסׄ   Mp

Com.: See **Judg 4:15.**

5:15   שְׁלַח

Three times   גׄ   Mp

Judg 5: 15; <u>Obad 1</u> (שְׁלָח)**; Job 18:8**

Com.: The Masorah notes the *three* occurrences of this lemma with a *šureq* under the שׁ, possibly to distinguish them from its more numerous occurrences with other vowels under the שׁ, such as שָׁלַח (17x), or שִׁלַּח (11x).

5:15   בִּפְלַגּוֹת

Twice   בׄ   Mp

Judg 5:15; Job 20:17

Com.: The Masorah notes the *two* occurrences of this lemma with the prep. בּ, to distinguish it from its *sole* occurrence with the prep. ל (לִפְלַגּוֹת) in v. 16.

┌───┐

JUDGES 5:16

לָמָּה יָשַׁבְתָּ בֵּין הַמִּשְׁפְּתַיִם לִשְׁמֹעַ שְׁרִקוֹת עֲדָרִים לִפְלַגּוֹת רְאוּבֵן גְּדוֹלִים חִקְרֵי־לֵב׃

└───┘

5:16   הַמִּשְׁפְּתָיִם

Twice   בׄ   Mp

Gen 49:14 (הַמִּשְׁפְּתָיִם)**; Judg 5:16**

Com.: The Masorah notes the *two* occurrences of this lemma written *once* with a *pataḥ* (here), and *once* with a *qameṣ* under the ת (Gen 49:14).

The Mp heading at Gen 49:14 reads *unique* reflecting the *sole* occurrence of this lemma with a *qameṣ* under the ת.

This lemma is featured in a Masoretic list of doublets with an initial הַ; see Frensdorff, *Ochlah*, §64, and Díaz-Esteban, *Sefer Oklah we-Oklah*, §65.

5:16   שְׁרִקוֹת

Twice   בֹּ   Mp

Judg 5:16; Jer 18:16 (שְׁרִיקוֹת, *qərê*)

Com.: The Masorah notes the *two* occurrences of this lemma written *one* plene י (Jer 18:16), and *one* defective י (here).

The Mp note has been written on the line above.

5:16   גְּדוֹלִים

Six times plene   ו מל   Mp

1–5   **Judg 5:16; Jer 25:14; Qoh 10:4; Neh 11:14** (הַגְּדוֹלִים); **12:43**
6   **1 Chr 17:8** (הַגְּדוֹלִים)

גְּדוֹלִים *six times* plene   גדולים ו מל   Mm

1–5	Judg 5:16, difference of opinion	חקר לב (פולג) [פלוגתא]
	Jer 25:14	כי עבדו בם
	כְּשֵׁם הַגְּדוֹלִים *of Chronicles* (1 Chr 17:8)	כשם (הגדולים) [הגדולים] דדבר ימֹ
	Qoh 10:4	כי מרפא יניח
	Neh 12:43	ויזבחו ביום
6	Neh 11:14	זבדיאל בן הגדולים

Com.: The Masorah notes the *six* occurrences of this lemma in various forms, written plene ו, to distinguish them from its more numerous occurrences (32x) in various forms written defective ו (גְּדֹלִים), *one* of which is in the previous verse.

This distinction is implied in the Mm in the additional notation *of Chronicles* to the 1 Chr 17:8 reference, which distinguishes it from the parallel passage in 2 Sam 7:9, where the lemma occurs as הַגְּדֹלִים.

In the Mm note at the Judg 5:16 reference, mention is made of a difference of opinion (פלוגתא) concerning the vocalization of this lemma in this verse; see also Breuer, *The Biblical Text*, 37, n. 7*. However, the plene writing is what is found in both M^C and M^A.

The Mp note has been written on the line above.

JUDGES 5:17

גִּלְעָד בְּעֵבֶר הַיַּרְדֵּן שָׁכֵן וְדָן לָמָּה יָגוּר אֳנִיּוֹת אָשֵׁר יָשַׁב לְחוֹף יַמִּים וְעַל מִפְרָצָיו יִשְׁכּוֹן׃

5:17   וְדָן

Twice   בֿ   Mp

Judg 5:17; Ezek 27:19

Com.: This lemma is featured in a Masoretic list of homonyms; see Frensdorff, *Ochlah*, §59, and Díaz-Esteban, *Sefer Oklah we-Oklah*, §60. Here the meaning is *and Dan*, whereas in Ezek 27:19 the meaning is another name *Vedan*.

5:17   יָשַׁב

יָשַׁב *fifteen times*, and (their) references   ישב הֿיֿ וסימֿ   Mm

1–5	<u>Gen 13:12</u>^a	אברם
	Twice in it (Gen 13:12^b)	בֿ בו
	Gen 19:29	בשחת
	<u>Judg 5:17</u>	גלעד
	1 Sam 27:7	מספר
6–10	1 Sam 27:11	ואיש ואשה
	2 Sam 7:1	ויהי
	And its companion (1 Chr 17:1)	וחביר
	<u>1 Kgs 1:46</u>	שלמה
	1 Kgs 2:12	ושלמה
11–15	<u>1 Kgs 11:16</u>	כי ששת
	2 Kgs 13:13	וירעבם
	Jer 2:6	המעלה
	1 Chr 5:9	ולמזרח
	Ps 47:9	מלך אלהים

And *five times* with *qameṣ*   וֹה קמצין

1–5	2 Sam 19:38	עבדך
	Jer 49:1	הבנים
	Dan 9:16	אפך
	Ps 1:1	בעצת רשעים
	Ps 29:10	למבול

Com.: The Masorah notes the *fifteen* occurrences of this lemma pointed with a *pataḥ* under the שׁ, to distinguish them from the *five* occurrences pointed with a *qameṣ* under the שׁ (יֹשָׁב).

5:17   מִפְרָצָיו

Unique   ל   Mp

5:17   יִשְׁכּוֹן

Twice plene   ב מל   Mp

Judg 5:17; **Ps 104:12**

יִשְׁכּוֹן *twice* plene   ב מל   Mm

| Ps 104:12 | עליהם עוף השמים |
| Judg 5:17 | אשר ישב |

Com.: The Masorah notes the *two* occurrences of this lemma written plene וֹ, to distinguish them from its more numerous occurrences (12x) written defective וֹ (יִשְׁכֹּן).

JUDGES 5:18

זְבֻלוּן עַם חֵרֵף נַפְשׁוֹ לָמוּת וְנַפְתָּלִי עַל מְרוֹמֵי שָׂדֶה׃

5:18   וְנַפְתָּלִי

Seven times   ז   Mp

1–5   Gen 35:25; Exod 1:4; Deut 27:13; **Judg 5:18**; 1 Chr 12:41

Com.: The Mp heading here of *seven times* is incorrect since there are only *five* occurrences of this lemma.

The Masorah notes the *five* occurrences with a וֹ cj., to distinguish them from its more numerous occurrences (39x) without a cj.

Neither M^C nor M^A has a note on this lemma here.

5:18   מְרוֹמֵי

Three times, once plene and *twice* defective   ג̇ הד מל וב̇ חס̇   Mp

Judg 5:18; Prov 9:3 (מְרֹמֵי); 9:14 (מְרֹמֵי)

Com.: The Masorah notes the *three* occurrences of this lemma *twice* written defective וֹ (Prov 9:3 and 9:14), and *once* written plene וֹ (here).

> ## JUDGES 5:19
>
> בָּ֣אוּ מְלָכִים֮ נִלְחָ֒מוּ֒ אָ֤ז נִלְחֲמוּ֙ מַלְכֵ֣י כְנַ֔עַן בְּתַעְנַ֖ךְ עַל־מֵ֣י מְגִדּ֑וֹ בֶּ֥צַע כֶּ֖סֶף לֹ֥א לָקָֽחוּ׃

5:19   בָּאוּ

Twice at the beginning of verse   ב̇ ראש פסוק   Mp

Judg 5:19; <u>Hos 9:7</u>

Com.: The Masorah notes the *two* occurrences of this lemma at the beginning of a verse without a וֹ cj., to distinguish them from its more numerous occurrences (13x) that occur at the beginning of a verse with a וֹ cj.; see Frensdorff, *Ochlah*, §171, and Ognibeni, *'Oklah*, §95.

> ## JUDGES 5:20
>
> מִן־שָׁמַ֖יִם נִלְחָ֑מוּ הַכּֽוֹכָבִים֙ מִמְּסִלּוֹתָ֔ם נִלְחֲמ֖וּ עִם־סִֽיסְרָֽא׃

5:20   מִן־שָׁמַיִם

Twice   ב̇   Mp

Judg 5:20; 2 Sam 22:14

Com.: The Masorah notes the *two* occurrences of this lemma without the def. article, to distinguish them from its more numerous occurrences (29x) with the def. article (מִן הַשָּׁמַיִם).

The Mp heading at 2 Sam 22:14 incorrectly reads *three times*.

5:20   מִמְסִלּוֹתָם

Unique   ל   Mp

Com.: The Masorah notes the *sole* occurrence of this lemma with the prep. מ, to distinguish it from its occurrence with the prep. ב (בִּמְסִלּוֹתָם) at Isa 59:7.

JUDGES 5:21

נַחַל קִישׁוֹן גְּרָפָם נַחַל קְדוּמִים נַחַל קִישׁוֹן תִּדְרְכִי נַפְשִׁי עֹז׃

5:21   גְּרָפָם

Unique   ל   Mp

5:21   קְדוּמִים

Unique   ל   Mp

5:21   תִּדְרְכִי

Unique   ל   Mp

JUDGES 5:22

אָז הָלְמוּ עִקְּבֵי־סוּס מִדַּהֲרוֹת דַּהֲרוֹת אַבִּירָיו׃

5:22   דַּהֲרוֹת

Unique   ל   Mp

Com.: This lemma is featured in a Masoretic list of *hapax legomena* that start with consecutive letters of the alphabet, here דה; see Frensdorff, *Ochlah*, §37, and Díaz-Esteban, *Sefer Oklah we-Oklah*, §38.

JUDGES 5:23

אֹ֣ורוּ מֵר֗וֹז אָמַר֙ מַלְאַ֣ךְ יְהֹוָ֔ה אֹ֖רוּ אָר֣וֹר יֹשְׁבֶ֑יהָ כִּ֤י לֹֽא־בָ֙אוּ֙ לְעֶזְרַ֣ת יְהֹוָ֔ה לְעֶזְרַ֥ת יְהֹוָ֖ה בַּגִּבּוֹרִֽים׃

5:23　　אֹ֣ורוּ

Three times　　ג̇　　Mp

Judg 5:23ᵃ; 5:23ᵇ (אֹרוּ); **1 Sam 14:29** (אֹרוּ)

אורו *three times, once* plene *and* twice　　אורו ג̇ חד מל וב̇ חס̇ וסימנהון　　Mm
defective, *and their references*

Judg 5:23ᵃ　　　　　　　　　　　　　　　אורו מרוז
Twice in the verse (Judg 5:23ᵇ)　　　　שנים בפס̇
1 Sam 14:29　　　　　　　　　　　　　ראו נא כי ארו

Com.: The Masorah notes the *three* occurrences of this lemma, *once* plene וֹ (here) and
twice defective וֹ (Judg 5:23ᵇ and 1 Sam 14:29).

5:23　　מֵר֗וֹז

Unique　　ל̇　　Mp

5:23　　לְעֶזְרַת²

Twice　　ב̇　　Mp

Judg 5:23ᵃ; **5:23ᵇ**

Com.: This lemma is featured in a Masoretic list of doublets that occur in the same
verse; see Frensdorff, *Ochlah*, §58, and Díaz-Esteban, *Sefer Oklah we-Oklah*, §59.

5:23　　בַּגִּבּוֹרִים

Four times　　ד̇　　Mp

Judg 5:13; **5:23; Amos 2:16; 1 Chr 12:1**

Com.: The Masorah notes the *four* occurrences of this lemma with the prep. בְּ, to
distinguish them from its more numerous occurrences (13x) without this preposition.

JUDGES 5:24

תְּבֹרַךְ מִנָּשִׁים יָעֵל אֵשֶׁת חֶבֶר הַקֵּינִי מִנָּשִׁים בָּאֹהֶל תְּבֹרָךְ׃

5:24   תְּבֹרַךְ

Three times   גׄ   Mp

Judg 5:24ᵃ; 5:24ᵇ (תְּבֹרָךְ)**; Prov 20:21** (תְּבֹרַךְ)

Com.: The Masorah notes the *three* occurrences of this lemma, *twice* written with a *qameṣ* and *once* with a *pataḥ*, possibly to distinguish them from the *four* occurrences pointed as תְּבָרֵךְ.

5:24   מִנָּשִׁים¹

Three times   גׄ   Mp

Judg 5:24ᵃ; 5:24ᵇ; 1 Sam 15:33

Com.: The Masorah notes the *three* occurrences of this lemma with the prep. מ, to distinguish them from its more numerous occurrences (58x) without this preposition.

The Mp note has been placed in the line above.

5:24   מִנָּשִׁים²

Three times   גׄ   Mp

Com.: See directly above.

5:24   בָּאֹהֶל

Six times   וׄ   Mp

1–5	Gen 18:9; **Num 19:14**; Deut 31:15; **Judg 5:24; 1 Kgs 8:4**
6	**2 Chr 5:5**

Com.: The Masorah notes the *six* occurrences of this lemma with the def. prep., to distinguish them from its more numerous occurrences (41x) with the indef. prep. (בְּאֹהֶל).

5:24   תְּבֹרָךְ

Three times   ג̇   Mp

Com.: See directly above at תְּבֹרַךְ.

JUDGES 5:25

מַ֤יִם שָׁאַל֙ חָלָ֣ב נָתָ֔נָה בְּסֵ֥פֶל אַדִּירִ֖ים הִקְרִ֥יבָה חֶמְאָֽה׃

5:25   נָתָ֔נָה

Unique   ל̇   Mp

Com.: The Masorah notes the *sole* occurrence of this lemma with a *qameṣ* under the ת (pausal form), to distinguish it from its more numerous occurrences (8x) with a *šəwâ* (נְתָנָה, non-pausal form).

5:25   בְּסֵ֥פֶל

Unique   ל̇   Mp

5:25   הִקְרִ֥יבָה

Unique   ל̇   Mp

Com.: This lemma is featured in a Masoretic list of words that occur *twice*, *once* with a ו cj. (Num 15:27), and *once* without (here); see Frensdorff, *Ochlah*, §1, and Díaz-Esteban, *Sefer Oklah we-Oklah*, §1.

JUDGES 5:26

יָדָהּ֙ לַיָּתֵ֣ד תִּשְׁלַ֔חְנָה וִֽימִינָ֖הּ לְהַלְמ֣וּת עֲמֵלִ֑ים וְהָלְמָ֤ה סִֽיסְרָא֙ מָחֲקָ֣ה רֹאשׁ֔וֹ וּמָחֲצָ֥ה וְחָלְפָ֖ה רַקָּתֽוֹ׃

5:26   לְהַלְמ֣וּת

Unique   ל̇   Mp

5:26 עֲמֵלִים

Unique ל Mp

Com.: The Masorah notes the *sole* occurrence of this lemma in the pl., to distinguish it from its more numerous occurrences (7x) in the sg. (עָמֵל).

5:26 וְהָלְמָה

Unique ל Mp

The Mp note has been placed in the line above.

5:26 מָחֲקָה

Unique ל Mp

5:26 וּמָחֲצָה

Unique ל Mp

Com.: This lemma is featured in a Masoretic list of *hapax legomena* that start with ומ; see Frensdorff, *Ochlah*, §18, and Díaz-Esteban, *Sefer Oklah we-Oklah*, §19.

5:26 וְחָלְפָה

Unique ל Mp

The Mp note has been placed in the line above.

JUDGES 5:27

בֵּ֣ין רַגְלֶ֐יהָ כָּרַ֤ע נָפַ֣ל שָׁכָ֔ב בֵּ֚ין רַגְלֶ֙יהָ֙ כָּרַ֣ע נָפָ֔ל בַּאֲשֶׁ֣ר כָּרַ֔ע שָׁ֖ם נָפַ֥ל שָׁדֽוּד׃

5:27 נָפָ֔ל

Unique ẓaqep̄ qames ל זק קׁמׁ Mp

Com.: The Masorah notes the *sole* occurrence of this lemma with a *qames* under a *ẓaqep̄*, to distinguish them from its more numerous occurrences (5x) with an *'atnah* or *sôp̄ pasûq*.

This lemma is featured in a Masoretic list of words occurring only *once* with a *qames* and *ẓaqep̄*; see Frensdorff, *Ochlah*, §21, and Díaz-Esteban, *Sefer Oklah we-Oklah*, §22.

5:27   בַּאֲשֶׁר

Fifteen times   הֹי   Mp

1–5   **Gen 21:17; 39:9; 39:23; Judg 5:27**; 17:8
6–10   Judg 17:9; 1 Sam 23:13; **2 Kgs 8:1**; <u>Isa 47:12</u>; <u>56:4</u>
11–15   **Jonah 1:8; Ruth 1:17; Qoh 3:9; 7:2; 8:4**

Com.: The Masorah notes the *fifteen* occurrences of this lemma with the prep. בּ, to distinguish them from its almost *five-hundred* occurrences written with the prep. כּ (כַּאֲשֶׁר); see Ognibeni, *'Oklah*, §164.

All the Mp headings highlighted above read *fifteen* apart from those at Ruth 1:17 and Qoh 8:4, which correctly read *twice at the beginning of a verse*.

JUDGES 5:28

בְּעַד הַחַלּוֹן נִשְׁקְפָה וַתְּיַבֵּב אֵם סִיסְרָא בְּעַד הָאֶשְׁנָב מַדּוּעַ בֹּשֵׁשׁ רִכְבּוֹ לָבוֹא מַדּוּעַ אֶחֱרוּ פַּעֲמֵי מַרְכְּבוֹתָיו:

5:28   וַתְּיַבֵּב

Unique   ל   Mp

5:28   הָאֶשְׁנָב

Unique   ל   Mp

5:28   בֹּשֵׁשׁ

Twice   בּ   Mp

Exod 32:1; Judg 5:28

Com.: The Mp heading at Exod 32:1 adds catchwords מדוע בשש רכבו (מַדּוּעַ בֹּשֵׁשׁ רִכְבּוֹ) to refer the reader to this verse.

5:28   אֶחֱרוּ

Unique   ל   Mp

Com.: This lemma is featured in a Masoretic list of *hapax legomena* pairings, *one* of which occurs in the Torah (אָחֹן, Exod 33:19), *one* in the Prophets (אֶחֱרוּ, here), and *one* in the Writings (אֲעֶנֶה, Job 32:17); see Frensdorff, *Ochlah*, §57, and Díaz-Esteban, *Sefer Oklah we-Oklah*, §58. The relationship between each set of triple pairings in this list, apart from starting with the same letter of the alphabet, is unclear.

5:28	מַרְכְּבוֹתָיו

Twice	בֹ	Mp

Judg 5:28; **Jer 4:13**

Com.: The Masorah notes the *two* occurrences of this lemma written plene י, to distinguish them from its *two* occurrences written defective ו (מֶרְכְּבֹתָיו) at Exod 14:25 and Isa 66:15.

This distinction is implied in the heading of the Mp and Mm at Jer 4:13, which reads *twice plene*, thereby contrasting these forms with forms that occur defective.

JUDGES 5:29

חַכְמוֹת שָׂרוֹתֶיהָ תַּעֲנֶינָה אַף־הִיא תָּשִׁיב אֲמָרֶיהָ לָהּ׃

5:29	חַכְמוֹת

Twice	בֹ	Mp

Judg 5:29; **Prov 14:1**

חַכְמוֹת *twice*, and their references	חכמות בֹ וסימנה	Mm

Judg 5:29	(שרים) [שרותיה]
Prov 14:1	נשים בנתה

Com.: The Masorah notes the *two* occurrences of this lemma with a *pataḥ* under ח, to distinguish them from its more numerous occurrences (4x) with a *qameṣ* under the ח (חָכְמוֹת).

This lemma is also featured in a Masoretic list of doublets that have a *pataḥ*; see Frensdorff, *Ochlah*, §24, and Díaz-Esteban, *Sefer Oklah we-Oklah*, §25.

This lemma occurs in the ms. on folio 139v, but the Mm note appears on the top right of the preceding folio 139r.

5:29   תַּעֲנֶינָה

Unique   לֹ   Mp

Com.: This lemma is featured in *three* Masoretic lists. One is in a list of words that occur *three times*, *twice* with a וֹ cj. (1 Sam 9:12 and 18:7), and *once* without (here); see Frensdorff, *Ochlah*, §14, and Díaz-Esteban, *Sefer Oklah we-Oklah*, §15.

The second is in a list of *hapax legomena* that begin with a תּ; see Frensdorff, *Ochlah*, §74, and the third is in a list of *hapax legomena* that end in נָה; see Frensdorff, *Ochlah*, §369, and Ognibeni, *'Oklah*, §227.

5:29   תָּשִׁיב

Ten times   יֹ   Mp

1–5   **Gen 24:6**; Deut 24:13; **Judg 5:29**; 2 Kgs 18:24; Isa 36:9
6–10   **Isa 58:13; Ps 74:11; 89:44; Job 15:13**; Lam 3:64

תָּשִׁיב *ten times*   יֹ   תשיב   Mm

1–5	Gen 24:6	השמר לך פן ‹תשיב› את בני
	Deut 24:13	השב תשיב לו את העבוט
	Judg 5:29	חכמות שרותיה
	2 Kgs 18:24	ואיך תשיב
	And its companion (Isa 36:9)	וחביר׳
6–10	Isa 58:13	אם תשיב משבת רגלך
	Ps 89:44	צור חרבו
	Ps 74:11	למה תשיב ידך
	Job 15:13	כי תשיב אל אל
	Lam 3:64	תשיב

Com.: The Masorah notes the *ten* occurrences of this lemma in the *hiphil*, to distinguish them from its more numerous occurrences (33x) in the *qal* (תָּשׁוּב); see Ognibeni, *'Oklah*, §3G.

JUDGES 5:30

הֲלֹא יִמְצְאוּ יְחַלְּקוּ שָׁלָל רַחַם רַחֲמָתַ֫יִם לְרֹאשׁ גֶּבֶר שְׁלַל צְבָעִים לְסִיסְרָא שְׁלַל צְבָעִים רִקְמָה צֶבַע רִקְמָתַ֫יִם לְצַוְּארֵי שָׁלָל:

5:30   יְחַלְּקוּ

Unique   ל   Mp

1–2   **Judg 5:30**; Ps 22:19

Com.: The Mp heading here *of unique* is inexact since there are *two* occurrences of this lemma. The note more precisely should have read *unique in the book*.

Neither M^C nor M^A has a note on this lemma here.

In M^L the note has been placed in the left margin but it belongs in the right one.

5:30   רַחַם

Five times ה   Mp

1–5   **Judg 5:30**; **Isa 46:3** (רְחַם); **Ezek 20:26** (רְחַם); Prov 30:16 (רְחַם); **1 Chr 2:44**

רַחַם *five times,* *twice* with a *paṭaḥ* and *three times* with a *qameṣ*   רחם ה̇ ב̇ פת̇ וג̇ קמצין   Mm^1

1–5   Judg 5:30   הלא ימצאו יחלקו
         Isa 46:3   שמעו אלי בית יעקב
         1 Chr 2:44   ושמע (הליד) [הוליד]
         Ezek 20:26   ואטמא אותם
         Prov 30:16   שאול

And *once* (וְרֶחֶם): Gen 49:25   וחד ברכת שדים

רַחַם *four times*   ד̇   Mm^2

1–5   Isa 46:3   (העמוסים) [העמסים]
         Ezek 20:26   במתנותם
         1 Chr 2:44   ישמע
         Prov 30:16   ועצר

Com.: The Masorah notes the *five* occurrences of this lemma, *three times* written with a *qameṣ* under the ר (Isa 46:3, Ezek 20:26, and Prov 30:16), and *twice* with a *pataḥ* (here and 1 Chr 2:44).

The first Mm note adds the additional information about the occurrence of this lemma with a ו cj. (וְרָחַם) at Gen 49:25. Curiously, the second Mm note has omitted the Judg 5:30 reference in its list, and its heading just reads *four times*.

The headings in the Mp at 1 Chr 2:44 (ה) and in the Mm at <u>Prov 30:16</u> and <u>1 Chr 2:44</u> read *five times with a pataḥ*, thereby assuming a contrast with a form with a different vowel under the ח, which could possibly be a *səḡōl* (רְחֶם).

This note occurs *twice* on the same folio, the first one at the upper left of fol. 139v, and the second at the bottom right.

In M[L] the circellus has been placed between רַחַם and the following word רַחֲמָתַיִם, but it belongs only on רַחַם. Also the note has been placed in the right margin, but it belongs in the left one.

5:30   לְרֹאשׁ

Twenty-one times   כֹּא   Mp

1–5	Gen 49:26; Num 17:18; Deut 28:13; 28:44; 33:16
6–10	**Judg 5:30; 10:18; 11:8; 11:9**; 11:11
11–15	**2 Sam 22:44;** Jer 13:21; Amos 6:12; Ps 18:44; 118:22
16–20	Prov 10:6; 11:26; Lam 1:5; 2:19; **1 Chr 11:6**[a]
21–24	**1 Chr 11:6**[b]; 26:10; 29:11; 2 Chr 25:12

Com.: The Mp heading here of *twenty-one times* is incorrect since there are *twenty-four* occurrences of this lemma as correctly noted in the Mp headings at Judg 10:18, 11:9, 2 Sam 22:44, 1 Chr 11:6[a] and 11:6[b].

The Masorah notes the *twenty-four* occurrences of this lemma with the prep. ל, to distinguish them from its more numerous occurrences (100+) without this preposition.

The Mp heading at Judg 11:8 correctly notes the *five* occurrences of this lemma in the book of Judges (**5:30, 10:18, 11:8, 11:9**, and 11:11).

Neither M[C] nor M[A] has a note on this lemma here.

5:30   צְבָעִים לְסִיסְרָא

Unique   ל   Mp

Com.: The first part of this phrase צְבָעִים is featured in a Masoretic list of doublets that occur in the same verse; see Frensdorff, *Ochlah*, §58, and Díaz-Esteban, *Sefer Oklah we-Oklah*, §59.

5:30   צְבָעִים רִקְמָה

Unique   ל   Mp

Com.: The first part of this phrase צְבָעִים is featured in a Masoretic list of doublets that occur in the same verse; see directly above.

JUDGES 5:31

כֵּן יֹאבְדוּ כָל־אוֹיְבֶיךָ יְהוָה וְאֹהֲבָיו כְּצֵאת הַשֶּׁמֶשׁ בִּגְבֻרָתוֹ וַתִּשְׁקֹט הָאָרֶץ אַרְבָּעִים שָׁנָה: פ

5:31   אוֹיְבֶיךָ

Twice plene   ב מל   Mp

1–5   **Judg 5:31; Ps 83:3; <u>89:11</u>; 89:52; 1 Chr 17:8**
6–7   **1 Chr 17:10**; 21:12*

Com.: The Mp heading here of *twice plene* is incorrect since, as listed above, there are *seven* occurrences of this lemma. The correct heading of *seven times plene* is given in the other *four* Mp headings.

The Masorah notes the *seven* occurrences of this lemma written plene ו, to distinguish them from its more numerous occurrences (33x) written defective ו (אִיְבֶיךָ).

* M^L, contrary to M (אוֹיְבֶיךָ), writes the form at 1 Chr 21:12 defective ו (אִיְבֶיךָ); see Breuer, *The Biblical Text*, 369.

Both M^C and M^A correctly read here *seven times* plene.

5:31   כְּצֵאת

Three times   ג   Mp

Exod 21:7; 33:8; <u>Judg 5:31</u>

כְּצֵאת *three times*, and (their) references   כצאת ג̇ וסימנ̇   Mm

Exod 21:7	ימכר
Exod 33:8	כצאת
<u>Judg 5:31</u>	יאבדו כל אויביך

Com.: The Masorah notes the *three* occurrences of this lemma written with the prep. כ, to distinguish them from its more numerous occurrences (9x) with the prep. ב (בְּצֵאת); see Ognibeni, *'Oklah*, §2N.

5:31   בִּגְבֻרָתוֹ

Unique defective   ל חס̇   Mp

Com.: The Masorah notes the *single* occurrence of this lemma written defective ו, to distinguish them from its *two* occurrences written plene ו (בִּגְבוּרָתוֹ) at Jer 9:22 and Ps 66:7.

JUDGES 6:2
וַתָּעָז יַד־מִדְיָן עַל־יִשְׂרָאֵל מִפְּנֵי מִדְיָן עָשׂוּ לָהֶם ׀ בְּנֵי יִשְׂרָאֵל אֶת־הַמִּנְהָרוֹת אֲשֶׁר בֶּהָרִים וְאֶת־הַמְּעָרוֹת וְאֶת־הַמְּצָדוֹת:

6:2   וַתָּעָז

Twice   ב̇   Mp

Judg 3:10; **6:2**

Com.: The Masorah notes the *two* occurrences of this lemma with a ו consec., to distinguish them from its *two* occurrences written without a ו (תָּעָז) at Ps 89:14 and Qoh 7:19.

6:2   הַמִּנְהָרוֹת

Unique   ל   Mp

6:2   הַמְּצָדוֹת

Eight times   ח̇   Mp

| 1–5 | **Judg 6:2**; **1 Sam 23:14**; <u>23:19</u>; **24:1**; Isa 33:16 |
| 6–8 | **Jer 48:41**; 51:30; Ezek 33:27 |

Com.: The Masorah notes the *eight* occurrences of this lemma in various forms with a *qameṣ* under the **צ**, to distinguish them from its *sole* occurrence with a *ḥolem* after the **צ** (בִּמְצֹדוֹת) at Ezek 19:9.

This distinction is implied in the heading of the Mp at 1 Sam 23:14 which reads *eight times with qameṣ* (חָ), thereby assuming a contrast with a form with a different vowel with the **צ**, which can only be a *ḥolem*.

The Mp heading at 1 Sam 24:1 reads *unique* for its particular form with the indef. prep. **ב** (בִּמְצָדוֹת).

The Mm note at 1 Sam 23:19 is given in the form of an Aramaic mnemonic "he hides in the wilderness in the cave of the kid; death was hard for lofty Babylon"; see Marcus, *Scribal Wit*, 72–73.

JUDGES 6:3

וְהָיָה אִם־זָרַע יִשְׂרָאֵל וְעָלָה מִדְיָן וַעֲמָלֵק וּבְנֵי־קֶדֶם וְעָלוּ עָלָיו׃

6:3   זָרַע

Unique accented (*milraʿ*)   ל בטע   Mp

Com.: The Masorah notes the *single* occurrence of this lemma accented *milraʿ* (a verbal form, *sowed*), to distinguish it from its more numerous occurrences (12x accented *milʿêl* (a noun, *seed*); see Frensdorff, *Ochlah*, §373.

JUDGES 6:4

וַיַּחֲנוּ עֲלֵיהֶם וַיַּשְׁחִיתוּ אֶת־יְבוּל הָאָרֶץ עַד־בּוֹאֲךָ עַזָּה וְלֹא־יַשְׁאִירוּ מִחְיָה בְּיִשְׂרָאֵל וְשֶׂה וָשׁוֹר
וַחֲמוֹר׃

6:4   יְבוּל

Five times   הֿ   Mp

1–3   **Judg 6:4**; Hab 3:17; Job 20:28

Com.: The Mp heading here of *five times* is incorrect since there are only *three* occurrences of this lemma.

The Masorah notes these *three* occurrences without a sfx., to distinguish them from the numerous occurrences (9x) of this lemma with a sfx., such as יְבוּלָהּ and יְבוּלָם; see Ginsburg, 4, י, §56.

Dotan/Reich (*Masora Thesaurus, ad loc.*) suggest that the note has been misplaced and belongs with the second preceding word וַיַּשְׁחִיתוּ, which does occur *five times*.

Neither M^C nor M^A has a note on this lemma here.

6:4   בֹּאֲךָ

Five times plene   ה מל   Mp

Judg 6:4; 1 Sam 15:7; 17:52; 27:8; Isa 37:28 (וּבוֹאֲךָ)

Com.: The Masorah notes the *five* occurrences of this lemma in various forms written plene וֹ, to distinguish them from the *six* occurrences in various forms written defective וֹ (בֹּאֲךָ/וּבֹאֲךָ).

M^L, contrary to M (בֹּאֲךָ), has a *sixth* occurrence of this lemma since it writes the form at Judg 11:33 plene וֹ (בֹוֹאֲךָ); see Breuer, *The Biblical Text*, 62. However, all the Mp headings, apart from that Isa 37:28, read *five times*, thus supporting the enumeration inherent in the text of M.

The number *six* that is given in the heading of the Mp at Isa 37:28 is thought to be an error, a confusion with the similar form בָּאֲכָה for which the note *six times plene* (that is, plene ה) is also given; see Breuer, *The Aleppo Codex*, 274–75.

JUDGES 6:5

כִּי הֵם֩ וּמִקְנֵיהֶ֨ם יַעֲל֜וּ וְאָהֳלֵיהֶ֗ם יָבֹ֤אוּ כְדֵי־אַרְבֶּה֙ לָרֹ֔ב וְלָהֶ֥ם וְלִגְמַלֵּיהֶ֖ם אֵ֣ין מִסְפָּ֑ר וַיָּבֹ֥אוּ בָאָ֖רֶץ לְשַׁחֲתָֽהּ׃

6:5   יבאו

Read וּבָאוּ   ובאו קׄ   Mp

Com.: The *kĕṯîḇ* (יבאו), and the *qĕrê* (וּבָאוּ) represents a variation between a י of the 3rd pers. impf. and the ו of the ו consec.; see Gordis, *The Biblical Text*, 145.

This lemma is featured in a Masoretic list of words that have a י at the beginning of a word, which is read as a ו; see Frensdorff, *Ochlah*, §134, and Díaz-Esteban, *Sefer Oklah we-Oklah*, §118.

6:5   וְלָהֶם

Eight times   ח֗   Mp

1–5   **Gen 6:21**; **43:32**; <u>**Deut 1:39**</u>; <u>**Judg 6:5**</u>; **Ezra 2:65**
6–8   <u>**Ezra 6:20**</u>; **Neh 7:67**; <u>**2 Chr 25:14**</u>

וְלָהֶם *eight times*   ולהם ח֗   Mm

1–5	Gen 6:21	מאכל
	Gen 43:32	לבדם
	<u>Deut 1:39</u>	אתננה
	<u>Judg 6:5</u>	ולגמליהם
	<u>2 Chr 25:14</u>	יקטר
6–8	<u>Ezra 6:20</u>	הטהרו
	Ezra 2:65	משררים
	and its companion (Neh 7:67)	וחבירו

Com.: The Masorah notes the *eight* occurrences of this lemma with a ו cj., to distinguish them from its more numerous occurrences (600+) without a cj.

> ### JUDGES 6:7
>
> וַיְהִי כִּי־זָעֲקוּ בְנֵי־יִשְׂרָאֵל אֶל־יְהוָה עַל אֹדוֹת מִדְיָן׃

6:7   וַיְהִי

Twice with the accent (*zaqep gadôl*) in the book   ב֞ בטע בסיפ   Mp

Judg 6:7; <u>**11:5**</u>

Com.: The Masorah notes the *two* occurrences of this lemma in the book with the accent *zaqep gadôl*.

JUDGES 6:8

וַיִּשְׁלַ֧ח יְהֹוָ֛ה אִ֥ישׁ נָבִ֖יא אֶל־בְּנֵ֣י יִשְׂרָאֵ֑ל וַיֹּ֨אמֶר לָהֶ֜ם כֹּה־אָמַ֥ר יְהֹוָ֣ה ׀ אֱלֹהֵ֣י יִשְׂרָאֵ֗ל אָנֹכִ֞י
הֶעֱלֵ֤יתִי אֶתְכֶם֙ מִמִּצְרַ֔יִם וָאֹצִ֥יא אֶתְכֶ֖ם מִבֵּ֥ית עֲבָדִֽים׃

6:8   וָאֹצִ֥יא

Three times   גֿ   Mp

Com.: See **Josh 24:6**.

JUDGES 6:9

וָאַצִּ֤ל אֶתְכֶם֙ מִיַּ֣ד מִצְרַ֔יִם וּמִיַּ֖ד כׇּל־לֹחֲצֵיכֶ֑ם וָאֲגָרֵ֤שׁ אוֹתָם֙ מִפְּנֵיכֶ֔ם וָאֶתְּנָ֥ה לָכֶ֖ם אֶת־אַרְצָֽם׃

6:9   וָאַצִּ֤ל

Three times   גֿ   Mp

Josh 24:10; **Judg 6:9**; **1 Sam 10:18** (וָאַצִּ֖יל)

וָאַצִּל *three times, twice* defective and   (וַאַצִיל) [וַאַצל] גֿ בֿ חסֿ וחד מלֿ וסימנהון   Mm
once plene, and their references

Josh 24:10   ולא אביתי
Judg 6:9   מיד מצרים
1 Sam 10:18   העליתי

Com.: The Masorah notes the *three* occurrences of this lemma, *twice* written defective
י (Josh 24:10 and Judg 6:9), and *once* written plene י (1 Sam 10:18).

JUDGES 6:10

וָאֹמְרָ֣ה לָכֶ֗ם אֲנִי֙ יְהֹוָ֣ה אֱלֹהֵיכֶ֔ם לֹ֤א תִֽירְאוּ֙ אֶת־אֱלֹהֵ֣י הָאֱמֹרִ֔י אֲשֶׁ֥ר אַתֶּ֖ם יוֹשְׁבִ֣ים
בְּאַרְצָ֑ם וְלֹ֥א שְׁמַעְתֶּ֖ם בְּקוֹלִֽי׃ פ

6:10   יוֹשְׁבִ֣ים

Ten times plene   יֿ מלֿ   Mp

1–5   **Judg 6:10**; Isa 10:13; **Jer 36:12**; **44:13** (הַיֹּשְׁבִים); Ezek 3:15
6–10   **Ezek 8:1**; **1 Chr 9:2** (וְהַיֹּשְׁבִים); **2 Chr 18:9**; **2 Chr 30:25** (וְהַיֹּשְׁבִים);
       31:6 (הַיֹּשְׁבִים)

Com.: The Masorah notes the *ten* occurrences of this lemma in various forms written plene וֹ, to distinguish them from its more numerous occurrences (61x) in various forms written defective וֹ, such as יֹשְׁבִים and הַיֹּשְׁבִים.

Four of the Mp headings highlighted above (Judg 6:10; Jer 36:12; Ezek 8:1; 2 Chr 18:9) read *ten times plene*. The other *four* read as follows:

Jer 44:13 (הַיּוֹשְׁבִים)	*Twice plene*, referring to the *two* occurrences of הַיּוֹשְׁבִים here, and at 2 Chr 31:6.
1 Chr 9:2 (וְהַיּוֹשְׁבִים)	*Twice*, referring to the *two* occurrences of וְהַיּוֹשְׁבִים here, and at 2 Chr 30:25.
2 Chr 30:25 (וְהַיּוֹשְׁבִים)	*Three times*. Since there are *four* occurrences of this lemma with the def. article, with and without the וֹ cj., this note must be referring to the *three* forms of הַיּוֹשְׁבִים with and without וֹ cj., only in the book of Chronicles (1 Chr 9:2, 2 Chr 30:25 and 31:6). Thus the note more precisely should have read *three times in the book*.
2 Chr 31:6 (הַיּוֹשְׁבִים)	*Unique plene in the Writings*. Referring to the only form in the Writings with the def. article but without the וֹ cj.

JUDGES 6:11

וַיָּבֹא מַלְאַךְ יְהֹוָה וַיֵּשֶׁב תַּחַת הָאֵלָה אֲשֶׁר בְּעָפְרָה אֲשֶׁר לְיוֹאָשׁ אֲבִי הָעֶזְרִי וְגִדְעוֹן בְּנוֹ חֹבֵט חִטִּים בַּגַּת לְהָנִיס מִפְּנֵי מִדְיָן:

6:11   חֹבֵט

Unique   ל   Mp

6:11   בַּגַּת

Unique   ל   Mp

Com.: The Masorah notes the *sole* occurrence of this lemma with the def. prep. בַּ, to distinguish it from its more numerous occurrences (11x) with the indef. prep. בְּ (בְּגַת).

6:11   לְהָנִיס

Unique   ל   Mp

JUDGES 6:12

וַיֵּרָא אֵלָיו מַלְאַךְ יְהוָה וַיֹּאמֶר אֵלָיו יְהוָה עִמְּךָ גִּבּוֹר הֶחָיִל:

6:12   וַיֵּרָא

<Twenty>   *<כֹֿ>*   Mp

1–5   **Gen 12:7; 17:1**; 18:1; 26:2; 26:24
6–10   **Gen 35:9**; 46:29; Exod 3:2; **Lev 9:23**; Num 16:19
11–15   Num 17:7; 20:6; <u>**Deut 31:15**</u>; Judg 6:12; 13:3
16–20   **2 Sam 22:11**; 1 Kgs 9:2; <u>Ezek 10:8</u>; 19:11; **2 Chr 7:12**

Com.: The Masorah notes the *twenty* occurrences of this lemma in the *niphal*, to distinguish them from its more numerous occurrences (100+) in the *qal* וַיַּרְא.

All the Mp headings highlighted above read *twenty times* apart from that at 2 Chr 7:12, which mistakenly reads *twice*, an obvious confusion of the letters ב *twice* and כ *twenty*.

In M[L] this lemma has a circellus but no note. However, the note reading *twenty times* does occur in the Mp notes here in M[C] and M[A].

JUDGES 6:13

וַיֹּאמֶר אֵלָיו גִּדְעוֹן בִּי אֲדֹנִי וְיֵשׁ יְהוָה עִמָּנוּ וְלָמָּה מְצָאַתְנוּ כָּל־זֹאת וְאַיֵּה כָל־נִפְלְאֹתָיו אֲשֶׁר
סִפְּרוּ־לָנוּ אֲבוֹתֵינוּ לֵאמֹר הֲלֹא מִמִּצְרַיִם הֶעֱלָנוּ יְהוָה וְעַתָּה נְטָשָׁנוּ יְהוָה וַיִּתְּנֵנוּ בְּכַף־מִדְיָן:

6:13   בִּי אֲדֹנִי

Seven times   ז̇   Mp

1–5   **Gen 43:20**; <u>**44:18**</u>; Num 12:11; **Judg 6:13**; 1 Sam 1:26
6–7   <u>**1 Kgs 3:17**</u>; 3:26

Com.: The Masorah notes the *seven* occurrences of בִּי with אֲדֹנִי, to distinguish them from its *four* occurrences with אֲדֹנָי (בִּי אֲדֹנָי); see **Josh 7:8**.

6:13   וְיֵשׁ יְהוָה

Unique   ל̇   Mp

Com.: This lemma is featured in a Masoretic list of words occurring *twice* combined with the Tetragrammaton, *once* with a ו cj. (here), and *once* without a cj. (יֵשׁ יְהוָה, Gen 28:16); see Frensdorff, *Ochlah*, §186, and Díaz-Esteban, *Sefer Oklah we-Oklah*, §152FF.

6:13   מְצָאַתְנוּ

Three times   גׄ   Mp

Num 20:14 (מְצָאַתְנוּ); **Judg 6:13**; **Neh 9:32**

———————————————

מְצָאַתְנוּ *three times*   מצאתנו גׄ   Mm

Num 20:14   וישלה משה
Judg 6:13   אליו גדעון
Neh 9:32   ועתה אלהינו

Com.: The Masorah notes the *three* occurrences of this lemma, *twice* written with *paṭaḥ* under the א (here and Neh 9:32), and *once* written with *qameṣ* under the א (מְצָאַתְנוּ, Num 20:14).

The Mp heading at Neh 9:32 reads *three times, twice with paṭaḥ*, and the headings of the Mm at Num 20:14 and Neh 9:32 add *and once with qameṣ*.

6:13   בְּכַף־מִדְיָן

Unique   לׄ   Mp

Com.: The Masorah notes the *sole* occurrence of this lemma with the prep. בּ, to distinguish it from its occurrence with the prep. מ (מִכַּף מִדְיָן) in v. 14.

JUDGES 6:14

וַיִּפֶן אֵלָיו יְהֹוָה וַיֹּאמֶר לֵךְ בְּכֹחֲךָ זֶה וְהוֹשַׁעְתָּ אֶת־יִשְׂרָאֵל מִכַּף מִדְיָן הֲלֹא שְׁלַחְתִּיךָ׃

6:14   וַיִּפֶן אֵלָיו

Unique   לׄ   Mp

1–2   **Judg 6:14**; 2 Chr 26:20

Com.: The Mp heading here *of unique* is inexact since there are *two* occurrences of this lemma. The note more precisely should have read *unique in the book*.

Neither M^C nor M^A has a note on this lemma here.

6:14   וְהוֹשַׁעְתָּ

Twice   בֹּ   Mp

Judg 6:14; 1 Sam 23:2

Com.: The Masorah notes the *two* occurrences of this lemma with a וֹ consec., to distinguish them from its *sole* occurrence without a וֹ (הוֹשַׁעְתָּ) at Job 26:2.

6:14   מִכַּף מִדְיָן

Unique   לֹ   Mp

Com.: The Masorah notes the *sole* occurrence of this lemma with the prep. מ, to distinguish it from its occurrence with the prep. ב (בְּכַף־מִדְיָן) in v. 13.

JUDGES 6:15
וַיֹּאמֶר אֵלָיו בִּי אֲדֹנָי בַּמֶּה אוֹשִׁיעַ אֶת־יִשְׂרָאֵל הִנֵּה אַלְפִּי הַדַּל בִּמְנַשֶּׁה וְאָנֹכִי הַצָּעִיר בְּבֵית אָבִי:

6:15   בִּי אֲדֹנָי

Five times   הֹ   Mp

Com.: See **Josh 7:8**.

6:15   בַּמֶּה

Eight times   חֹ   Mp

1–5   **Gen 15:8**; **Judg 6:15**; 1 Sam 14:38; 1 Kgs 22:21; **Mic 6:6**
6–8   **Mal 1:2**; **2:17**; 2 Chr 18:20

בַּמֶּה *eight times*   במה חֹ   Mm

1–5	Gen 15:8	אדע
	Judg 6:15	אושיע
	1 Sam 14:38	היתה
	1 Kgs 22:21	אפתנו
	And its companion (2 Chr 18:20)	וחביר׳
6–8	Mic 6:6	אקדם
	Mal 1:2	אהבתנו
	Mal 2:17	הוגעתם

And once (וּבָמֶה): 2 Sam 21:3   וחד ובמה אכפר

Com.: The Masorah notes the *eight* occurrences of this lemma written with a *qameṣ*, to distinguish them from its more numerous occurrences (15x) written with a *səḡôl*; see Ognibeni, *'Oklah*, §32B.

This distinction is implied in the headings of the Mp at 1 Sam 14:38 (ח קמֹ), 1 Kgs 22:21 (חָ), 2 Chr 18:20 (חָ), and the Mm headings at <u>Gen 15:8</u> and <u>Mic 6:6</u>, all of which read *eight times with qameṣ*, thereby assuming a contrast with a form with a different vowel under the ח , which can only be a *səḡôl*.

The Mm note adds the additional information about the occurrence of this lemma with a ו cj. at 2 Sam 21:3.

6:15   הַדַּל

Unique   ל   Mp

Com.: This lemma is featured in a Masoretic list of words that occur *twice*, once with a ו cj. (Exod 30:15), and *once* without (here); see Frensdorff, *Ochlah*, §1, and Díaz-Esteban, *Sefer Oklah we-Oklah*, §1.

> ### JUDGES 6:16
>
> וַיֹּאמֶר אֵלָיו יְהֹוָה כִּי אֶהְיֶה עִמָּךְ וְהִכִּיתָ אֶת־מִדְיָן כְּאִישׁ אֶחָד:

6:16   וְהִכִּיתָ

Twice with the accent (*mêrəḵâ*)   ב בט   Mp

1–5   Deut 20:13; Judg 6:16

Com.: The Masorah notes the *two* occurrences of this lemma with the accent *mêrəḵâ*, to distinguish them from its *sole* occurrence with the accent *darḡâ* at 2 Kgs 13:17; see Dotan/Reich, *Masora Thesaurus, ad loc.*

The Mp heading at Deut 20:13 reads *five times with the accent* referring to the *five* occurrences of this lemma, written plene and defective ה, which are accented *milraʿ*; see **2 Kgs 13:17.**

6:16   כְּאִישׁ

Twenty times   כ   Mp

1–5   **Num 14:15; Judg 6:16**; 20:1; <u>20:8</u>; **20:11**
6–10   **1 Sam 11:7**; <u>2 Sam 19:15</u>; **Isa 42:13**; <u>66:13</u>; Jer 6:23
11–15   **Jer 14:9; 23:9**; 50:42; **Zech 4:1; Ps 38:15**
16–20   Prov 6:11; 24:34; Ezra 3:1; **Neh 7:2; 8:1**

Com.: The Masorah notes the *twenty* occurrences of this lemma with a *šəwâ* under the ב, possibly to distinguish them from its *sole* occurrence with a *qameṣ* (כָּאִישׁ) at **Judg 8:21**.

JUDGES 6:17

וַיֹּאמֶר אֵלָיו אִם־נָא מָצָאתִי חֵן בְּעֵינֶיךָ וְעָשִׂיתָ לִּי אוֹת שָׁאַתָּה מְדַבֵּר עִמִּי׃

6:17   שָׁאַתָּה

Unique   ל   Mp

JUDGES 6:18

אַל־נָא תָמֻשׁ מִזֶּה עַד־בֹּאִי אֵלֶיךָ וְהֹצֵאתִי אֶת־מִנְחָתִי וְהִנַּחְתִּי לְפָנֶיךָ וַיֹּאמַר אָנֹכִי אֵשֵׁב עַד שׁוּבֶךָ׃

6:18   תָמֻשׁ

Three times   ג   Mp

Judg 6:18; Isa 22:25 (תָּמוּשׁ); **Prov 17:13** (תָּמוּשׁ, *qərê*)

תָמֻשׁ *three times, once written* תָמֻשׁ,	תמש ג חד כת תמש		Mm
and once written תָמוּשׁ,	וחד כת תמוש		
and once written תמיש	וחד כת תמיש		

<u>Judg 6:18</u>   אל נא תמש מזה עד באי
Isa 22:25   תמוש היתד
<u>Prov 17:13</u>   לא תמיש רעה

Com.: The Masorah notes the *three* occurrences of this lemma written in *three* different ways, *once* plene וֹ (תָּמוּשׁ) at Isa 22:25, *once* defective וֹ (תָּמֻשׁ) here, and *once* plene יֹ (תמיש), the *kᵊṯîḇ* form at Prov 17:13 (the *qᵊrê* form is תָּמוּשׁ).

This lemma occurs in the ms. on folio 139v, but the Mm note appears on the bottom right of the following folio 140r.

6:18   וְהֹצֵאתִי

Twice defective   ב חס   Mp

Judg 6:18; Jer 51:44

Com.: The Masorah notes the *two* occurrences of this lemma written defective וֹ, to distinguish them from its more numerous occurrences (8x) written plene וֹ (וְהוֹצֵאתִי).

6:18   וְהִנַּחְתִּי

Three times   גׄ   Mp

Judg 6:18; <u>Ezek 22:20</u>; 37:14

Com.: The Masorah notes the *three* occurrences of this lemma, possibly to distinguish them from the *two* occurrences of its parallel form וְהֵנַחֹתִי at Exod 33:14 and Ezek 16:42.

The Mp and Mm headings at <u>Ezek 22:20</u> read *twice*. But, if referring to the *two* occurrences in Ezekiel, the note more precisely should have read *twice in the book*.

6:18   עַד

Twelve times with the accent (*mêrᵊḵâ*)   יֵׄב בטע   Mp

1–5   **<u>Gen 38:17</u>**; Deut 20:20; **28:22**; 28:35 (וְעַד); <u>Josh 5:8</u>
6–10   **Judg 6:18**; **Job 2:7** (*וְעַד, qᵊrê*); **Cant 2:7**; **3:5**; **8:4**
11   **<u>Ezra 9:6</u>**

Com.: The Mp heading here of *twelve times* is incorrect since there are only *eleven* occurrences of this lemma. The Masorah notes the *eleven* occurrences of the prep. עַד, with the accent *mêrᵊḵâ* as the penultimate word at the end of a verse, to distinguish them from its more numerous occurrences (18x) of this lemma with this accent in the middle of a verse.

This distinction is implied in the Mp heading at Cant 2:7 and the Mp and Mm
headings at <u>Ezra 9:6</u>, which read *eleven times with this accent at the end of a verse*.

The Mm at <u>Ezra 9:6</u> reads *eleven times accented mêrəkâ* (דמארכֹ) *at the end of a verse*.

Both M^C and M^A correctly read here *eleven times with this accent*.

JUDGES 6:19

וְגִדְעוֹן בָּא וַיַּעַשׂ גְּדִי־עִזִּים וְאֵיפַת־קֶמַח מַצּוֹת הַבָּשָׂר שָׂם בַּסַּל וְהַמָּרַק שָׂם בַּפָּרוּר וַיּוֹצֵא אֵלָיו
אֶל־תַּחַת הָאֵלָה וַיִּגַּשׁ׃ ס

6:19   וַיּוֹצֵא

Twelve times plene   יב מל   Mp

1–5   **Gen 15:5; 24:53; 43:23; 48:12; Exod 19:17**
6–10   **Judg 6:19; <u>2 Kgs 24:13</u>; Jer 10:13; 50:25; 51;16***
11–12   **<u>Ps 136:11</u>; 2 Chr 23:14**

Com.: The Masorah notes the *twelve* occurrences of this lemma written plene וֹ, to
distinguish them from its *thirteen* occurrences written defective וֹ (וַיֹּצֵא); see <u>Judg
19:25</u>.

This distinction is implied in the additional notation in the Mm at <u>Ps 136:11</u> which,
after listing the *twelve* plene forms, states that there are also *thirteen* defective forms
making a total of *twenty-five* such forms in the Bible.

* M^L, contrary to M (וַיּוֹצֵא), has only *eleven* occurrences since it writes this lemma
defective at Jer 51:16 (וַיֹּצֵא); see Breuer, *The Biblical Text*, 196 and 394. However, all
the Mp headings highlighted above and the Mm heading here read *twelve times*, thus
supporting the enumeration inherent in the text of M.

JUDGES 6:20

וַיֹּאמֶר אֵלָיו מַלְאַךְ הָאֱלֹהִים קַח אֶת־הַבָּשָׂר וְאֶת־הַמַּצּוֹת וְהַנַּח אֶל־הַסֶּלַע הַלָּז וְאֶת־הַמָּרַק
שְׁפוֹךְ וַיַּעַשׂ כֵּן׃

6:20   מַלְאַךְ הָאֱלֹהִים

Eight times   ח   Mp

1–5   **Gen 31:11; Exod 14:19; Judg 6:20; 13:6; 13:9**
6–8   **2 Sam 14:17** (כְּמַלְאַךְ)**; 14:20; 19:28** (כְּמַלְאַךְ)

Com.: The Masorah notes the *eight* occurrences of מַלְאַךְ with הָאֱלֹהִים, to distinguish them from its *sole* occurrence with אֱלֹהִים (מַלְאַךְ אֱלֹהִים) at Gen 21:17, and from its more numerous occurrences (49x) with the Tetragrammaton (מַלְאַךְ יְהוָה).

All the Mp headings highlighted above read *eight times* apart from that at 2 Sam 14:17, which reads *twice* counting just the *two* forms with the prep. כ at that reference and at 2 Sam 19:28.

6:20   וְהַנַּח

Twice   ב   Mp

Exod 16:33; Judg 6:20

Com.: The Masorah notes the *sole* occurrence of this lemma with a ו cj., to distinguish it from its occurrence without a cj. at Hos 4:17.

6:20   שְׁפוֹךְ

Twice plene   ב מל   Mp

Judg 6:20; Jer 22:17(לִשְׁפּוֹךְ)

Com.: The Masorah notes the *two* occurrences of this lemma written plene ו, to distinguish them from its more numerous occurrences (9x) written defective ו (שְׁפֹךְ/לִשְׁפֹּךְ).

JUDGES 6:21

וַיִּשְׁלַח מַלְאַךְ יְהוָה אֶת־קְצֵה הַמִּשְׁעֶנֶת אֲשֶׁר בְּיָדוֹ וַיִּגַּע בַּבָּשָׂר וּבַמַּצּוֹת וַתַּעַל הָאֵשׁ מִן־הַצּוּר וַתֹּאכַל אֶת־הַבָּשָׂר וְאֶת־הַמַּצּוֹת וּמַלְאַךְ יְהוָה הָלַךְ מֵעֵינָיו׃

6:21   וּבַמַּצּוֹת

Unique   ל   Mp

6:21   וַתַּעַל הָאֵשׁ

Unique   ל   Mp

6:21   מֵעֵינָיו

Unique   ל   Mp

Com.: The Masorah notes the *sole* occurrence of this lemma with the prep. מ, to distinguish it from its more numerous occurrences (51x) with the prep. ב (בְּעֵינָיו).

JUDGES 6:22

וַיַּרְא גִּדְעֹון כִּי־מַלְאַךְ יְהוָה הוּא ס וַיֹּאמֶר גִּדְעֹון אֲהָהּ אֲדֹנָי יְהוִה כִּי־עַל־כֵּן רָאִיתִי מַלְאַךְ יְהוָה פָּנִים אֶל־פָּנִים:

6:22   פָּנִים אֶל־פָּנִים

Five times   ה   Mp

1–5   **Gen 32:31; Exod 33:11; Deut 34:10; Judg 6:22; Ezek 20:35**

פָּנִים אֶל־פָּנִים *five times*   פנים אל פנים ה   Mm

1–5	Exod 33:11	ודבר יהוה
	Deut 34:10	ולא קם נביא
	Gen 32:31	כי ראיתי (אל) [אלהים]
	Judg 6:22	כי על כן
	Ezek 20:35	ונשפטתי

Com.: The Masorah notes the *five* occurrences of this lemma, to distinguish them from the *sole* occurrence of its parallel phrase פֶּה אֶל פֶּה at Num 12:8.

The heading of the Mp at Deut 34:10 mistakenly reads *four times*, though the Mm there lists *five* references.

JUDGES 6:23

וַיֹּאמֶר לֹו יְהוָה שָׁלֹום לְךָ אַל־תִּירָא לֹא תָּמוּת:

6:23   וַיֹּאמֶר לֹו יְהוָה

Four times   ד   Mp

Gen 4:15; **Judg 6:23; 6:25; 1 Chr 14:10**

Com.: The Masorah notes the *four* occurrences of the phrase וַיֹּאמֶר לוֹ with the Tetragrammaton, to distinguish them from its *three* occurrences with אֱלֹהִים or הָאֱלֹהִים (וַיֹּאמֶר לוֹ אֱלֹהִים/הָאֱלֹהִים).

The Mp heading at Judg 6:25 reads *twice with these accents*, and refers to the fact that at both Gen 4:15 and Judg 6:25 the accents on this phrase are identical, having the combination *dargâ mûnaḥ rəḇîaʿ* (וַיֹּאמֶר לוֹ יְהֹוָה).

In Mᴸ only one circellus has been placed on לוֹ יְהֹוָה but, since this phrase occurs *nine times*, it is clear that the lemma should be the *three* words וַיֹּאמֶר לוֹ יְהֹוָה, as it is in v. 25 where there are *two* circelli.

6:23   שָׁלוֹם לְךָ

Twice   בֹ   Mp

1–3   **Judg 6:23**; **1 Sam 20:21**; 1 Chr 12:19

Com.: The Mp heading here, and in Mᴬ, of *twice* is inexact since there are *three* occurrences of this lemma. The note more precisely should have read *twice in the Prophets*.

The Masorah notes the *three* occurrences of שָׁלוֹם with לְךָ, to distinguish them from its *two* occurrences written with לָךְ (שָׁלוֹם לָךְ) at **Judg 19:20** and Dan 10:19.

The Mp heading at 1 Sam 20:21 correctly reads *three times*.

Mᶜ has no note here.

JUDGES 6:24

וַיִּבֶן שָׁם גִּדְעוֹן מִזְבֵּחַ לַיהוָה וַיִּקְרָא־לוֹ יְהוָה שָׁלוֹם עַד הַיּוֹם הַזֶּה עוֹדֶנּוּ בְּעָפְרָת אֲבִי הָעֶזְרִי: פ

6:24   בְּעָפְרָת

Unique   לֹ   Mp

Com.: The Masorah notes the *sole* occurrence of this lemma in the cstr., to distinguish it from its *three* occurrences in the absol. (בְּעָפְרָה), *one* of which occurs in v. 11.

JUDGES 6:25

וַיְהִי֩ בַּלַּ֨יְלָה הַה֜וּא וַיֹּ֧אמֶר ל֣וֹ יְהֹוָ֗ה קַ֣ח אֶת־פַּר־הַשּׁוֹר֩ אֲשֶׁ֨ר לְאָבִ֜יךָ וּפַ֨ר הַשֵּׁנִ֜י שֶׁ֣בַע שָׁנִ֗ים וְהָרַסְתָּ֞ אֶת־מִזְבַּ֤ח הַבַּ֨עַל֙ אֲשֶׁ֣ר לְאָבִ֔יךָ וְאֶת־הָאֲשֵׁרָ֥ה אֲשֶׁר־עָלָ֖יו תִּכְרֹֽת׃

6:25   וַיֹּ֧אמֶר ל֣וֹ יְהֹוָ֗ה

Twice with these accents (*dargâ mûnaḥ rᵊbîaʿ*)   בׄ בטע   Mp

Com.: See directly above at **Judg 6:23**.

6:25   וּפַ֨ר הַשֵּׁנִ֜י

Unique   לׄ   Mp

Com.: This lemma is featured in a Masoretic list of two-word phrases whose second word occurs *once* with the def. article (here), and *once* without (וּפַר שֵׁנִי, Num 8:8); see Frensdorff, *Ochlah*, §3, and Díaz-Esteban, *Sefer Oklah we-Oklah*, §3.

6:25   וְהָרַסְתָּ֞

Unique   לׄ   Mp

6:25   וְאֶת־הָאֲשֵׁרָ֥ה

Unique   לׄ   Mp

Com.: The Masorah notes the *sole* occurrence of this lemma with a ו cj., to distinguish it from its *three* occurrences without a cj.

JUDGES 6:26

וּבָנִ֨יתָ מִזְבֵּ֜חַ לַיהֹוָ֣ה אֱלֹהֶ֗יךָ עַ֣ל רֹ֧אשׁ הַמָּע֛וֹז הַזֶּ֖ה בַּמַּֽעֲרָכָ֑ה וְלָֽקַחְתָּ֙ אֶת־הַפָּ֣ר הַשֵּׁנִ֔י וְהַעֲלִ֣יתָ עוֹלָ֔ה בַּעֲצֵ֥י הָאֲשֵׁרָ֖ה אֲשֶׁ֥ר תִּכְרֹֽת׃

6:26   הַמָּע֛וֹז

הַמָּעוֹז *twice*   בׄ   Mm

<u>\<Judg 6:26\></u>
Dan 11:31   וזרעים (ממנה) ממנו יעמדו

Com.: The Masorah notes the *two* occurrences of this lemma with a def. article, to distinguish them from its more numerous occurrences (11x) without a def. article.

This lemma is featured in a Masoretic list of doublets with an initial הַ; see Frensdorff, *Ochlah*, §64, and Díaz-Esteban, *Sefer Oklah we-Oklah*, §65.

6:26   וְהַעֲלֵיתָ

Three times   גֿ   Mp

Deut 27:6; Judg 6:26; Jer 38:10

וְהַעֲלֵיתָ   *three times*   והעלית גֿ   Mm

Deut 27:6	והעלית עליו (עלות) [עולת]
Judg 6:26	והעלית עולה בעצי
Jer 38:10	והעלית את ירמיהו הנביא

Com.: The Masorah notes the *three* occurrences of this lemma pointed with a *ḥîreq* under the ל, and accented *milʿêl*, to distinguish them from the *sole* occurrence of its parallel form pointed with a *ṣerê* under the ל, and accented *milraʿ* (וְהַעֲלֵיתָ) at Exod 40:4; see Ognibeni, *'Oklah*, §8H.

At Exod 40:4 the Mp heading reads *unique*, and adds וטעם בתיו *and accented on the* ת, e.g., accented *milraʿ*.

6:26   עוֹלָה

Unique plene in the book   ל מל בסֿ   Mp

Com.: The Masorah notes the *sole* occurrence of this lemma in the book written plene וֹ, to distinguish it from its more numerous occurrences (4x) in the book written defective וֹ (עֹלָה).

JUDGES 6:27

וַיִּקַּח גִּדְעוֹן עֲשָׂרָה אֲנָשִׁים מֵעֲבָדָיו וַיַּעַשׂ כַּאֲשֶׁר דִּבֶּר אֵלָיו יְהוָה וַיְהִי כַּאֲשֶׁר יָרֵא אֶת־בֵּית אָבִיו
וְאֶת־אַנְשֵׁי הָעִיר מֵעֲשׂוֹת יוֹמָם וַיַּעַשׂ לָיְלָה:

6:27   וְאֶת־אַנְשֵׁי

Unique   ל   Mp

Com.: The Masorah notes the *sole* occurrence of this lemma with a ו cj., to distinguish it from its more numerous occurrences (7x) without a cj.

JUDGES 6:28

וַיַּשְׁכִּימוּ אַנְשֵׁי הָעִיר בַּבֹּקֶר וְהִנֵּה נֻתַּץ מִזְבַּח הַבַּעַל וְהָאֲשֵׁרָה אֲשֶׁר־עָלָיו כֹּרָתָה וְאֵת הַפָּר הַשֵּׁנִי
הֹעֲלָה עַל־הַמִּזְבֵּחַ הַבָּנוּי:

6:28   נֻתַּץ

Unique   ל   Mp

Com.: This lemma is featured in a Masoretic list of doublets with different hierarchial vowels, in a list termed *mil'êl* and *milra'*; see Yeivin, *Introduction*, §132, p. 103. In this connection, the higher vowel, the *mil'êl*, is the vowel *qibbûṣ*, and the lower vowel, the *milra'*, is the vowel *ḥîreq*. Thus נֻתַּץ (here) with *qibbûṣ* is *mil'êl*, but נִתַּץ (2 Chr 33:3) with *ḥîreq* is *milra'*; see Frensdorff, *Ochlah*, §5, and Díaz-Esteban, *Sefer Oklah we-Oklah*, §5.

6:28   כֹּרָתָה

Unique and defective   ל וחס   Mp

Com.: By noting that this lemma is *unique* and written defective ו, the Masorah is also implying (correctly) that this lemma does not occur elsewhere written plene ו.

6:28   וְאֵת הַפָּר

וְאֵת הַפָּר *three times*   ואת הפר גׄ   Mm

Exod 29:3	ואת הפר ואת שני (האילים) [האילם]
Lev 8:17	ואת ערו ואת בשרו
Judg 6:28	העלה על המזבח

Com.: The Masorah notes the *three* occurrences of this lemma with the def. article, to distinguish them from its *two* occurrences in the cstr. without the def. article (וְאֵת פַּר) at Lev. 8:2 and 16:27.

6:28   הֶעָלָה

Three times   גֹ   Mp

<u>Judg 6:28</u>; Hab 1:15 (הֶעֱלָה); <u>2 Chr 20:34</u>

הֶעָלָה *twice* and defective   העלה בֹ וחֹס   Mm

<u>Judg 6:28</u>   ואת הפר השני
<u>2 Chr 20:34</u>   העלה על ספר מלכי ישראל

And *once* (הֶעֱלָה): Hab 1:15   וחד (כלו) [כלה] בחכה העלה

Com.: The Mp notes the *three* occurrences of this lemma, *two* of them are *hophal*s pointed as הֶעָלָה, and *one* of them is a *hiphil* pointed as הֶעֱלָה.

The Mp heading at Hab 1:15 (הֶעֱלָה) reads *unique* noting the singularity of its particular form.

The heading of the Mm notes that the *two hophal* forms are written defective (וֹ), and the Mm additionally notes the occurrence of the *hiphil* form (הֶעֱלָה) at Hab 1:15.

The Mp and Mm headings at 2 Chr 20:34 read *twice*, and the Mm lists the *two hophal* forms.

6:28   הַבָּנוּי

Unique   לֹ   Mp

Com.: The Masorah notes the *sole* occurrence of this lemma with a def. article, to distinguish it from its occurrence without a def. article (בָּנוּי) at Cant 4:4.

JUDGES 6:30

וַיֹּאמְרוּ אַנְשֵׁי הָעִיר אֶל־יוֹאָשׁ הוֹצֵא אֶת־בִּנְךָ וְיָמֹת כִּי נָתַץ אֶת־מִזְבַּח הַבַּעַל וְכִי כָרַת הָאֲשֵׁרָה אֲשֶׁר־עָלָיו:

6:30   הוֹצֵא

Five times   הֹ   Mp

1–5   **Gen 19:12; <u>Lev 24:14</u>; Judg 6:30; 19:22; 2 Kgs 10:22**

Com.: The Masorah notes the *five* occurrences of this lemma, a *hiphil* imper., to distinguish them from its *sole* occurrence of the alternate *hiphil* imper. form הַיְצֵא (*qərê*) at Gen 8:17.

6:30   וְיָמֹת

Twice   בֹ   Mp

Judg 6:30; 1 Kgs 21:10

Com.: The Masorah notes the *two* occurrences of this lemma with a ו cj., to distinguish them from its *sole* occurrence without a cj. at Deut 33:6.

The Mp heading at 1 Kgs 21:10 reads *twice and defective* ו implying (correctly) that this lemma does not occur elsewhere written plene ו.

This lemma is featured in a Masoretic list of words occurring *three times*, *twice* with a ו cj., and *once* without it (Deut 33:6); see Frensdorff, *Ochlah*, §14, and Díaz-Esteban, *Sefer Oklah we-Oklah*, §15.

JUDGES 6:31

וַיֹּאמֶר יוֹאָשׁ לְכֹל אֲשֶׁר־עָמְדוּ עָלָיו הַאַתֶּם | תְּרִיבוּן לַבַּעַל אִם־אַתֶּם תּוֹשִׁיעוּן אוֹתוֹ אֲשֶׁר יָרִיב לוֹ יוּמַת עַד־הַבֹּקֶר אִם־אֱלֹהִים הוּא יָרֶב לוֹ כִּי נָתַץ אֶת־מִזְבְּחוֹ:

6:31   הַאַתֶּם

Unique   ל   Mp

Com.: The Masorah notes the *sole* occurrence of this lemma with the interrog. הֹ, to distinguish it from its more numerous occurrences (200+) without this interrogative (אַתֶּם), *one* of which is in this verse and *another* is in v. 10.

6:31   תְּרִיבוּן

Three times   גֿ   Mp

Exod 17:2; **Judg 6:31**; Job 13:8

תְּרִיבוּן *three times* and plene   תריבון גֿ ומל   Mm

Exod 17:2   עמדו מה
Judg 6:31   האתם
Job 13:8   הפניו תשאון

Com.: By noting that this lemma occurs *three times* and written plene יֿ, the Masorah is also implying (correctly) that this lemma does not occur elsewhere written defective יֿ.

6:31   תּוֹשִׁיעוּן

Unique   לֿ   Mp

6:31   מִזְבְּחוֹ

Three times   גֿ   Mp

Judg 6:31; 6:32; Lam 2:7

Com.: The Masorah notes the *three* occurrences of this lemma, possibly to distinguish them from its *sole* occurrence pointed differently (מִזְבְּחוֹ), and with a different meaning (*from its [= their] sacrifice*) at Exod 34:15.

JUDGES 6:34

וְרוּחַ יְהוָה לָבְשָׁה אֶת־גִּדְעוֹן וַיִּתְקַע בַּשּׁוֹפָר וַיִּזָּעֵק אֲבִיעֶזֶר אַחֲרָיו׃

6:34   וְרוּחַ יְהוָה

Three times   גֿ   Mp

Judg 6:34; 1 Sam 16:14; **1 Kgs 18:12**

Com.: The Masorah notes the *three* occurrences of this lemma with a וֿ cj., to distinguish them from its more numerous occurrences (23x) without a cj.

JUDGES 6:35

וּמַלְאָכִים שָׁלַח בְּכָל־מְנַשֶּׁה וַיִּזָּעֵק גַּם־הוּא אַחֲרָיו וּמַלְאָכִים שָׁלַח בְּאָשֵׁר וּבִזְבֻלוּן וּבְנַפְתָּלִי
וַיַּעֲלוּ לִקְרָאתָם:

6:35   וּבִזְבֻלוּן

Nine times written this way   טֹ כת כן   Mp

Com.: See **Josh 19:27**.

JUDGES 6:36

וַיֹּאמֶר גִּדְעוֹן אֶל־הָאֱלֹהִים אִם־יֶשְׁךָ מוֹשִׁיעַ בְּיָדִי אֶת־יִשְׂרָאֵל כַּאֲשֶׁר דִּבַּרְתָּ:

6:36   וַיֹּאמֶר גִּדְעוֹן אֶל־הָאֱלֹהִים

Twice   בֿ   Mp

Judg 6:36; 6:39

Com.: The Masorah notes the *two* occurrences of the phrase וַיֹּאמֶר גִּדְעוֹן with אֶל־
הָאֱלֹהִים to distinguish them from its *two* occurrences without (וַיֹּאמֶר אֶל־הָאֱלֹהִים
גִּדְעוֹן) in v. 22 and Judg 8:7.

In M^L only one circellus has been placed here and in v. 39 on the words אֶל־הָאֱלֹהִים
but, since this phrase occurs more than twice, it is most likely that the note refers to
the entire phrase וַיֹּאמֶר גִּדְעוֹן אֶל־הָאֱלֹהִים, that only occurs *twice*.

JUDGES 6:37

הִנֵּה אָנֹכִי מַצִּיג אֶת־גִּזַּת הַצֶּמֶר בַּגֹּרֶן אִם טַל יִהְיֶה עַל־הַגִּזָּה לְבַדָּהּ וְעַל־כָּל־הָאָרֶץ חֹרֶב וְיָדַעְתִּי
כִּי־תוֹשִׁיעַ בְּיָדִי אֶת־יִשְׂרָאֵל כַּאֲשֶׁר דִּבַּרְתָּ:

6:37   עַל־הַגִּזָּה

Unique   ל   Mp

Com.: This form is featured in a Masoretic list of words that only occur *once* preceded
by the prep. עַל; see Frensdorff, *Ochlah*, §76, and Díaz-Esteban, *Sefer Oklah we-Oklah*,
§155.

6:37 וְעַל־כָּל־הָאָֽרֶץ

Three times גׄ Mp

1–4 **Judg 6:37; 6:39; 6:40**; Ps 108:6

Com.: The Mp heading here, and in Mᶜ, *of three times* is inexact since there are *four* occurrences of this lemma. The note more precisely should have read *three times in this section* or *three times in the book*.

The Masorah notes the *three* occurrences of this lemma with כָּל, to distinguish them from its more numerous occurrences (7x) without כָּל (וְעַל הָאָֽרֶץ).

Mᴬ reads here *seven times and similarly all Psalms apart from two* to include the *four* occurrences of this lemma without an initial ו cj. (עַל־כָּל־הָאָֽרֶץ).

6:37 חֹֽרֶב

Sixteen times יׄוׄ Mp

1–5 Gen 31:40; **Judg 6:37**; 6:39; 6:40; Isa 4:6 (מֵחֹֽרֶב)
6–10 Isa 25:4 (מֵחֹֽרֶב); 25:5ᵃ (כְּחֹֽרֶב); 25:5ᵇ; **61:4**; Jer 36:30 (לַחֹֽרֶב)
11–15 Jer 49:13 (לְחֹֽרֶב); 50:38; Ezek 29:10; Zeph 2:14; Hag 1:11
16 **Job 30:30**

Com.: The Masorah notes the *sixteen* occurrences of this lemma in various forms with a *saġôl* under the ר, to distinguish them from its *fifteen* occurrences in various forms with a *ṣerê* under the ר (חֹֽרֶב/בְּחֹֽרֶב/מֵחֹֽרֶב).

The Mp heading at Job 30:30 reads more expansively *sixteen times in various forms*.

JUDGES 6:38

וַיְהִי־כֵן וַיַּשְׁכֵּם מִֽמָּחֳרָת וַיָּ֫זַר אֶת־הַגִּזָּה וַיִּמֶץ טַל מִן־הַגִּזָּה מְלוֹא הַסֵּ֫פֶל מָֽיִם׃

6:38 וַיָּ֫זַר

Unique לׄ Mp

6:38 וַיִּ֫מֶץ

Unique לׄ Mp

6:38   מְלוֹא

Twice plene   ב מל   Mp

Lev 5:12; Judg 6:38

Com.: The Masorah notes the *two* occurrences of this lemma written plene וֹ, to distinguish them from its more numerous occurrences (15x) written defective וֹ (מְלֹא).

JUDGES 6:39

וַיֹּאמֶר גִּדְעוֹן אֶל־הָאֱלֹהִים אַל־יִחַר אַפְּךָ בִּי וַאֲדַבְּרָה אַךְ הַפָּעַם אֲנַסֶּה נָּא־רַק־הַפַּעַם בַּגִּזָּה יְהִי־נָא חֹרֶב אֶל־הַגִּזָּה לְבַדָּהּ וְעַל־כָּל־הָאָרֶץ יִהְיֶה־טָּל׃

6:39   וַיֹּאמֶר גִּדְעוֹן אֶל־הָאֱלֹהִים

Twice   ב   Mp

Com.: See directly above at **Judg 6:36**.

6:39   וְעַל־כָּל־הָאָרֶץ

Three times   ג   Mp

Com.: See directly above at **Judg 6:37.**

JUDGES 6:40

וַיַּעַשׂ אֱלֹהִים כֵּן בַּלַּיְלָה הַהוּא וַיְהִי־חֹרֶב אֶל־הַגִּזָּה לְבַדָּהּ וְעַל־כָּל־הָאָרֶץ הָיָה טָל׃ פ

6:40   וַיַּעַשׂ אֱלֹהִים

וַיַּעַשׂ אֱלֹהִים *four times* ד ויעש אלהים   Mm

Gen 1:7	את הרקיע ויבדל
Gen 1:16	את שני המארת
Gen 1:25	את חית (הא) [הארץ]
Judg 6:40	בלילה ההוא

Com.: The Masorah notes the *four* occurrences of this lemma with אֱלֹהִים, to distinguish them from its more numerous occurrences (11x) with the Tetragrammaton (וַיַּעַשׂ יְהוָה).

6:40 וְעַל־כָּל־הָאָֽרֶץ

Three times גׄ Mp

Com.: See directly above at **Judg 6:37**.

JUDGES 7:1

וַיַּשְׁכֵּם יְרֻבַּעַל הוּא גִדְעוֹן וְכָל־הָעָם אֲשֶׁר אִתּוֹ וַיַּחֲנוּ עַל־עֵין חֲרֹד וּמַחֲנֵה מִדְיָן הָיָה־לוֹ מִצָּפוֹן
מִגִּבְעַת הַמּוֹרֶה בָּעֵֽמֶק׃

7:1 חֲרֹד

Unique לׄ Mp

7:1 מִגִּבְעַת הַמּוֹרֶה

Unique לׄ Mp

JUDGES 7:2

וַיֹּאמֶר יְהוָה אֶל־גִּדְעוֹן רַב הָעָם אֲשֶׁר אִתָּךְ מִתִּתִּי אֶת־מִדְיָן בְּיָדָם פֶּן־יִתְפָּאֵר עָלַי יִשְׂרָאֵל לֵאמֹר
יָדִי הוֹשִׁיעָה לִּֽי׃

7:2 מִתִּתִּי

Three times גׄ Mp

Gen 29:19; Judg 7:2; 1 Kgs 21:3

מִתִּתִּי *three times*, and their references   מתתי גׄ וסימנהון   Mm

Gen 29:19   אתה לאיש אחר
Judg 7:2   מדין בידם פן יתפאר
1 Kgs 21:3   נחלת (אבותי) [אבתי]

Com.: The Masorah notes the *three* occurrences of this lemma with the prep. מ, to distinguish them from its *three* occurrences without this prep. (תִּתִּי).

7:2   יִתְפָּאֵר

Unique   לֹ   Mp

Com.: The Masorah notes the *sole* occurrence of this lemma with a *ṣerê* under the א, to distinguish it from its occurrence with a *qameṣ* under the א (יִתְפָּאָר, pausal form) at Isa 44:23.

JUDGES 7:3

וְעַתָּה קְרָא נָא בְּאָזְנֵי הָעָם לֵאמֹר מִי־יָרֵא וְחָרֵד יָשֹׁב וְיִצְפֹּר מֵהַר הַגִּלְעָד וַיָּשָׁב מִן־הָעָם עֶשְׂרִים וּשְׁנַיִם אֶלֶף וַעֲשֶׂרֶת אֲלָפִים נִשְׁאָרוּ׃ ס

7:3   יָשֹׁב

Five times   הֹ   Mp

1–5   <u>Judg 7:3</u>; 1 Sam 20:5; 2 Sam 15:8 (יָשׁוּב, *qərê*); <u>Isa 12:1</u>; Ps 74:21

יָשֹׁב *five times* and defective, and their references   ישב ה וחס וסימנהון   Mm

1 Sam 20:5	ישב אשב עם (המצפה) [המלך]
<u>Judg 7:3</u>	ויצפר מהר
2 Sam 15:8	אם (ישב) [ישוב] ישיבני יהוה
<u>Isa 12:1</u>	ישב אפך ותנחמני
Ps 74:21	אל ישב דך נכלם

Com.: The Masorah notes the *five* occurrences of this lemma, written both plene and defective ו, pointed with a *ḥolem*, to distinguish them from its more numerous occurrences (56x) pointed with a *śûreq* or *qibbûṣ* (יָשׁוּב/יָשֻׁב).

Three of the above forms (Judg 7:3, Isa 12:1, and Ps 74:21) are jussives from שׁוּב, but the form in 1 Sam 20:5 is an infin. absol. from יָשֵׁב. The *qərê* form יָשׁוּב (from שׁוּב) in 2 Sam 15:8 does not fit the context, as one would expect before יְשִׁיבֵנִי a *hiphil* infin. absol. (הָשֵׁב).

The heading of the Mm here (and in M[C]) of *five times and defective* (ו) is incorrect as there are only *four* such forms. All of the Mp headings highlighted above and the heading to the Mm at <u>Isa 12:1</u> correctly just read *five times* (not *five times defective*). Similarly, the Mm of M[A] here just reads *five times*.

7:3 וְיִצְפֹּר

Unique ל Mp

7:3 מֵהַר הַגִּלְעָד

Unique ל Mp

Com.: This lemma is featured in a Masoretic list of two-word phrases that occur *once* with the def. article within the phrase (here) and *once* without this def. article (Cant 4:1); see Frensdorff, *Ochlah*, §3, and Díaz-Esteban, *Sefer Oklah we-Oklah*, §3.

> ## JUDGES 7:4
>
> וַיֹּאמֶר יְהוָה אֶל־גִּדְעוֹן עוֹד הָעָם רָב הוֹרֵד אוֹתָם אֶל־הַמַּיִם וְאֶצְרְפֶנּוּ לְךָ שָׁם וְהָיָה אֲשֶׁר אֹמַר
> אֵלֶיךָ זֶה ׀ יֵלֵךְ אִתָּךְ הוּא יֵלֵךְ אִתָּךְ וְכֹל אֲשֶׁר־אֹמַר אֵלֶיךָ זֶה לֹא־יֵלֵךְ עִמָּךְ הוּא לֹא יֵלֵךְ:

7:4 הוֹרֵד

Three times גׄ Mp

Exod 33:5; **Judg 7:4**; **Ps 56:8**

Com.: The Masorah notes the *three* occurrences of this lemma pointed with a *holem* and a *ṣerê*, possibly to distinguish them from its *two* occurrences pointed with a *šûreq* and a *pataḥ* (הוּרַד) at Gen 39:1 and Isa 14:11.

7:4 וְאֶצְרְפֶנּוּ

Unique ל Mp

7:4 יֵלֵךְ עִמָּךְ

Twice בׄ Mp

Judg 7:4; **2 Sam 13:26**

יֵלֵךְ עִמָּךְ *twice* ילך עמד בׄ   Mm

Judg 7:4   הורד אותם אל המים
2 Sam 13:26 למה ילך עמך

Com.: The Masorah notes the *two* occurrences of יֵלֵךְ with עִמָּךְ, to distinguish them from its *two* occurrences written with אִתָּךְ (יֵלֵךְ אִתָּךְ), which occur in this same verse.

JUDGES 7:5

וַיּוֹרֶד אֶת־הָעָם אֶל־הַמָּיִם ס וַיֹּאמֶר יְהֹוָה אֶל־גִּדְעוֹן כֹּל אֲשֶׁר־יָלֹק בִּלְשׁוֹנוֹ מִן־הַמַּיִם כַּאֲשֶׁר יָלֹק הַכֶּלֶב תַּצִּיג אוֹתוֹ לְבָד וְכֹל אֲשֶׁר־יִכְרַע עַל־בִּרְכָּיו לִשְׁתּוֹת׃

7:5 וַיּוֹרֶד

Six times וׄ Mp

1–5 **Judg 7:5**; 1 Sam 21:14; **Joel 2:23**; Ps 78:16; **Prov 21:22** (וַיֹּרֶד)
6   **2 Chr 23:20**

Com.: The Masorah notes the *six* occurrences of this lemma, written plene and defective ו, in the sg., to distinguish them from its *five* occurrences, written plene and defective ו, in the pl. (וַיּוֹרִידוּ/וַיֹּרִדוּ/וַיּוֹרִדוּ).

This distinction is implied in the Mm note at Joel 2:23 in the additional notation *of Chronicles* to the 2 Chr 23:20 reference, which distinguishes it from its parallel passage in 2 Kgs 11:19, where the lemma occurs as וַיֹּרִידוּ.

7:5 בִּלְשׁוֹנוֹ

Seven times plene זׄ מל Mp

1–5 **Judg 7:5**; Isa 30:27 (וּלְשׁוֹנוֹ); Zech 14:12 (וּלְשׁוֹנוֹ); Ps 10:7 (לְשׁוֹנוֹ);
    37:30 (וּלְשׁוֹנוֹ)
6–7 **Prov 17:20; 21:23** (וּלְשׁוֹנוֹ)

Com.: The Masorah notes the *seven* occurrences of this lemma in various forms, written plene ו, to distinguish them from its more numerous occurrences (9x) in various forms, written defective ו (e.g. לְשׁוֹנוֹ).

This enumeration does not include the *two* occurrences of this lemma in Esther (at 1:22 and 3:12).

The Mp heading at Prov 21:23 reads *four times* enumerating the *four* occurrences of the form with ו cj. (וּלְשׁוֹנוֹ) there, and at Isa 30:27, Zech 14:12, and Ps 37:30.

7:5   לְבָד

Unique and similarly all the Tabernacle   ל̇ וכל משכֿ ותרֿ עשֿ דכו̇   Mp
and The Twelve

Com.: The Masorah notes the *single* occurrence of this lemma, outside of the Tabernacle sections (Exod 25–31, 36–40) and The Twelve, written with a *qames*, to distinguish them from its more numerous occurrences (17x) written with a *patah* (לְבַד).

┌───┐

JUDGES 7:6

וַיְהִי מִסְפַּר הַֽמֲלַקְקִים בְּיָדָם אֶל־פִּיהֶם שְׁלֹשׁ מֵאוֹת אִישׁ וְכֹל יֶתֶר הָעָם כָּרְעוּ עַל־בִּרְכֵיהֶם לִשְׁתּוֹת מָֽיִם: ס

└───┘

7:6   הַֽמֲלַקְקִים

Twice   ב̇   Mp

Judg 7:6; 7:7

7:6   וְכֹל יֶתֶר

Unique   ל̇   Mp

Com.: The Masorah notes the *sole* occurrence of this lemma with a ו cj., to distinguish it from its occurrence without a cj. at Hab 2:8.

7:6   בִּרְכֵיהֶם

All forms of בִּרְכֵי, בִּרְכַּי   הַבִּרְכַּיִם have   כל לשון ברכי ברכי הברכים   Mm
a *dageš* apart from *two rapê*   דגש ב̇ מ̇ ב̇ רפי

בִּרְכֵיהֶם (Judg 7:6)	ברכיהם
בִּרְכוֹהִי (Dan 6:11)	ברכוהי

Com.: The Masorah notes that all forms of בִּרְכֵי (Gen 50:23), בִּרְכַּי (Gen 30:3, etc.) and הַבִּרְכַּיִם (Deut 28:35 and 1 Kgs 19:18) have a *dageš* in the letter כ, apart from *two* that are *rapê*, that is, without a *dageš*. These *two* forms are בִּרְכֵיהֶם (Judg 7:6) and בִּרְכוֹהִי (Dan 6:11).

JUDGES 7:7

וַיֹּ֤אמֶר יְהוָה֙ אֶל־גִּדְע֔וֹן בִּשְׁלֹשׁ֩ מֵא֨וֹת הָאִ֤ישׁ הַֽמֲלַקְקִים֙ אוֹשִׁ֣יעַ אֶתְכֶ֔ם וְנָתַתִּ֥י אֶת־מִדְיָ֖ן בְּיָדֶ֑ךָ
וְכָל־הָעָ֔ם יֵלְכ֖וּ אִ֥ישׁ לִמְקֹמֽוֹ׃

7:7   הַֽמֲלַקְקִים

Twice   בׄ   Mp

Judg 7:6; 7:7

7:7   לִמְקֹמֽוֹ

Three times defective   גׄ חס   Mp

1   *All* the Torah (Gen 18:33; 32:1; Num 24:25)
2   *All* Judges (**Judg 7:7; 9:55; 19:28**)
3   **2 Sam 19:40**

Com.: The Masorah notes the *three* occurrences of this lemma written defective first ו,
to distinguish them from its *five* occurrences written plene first ו (לִמְקוֹמוֹ).

This allocation of the references is according to Breuer, *The Biblical Text*, 68.

M^L, contrary to M (לִמְקוֹמוֹ), has *two* more occurrences of this lemma since it writes
the forms at 1 Sam 2:20 and 1 Sam 5:11 defective first ו (לִמְקֹמוֹ); see Breuer, *The
Biblical Text*, 68 and 70.

JUDGES 7:8

וַיִּקְח֣וּ אֶת־צֵדָה֩ הָעָ֨ם בְּיָדָ֜ם וְאֵ֣ת שׁוֹפְרֹֽתֵיהֶ֗ם וְאֵ֤ת כָּל־אִישׁ֙ יִשְׂרָאֵ֔ל שִׁלַּח֙ אִ֣ישׁ לְאֹֽהָלָ֔יו וּבִשְׁלֹשׁ־
מֵא֥וֹת הָאִ֖ישׁ הֶחֱזִ֑יק וּמַחֲנֵ֣ה מִדְיָ֔ן הָ֥יָה ל֖וֹ מִתַּ֥חַת בָּעֵֽמֶק׃ פ

7:8   צֵדָה

Three times defective   גׄ חס   Mp

1   *All* the Torah (Gen 42:25; 45:21; Exod 12:39)
2–3   **Judg 7:8; 20:10**

Com.: The Masorah notes the *three* occurrences of this lemma written defective יֹ, to distinguish them from its *four* occurrences written plene יֹ (צֵידָה).

The Masorah takes the *three* Torah occurrences as one unit; see Breuer, *The Biblical Text*, 43.

7:8   שׁוֹפְרֹתֵיהֶם

Unique   לֹ   Mp

7:8   וּבִשְׁלֹשׁ

Four times   דֹ   Mp

Com.: The Mp heading here of *four times* is incorrect since this is the lemma's only occurrence.

The Masorah notes the occurrences of this lemma with a ו cj., to distinguish it from its *two* occurrences without a cj., *one* of which is in the preceding verse, and the *other* is at Jer 1:2.

M^C correctly reads here *unique*, but M^A has no note here.

7:8   וּבִשְׁלֹשׁ־מֵאוֹת

Unique   לֹ   Mp

Com.: The Masorah notes the *sole* occurrence of this lemma with a ו cj, to distinguish it from its occurrence without a cj. (בִּשְׁלֹשׁ־מֵאוֹת) in the preceding verse.

> ## JUDGES 7:10
>
> וְאִם־יָרֵא אַתָּה לָרֶדֶת רֵד אַתָּה וּפֻרָה נַעַרְךָ אֶל־הַמַּחֲנֶה׃

7:10   וְאִם

Four times at the beginning of a verse in the book   דֹ רֹא פֹס בֹס   Mp

Judg 7:10; 9:19; 9:20; 14:13

Com.: The Masorah notes the *four* occurrences of this lemma at the beginning of a verse in the book, to distinguish them from its *five* occurrences in the middle of a verse in the book.

Usually such a note of a form with a וֹ cj. at the beginning of a verse in the book is contrasted with forms that do not have a וֹ cj.; see **1 Kgs 3:14**. But there are no occurrences of אִם at the beginning of a verse in the book.

JUDGES 7:11

וְשָׁמַעְתָּ מַה־יְדַבֵּרוּ וְאַחַר תֶּחֱזַקְנָה יָדֶיךָ וְיָרַדְתָּ בַּמַּחֲנֶה וַיֵּרֶד הוּא וּפֻרָה נַעֲרוֹ אֶל־קְצֵה הַחֲמֻשִׁים אֲשֶׁר בַּמַּחֲנֶה:

7:11   יָדֶיךָ

Eleven times plene   יא מל   Mp

Com.: See **Josh 10:6**.

7:11   וּפֻרָה

Twice and defective   ב וחס   Mp

Judg 7:10; **7:11**

Com.: By noting that this lemma occurs *twice* and is written defective וֹ, the Masorah is also implying (correctly) that this lemma does not occur elsewhere written plene וֹ.

JUDGES 7:12

וּמִדְיָן וַעֲמָלֵק וְכָל־בְּנֵי־קֶדֶם נֹפְלִים בָּעֵמֶק כָּאַרְבֶּה לָרֹב וְלִגְמַלֵּיהֶם אֵין מִסְפָּר כַּחוֹל שֶׁעַל־שְׂפַת הַיָּם לָרֹב:

7:12   וּמִדְיָן וַעֲמָלֵק

Unique   ל   Mp

Com.: This lemma is featured in a Masoretic list of word pairs occurring only *once* where both parts of the pair have a וֹ cj.; see Frensdorff, *Ochlah*, §253.

7:12   וְכָל־בְּנֵי

Six times   וֹ   Mp

1–5   **Exod 34:30; Num 27:21; Josh 3:1; Judg 7:12; 1 Kgs 8:63**
6   2 Chr 7:3

וְכָל־בְּנֵי   *six times*   וכל בני ו   Mm

1–5	Exod 34:30	וירא אהרן וכל
	Num 27:21	ולפני אלעזר הכהן
	Josh 3:1	יהושע בבקר
	Judg 7:12	ומדין ועמלק
	וַיַּחְנְכוּ אֶת־בֵּית *of Kings* (1 Kgs 8:63)	ויחנכו את בית דמלכים
6	2 Chr 7:3	ראים ברדת

Com.: The Masorah notes the *six* occurrences of this lemma with a וֹ cj., to distinguish them from its more numerous occurrences (41x) without a cj.

The additional notation *of Kings* to the 1 Kgs 8:63 reference distinguishes the wider lemma there (וְכָל־בְּנֵי יִשְׂרָאֵל) from its parallel passage in 2 Chr 7:5, where the lemma occurs as וְכָל הָעָם.

7:12   שֶׁעַל

Twice   בֿ   Mp

Judg 7:12; 8:26

Com.: The Masorah notes the *two* occurrences of עַל with the rel. pron. שֶׁ, to distinguish them from its more numerous occurrences (100+) with the rel. pron. אֲשֶׁר (אֲשֶׁר עַל).

JUDGES 7:13

וַיָּבֹא גִדְעוֹן וְהִנֵּה־אִישׁ מְסַפֵּר לְרֵעֵהוּ חֲלוֹם וַיֹּאמֶר הִנֵּה חֲלוֹם חָלַמְתִּי וְהִנֵּה צְלוֹל לֶחֶם שְׂעֹרִים מִתְהַפֵּךְ בְּמַחֲנֵה מִדְיָן וַיָּבֹא עַד־הָאֹהֶל וַיַּכֵּהוּ וַיִּפֹּל וַיַּהַפְכֵהוּ לְמַעְלָה וְנָפַל הָאֹהֶל:

7:13   הִנֵּה חֲלוֹם

Unique   לֿ   Mp

7:13   צְלוֹל

Read צְלִיל   צליל ק   Mp¹

Unique   לֿ   Mp²

Com.: The forms of the *kᵊṯîḇ* (צלול), and *qᵊrê* (צְלִיל) represent variants of the *qātîl/qātûl* type; see Gordis, *The Biblical Text*, 117

This lemma is featured in a Masoretic list of words where a ו in the middle of a word is read as a י; see Frensdorff, Ochlah, §81.

In M^C and M^A this form is written צְלִיל with no *kǝtîb/qǝrê*; see Breuer, *The Biblical Text*, 59.

In M^L there is only *one* circellus on this lemma but there are two Mp notes.

7:13	מִתְהַפֵּךְ

Twice   בֹּ   Mp

Judg 7:13; Job 37:12

מִתְהַפֵּךְ *twice*	מתהפך בֹ	Mm

| Judg 7:13 | במחנה מדין ויבא |
| Job 37:12 | [בתחבולתיו] (בתחבלתיו) |

7:13	וַיַּהַפְכֵהוּ

Unique   לֹ   Mp

JUDGES 7:14

וַיַּעַן רֵעֵהוּ וַיֹּאמֶר אֵין זֹאת בִּלְתִּי אִם־חֶרֶב גִּדְעוֹן בֶּן־יוֹאָשׁ אִישׁ יִשְׂרָאֵל נָתַן הָאֱלֹהִים בְּיָדוֹ אֶת־מִדְיָן וְאֶת־כָּל־הַמַּחֲנֶה: פ

7:14	נָתַן הָאֱלֹהִים

Twice   בֹּ   Mp

Judg 7:14; 2 Chr 9:23

Com.: The Masorah notes the *two* occurrences of נָתַן with הָאֱלֹהִים, to distinguish them from its more numerous occurrences (6x) with אֱלֹהִים (נָתַן אֱלֹהִים).

JUDGES 7:15

וַיְהִי֩ כִשְׁמֹ֨עַ גִדְע֜וֹן אֶת־מִסְפַּ֧ר הַחֲל֛וֹם וְאֶת־שִׁבְר֖וֹ וַיִּשְׁתָּ֑חוּ וַיָּ֙שָׁב֙ אֶל־מַחֲנֵ֣ה יִשְׂרָאֵ֔ל וַיֹּ֖אמֶר ק֑וּמוּ כִּֽי־נָתַ֧ן יְהֹוָ֛ה בְּיֶדְכֶ֖ם אֶת־מַחֲנֵ֥ה מִדְיָֽן׃

7:15   שִׁבְרוֹ

Twice: כֶּסֶף שִׁבְרוֹ   ב כסף שברו   Mp

Gen 44:2; Judg 7:15

Com.: The Masorah notes the *two* occurrences of this lemma written with a *ḥolem*, to distinguish them from its more numerous occurrences (4x) written with a *šûreq* (שִׁבְרוּ).

The catchwords כסף שברו (כֶּסֶף שִׁבְרוֹ), written in the Mp note, refer the reader to Gen 44:2, which has it own Mp note, and catchwords את מספר החלום (אֶת מִסְפַּר הַחֲלוֹם), that refer the reader back to this verse.

This lemma is featured in a Masoretic list of homonyms; see Frensdorff, *Ochlah*, §59, and Díaz-Esteban, *Sefer Oklah we-Oklah*, §60. In Gen 44:2 the meaning is *his grain*, whereas here it means *its interpretation*.

JUDGES 7:16

וַיַּ֜חַץ אֶת־שְׁלֹשׁ־מֵא֣וֹת הָאִ֗ישׁ שְׁלֹשָׁ֣ה רָאשִׁ֑ים וַיִּתֵּ֨ן שׁוֹפָר֤וֹת בְּיַד־כֻּלָּם֙ וְכַדִּ֣ים רֵקִ֔ים וְלַפִּדִ֖ים בְּת֥וֹךְ הַכַּדִּֽים׃

7:16   וַיַּחַץ

Three times   ג   Mp

Gen 32:8; 33:1; Judg 7:16

וַיַּחַץ *three times*   ויחץ ג   Mm

Gen 32:8   ויחץ את העם אשר
Gen 33:1   ויחץ את הילדים
Judg 7:16   ויחץ את שלש מאות

Com.: The Masorah notes the *three* occurrences of this lemma in an apocopated form with a ו consec., to distinguish them from its *sole* occurrence in an unapocopated form and without a ו (יֶחֱזֶה) at Isa 30:28.

רָאשִׁים   7:16

Twenty times   כ   Mp

1–5	Gen 2:10; Exod 18:25; Deut 1:15; **Judg 7:16**; 9:34
6–10	Judg 9:43; **1 Sam 11:11**; 13:17; **Prov 13:23**; Job 1:17
11–15	Ezra 7:28; 8:16; **Neh 11:13**; **1 Chr 5:24**; 7:2
16–20	**1 Chr 7:3**; 8:28; **9:13**; **9:34**; 24:4

Com.: The Masorah notes the *twenty* occurrences of this lemma without the def. article, to distinguish them from its *two* occurrences with the def. article (הָרָאשִׁים) at **Judg 7:20** and **Judg 9:44**.

JUDGES 7:17

וַיֹּאמֶר אֲלֵיהֶם מִמֶּנִּי תִרְאוּ וְכֵן תַּעֲשׂוּ וְהִנֵּה אָנֹכִי בָא בִקְצֵה הַמַּחֲנֶה וְהָיָה כַאֲשֶׁר־אֶעֱשֶׂה כֵּן תַּעֲשׂוּן׃

וְכֵן תַּעֲשׂוּ   7:17

Twice   ב   Mp

Exod 25:9; Judg 7:17

וְכֵן תַּעֲשׂוּ *twice*, and their references   וכן תעשו ב וסימנהון   Mm

Exod 25:9	ככל אשר אני מראה אותך את תבנית
Judg 7:17	ויאמר אליהם ממני תראו

Com.: The Masorah notes the *two* occurrences of this lemma with a ו cj. and without a paragogic נ, to distinguish them from its *sole* occurrence without a ו cj. but with a paragogic נ (כֵּן תַּעֲשׂוּן), which occurs in the same verse.

The Mp heading at Exod 25:9 adds catchwords ממני תראו (מִמֶּנִּי תִרְאוּ) to refer the reader to this verse.

7:17   וְהִנֵּה אָנֹכִי

Five times   הֿ   Mp

Com.: See **Josh 23:14**

7:17   תַּעֲשׂוּן

Fourteen times   יֿד   Mp

1–5   **Exod 4:15**; 20:23; Num 32:20; <u>32:23</u>; Deut 1:18
6–10   **Deut 12:4; 12:8; 29:8; Judg 7:17; 15:7**
11–14   **1 Sam 2:23; 2 Kgs 11:5; 2 Chr 19:9; 19:10**

Com.: The Masorah notes the *fourteen* occurrences of this lemma with a paragogic נ, to distinguish them from its more numerous occurrences (69x) written without this נ.

This distinction is implied in the Mm of <u>Exod 4:15</u> and <u>Num 32:23</u>, where there is an addition *of Kings* to the catchword of the 2 Kgs 11:5 reference, to distinguish this reference from its parallel passage in 2 Chr 23:4, where the lemma appears as תַּעֲשׂוּ.

JUDGES 7:18

וְתָקַעְתִּי בַּשּׁוֹפָר אָנֹכִי וְכָל־אֲשֶׁר אִתִּי וּתְקַעְתֶּם בַּשּׁוֹפָרוֹת גַּם־אַתֶּם סְבִיבוֹת כָּל־הַמַּחֲנֶה
וַאֲמַרְתֶּם לַיהוָה וּלְגִדְעוֹן: פ

7:18   סְבִיבוֹת כָּל־הַמַּחֲנֶה

Unique   לֿ   Mp

Com.: The Masorah notes the *sole* occurrence of this lemma with כָּל, to distinguish it from its *two* occurrences without כָּל (סְבִיבוֹת הַמַּחֲנֶה) at Num 11:31 and Num 11:32.

7:18   וּלְגִדְעוֹן

Three times   גֿ   Mp

Judg 7:18; 7:20; 8:30

Com.: This lemma is featured in a Masoretic list of words that occur *four times*, *three times* with a preceding ו, and *once* without it (**Judg 8:27**); see Frensdorff, *Ochlah*, §16, and Díaz-Esteban, *Sefer Oklah we-Oklah*, §17.

JUDGES 7:19

וַיָּבֹא גִדְעוֹן וּמֵאָה־אִישׁ אֲשֶׁר־אִתּוֹ בִּקְצֵה הַמַּחֲנֶה רֹאשׁ הָאַשְׁמֹרֶת הַתִּיכוֹנָה אַךְ הָקֵם הֵקִימוּ אֶת־הַשֹּׁמְרִים וַיִּתְקְעוּ בַּשּׁוֹפָרוֹת וְנָפוֹץ הַכַּדִּים אֲשֶׁר בְּיָדָם׃

7:19　　הַתִּיכוֹנָה

Twice plene　　ב מל　　Mp

Judg 7:19; Ezek 41:7 (לַתִּיכוֹנָה)

Com.: The Masorah notes the *two* occurrences of this lemma in various forms written plene ו, to distinguish them from its more numerous occurrences (5x) in various forms written defective ו (הַתִּיכֹנָה/וְהַתִּיכֹנָה).

7:19　　הֵקִימוּ

Five times　　ה　　Mp

1–5　　**Num 10:21** (וְהֵקִימוּ); **Judg 7:19**; Isa 23:13; Jer 34:18; **35:16**

Com.: The Masorah notes the *five* occurrences of this lemma, with and without a ו cj., possibly to distinguish them from its *single* occurrence of the Aramaic form with a ו cj. וַהֲקִימוּ at Ezra 6:18.

7:19　　וְנָפוֹץ

Three times plene　　ג מל　　Mp

Com.: The Mp heading here of *three times plene* is incorrect since this is the only occurrence of this lemma.

Both M^C and M^A correctly read here *unique and plene*.

JUDGES 7:20

וַיִּתְקְעוּ שְׁלֹשֶׁת הָרָאשִׁים בַּשּׁוֹפָרוֹת וַיִּשְׁבְּרוּ הַכַּדִּים וַיַּחֲזִיקוּ בְיַד־שְׂמאוֹלָם בַּלַּפִּדִים וּבְיַד־יְמִינָם הַשּׁוֹפָרוֹת לִתְקוֹעַ וַיִּקְרְאוּ חֶרֶב לַיהוָה וּלְגִדְעוֹן׃

7:20　　הָרָאשִׁים

Twice　　ב　　Mp

Judg 7:20; 9:44

Com.: The Masorah notes the *two* occurrences of this lemma with the def. article, to distinguish them from its more numerous occurrences (20x) without this article (רָאשִׁים); see directly above at **Judg 7:16.**

7:20   וַיַּחֲזִיקוּ

Six times   וֹ   Mp

1–5   Gen 19:16*; **Judg 7:20**; <u>2 Sam 2:16</u> (וַיַּחֲזִקוּ); **1 Kgs 9:9** (וַיַּחֲזִקוּ)
6   **2 Chr 7:22; 28:15**

Com.: The Masorah notes the *six* occurrences of this lemma, written plene and defective י, in the *hiphil*, to distinguish them from its *two* occurrences in the *piel* (וַיְחַזְּקוּ) at Neh 2:18 and 2 Chr 11:17.

* M^L, contrary to M (וַיַּחֲזִיקוּ), writes the form at Gen 19:16 defective י (וַיַּחֲזִקוּ); see Breuer, *The Biblical Text*, 4.

The Mp and Mm headings at 2 Sam 2:16 and the Mp heading at 1 Kgs 9:9 read *three times defective* (י), which according to the Mm list at <u>1 Sam 2:16</u>, includes both these references and Dan 11:32 (יַחֲזִקוּ).

7:20   שְׂמֹאולָם

Unique and plene   ל וּמל   Mp

Com.: By noting that this lemma is *unique* and written plene וּ, the Masorah is also implying (correctly) that this lemma does not occur elsewhere written defective וּ.

7:20   לִתְקוֹעַ

Unique   ל   Mp

Com.: The Masorah notes the *sole* occurrence of this lemma with the prep. לְ, to distinguish it from its *four* occurrences without this preposition.

7:20   וּלְגִדְעוֹן

Three times   גֹ   Mp

Com.: See directly above at **Judg 7:18.**

JUDGES 7:21

וַיַּעַמְדוּ אִישׁ תַּחְתָּיו סָבִיב לַמַּחֲנֶה וַיָּרָץ כָּל־הַמַּחֲנֶה וַיָּרִיעוּ וַיָּנִיסוּ׃

7:21   וַיָּרָץ כָּל הַמַּחֲנֶה

Unique   ל   Mp

7:21   וַיָּנִיסוּ

Read וַיָּנוּסוּ   וינוסו ק   Mp

Com.: The *kətîb* (ויניסו, *hiphil*), and the *qərê* (וַיָּנוּסוּ, *qal*) are examples of *kətîb/qərê* variations in different conjugations; see Gordis, *The Biblical Text*, 134.

This lemma is featured in a Masoretic list of words that have a י in the middle of word that is read as a ו; see the Mm at <u>Num 1:16</u> *sub* קריאי, Frensdorff, *Ochlah*, §80, and Díaz-Esteban, *Sefer Oklah we-Oklah*, §71.

JUDGES 7:22

וַיִּתְקְעוּ שְׁלֹשׁ־מֵאוֹת הַשּׁוֹפָרוֹת וַיָּשֶׂם יְהוָה אֵת חֶרֶב אִישׁ בְּרֵעֵהוּ וּבְכָל־הַמַּחֲנֶה וַיָּנָס הַמַּחֲנֶה עַד־בֵּית הַשִּׁטָּה צְרֵרָתָה עַד שְׂפַת־אָבֵל מְחוֹלָה עַל־טַבָּת׃

7:22   וּבְכָל־הַמַּחֲנֶה

Unique   ל   Mp

Com.: This lemma is featured in a Masoretic list of words that only occur *once* preceded by וּבְכָל or בְּכָל; see Frensdorff, *Ochlah*, §255.

7:22   הַשִּׁטָּה

Unique   ל   Mp

7:22   צְרֵרָתָה

Unique   ל   Mp

Com.: This lemma is featured in a Masoretic list of *hapax legomena* that occurs once with a ד (צְרֵדָתָה 2 Chr 4:17), and once with a ר (here); see Frensdorff, *Ochlah*, §7.

7:22   טַבָּת

Unique   ל   Mp

JUDGES 7:23

וַיִּצָּעֵק אִישׁ־יִשְׂרָאֵל מִנַּפְתָּלִי וּמִן־אָשֵׁר וּמִן־כָּל־מְנַשֶּׁה וַיִּרְדְּפוּ אַחֲרֵי מִדְיָן׃

7:23   וַיִּצָּעֵק

Three times   גֿ   Mp

Judg 7:23; 7:24; **12:1**

Com.: The Masorah notes the *three* occurrences of this lemma in the *niphal*, to distinguish them from its more numerous occurrences (8x) in the *qal* (וַיִּצְעַק).

7:23   וּמִן־כָּל

Twice, and similarly all Aramaic   בֿ וכל ארמֿ דכותֿ   Mp

Judg 7:23; Daniel 1:15 (מִן־כָּל)

Com.: The Masorah notes the *two* occurrences of this lemma where the prep. מִן or וּמִן is written separate from כָּל, to distinguish them from its more numerous occurrences (200+) where the prep. is joined with כָּל (מִכָּל/וּמִכָּל).

The Masorah also notes that this lemma is the norm in the Aramaic sections of the Bible, where מִן־כָּל occurs *five times* in Daniel.

Mᴬ reads, with Mᴸ here, but Mᶜ reads here *unique, and similarly all Aramaic.*

JUDGES 7:24

וּמַלְאָכִים שָׁלַח גִּדְעוֹן בְּכָל־הַר אֶפְרַיִם לֵאמֹר רְדוּ לִקְרַאת מִדְיָן וְלִכְדוּ לָהֶם אֶת־הַמַּיִם עַד בֵּית בָּרָה וְאֶת־הַיַּרְדֵּן וַיִּצָּעֵק כָּל־אִישׁ אֶפְרַיִם וַיִּלְכְּדוּ אֶת־הַמַּיִם עַד בֵּית בָּרָה וְאֶת־הַיַּרְדֵּן׃

7:24   ¹בָּרָה

Five times written like this   הֿ כתֿ כן   Mp

1–5   **Judg 7:24ᵃ**; 7:24ᵇ; Ps 19:9; **Cant 6:9**; 6:10

Com.: The Masorah notes the *five* occurrences of this lemma written with a ה, to distinguish them from its more numerous occurrences (16x) written with an א; see Ginsburg, 4, ב, §453b and §456.

The Mm at Cant 6:9 has an additional note that reads *and similarly all occurrences where the word refers to eating*, citing (וְאָבְרֶה) 2 Sam 13:10 and (אָבְרֶה) Job 39:13.

7:24   וְאֶת־הַיַּרְדֵּן²

Twice   בׄ   Mp

Judg 7:24ᵃ; **7:24ᵇ**

Com.: The Masorah notes the *sole* occurrence of this lemma with a ו cj., to distinguish it from its more numerous occurrences (44x) without a cj.

JUDGES 7:25

וַיִּלְכְּדוּ שְׁנֵי־שָׂרֵי מִדְיָן אֶת־עֹרֵב וְאֶת־זְאֵב וַיַּהַרְגוּ אֶת־עוֹרֵב בְּצוּר־עוֹרֵב וְאֶת־זְאֵב הָרְגוּ בְיֶקֶב־ זְאֵב וַיִּרְדְּפוּ אֶל־מִדְיָן וְרֹאשׁ־עֹרֵב וּזְאֵב הֵבִיאוּ אֶל־גִּדְעוֹן מֵעֵבֶר לַיַּרְדֵּן:

7:25   עוֹרֵב¹

Four times plene   ד מׄל   Mp

Judg 7:25ᵃ; 7:25ᵇ; Isa 10:26; Cant 5:11 (כְּעוֹרֵב)

Com.: The Masorah notes the *four* occurrences of this lemma written plene ו, to distinguish them from its more numerous occurrences (7x) written defective ו (עֹרֵב/בְּעֹרֵב).

The Mp heading at Cant 5:11 reads *unique and once* כערב noting the form with the def. prep. כָּ written plene ו (כָּעוֹרֵב), as well as the form with the indef. prep. כְּ written defective ו (כְּעֹרֵב) at Ps 83:12.

7:25   עוֹרֵב²

Four times plene   ד מׄל   Mp

Com.: See directly above.

7:25   וְרֹאשׁ

Eleven times   יֹֽא   Mp

1–5   **Deut 32:33; Judg 7:25**; 9:37; <u>1 Sam 5:4</u>; **17:57**
6–10   **2 Sam 15:30**; 1 Kgs 10:19; <u>**Isa 7:8**</u>; 7:9ᵃ; 7:9ᵇ
11   **Prov 8:26**

Com.: The Masorah notes the *eleven* occurrences of this lemma with a *šəwâ* under the ו, to distinguish them from its *two* occurrences with a *qameṣ* under the ו (וָרֹאשׁ) at Gen 46:21 and Lam 3:19.

All the Mp headings highlighted above read *eleven times* apart from that at 2 Sam 15:30, which mistakenly reads *twelve times*.

In Mᴸ the circellus has been placed between this word and the following word עֹרֵב but, since the phrase וְרֹאשׁ עֹרֵב occurs only this *once*, it is more likely that the note belongs solely with וְרֹאשׁ which does occur *eleven times*.

JUDGES 8:1

וַיֹּאמְרוּ אֵלָיו אִישׁ אֶפְרַיִם מָה־הַדָּבָר הַזֶּה עָשִׂיתָ לָּנוּ לְבִלְתִּי קְרֹאות לָנוּ כִּי הָלַכְתָּ לְהִלָּחֵם בְּמִדְיָן וַיְרִיבוּן אִתּוֹ בְּחָזְקָה׃

8:1   קְרֹאות

Unique   ל   Mp

Com.: The Masorah notes the *sole* occurrence of this infin. cstr. with an unusual ות ending, to distinguish it from its *four* occurrences of this infin. cstr. without this ending (קְרֹא).

8:1   וַיְרִיבוּן

Unique and plene   ל וּמל   Mp

Com.: By noting that this lemma is *unique* and written plene (י), the Masorah is also implying (correctly) that this lemma does not occur elsewhere written defective.

This lemma is featured in a Masoretic list of words that occur *twice*, once with a ו cj. (here), and *once* without (יְרִיבֻן) at Exod 21:18; see Frensdorff, *Ochlah*, §1, and Dí-az-Esteban, *Sefer Oklah we-Oklah*, §1.

8:1   בְּחָזְקָה

Four times   דֿ   Mp

Judg 4:3; 8:1; 1 Sam 2:16; Jonah 3:8

Mm   בחזקה דֿ וסימנהון   חָזְקָה *four times*, and their references

וייבון אתו   Judg 8:1
והוא לחץ את   Judg 4:3
ואם לא לקחתי בחזקה   1 Sam 2:16
ויקראו אל אלהים   Jonah 3:8

וחד ובחזקה רדיתם אתם (ובפֿ) [ובפרך]   And *once* (וּבְחָזְקָה): Ezek 34:4

Com.: The Masorah notes the *four* occurrences of this lemma, to distinguish them from the *sole* occurrence of its parallel form בְּחָזְק at Isa 40:10.

The Mm has an additional note that this lemma also occurs with a ו cj. (וּבְחָזְקָה) at Ezek 34:4.

┌───┐
│   **JUDGES 8:2**   │
│   │
│ וַיֹּאמֶר אֲלֵיהֶם מֶה־עָשִׂיתִי עַתָּה כָּכֶם הֲלוֹא טוֹב עֹלְלוֹת אֶפְרַיִם מִבְצִיר אֲבִיעֶזֶר׃ │
└───┘

8:2   עֹלְלוֹת

Unique written this way   לֿ כתֿ כן   Mp

Com.: The Masorah notes the *unique* occurrence of this lemma written this way to distinguish it from other writings such as עוֹלֵלֹת (Isa 17:6), עֹלֵלוֹת (Obad 5), and עוֹלֵלוֹת (Jer 49:9).

JUDGES 8:3

בְּיֶדְכֶם נָתַן אֱלֹהִים אֶת־שָׂרֵי מִדְיָן אֶת־עֹרֵב וְאֶת־זְאֵב וּמַה־יָּכֹלְתִּי עֲשׂוֹת כָּכֶם אָז רָפְתָה רוּחָם
מֵעָלָיו בְּדַבְּרוֹ הַדָּבָר הַזֶּה:

8:3   יָכֹלְתִּי

Three times   גׄ   Mp

Gen 30:8; Judg 8:3; Ps 40:13

יָכֹלְתִּי *three times* and defective, and their references   יכלתי גׄ וחסׄ וסימנהון   Mm

Gen 30:8   נפתולי אלהים נפתלתי
Judg 8:3   ומה יכלתי עשות ככם
Ps 40:13   השיגוני עונתי ולא

Com.: By noting that this lemma occurs *three times* and is written defective וֹ, the
Masorah is also implying (correctly) that this lemma does not occur elsewhere written
plene וֹ.

This 1st pers. sg. form may be contrasted with the 3rd pers. sg. form, which is written
both defective (יָכֹל) and plene (יָכוֹל).

8:3   רָפְתָה

Twice   בׄ   Mp

Judg 8:3; Jer 49:24

Com.: The Masorah notes the *two* occurrences of this lemma in the fem., to distinguish
it from its *two* occurrences in the masc. (רְפָה) at **Judg 19:9** and 1 Chr 8:37.

8:3   רוּחָם

Three times   גׄ   Mp

Judg 8:3; Ezek 13:3; Ps 104:29

Mm   רוחם ג ומל וסימנהון   רוֹחֵם *three times* and plene, and their references

Judg 8:3	אז רפתה רוחם מעליו
Ezek 13:3	אחר רוחם
Ps 104:29	(תוסף) [תסף] רוחם יגועון ואל עפרם

Com.: The Masorah notes that this lemma occurs *three* times and is written plene (וֹ), thereby implying (correctly) that this lemma does not occur elsewhere written defective ו.

JUDGES 8:4

וַיָּבֹא גִדְעוֹן הַיַּרְדֵּנָה עֹבֵר הוּא וּשְׁלֹשׁ־מֵאוֹת הָאִישׁ אֲשֶׁר אִתּוֹ עֲיֵפִים וְרֹדְפִים:

8:4   הַיַּרְדֵּנָה

Mm   הירדנה ד וסימנהון   הַיַּרְדֵּנָה *four times*, and their references

Num 34:12	וירד (גבול) [הגבול] הירדנה
Judg 8:4	ויבא גדעון הירדנה עבר
2 Kgs 2:6	כי יהוה שלחני הירדנה
2 Kgs 6:4	וילך אתם <ויבאו> הירדנה

Com.: The Masorah notes the *four* occurrences of this lemma with the locative ה, to distinguish them from its more numerous occurrences (100+) written without this adverbial form.

JUDGES 8:6

וַיֹּאמֶר שָׂרֵי סֻכּוֹת הֲכַף זֶבַח וְצַלְמֻנָּע עַתָּה בְּיָדֶךָ כִּי־נִתֵּן לִצְבָאֲךָ לָחֶם:

8:6   הֲכַף

Mp   בֿ   *Twice*

Judg 8:6; 8:15

Com.: This lemma is featured in a Masoretic list of doublets with an initial הַ or הֲ; see Frensdorff, *Ochlah*, §64, and Díaz-Esteban, *Sefer Oklah we-Oklah*, §65.

8:6   נָתַן

Six times   ו   Mp

1–5   **Gen 34:21**; **Judg 8:6**; **8:15**; 8:25; 1 Sam 30:22
6   **Neh 10:31**

נָתַן *six times*, and their references   נתן ו וסימנהון   Mm

1–5   Gen 34:21   ואת בנתינו נתן
        Judg 8:6   כי נתן לצבאך
        Judg 8:15   כי נתן לאנשיך
        Judg 8:25   ויאמרו נתן
        1 Sam 30:22   להם מהשלל
6   Neh 10:31   ואת (בנותינו) [בנתיהם]

Com.: The Masorah notes the *six* occurrences of this lemma pointed with a *ṣerê*, to distinguish them from its more numerous occurrences (15x) pointed with a *pataḥ* (נָתַן); see Ognibeni, *'Oklah*, §5F.

This note is repeated in an abbreviated fashion at v. 15.

8:6   לִצְבָאֶךָ

Unique   ל   Mp

Com.: The Masorah notes the *sole* occurrence of this lemma with the prep. ל, to distinguish it from its occurrence without this prep. at Judg 9:29.

JUDGES 8:7

וַיֹּאמֶר גִּדְעֹון לָכֵן בְּתֵת יְהוָה אֶת־זֶבַח וְאֶת־צַלְמֻנָּע בְּיָדִי וְדַשְׁתִּי אֶת־בְּשַׂרְכֶם אֶת־קוֹצֵי הַמִּדְבָּר
וְאֶת־הַבַּרְקֳנִים׃

8:7   וְדַשְׁתִּי

Unique   ל   Mp

8:7   אֶת־קוֹצֵי

Unique   ל   Mp

Com.: The Masorah notes the *sole* occurrence of this lemma without a ו cj., to distinguish it from its occurrence with a cj. (וְאֶת־קוֹצֵי) at v. 16.

8:7   אֶת־קוֹצֵי הַמִּדְבָּר

The *first*: Judg 8:7	קדמיה את קוצי המדבר	Mm
The *second*: Judg 8:16	תיניׄ ואת קוצי המדבר	
And their *síman*: Gen 1:1	וסימנהון בראשית ברא אלהים את	

Com.: The Masorah presents two parallel passages differing in their use of the ו cj. In the first passage (Judg 8:7), the phrase without the ו cj. reads אֶת־קוֹצֵי הַמִּדְבָּר; in the second passage (Judg 8:16), the phrase with the ו cj. reads וְאֶת־קוֹצֵי הַמִּדְבָּר.

To illustrate this difference the Masorah uses a third verse mnemonic of Gen 1:1 where the same words אֵת and וְאֵת appear in the same order (בְּרֵאשִׁית בָּרָא אֱלֹהִים אֵת הַשָּׁמַיִם וְאֵת הָאָרֶץ).

8:7   הַבַּרְקָנִים

Twice   בׄ   Mp

Judg 8:7; 8:16

> ### JUDGES 8:8
>
> וַיַּעַל מִשָּׁם פְּנוּאֵל וַיְדַבֵּר אֲלֵיהֶם כָּזֹאת וַיַּעֲנוּ אוֹתוֹ אַנְשֵׁי פְנוּאֵל כַּאֲשֶׁר עָנוּ אַנְשֵׁי סֻכּוֹת׃

8:8   פְּנוּאֵל²

Eight times   חׄ   Mp

1–5   Gen 32:32; Judg 8:8ᵃ; **8:8ᵇ; 8:9; 8:17**

6–8   **1 Kgs 12:25**; 1 Chr 4:4 (וּפְנוּאֵל); 8:25 (וּפְנוּאֵל, *qerê*)

Com.: The Masorah notes the *eight* occurrences of this lemma in various forms written with a ו, to distinguish them from its *two* occurrences in various forms written with a י (פְּנִיאֵל) at Gen 32:31, and in the *kᵉtîb* (ופניאל) at 1 Chr 8:25.

JUDGES 8:9

וַיֹּ֡אמֶר גַּם־לְאַנְשֵׁ֣י פְנוּאֵל֩ לֵאמֹ֨ר בְּשׁוּבִ֤י בְשָׁלוֹם֙ אֶתֹּ֔ץ אֶת־הַמִּגְדָּ֖ל הַזֶּֽה׃ פ

8:9   פְנוּאֵל

Eight times   ח̇   Mp

Com.: See directly above at **Judg 8:8**.

8:9   אֶת־הַמִּגְדָּל

Unique   ל   Mp

Com.: The Masorah notes the *sole* occurrence of this lemma without a ו cj., to distinguish it from its occurrence with a ו cj. (וְאֶת־הַמִּגְדָּל) at Gen 11:5.

JUDGES 8:10

וְזֶ֨בַח וְצַלְמֻנָּ֜ע בַּקַּרְקֹ֗ר וּמַחֲנֵיהֶ֣ם עִמָּ֗ם כַּחֲמֵ֤שֶׁת עָשָׂר֙ אֶ֔לֶף כֹּ֚ל הַנּ֣וֹתָרִ֔ים מִכֹּ֖ל מַחֲנֵ֣ה בְנֵי־קֶ֑דֶם וְהַנֹּ֣פְלִ֗ים מֵאָ֤ה וְעֶשְׂרִים֙ אֶ֔לֶף אִ֖ישׁ שֹׁ֥לֵֽף חָֽרֶב׃

8:10   וְזֶבַח וְצַלְמֻנָּע

Unique   ל   Mp

Com.: This lemma is featured in a Masoretic list of word pairs in which both parts of the pair have a ו cj.; see Frensdorff, *Ochlah*, §253.

In M[L] the circellus has been placed only on וְצַלְמֻנָּע, but since there are *seven* occurrences of this lemma (see v. 21), the note must refer, as it does in M[C] and M[A], to both words, which only occur this *once*.

8:10   בַּקַּרְקֹר

Unique   ל   Mp

8:10   כַּחֲמֵשֶׁת עָשָׂר

Unique   ל   Mp

Com.: The Masorah notes the *sole* occurrence of this lemma with the prep. כ, to distinguish it from its occurrence with a ו cj. (וַחֲמֵשֶׁת עָשָׂר) at 2 Sam 19:18

8:10   מִכֹּל מַחֲנֵה בְנֵי־קֶדֶם

Unique   ל   Mp

Com.: In M[L] there are only two circelli on this four-word phrase, one on מִכֹּל מַחֲנֵה and one on בְנֵי־קֶדֶם. With *four- or five-word* phrases it is not unusual for only *two* circelli to be given; see **Josh 1:6** and *passim*.

JUDGES 8:11

וַיַּעַל גִּדְעוֹן דֶּרֶךְ הַשְּׁכוּנֵי בָאֳהָלִים מִקֶּדֶם לְנֹבַח וְיָגְבֳּהָה וַיַּךְ אֶת־הַמַּחֲנֶה וְהַמַּחֲנֶה הָיָה בֶטַח׃

8:11   הַשְּׁכוּנֵי

Unique   ל   Mp

8:11   בָאֳהָלִים

Four times   דֿ   Mp

Judg 8:11; **Jer 35:7**; 35:10; **Hos 12:10**

Com.: The Masorah notes the *four* occurrences of this lemma with the prep. בְּ, to distinguish them from its *three* occurrences without this prep. (אֹהָלִים).

The Mp heading at Hos 12:10, which reads *unique written with* א, represents a tradition that has the א of בָאֳהָלִים written with a *qameṣ* and not a *ḥaṭep qameṣ*; see Dotan/Reich, *Masora Thesaurus, ad loc.*

8:11   לְנֹבַח

Unique   ל   Mp

Com.: The Masorah notes the *sole* occurrence of this lemma with the prep. לְ, to distinguish it from its occurrence with a ו cj. (וְנֹבַח) at Num 32:42, and from its occurrence without any prefix (נֹבַח) also at Num 32:42.

8:11   וְיָגְבֳּהָה

Twice   בֿ   Mp

Num 32:35; Judg 8:11

JUDGES 8:12

וַיָּנֻוסוּ זֶבַח וְצַלְמֻנָּע וַיִּרְדֹּף אַחֲרֵיהֶם וַיִּלְכֹּד אֶת־שְׁנֵי | מַלְכֵי מִדְיָן אֶת־זֶבַח וְאֶת־צַלְמֻנָּע וְכָל־
הַמַּחֲנֶה הֶחֱרִיד:

8:12   וְאֶת־צַלְמֻנָּע

Three times   נ֗   Mp

Judg 8:7; **8:12**; 8:21

8:12   וְכָל־הַמַּחֲנֶה

Unique   ל   Mp

Com.: The Masorah notes the *sole* occurrence of this lemma with a ו cj., to distinguish it from its more numerous occurrences (6x) without a cj.

JUDGES 8:13

וַיָּשָׁב גִּדְעוֹן בֶּן־יוֹאָשׁ מִן־הַמִּלְחָמָה מִלְמַעֲלֵה הֶחָרֶס:

8:13   מִלְמַעֲלֵה

Unique   ל   Mp

Com.: This lemma is featured in a Masoretic list of *hapax legomena* in a similar unit where *one* has a prefixed ל (here), and the *other* does not have this ל (מִמַּעֲלֵה, Judg 1:36); see Frensdorff, *Ochlah*, §245, and Ognibeni, *'Oklah*, §136.

8:13   הֶחָרֶס

Unique   ל   Mp

JUDGES 8:14

וַיִּלְכָּד־נַעַר מֵאַנְשֵׁי סֻכּוֹת וַיִּשְׁאָלֵהוּ וַיִּכְתֹּב אֵלָיו אֶת־שָׂרֵי סֻכּוֹת וְאֶת־זְקֵנֶיהָ שִׁבְעִים וְשִׁבְעָה
אִישׁ:

8:14   וַיִּשְׁאָלֵהוּ

Three times   נ֗   Mp

Gen 37:15; **Judg 8:14; Jer 37:17**

8:14   וְאֶת־זְקֵנֶיהָ

Unique   ל   Mp

JUDGES 8:15

וַיָּבֹא אֶל־אַנְשֵׁי סֻכּוֹת וַיֹּאמֶר הִנֵּה זֶבַח וְצַלְמֻנָּע אֲשֶׁר חֵרַפְתֶּם אוֹתִי לֵאמֹר הֲכַף זֶבַח וְצַלְמֻנָּע עַתָּה בְּיָדֶךָ כִּי נִתֵּן לַאֲנָשֶׁיךָ הַיְעֵפִים לָחֶם׃

8:15   זֶבַח וְצַלְמֻנָּע¹

Four times   ד   Mp

1–5   Judg 8:5; 8:6; 8:12; **8:15**[a]; 8:15[b];
6   Judg 8:21

Com.: The Mp heading here of *four times* is incorrect since there are *six* occurrences of this lemma.

Neither M[C] nor M[A] has a note on this lemma here.

8:15   נִתֵּן

Six times   ו   Mp

1–5   **Gen 34:21**; **Judg 8:6**; **8:15**; 8:25; 1 Sam 30:22
6   **Neh 10:31**

נִתֵּן *six times*   נתן ו   Mm

1–5   Gen 34:21   שלמים
       Judg 8:15   לאנשיך
       Judg 8:6   לצבאך
       Judg 8:25   ויפרשו
       1 Sam 30:22 מהשלל
6   Neh 10:31   (בנותינו) [בנתינו]

Com.: See directly above at **Judg 8:6**.

8:15   לַאֲנָשֶׁיךָ הַיְעֵפִים

Unique   ל   Mp

JUDGES 8:16

וַיִּקַּח֙ אֶת־זִקְנֵ֣י הָעִ֔יר וְאֶת־קוֹצֵ֥י הַמִּדְבָּ֖ר וְאֶת־הַֽבַּרְקָנִ֑ים וַיֹּ֣דַע בָּהֶ֔ם אֵ֖ת אַנְשֵׁ֥י סֻכּֽוֹת׃

8:16   הַֽבַּרְקָנִ֑ים

Twice   בֹ   Mp

Judg 8:7; 8:16

8:16   וַיֹּ֣דַע

Unique   ל   Mp

Com.: This lemma is featured in a Masoretic list of doublets that occur *once* with a ו cj. (Num 16:5), and *once* with a ו consec. (here); see Frensdorff, *Ochlah*, §46, Dí-az-Esteban, *Sefer Oklah we-Oklah*, §47, and Ognibeni, *'Oklah*, §7T.

JUDGES 8:17

וְאֶת־מִגְדַּ֥ל פְּנוּאֵ֖ל נָתָ֑ץ וַֽיַּהֲרֹ֖ג אֶת־אַנְשֵׁ֥י הָעִֽיר׃

8:17   וְאֶת־מִגְדַּ֥ל

Unique   ל   Mp

Judg 8:17; Neh 3:11

Com.: The Mp heading here *of unique* is inexact since there are *two* occurrences of this lemma. The note more precisely should have read *unique in the book*.

Neither M[C] nor M[A] has a note on this lemma here.

8:17   פְּנוּאֵ֖ל

Eight times   ח   Mp

Com.: See above at **Judg 8:8**.

JUDGES 8:18

וַיֹּאמֶר אֶל־זֶבַח וְאֶל־צַלְמֻנָּע אֵיפֹה הָאֲנָשִׁים אֲשֶׁר הֲרַגְתֶּם בְּתָבוֹר וַיֹּאמְרוּ כָּמוֹךָ כְמוֹהֶם אֶחָד כְּתֹאַר בְּנֵי הַמֶּלֶךְ׃

8:18   אֶל־זֶבַח

Unique   ל   Mp

Com.: This lemma is featured in a Masoretic list of words that only occur *once* with the prep. אֶל; see Frensdorff, *Ochlah*, §77, and Díaz-Esteban, *Sefer Oklah we-Oklah*, §156A.

8:18   אֵיפֹה

Ten times written   ה   י כתב ה֯   Mp

1–5   Gen 37:16; **Judg 8:18**; 1 Sam 19:22; <u>**2 Sam 9:4**</u>; Isa 49:21
6–10   **Jer 3:2**; 36:19; **Job 4:7**; (וְאֵיפֹה); **38:4**; Ruth 2:19

Com.: The Masorah notes the *ten* occurrences of this lemma written with a ה, to distinguish them from its *eleven* occurrences written with an א (אֵפוֹא).

The Mp note at Job 4:7 correctly reads *twice written with* ה *in the book* (of Job); here and at Job 38:4.

8:18   כְמוֹהֶם

Three times and plene   ג ומל֯   Mp

Judg 8:18; Ps 115:8; <u>135:18</u>

Com.: The Masorah notes the *three* occurrences of this lemma that are only written plene ו, unlike other forms of this prep. which can be written defective ו (e.g. כְּמֹנִי and כְּמֹנוּ).

8:18   כְּתֹאַר

Unique   ל   Mp

Com.: The Masorah notes the *sole* occurrence of this lemma with the prep. כ, to distinguish it from its more numerous occurrences (11x) without this preposition.

JUDGES 8:19

וַיֹּאמַר אֶחַי בְּנֵי־אִמִּי הֵם חַי־יְהוָה לוּ הַחֲיִתֶם אוֹתָם לֹא הָרַגְתִּי אֶתְכֶם:

8:19   לוּ

Twenty-two times   לו כֹב   Mm

1–5	Gen 17:18	(יִשְׁמָעֵאל =)	ישמעאל
	Gen 23:13	(מֵתִי =)	מיתא
	Gen 30:34	(לָבָן =)	לבן
	Gen 50:15	(יִשְׂטְמֵנוּ =)	סטימא
	Num 22:29	(בִּלְעָם =)	בלעם
6–10	Deut 32:29	(חָכְמוּ =)	חכימא
	Josh 7:7	(יְהוֹשֻׁעַ =)	יהושע
	Judg 13:23	(לַהֲמִיתֵנוּ =)	קטלה
	Judg 8:19	(אֶחַי =)	אחוו
	1 Sam 14:30	(אָכֹל אָכַל =)	בזונה
11–15	Num 20:3	(גָוַעְנוּ =)	יסופון
	Num 14:2	(בְּאֶרֶץ =)	מן ארעא
	Num 14:2	(בַּמִּדְבָּר =)	ומן מדברה
	Isa 48:18	(וְצִדְקָתְךָ =)	בזכותה
	2 Sam 19:7	(אַבְשָׁלוֹם =)	דאבשלום
16–20	Isa 63:19	(לֹא־מָשַׁלְתָּ בָּם =)	לא שלטת בה
	Ezek 14:15	(חַיָּה רָעָה =)	חיותא בישתא
	<2 Sam 18:12	(שָׁקֵל =)>	<אתקיל>
	Mic 2:11	(אִישׁ =)	גוברא
	Ps 81:14	(שֹׁמֵעַ =)	דשמע
21–22	Job 6:2	(כַּעְשִׂי =)	ולא מתכעסה
	Job 16:4	(נַפְשְׁכֶם =)	נפשה

Com.: The Masorah notes the *twenty-two* occurrences of this lemma pointed with a *šûreq*, to distinguish them from its more numerous occurrences pointed with a *ḥolem* (לֹו); see Ognibeni, *'Oklah*, §19D.

The catchwords are given in the form of an Aramaic mnemonic: "Ishmael the dead one, Laban the begrudger, Balaam the wise. Joshua killed his brothers with his belt. They will perish from the land and from the wilderness. By the merit of Absalom the evil beast had no power over him. <He weighed> the man who heard, and did not himself get angry"; see Marcus, *Scribal Wit*, 57–64.

The lemma לו occurs *twenty-two* times, but there are only *twenty-one* catchwords listed in the note. However, the missing catchword for 2 Sam 18:22 (אתקיל, *he weighed*) is listed in *Miqra'ot Gedolot* (at Gen 17:18, and in the *Mf*) and (incorrectly as אתקטל) in Ginsburg (2, לֹ, §304).

8:19   הַחֲיִתֶם

Unique   ל   Mp

Com.: This lemma is featured in a Masoretic list of *hapax legomena* starting with ה or הַ; see Frensdorff, *Ochlah*, §65, and Díaz-Esteban, *Sefer Oklah we-Oklah*, §66.

JUDGES 8:20

וַיֹּאמֶר לְיֶתֶר בְּכוֹרוֹ קוּם הֲרֹג אוֹתָם וְלֹא־שָׁלַף הַנַּעַר חַרְבּוֹ כִּי יָרֵא כִּי עוֹדֶנּוּ נָעַר׃

8:20   בְּכוֹרוֹ

Three times plene   ג מל   Mp

Gen 38:6; Judg 8:20; 2 Sam 3:2

Com.: The Masorah notes the *three* occurrences of this lemma written plene first ו, to distinguish them from its more numerous occurrences (8x) written defective first ו (בְּכֹרוֹ).

JUDGES 8:21

וַיֹּאמֶר זֶבַח וְצַלְמֻנָּע קוּם אַתָּה וּפְגַע־בָּנוּ כִּי כָאִישׁ גְּבוּרָתוֹ וַיָּקָם גִּדְעוֹן וַיַּהֲרֹג אֶת־זֶבַח וְאֶת־צַלְמֻנָּע וַיִּקַּח אֶת־הַשַּׂהֲרֹנִים אֲשֶׁר בְּצַוְּארֵי גְמַלֵּיהֶם׃

8:21   וְצַלְמֻנָּע

Five times   ה   Mp

1–5   Judg 8:5; 8:6; 8:10; 8:12; 8:15[a]
6–7   Judg 8:15[b]; **8:21**

Com.: The Mp heading here of *five times* is incorrect since there are *seven* occurrences of this lemma.

The Masorah notes the *seven* occurrences of this lemma with a ו cj., to distinguish them from its *four* occurrences without a cj.

Neither M[C] nor M[A] has a note on this lemma here.

8:21   וּפְגַע־בָּנוּ

Unique   ל   Mp

Com.: The Masorah notes the *sole* occurrence of this lemma with a 1st pers. pl. sfx., possibly to distinguish it from its occurrence with a 3rd pers. sg. sfx. (וּפְגַע־בּוֹ) at 1 Kgs 2:31.

8:21   כָּאִישׁ

Unique   ל   Mp

Com.: The Masorah notes the *sole* occurrence of this lemma with a *qameṣ* under the כ, to distinguish it from its *twenty* occurrences with a *šəwâ* under the כ (כְּאִישׁ); see **Judg 6:16.**

8:21   הַשַּׂהֲרֹנִים

Three times   ג   Mp

Judg 8:21; 8:26; Isa 3:18 (וְהַשַּׂהֲרֹנִים)

Com.: The Masorah notes the *three* occurrences of this lemma, *once* with a ו cj. (Isa 3:18), and *twice* without a cj. (here and v. 26).

JUDGES 8:22

וַיֹּאמְרוּ אִישׁ־יִשְׂרָאֵל אֶל־גִּדְעוֹן מְשָׁל־בָּנוּ גַּם־אַתָּה גַּם־בִּנְךָ גַּם בֶּן־בְּנֶךָ כִּי הוֹשַׁעְתָּנוּ מִיַּד מִדְיָן׃

8:22   וַיֹּאמְרוּ אִישׁ־יִשְׂרָאֵל

Unique   ל   Mp

Com.: The Masorah notes the *sole* occurrence of the phrase אִישׁ־יִשְׂרָאֵל with וַיֹּאמְרוּ, to distinguish it from its *two* occurrences with וַיֹּאמֶר (וַיֹּאמֶר אִישׁ־יִשְׂרָאֵל) at Josh 9:7 (*qərê*, the *kəṯîḇ* form is ויאמרו), and 1 Sam 17:25.

8:22   הוֹשַׁעְתָּנוּ

Twice   ב   Mp

Judg 8:22; Ps 44:8

Judges 8:23

וַיֹּאמֶר אֲלֵהֶם גִּדְעוֹן לֹא־אֶמְשֹׁל אֲנִי בָּכֶם וְלֹא־יִמְשֹׁל בְּנִי בָּכֶם יְהוָה יִמְשֹׁל בָּכֶם:

8:23   אֲלֵהֶם

Twenty-nine times defective in the Prophets   בֿט חֿס בנֿב   Mp

1–5   **Josh 6:6**; **23:2**; **Judg 3:28**; **8:23**; 8:24
6–10   Judg 18:2; 18:4; **19:23**[b]; <u>**1 Kgs 12:16**</u>*; 12:28
11–15   **1 Kgs 13:12**; **22:6**; 2 Kgs 1:2; 1:3; 1:7
16–20   **2 Kgs 2:18**; **6:19**; **9:19**; **10:18**; 12:8
21–25   **2 Kgs 18:18**; Ezek 16:37; 20:3; 20:7; 20:29
26–29   <u>Ezek 33:25</u>*; **33:27**; 37:19; Zech 1:3

Com.: The Masorah notes the *twenty-nine* occurrences of this lemma in the Prophets written defective יֿ, to distinguish them from its more numerous occurrences (100+) in the Prophets written plene י (אֲלֵיהֶם).

* M[L], contrary to M (אֲלֵהֶם), writes the *two* forms at 1 Kgs 12:16 and Ezek 33:25 plene י (אֲלֵיהֶם); see Breuer, *The Biblical Text*, 112 and 218. On the other hand, M[L], contrary to M (אֲלֵיהֶם), writes the forms at Josh 9:8 and 2 Kgs 18:19 defective י (אֲלֵהֶם); see Breuer, *The Biblical Text*, 46 and 131.

Of the *sixteen* highlighted Mp headings above, only Judg 8:23 and Ezek 33:27 read *twenty-nine times defective in the Prophets*.

All the other Mp headings relate to specific books, thus every one of the *ten* highlighted Mp headings in Kings note the *thirteen* occurrences in Kings; the headings at Josh 6:6 and 23:2 note the *two* occurrences in Joshua, and those at Judg 3:28 and 19:23[b] note the *six* occurrences in Judges.

8:23   וְלֹא־יִמְשֹׁל

Unique   ל   Mp

Com.: This lemma is featured in a Masoretic list of *hapax legomena* phrases that occur *once* with a ו cj., and *once* without a cj. (Exod 21:8); see the Mm to <u>Lev 1:17</u>.

JUDGES 8:24

וַיֹּאמֶר אֲלֵהֶם גִּדְעוֹן אֶשְׁאֲלָה מִכֶּם שְׁאֵלָה וּתְנוּ־לִי אִישׁ נֶזֶם שְׁלָלוֹ כִּי־נִזְמֵי זָהָב לָהֶם כִּי יִשְׁמְעֵאלִים הֵם:

8:24   אִישׁ נֶזֶם

Unique   ל   Mp

Com.: The Mp heading here of *unique* is incorrect since there is another occurrence of this lemma in the following verse.

Neither M^C nor M^A has a note on this lemma here.

The circellus between these two words is not clear.

8:24   הֵם

Twelve times at the end of a verse   יב סוף פסו   Mp

1–5   **Gen 40:12**; 40:18; Exod 18:26; 29:33; Lev 11:42
6–10   **Num 1:16**; **Judg 8:24**; 1 Kgs 20:3; Isa 49:21; Ezek 12:2
11–12   **Ezra 2:59**; Neh 7:61

הֵם *twelve times* at the end of a verse, and their references   הם יב סוף פסוק וסימנהון   Mm

1–5	Gen 40:12	[השריגים] (השריגים)
	Gen 40:18	הסלים
	Exod 18:26	ישפוטו
	Exod 29:33	כפר
	Lev 11:42	גחון
6–10	Num 1:16	קרואי
	Judg 8:24	אשאלה
	1 Kgs 20:3	כספך
	Isa 49:21	(גלמודה) [וגלמודה]
	Ezek 12:2	בן אדם
11–12	Ezra 2:59	חרשא
	And its companion (Neh 7:61)	(וחב) [וחבירו]

Com.: The Masorah notes the *twelve* occurrences at the end of a verse of this lemma, to distinguish them from the more numerous occurrences (28x) at the end of a verse of its alternate form הֵמָּה; see Ognibeni, *'Oklah*, §106.

JUDGES 8:25

וַיֹּאמְרוּ נָתוֹן נִתֵּן וַיִּפְרְשׂוּ אֶת־הַשִּׂמְלָה וַיַּשְׁלִיכוּ שָׁמָּה אִישׁ גֶזֶם שְׁלָלוֹ:

8:25   וַיַּשְׁלִיכוּ

Four times plene   ד מל֞   Mp

Com.: See **Josh 8:29**.

JUDGES 8:26

וַיְהִי מִשְׁקַל נִזְמֵי הַזָּהָב אֲשֶׁר שָׁאָל אֶלֶף וּשְׁבַע־מֵאוֹת זָהָב לְבַד מִן־הַשַּׂהֲרֹנִים וְהַנְּטִפוֹת וּבִגְדֵי
הָאַרְגָּמָן שֶׁעַל מַלְכֵי מִדְיָן וּלְבַד מִן־הָעֲנָקוֹת אֲשֶׁר בְּצַוְּארֵי גְמַלֵּיהֶם:

8:26   שָׁאָל

Three times   ג֞   Mp

Josh 19:50; <u>Judg 8:26</u>; <u>1 Chr 4:10</u>

שָׁאָל   *three times* with *qameṣ*, and their references   שאל ג֞ קמ֞ וסימנהון   Mm

Josh 19:50	תמנת
<u>Judg 8:26</u>	נזמי
<u>1 Chr 4:10</u>	יעבץ

Com.: The Masorah notes the *three* occurrences of this lemma written with a *qameṣ* under the א, to distinguish them from its more numerous occurrences with a *pataḥ* under the א (שַׁאַל).

8:26   הַשַּׂהֲרֹנִים

Three times   ג֞   Mp

Com.: See directly above at **Judg 8:21**.

8:26   וְהַנְּטִפוֹת

Twice   בֿ   Mp

Judg 8:26 (וְהַנְּטִיפוֹת)*; **Isa 3:19** (הַנְּטִפוֹת)*

Com.: The Masorah notes the *two* occurrences of this lemma, *one* written plene י and with a ו cj.(here), and *one* written defective י without a ו cj. (Isa 3:19).

* Mᴸ, contrary to M (וְהַנְּטִפוֹת), writes the form here defective י וְהַנְּטִפֹת; see Breuer, *The Biblical Text*, 60. On the other hand, Mᴸ, contrary to M (הַנְּטִפוֹת), writes the form at Isa 3:19 plene י (הַנְּטִיפוֹת).

Mᴬ reads the text here וְהַנְּטִיפוֹת and has a Mp note *twice, once plene and once defective* (י). Mᶜ likewise reads the text here וְהַנְּטִיפוֹת, but its Mp note reads *twice and plene* (י), notwithstanding the fact that it writes the lemma defective at Isa 3:19, and has a note there *unique defective.*

8:26   וּבִגְדֵי הָאַרְגָּמָן

Twice   בֿ   Mp

Com.: The Mp heading here of *twice* is incorrect since this is the *only* occurrence of this lemma.

Neither Mᶜ nor Mᴬ has a note on this lemma here.

8:26   וּלְבַד

Unique   לֿ   Mp

Com.: The Masorah notes the *sole* occurrence of this lemma with a ו cj., to distinguish it from its more numerous occurrences (17x) without a cj., *one* of which is in this very verse.

8:26   הָעֲנָקוֹת

Unique   לֿ   Mp

JUDGES 8:27

וַיַּעַשׂ אוֹתוֹ גִדְעוֹן לְאֵפוֹד וַיַּצֵּג אוֹתוֹ בְעִירוֹ בְּעָפְרָה וַיִּזְנוּ כָל־יִשְׂרָאֵל אַחֲרָיו שָׁם וַיְהִי לְגִדְעוֹן
וּלְבֵיתוֹ לְמוֹקֵשׁ:

8:27   לְאֵפוֹד

Unique   לֹ   Mp

Com.: This lemma is featured in a Masoretic list of *hapax legomena* that begin with לֹ; see Frensdorff, *Ochlah*, §27, and Díaz-Esteban, *Sefer Oklah we-Oklah*, §28.

8:27   וַיַּצֵּג

Three times   גֹ   Mp

Gen 30:38; Judg 8:27

Com.: The Mp heading here of *three times* is incorrect since there are only *two* occurrences of this lemma.

The Mp heading at Gen 30:38 correctly reads *twice*, and adds the catchwords אותו בעירו (אותו בעירו) referring the reader back to this verse.

M^A correctly reads here *twice*, and adds catchwords referring the reader to Gen 30:28. M^C has no note here.

8:27   לְגִדְעוֹן

Unique   לֹ   Mp

Com.: This lemma is featured in a Masoretic list of words that occur *four times, three times* with a preceding ו (see **Judg 7:18**), and *once* without it (here); see Frensdorff, *Ochlah*, §16, and Díaz-Esteban, *Sefer Oklah we-Oklah*, §17.

JUDGES 8:28

וַיִּכָּנַע מִדְיָן לִפְנֵי בְּנֵי יִשְׂרָאֵל וְלֹא יָסְפוּ לָשֵׂאת רֹאשָׁם וַתִּשְׁקֹט הָאָרֶץ אַרְבָּעִים שָׁנָה בִּימֵי גִדְעוֹן:
פ

8:28   וַיִּכָּנַע

Three times   גֹ   Mp

Judg 8:28; 2 Chr 32:26; 33:12

Com.: The Masorah notes the *three* occurrences of this lemma in the *niphal*, to distinguish them from its *two* occurrences in the *hiphil* (וַיִּכָּנַע) at **Judg 4:23** and Ps 107:12.

8:28   וְלֹא יָסְפוּ

Four times   דֿ   Mp

Judg 8:28; 1 Sam 7:13; 2 Sam 2:28; 2 Kgs 6:23

Com.: The Masorah notes the *four* occurrences of this lemma with a *šawâ* under the ס, to distinguish them from its *sole* occurrence with a *qameṣ* under the ס (וְלֹא יָסָפוּ) at Num 11:25.

JUDGES 8:30

וּלְגִדְעוֹן הָיוּ שִׁבְעִים בָּנִים יֹצְאֵי יְרֵכוֹ כִּי־נָשִׁים רַבּוֹת הָיוּ לוֹ׃

8:30   וּלְגִדְעוֹן

Three times   גֿ   Mp

Com.: See **Judg 7:18**.

JUDGES 8:31

וּפִילַגְשׁוֹ אֲשֶׁר בִּשְׁכֶם יָלְדָה־לּוֹ גַם־הִיא בֵּן וַיָּשֶׂם אֶת־שְׁמוֹ אֲבִימֶלֶךְ׃

8:31   וּפִילַגְשׁוֹ

Twice at the beginning of a verse   בֿ רֿא פֿס   Mp

Gen 22:24; Judg 8:31

וּפִילַגְשׁוֹ *twice* at the beginning of a verse,   ופילגשו בֿ ראש פסוק וסימנהון   Mm
and their references

Gen 22:24   ופילגשו ושמה ראומה
Judg 8:31   בשכם ילדה לו גם היא

Com.: The Masorah notes the *two* occurrences of this lemma at the beginning of a verse, to distinguish them from its *two* occurrences in the middle of a verse at Judg 19:9 and 19:10.

Normally such a note indicates the presence or absence of a ו cj. at the beginning of a verse, but there are no examples of פִּילַגְשׁוֹ at the beginning of a verse.

JUDGES 8:32

וַיָּמָת גִּדְעוֹן בֶּן־יוֹאָשׁ בְּשֵׂיבָה טוֹבָה וַיִּקָּבֵר בְּקֶבֶר יוֹאָשׁ אָבִיו בְּעָפְרָה אֲבִי הָעֶזְרִי׃ פ

8:32   וַיָּמָת גִּדְעוֹן

Unique   לֹ   Mp

Com.: The Masorah notes the *sole* occurrence of this lemma with the impf. and ו consec., to distinguish it from its occurrence with the perf. (מֵת גִּדְעוֹן) in the following verse.

8:32   בְּשֵׂיבָה טוֹבָה

Four times   דֹ   Mp

Gen 15:15; 25:8; Judg 8:32; 1 Chr 29:28

בְּשֵׂיבָה טוֹבָה *four times*, and their references   בשיבה טובה ד וסימנהון   Mm

Gen 15:15	ואתה תבוא אל אבתיך
Gen 25:8	ויגוע וימת אברהם
Judg 8:32	וימת גדעון בן יואש
1 Chr 29:28	וימת בשיבה טובה שבע

Com.: The Masorah notes the *four* occurrences of בְּשֵׂיבָה with טוֹבָה, to distinguish them from its *sole* occurrence without טוֹבָה at Ps 92:15.

The Mp heading at Gen 25:8 mistakenly reads *five times*, but the Mm there correctly reads *four times*, as do the other *three* Mp headings highlighted above.

8:32   הָעֶזְרִי

Three times   גׄ   Mp

Judg 6:11; 6:24; **8:32**

Com.: The Masorah notes the *three* occurrences of this lemma with the def. article, to distinguish them from its *four* occurrences without it.

JUDGES 8:33

וַיְהִ֗י כַּאֲשֶׁר֙ מֵ֣ת גִּדְע֔וֹן וַיָּשׁ֙וּבוּ֙ בְּנֵ֣י יִשְׂרָאֵ֔ל וַיִּזְנ֖וּ אַחֲרֵ֣י הַבְּעָלִ֑ים וַיָּשִׂ֧ימוּ לָהֶ֛ם בַּ֥עַל בְּרִ֖ית לֵאלֹהִֽים׃

8:33   וַיָּשׁוּבוּ

Six times plene   ו מלׄ   Mp

1–5	**Judg 8:33**; 21:23; 1 Kgs 22:33; 2 Kgs 1:5; **Jer 34:11**
6	Zech 1:6

Com.: The Masorah notes the *six* occurrences of this lemma in the Prophets written plene first וֹ, to distinguish them from its more numerous occurrences (26x) in the Prophets written defective ו (וַיָּשֻׁבוּ). That this lemma is limited to the Prophets is clear from the Mp headings at Judg 21:23, 1 Kgs 22:33 and Zech 1:6, all of which read *six times plene in the Prophets*.

The heading at Jer 34:11 of *unique plene in the Prophets* should be *unique plene in the book*, since this is the only occurrence of this lemma in Jeremiah.

JUDGES 8:34

וְלֹ֤א זָֽכְרוּ֙ בְּנֵ֣י יִשְׂרָאֵ֔ל אֶת־יְהוָ֖ה אֱלֹהֵיהֶ֑ם הַמַּצִּ֥יל אוֹתָ֛ם מִיַּ֥ד כָּל־אֹיְבֵיהֶ֖ם מִסָּבִֽיב׃

8:34   וְלֹא זָכְרוּ

Three times   גׄ   Mp

Judg 8:34; Amos 1:9; Neh 9:17

וְלֹא זָכְרוּ *three times*, and their references   ולא זכרו גֿ וסימנהון   Mm

<u>Judg 8:34</u>	המציל
<u>Amos 1:9</u>	ברית
<u>Neh 9:17</u>	נפלאתיך

Com.: The Masorah notes the *three* occurrences of this lemma with a ו cj., to distinguish them from its *two* occurrences without a cj. at Ps 78:42 and Ps 106:7.

8:34   מִיַּד כָּל־אֹיְבֵיהֶם

Twice   בֿ   Mp

Judg 8:34; 2 Sam 3:18 (וּמִיַּד)

Com.: The Masorah notes the *two* occurrences of this lemma with כָּל, to distinguish them from its *sole* occurrence without כָּל at Judg 2:18.

The Mp heading at 2 Sam 3:18 reads *unique* reflecting the *sole* occurrence there of this lemma with a ו cj.

In M^L the circellus has been placed only on כָּל־אֹיְבֵיהֶם but, since this phrase occurs *three* times, it is most likely that, as in M^A, the note belongs with the preceding word as well since the wider phrase מִיַּד כָּל־אֹיְבֵיהֶם only occurs *twice*. M^C has no note here.

JUDGES 8:35

וְלֹא־עָשׂוּ חֶסֶד עִם־בֵּית יְרֻבַּעַל גִּדְעוֹן כְּכָל־הַטּוֹבָה אֲשֶׁר עָשָׂה עִם־יִשְׂרָאֵל׃ פ

8:35   וְלֹא־עָשׂוּ

Five times   הֿ   Mp

1–5   **Exod 1:17; Judg 8:35; 2 Kgs 18:12; <u>Jer 11:8</u>; <u>2 Chr 21:19</u>**

Com.: The Masorah notes the *five* occurrences of this lemma with a ו cj., to distinguish them from its more numerous occurrences (8x) of this form written without a cj.

JUDGES 9:1

וַיֵּ֨לֶךְ אֲבִימֶ֤לֶךְ בֶּן־יְרֻבַּ֙עַל֙ שְׁכֶ֔מָה אֶל־אֲחֵ֣י אִמּ֑וֹ וַיְדַבֵּ֣ר אֲלֵיהֶ֔ם וְאֶל־כָּל־מִשְׁפַּ֖חַת בֵּית־אֲבִ֣י אִמּ֑וֹ
לֵאמֹֽר׃

9:1   שְׁכֶ֔מָה

Six times   ו   Mp

1–5   **Gen 37:14**; Josh 24:1; **Judg 9:1; 9:31;** 21:19
6   **2 Chr 10:1**

Com.: The Masorah notes the *six* occurrences of this lemma with the locative ה, to distinguish them from its more numerous occurrences (50x) without this adverbial form (שְׁכֶם).

This distinction is implied in the Mm of **Judg 9:31** in the additional notation *of Chronicles* to the 2 Chr 10:1 reference, which distinguishes it from its parallel passage in 1 Kgs 12:1, where the lemma occurs as שְׁכֶם.

9:1   וְאֶל־כָּל

Twice in the book   ב בסֹ   Mp

Com.: See **Judg 2:4**.

JUDGES 9:2

דַּבְּרוּ־נָ֞א בְּאָזְנֵ֣י כָל־בַּעֲלֵ֣י שְׁכֶם֮ מַה־ט֣וֹב לָכֶם֒ הַמְשֹׁ֙ל בָּכֶ֜ם שִׁבְעִ֣ים אִ֗ישׁ כֹּ֚ל בְּנֵ֣י יְרֻבַּ֔עַל אִם־מְשֹׁ֥ל
בָּכֶ֖ם אִ֣ישׁ אֶחָ֑ד וּזְכַרְתֶּ֕ם כִּי־עַצְמְכֶ֥ם וּבְשַׂרְכֶ֖ם אָנִֽי׃

9:2   בְּאָזְנֵ֣י

Thirty-seven times   לֿז   Mp

Com.: See **Josh 20:4**.

9:2   הַמְשֵׁל

Unique   ל   Mp

Com.: This lemma is featured in a Masoretic list of doublets with different hierarchial vowels, in the list termed *mil'êl* and *milra'*; see Yeivin, *Introduction*, §132, p. 103. In this connection, the higher vowel, the *mil'êl*, is the vowel *ḥolem*, and the lower vowel, the *milra'*, is the vowel *ṣerê*. Thus הַמְשֵׁל (here) with the *ḥolem* is *mil'êl*, but הַמְשֵׁל (Job 25:2) with the *ṣerê* is *milra'*; see Frensdorff, *Ochlah*, §5, and Díaz-Esteban, *Sefer Oklah we-Oklah*, §5.

9:2   עַצְמֵכֶם וּבְשַׂרְכֶם

Unique   ל   Mp

> ## JUDGES 9:3
>
> וַיְדַבְּרוּ אֲחֵי־אִמּוֹ עָלָיו בְּאָזְנֵי כָּל־בַּעֲלֵי שְׁכֶם אֵת כָּל־הַדְּבָרִים הָאֵלֶּה וַיֵּט לִבָּם אַחֲרֵי אֲבִימֶלֶךְ כִּי אָמְרוּ אָחִינוּ הוּא׃

9:3   בְּאָזְנֵי

Thirty-seven times   לז   Mp

Com.: See **Josh 20:4**.

9:3   אֵת כָּל־הַדְּבָרִים הָאֵלֶּה

Thirteen times   יג   Mp

1–5	Gen 20:8; 29:13; Exod. 19:7; 20:1; Num 16:31
6–10	Deut 12:28; **32:45**; **Judg 9:3**; 1 Sam 19:7; **2 Sam 13:21**
11–12	**2 Sam 14:19**;1 Kgs 18:36; **Jer 7:27**; 11:6; **16:10**
16–20	Jer 25:30; 26:15; 34:6; 36:16; 36:17
20–25	Jer 36:18; 36:24; 43:1; **51:60**; 51:61

Com.: The Masorah note here is in error since there are *twenty-five* occurrences of this lemma. The number *thirteen* refers to the number of occurrences of this phrase without הָאֵלֶּה; see the Mm at <u>Lev 8:36</u> and <u>Deut 1:18</u>. The error no doubt was occasioned by the fact that in M^{L} there are circelli only on the words אֵת כָּל־הַדְּבָרִים instead of on the full phrase אֵת כָּל־הַדְּבָרִים הָאֵלֶּה.

The Mp heading at Deut 32:45 reads *seven times in the Torah* and correctly enumerates the *seven* occurrences in the Torah.

Neither M^C or M^A has a note here.

JUDGES 9:4

וַיִּתְּנוּ־לוֹ שִׁבְעִים כֶּסֶף מִבֵּית בַּעַל בְּרִית וַיִּשְׂכֹּר בָּהֶם אֲבִימֶלֶךְ אֲנָשִׁים רֵיקִים וּפֹחֲזִים וַיֵּלְכוּ אַחֲרָיו:

9:4	וַיִּשְׂכֹּר בָּהֶם

Unique   ל   Mp

Com.: The Masorah notes the *sole* occurrence of וַיִּשְׂכֹּר with בָּהֶם, to distinguish it from its occurrence with עָלָיו (וַיִּשְׂכֹּר עָלָיו) at Neh 13:2.

In M^L only the very tip of the ל is visible in the ms.

9:4	וּפֹחֲזִים

Unique   ל   Mp

Com.: The Masorah notes the *sole* occurrence of this lemma with a ו cj., to distinguish it from its occurrence without a cj. at Zeph 3:4.

JUDGES 9:5

וַיָּבֹא בֵית־אָבִיו עָפְרָתָה וַיַּהֲרֹג אֶת־אֶחָיו בְּנֵי־יְרֻבַּעַל שִׁבְעִים אִישׁ עַל־אֶבֶן אֶחָת וַיִּוָּתֵר יוֹתָם בֶּן־יְרֻבַּעַל הַקָּטֹן כִּי נֶחְבָּא: ס

9:5	עָפְרָתָה

Unique   ל   Mp

Com.: The Masorah notes the *sole* occurrence of this lemma with the locative ה, to distinguish it from its *two* occurrences without this adverbial ending (עָפְרָה) at 1 Sam 13:17 and 1 Chr 4:14.

JUDGES 9:6

וַיֵּאָסְפ֞וּ כָּל־בַּעֲלֵ֣י שְׁכֶם֮ וְכָל־בֵּ֣ית מִלּוֹא֒ וַיֵּלְכ֗וּ וַיַּמְלִ֤יכוּ אֶת־אֲבִימֶ֙לֶךְ֙ לְמֶ֔לֶךְ עִם־אֵל֥וֹן מֻצָּ֖ב אֲשֶׁ֥ר בִּשְׁכֶֽם׃

9:6   וַיֵּאָסְפ֞וּ

Twelve times   יֹב   Mp

1–5   Exod 32:26; Josh 10:5; **Judg 9:6; 10:17**; 20:14
6–10   **1 Sam 17:1; 2 Sam 10:15**; 23:11; **Ezra 3:1**; Neh 8:1
11–12   Neh 12:28; **2 Chr 30:13**

Com.: The Masorah notes the *twelve* occurrences of this lemma with a וֹ consec., to distinguish them from its *four* occurrences without this וֹ (וַיֵּאָסְפוּ).

The Mp heading at 2 Chr 30:13 mistakenly reads *fourteen times*. Dotan/Reich (*Masora Thesaurus, ad loc.*) suggest that this note belongs in the previous verse on the word וְהַשֹּׁרְרִים, which does occur *fourteen times*.

9:6   וְכָל־בֵּ֣ית

וְכָל־בֵּ֣ית   *twelve times*   וכל בית יֹב   Mm

1–5	<Gen 50:8>	
	<u>Judg 9:6</u>	מלוא
	Judg 16:31	אביהו
	1 Sam 22:1	וימלט
	1 Sam 22:16	ויאמר המלך
6–10	2 Sam 6:5	(משחקים) [משחקים]
	2 Sam 6:15	מעלים
	1 Kgs 4:12	בענא בן אחילוד
	Jer 52:9	כי כל הגוים
	Ezek 11:15	אחיך אחיך
11–12	Ezek 37:16	חבריו
	Ezek 12:10	הנשיא

Com.: The Masorah notes the *twelve* occurrences of this lemma with a וֹ cj., to distinguish them from its more numerous occurrences (34x) without a cj.

9:6 אֵלוֹן

Three times defective   ג̇ חס   Mp

1–5   **Josh 19:33** (מֵאֵלוֹן); Judg 4:11; **9:6**; 9:37; **1 Sam 10:3**

אֵלוֹן *three times*, and defective in the Prophets   אלון ג̇ וחס בנב   Mm

Judg 9:6	עם אלון מצב
Judg 9:37	וראש אחד בא
1 Sam 10:3	(והלכת) [וחלפת] משם והלאה ובאת עד אלון

Com.: The heading of the Mp here of *three times* is incorrect, as are the heading and list in the Mm, since there are *five* occurrences of this lemma. The correct enumeration is found in the Mp headings of Josh 19:33 and 1 Sam 10:3.

The Masorah notes the *five* occurrences of this lemma in various forms in the Prophets written defective י, to distinguish them from its *five* occurrences in various forms in the Prophets written plene י (אֵילוֹן/וְאֵילוֹן).

Since there are other occurrences of this lemma in the Prophets written plene י, the Mm heading is also incorrect in writing *and defective in the Prophets* with its implication that there are only defective forms in the Prophets. It should read simply *defective in the Prophets*.

Neither M^C nor M^A has a note on this lemma here.

9:6 מַצָּב

Three times   ג̇   Mp

Gen 28:12; **Judg 9:6**; Isa 29:3

מַצָּב *three times*, and defective   מצב ג̇ וחס   Mm

Gen 28:12	והנה סלם מצב
Judg 9:6	עם אלון מצב
Isa 29:3	והקימתי עליך

Com.: By noting that this lemma occurs *three times* and written defective וֹ, the Masorah is also implying (correctly) that this lemma does not occur elsewhere written plene וֹ.

The Mm at Isa 29:3 is given in the form of an Aramaic mnemonic "the ladder of Shechem is raised"; see Marcus, *Scribal Wit*, 89.

The Mp heading at Gen 28:12 mistakenly reads *twice*. For some suggestions as to how this problem might be resolved, see Dotan/Reich, *Masora Thesaurus, ad loc.*

JUDGES 9:7

וַיַּגִּדוּ לְיוֹתָם וַיֵּלֶךְ וַיַּעֲמֹד בְּרֹאשׁ הַר־גְּרִזִים וַיִּשָּׂא קוֹלוֹ וַיִּקְרָא וַיֹּאמֶר לָהֶם שִׁמְעוּ אֵלַי בַּעֲלֵי שְׁכֶם וְיִשְׁמַע אֲלֵיכֶם אֱלֹהִים׃

9:7   וְיִשְׁמַע

Three times   גֵ   Mp

Judg 9:7; <u>Isa 42:23</u>; **Jer 23:18**

וְיִשְׁמַע *three times*, and their references   וישמע גׄ וסימנהון   Mm

<u>Judg 9:7</u>	אליכם
<u>Isa 42:23</u>	יקשיב] [יקשב
Jer 23:18	וירא וישמע

Com.: The Masorah notes the *three* occurrences of this lemma with a וֹ cj., to distinguish them from its more numerous occurrences (88x) with a וֹ consec. (וַיִּשְׁמַע); see Ognibeni, *'Oklah*, §12E.

JUDGES 9:8

הָלוֹךְ הָלְכוּ הָעֵצִים לִמְשֹׁחַ עֲלֵיהֶם מֶלֶךְ וַיֹּאמְרוּ לַזַּיִת מָלוֹכָה עָלֵינוּ׃

9:8   מָלוֹכָה

Read מָלְכָה   מלכה קרי   Mp

Com.: The *katîb* (מלוכה, *rule*) represents an older form of the imper. with cohortative ה, whereas the *qarê* (מָלְכָה) has the later form; see Gordis, *The Biblical Text*, 107.

JUDGES 9:9

וַיֹּאמֶר לָהֶם הַזַּיִת הֶחֳדַלְתִּי אֶת־דִּשְׁנִי אֲשֶׁר־בִּי יְכַבְּדוּ אֱלֹהִים וַאֲנָשִׁים וְהָלַכְתִּי לָנוּעַ עַל־הָעֵצִים:

9:9   דִּשְׁנִי

Unique   ל   Mp

9:9   יְכַבְּדוּ אֱלֹהִים

Unique   ל   Mp

9:9   וַאֲנָשִׁים

Ten times   י   Mp

1–5   Num 16:2; **Judg 9:9**; 9:13; **1 Sam 22:6**; 1 Kgs 11:17
6–10   Jer 26:22; <u>Ezek 23:45</u>; Qoh 9:14; Neh 1:2; 2:12

Com.: The Masorah notes the *ten* occurrences of this lemma, which is indef., to distinguish them from its more numerous occurrences (16x) of the def. noun (וְהָאֲנָשִׁים).

9:9   לָנוּעַ

Four times   ד   Mp

Judg 9:9; **9:11**; 9:13; **Jer 14:10**

JUDGES 9:10

וַיֹּאמְרוּ הָעֵצִים לַתְּאֵנָה לְכִי־אַתְּ מָלְכִי עָלֵינוּ:

9:10   מָלְכִי

Twice   ב   Mp

Judg 9:10; **9:12** (*qərê*)

JUDGES 9:11

וַתֹּאמֶר לָהֶם הַתְּאֵנָה הֶחֳדַלְתִּי אֶת־מָתְקִי וְאֶת־תְּנוּבָתִי הַטּוֹבָה וְהָלַכְתִּי לָנוּעַ עַל־הָעֵצִים:

9:11   מָתְקִי

Unique   ל   Mp

Com.: This lemma is featured in a Masoretic list of *hapax legomena* arranged alphabetically, *one* of which occurs in the Torah (מִקְדָּשִׁי, Lev 21:23), *one* in the Prophets (מָתְקִי, here), and *one* in the Writings (מָתְקוּ, Job 21:33); see Frensdorff, *Ochlah*, §57, and Díaz-Esteban, *Sefer Oklah we-Oklah*, §58.

9:11   לָנוּעַ

Four times   ד   Mp

Judg 9:9; 9:11; 9:13; Jer 14:10

JUDGES 9:12

וַיֹּאמְרוּ הָעֵצִים לַגֶּפֶן לְכִי־אַתְּ מָלוֹכִי עָלֵינוּ׃

9:12   לַגֶּפֶן

Unique with *qameṣ*   ל   Mp

Com.: The Masorah notes the *sole* occurrence of this lemma with a *qameṣ* under the ג, to distinguish it from its other occurrence with a *səḡôl* (לַגֶּפֶן) at Gen 49:11.

This lemma is featured in a Masoretic list of *doublets* that begin with ל and a vowel; see Frensdorff, *Ochlah*, §28, and Díaz-Esteban, *Sefer Oklah we-Oklah*, §29.

9:12   מָלוֹכִי

Read   מָלְכִי ק   מלכי ק   Mp

Com.: The *kəṯîḇ* (מלוכי, *rule*) represents an older form of the imper., whereas the *qərê* (מָלְכִי) has the later form; see Gordis, *The Biblical Text*, 107.

In M[L] this lemma has no circellus.

JUDGES 9:13

וַתֹּאמֶר לָהֶם הַגֶּפֶן הֶחֳדַלְתִּי אֶת־תִּירוֹשִׁי הַמְשַׂמֵּחַ אֱלֹהִים וַאֲנָשִׁים וְהָלַכְתִּי לָנוּעַ עַל־הָעֵצִים׃

9:13   הַמְשַׂמֵּחַ

Unique   ל   Mp

JUDGES 9:14

וַיֹּאמְר֥וּ כָל־הָעֵצִ֖ים אֶל־הָאָטָ֑ד לֵ֥ךְ אַתָּ֖ה מְלָךְ־עָלֵֽינוּ׃

9:14 כָל־הָעֵצִ֖ים

Unique ל Mp

Com.: The Masorah notes the *sole* occurrence of הָעֵצִים with כָּל, to distinguish it from its more numerous occurrences (30x) without כָּל, *seven* of which occur in this chapter in vv. 8, 9, 10, 11, 12, 13 and 15.

JUDGES 9:15

וַיֹּ֣אמֶר הָאָטָד֮ אֶל־הָעֵצִים֒ אִם־בֶּאֱמֶ֗ת אַתֶּ֜ם מֹשְׁחִ֥ים אֹתִ֛י לְמֶ֖לֶךְ עֲלֵיכֶ֑ם בֹּ֚אוּ חֲס֣וּ בְצִלִּ֔י וְאִם־אַ֕יִן תֵּ֤צֵא אֵשׁ֙ מִן־הָ֣אָטָ֔ד וְתֹאכַ֖ל אֶת־אַרְזֵ֥י הַלְּבָנֽוֹן׃

9:15 אֹתִ֛י

Unique defective in the book ל חס֔ בסיפֿ Mp

Com.: The Masorah notes the *sole* occurrence of this lemma in the book written defective ו, to distinguish them from its more numerous occurrences (8x) in the book written plene ו (אוֹתִי); see the Mm at <u>Deut 32:51</u> *sub* אוֹתִֽי.

JUDGES 9:16

וְעַתָּ֞ה אִם־בֶּאֱמֶ֤ת וּבְתָמִים֙ עֲשִׂיתֶ֔ם וַתַּמְלִ֖יכוּ אֶת־אֲבִימֶ֑לֶךְ וְאִם־טוֹבָ֣ה עֲשִׂיתֶ֗ם עִם־יְרֻבַּ֙עַל֙ וְעִם־בֵּית֔וֹ וְאִם־כִּגְמ֥וּל יָדָ֖יו עֲשִׂ֥יתֶם לֽוֹ׃

9:16 וְאִם־טוֹבָ֣ה

Unique ל Mp

9:16 כִּגְמ֥וּל

Twice ב֗ Mp

Judg 9:16; 2 Chr 32:25 (כִּגְמֻ֖ל)

Com.: The Masorah notes the *two* occurrences of this lemma in various forms with the prep. ב, to distinguish them from its more numerous occurrences (8x) without this preposition.

JUDGES 9:17

אֲשֶׁר־נִלְחַם אָבִי עֲלֵיכֶם וַיַּשְׁלֵךְ אֶת־נַפְשׁוֹ מִנֶּגֶד וַיַּצֵּל אֶתְכֶם מִיַּד מִדְיָן:

9:17   נִלְחַם

Twelve times   יֹב   Mp

1–5	**Num 21:26; Judg 9:17; 11:25;** <u>2 Sam 8:10</u>; **1 Kgs 14:19**
6–10	**2 Kgs 13:12;** <u>14:15</u>; Isa 30:32; 63:10; **1 Chr 18:10**
11–12	**2 Chr 20:29; 27:5**

Com.: The Masorah notes the *twelve* occurrences of this lemma with a *paṭaḥ* (perf.), to distinguish them from its occurrences (11x) with a *qameṣ* (נִלְחָם, ptcp.); see Ognibeni, *'Oklah*, §182A.

This distinction is implied in the Mm lists of <u>2 Sam 8:10</u> and <u>2 Kgs 14:15</u>, where there is an additional notation of the *first occurrence* of a catchword in the 1 Kgs 14:19 reference, to distinguish this reference from its *second occurrence* of this catchword in 2 Kgs 14:28, where the lemma appears as נִלְחָם.

JUDGES 9:18

וְאַתֶּם קַמְתֶּם עַל־בֵּית אָבִי הַיּוֹם וַתַּהַרְגוּ אֶת־בָּנָיו שִׁבְעִים אִישׁ עַל־אֶבֶן אֶחָת וַתַּמְלִיכוּ אֶת־
אֲבִימֶלֶךְ בֶּן־אֲמָתוֹ עַל־בַּעֲלֵי שְׁכֶם כִּי אֲחִיכֶם הוּא:

9:18   וְאַתֶּם

Seven times with the accent (*gerśayim*)   ז בטע   Mp

1–4   **Josh 18:6;** <u>Judg 9:18</u>; <u>Ezek 36:8</u>; <u>Neh 13:18</u>

וְאַתֶּם *four times* with the accent (*gerśayim*)   ואתם ד בטע   Mm

<u>Judg 9:18</u>	(= קַמְתֶּם)	קמון
<u>Ezek 36:8</u>	(= יִשְׂרָאֵל)	ישראל
Josh 18:6	(= תִּכְתְּבוּ)	וכתבון
Neh 13:18	(= הַשַּׁבָּת)	בשיבתה

Com.: The Mp heading here of *seven times with the accent* is incorrect since there are only *four* occurrences of this lemma. The correct number is given in the Mm here, and in the *three* other Mp headings highlighted above.

The Masorah notes the *four* occurrences of this lemma with the accent *geršayim*, to distinguish them from occurrences with other accents. The catchwords are given in the form of an Aramaic mnemonic: "Israel rose up and wrote on the Sabbath"; see Marcus, *Scribal Wit*, 62–63.

Both Mᶜ and Mᴬ correctly read here *four times with the accent.*

9:18   עַל־בַּעֲלֵי

Unique   ל   Mp

Com.: The Masorah notes the *sole* occurrence of this lemma without a ו cj., to distinguish it from its occurrence with a ו cj. (וְעַל־בַּעֲלֵי) in v. 24.

JUDGES 9:19

וְאִם־בֶּאֱמֶת וּבְתָמִים עֲשִׂיתֶם עִם־יְרֻבַּעַל וְעִם־בֵּיתוֹ הַיּוֹם הַזֶּה שִׂמְחוּ בַּאֲבִימֶלֶךְ וְיִשְׂמַח גַּם־הוּא בָּכֶם:

9:19   וְיִשְׂמַח

Unique   ל   Mp

Com.: The Masorah notes the *sole* occurrence of this lemma with a ו cj., to distinguish them from its occurrence with a ו consec. (וַיִּשְׂמַח) at Judg 19:3.

JUDGES 9:20

וְאִם־אַיִן תֵּצֵא אֵשׁ מֵאֲבִימֶלֶךְ וְתֹאכַל אֶת־בַּעֲלֵי שְׁכֶם וְאֶת־בֵּית מִלּוֹא וְתֵצֵא אֵשׁ מִבַּעֲלֵי שְׁכֶם וּמִבֵּית מִלּוֹא וְתֹאכַל אֶת־אֲבִימֶלֶךְ:

9:20   וְתֹאכַל¹

Six times   ו   Mp

1–5   Judg 9:15; **9:20ᵃ; 9:20ᵇ; 2 Kgs 1:10; 1:12**
6   **Zech 11:1**

Com.: The Masorah notes the *six* occurrences of this lemma with a ו cj., to distinguish them from its more numerous occurrences (21x) written with a ו consec. (וַתֹּאכַל).

This distinction is implied in the heading of the Mm at Zech 11:1, which reads *seven times rapê*, that is, *seven times* without *dageš*.

9:20   ²וְתֹאכַל

Six times   וֹ   Mp

Com.: See directly above.

JUDGES 9:21

וַיָּ֣נָס יוֹתָ֗ם וַיִּבְרַ֚ח וַיֵּ֙לֶךְ֙ בְּאֵ֔רָה וַיֵּ֣שֶׁב שָׁ֔ם מִפְּנֵ֖י אֲבִימֶ֥לֶךְ אָחִֽיו׃ פ

9:21   בְּאֵ֔רָה

Four times   ד֔   Mp

Gen 46:1; Num 21:16; **Judg 9:21**; **1 Chr 5:6**

בְּאֵ֔רָה *four times*   בארה ד   Mm

Num 21:16	ומשם בארה הוא
Judg 9:21	וינֹּ֗ס יותֹּם ויברח
Gen 46:1	ויסע ישראל וכל אשר לו
1 Chr 5:6	בארה בנו אשר

Com.: The Masorah notes the *four* occurrences of this lemma, *three times* as the name of a place (*Beer*) with a locative ה, and *once* (1 Chr 5:6) as the name of a person (*Beerah*),

The Mp heading at 1 Chr 5:6 reads *unique as the name of a person*, whereas the heading to the Mm at 1 Chr 5:6 reads *four times, three times as the name of a place, and once as the name of a person.*

JUDGES 9:22

וַיָּ֧שַׂר אֲבִימֶ֛לֶךְ עַל־יִשְׂרָאֵ֖ל שָׁלֹ֥שׁ שָׁנִֽים׃

9:22   וַיָּ֧שַׂר

Three times written שׂ   ג֔ כת שׂ   Mp

Judg 9:22; Hos 12:5; 1 Chr 20:3

Com.: The Masorah notes the *three* occurrences of this lemma written with a שׂ, to distinguish them from its more numerous occurrences (22x) written with a ס (וַיָּ֫סַר).

JUDGES 9:23

וַיִּשְׁלַח אֱלֹהִים רוּחַ רָעָה בֵּין אֲבִימֶלֶךְ וּבֵין בַּעֲלֵי שְׁכֶם וַיִּבְגְּדוּ בַעֲלֵי־שְׁכֶם בַּאֲבִימֶלֶךְ׃

9:23   וַיִּשְׁלַח אֱלֹהִים

Unique   ל   Mp

Com.: This phrase is featured in a Masoretic list of two-word phrases that occur *once* with a def. article between them (1 Chr 21:15), and *once* without (here); see Frensdorff, *Ochlah*, §3, and Díaz-Esteban, *Sefer Oklah we-Oklah*, §3.

9:23   וַיִּבְגְּדוּ

Twice   ב   Mp

Judg 9:23; Ps 78:57

Com.: The Masorah notes the *two* occurrences of this lemma with a ו consec., to distinguish them from its *sole* occurrence without a ו (יִבְגְּדוּ) at Isa 33:1.

JUDGES 9:24

לָבוֹא חֲמַס שִׁבְעִים בְּנֵי־יְרֻבַּעַל וְדָמָם לָשׂוּם עַל־אֲבִימֶלֶךְ אֲחִיהֶם אֲשֶׁר הָרַג אוֹתָם וְעַל בַּעֲלֵי שְׁכֶם אֲשֶׁר־חִזְּקוּ אֶת־יָדָיו לַהֲרֹג אֶת־אֶחָיו׃

9:24   עַל־אֲבִימֶלֶךְ

Unique   ל   Mp

Com.: This lemma is featured in a Masoretic list of words that only occur *once* preceded by the prep. עַל; see Frensdorff, *Ochlah*, §76, and Díaz-Esteban, *Sefer Oklah we-Oklah*, §155.

9:24   אֲחִיהֶם

Four times   ד   Mp

Judg 9:24; 2 Sam 3:30; Job 1:13; 1:18

Com.: The Masorah notes the *four* occurrences of this lemma with a *ḥîreq* under the ח (sg.), to distinguish them from its more numerous occurrences (37x) with a *ṣerê* (אֲחֵיהֶם, pl.).

The Mp heading at Job 1:18 reads *four times and once* ואחיהם, and this form is featured
in a Masoretic list of words that occur *five times*, *four times* without a ו cj. and *once* (1 Chr
9:17) with a cj.; see Frensdorff, *Ochlah*, §17, and Díaz-Esteban, *Sefer Oklah we-Oklah*,
§18.

9:24   חִזְּקוּ

Four times   דֹ   Mp

Judg 9:24; 2 Kgs 12:7; Jer 5:3; Ezra 1:6

חִזְּקוּ *four times*   חזקו ד   Mm

Judg 9:24   אשר חזקו את ידיו
Jer 5:3   חזקו פניהם מסלע
2 Kgs 12:7   לא חזקו הכהנים
Ezra 1:6   וכל (סביבותיהם) [סביבתיהם] חזקו בידיהם

Com.: The Masorah notes the *four* occurrences of this lemma with a *dageš* in the ז (*piel*),
to distinguish them from its more numerous occurrences (8x) without this *dageš*
(חִזְקוּ, *qal*); see Ognibeni, *'Oklah*, §40C.

JUDGES 9:25

וַיָּשִׂ֣ימוּ לוֹ֩ בַעֲלֵ֨י שְׁכֶ֜ם מְאָרְבִ֗ים עַ֚ל רָאשֵׁ֣י הֶֽהָרִ֔ים וַיִּגְזְל֗וּ אֵ֛ת כָּל־אֲשֶׁר־יַעֲבֹ֥ר עֲלֵיהֶ֖ם בַּדָּ֑רֶךְ וַיֻּגַּ֖ד
לַאֲבִימֶֽלֶךְ׃ פ

9:25   וַיֻּגַּד

Twenty-four times   כֹד   Mp

Com.: See **Josh 10:17**.

JUDGES 9:26

וַיָּבֹ֞א גַּ֤עַל בֶּן־עֶ֙בֶד֙ וְאֶחָ֔יו וַיַּעַבְר֖וּ בִּשְׁכֶ֑ם וַיִּבְטְחוּ־ב֖וֹ בַּעֲלֵ֥י שְׁכֶֽם׃

9:26   וַיַּעַבְרוּ בִּשְׁכֶם

Unique   לֹ   Mp

JUDGES 9:27

וַיֵּצְאוּ הַשָּׂדֶה וַיִּבְצְרוּ אֶת־כַּרְמֵיהֶם וַיִּדְרְכוּ וַיַּעֲשׂוּ הִלּוּלִים וַיָּבֹאוּ בֵּית אֱלֹהֵיהֶם וַיֹּאכְלוּ וַיִּשְׁתּוּ
וַיְקַלְלוּ אֶת־אֲבִימֶלֶךְ:

9:27   וַיִּבְצְרוּ

Unique   ל   Mp

9:27   וַיִּדְרְכוּ

Unique   ל   Mp

9:27   הִלּוּלִים

Twice plene   ב מל   Mp

Lev 19:24; Judg 9:27

הִלּוּלִים   *twice*   הלולים ב   Mm

Lev 19;24   יהיה כל פריו
Judg 9:27   ויבצרו את כרמיהם

Com.: The Mp heading here of *twice plene* (וֹ) is not exact since there are no occurrences of this lemma written defective וֹ. The more precise heading is given in the Mp heading at Lev 19:24, which reads *twice and plen*e (וֹ) correctly implying that this lemma does not occur elsewhere written defective וֹ.

JUDGES 9:28

וַיֹּאמֶר ׀ גַּעַל בֶּן־עֶבֶד מִי־אֲבִימֶלֶךְ וּמִי־שְׁכֶם כִּי נַעַבְדֶנּוּ הֲלֹא בֶן־יְרֻבַּעַל וּזְבֻל פְּקִידוֹ עִבְדוּ אֶת־
אַנְשֵׁי חֲמוֹר אֲבִי שְׁכֶם וּמַדּוּעַ נַעַבְדֶנּוּ אֲנָחְנוּ:

9:28   וּזְבֻל

Unique   ל   Mp

Com.: The Masorah notes the *sole* occurrence of this lemma with a וֹ cj., to distinguish it from its more numerous occurrences (7x) without a cj., *five* of which occur in this chapter in vv. 30, 36[a], 36[b], 38, and 41.

9:28   פְּקִידוֹ

Unique   לֹ   Mp

9:28   וּמַדּוּעַ

Ten times   יֹ   Mp

1–5   **Num 12:8; 16:3; Judg 9:28; 11:7; 11:26**
6–10 **1 Sam 20:2; 2 Sam 18:11; 19:44; 1 Kgs 1:13; 2:43**

וּמַדּוּעַ *ten times*, and their references   ומדוע יֹ וסימנהון   Mm

1–5	Num 12:8	ומדוע לא יראתם
	Num 16:3	תתנשאו על קהל
	Judg 9:28	נעבדנו
	Judg 11:7	באתם
	Judg 11:26	הצלתם
6–10	1 Sam 20:2	יסתיר
	2 Sam 18:11	הכיתו
	2 Sam 19:44	הקלתני
	{2 Sam 18:11}	{הכיתו שם}
	<1 Kgs 1:13>	
	1 Kgs 2:43	לא שמרת

Com.: The Masorah notes the *ten* occurrences of this lemma with a ו cj., to distinguish them from its more numerous occurrences (61x) without a cj.

In the Mm, list *two* sets of catchwords have been given for the 2 Sam 18:11 reference, but none has been given for the 1 Kgs 1:13 reference.

JUDGES 9:29

וּמִי יִתֵּן אֶת־הָעָם הַזֶּה בְּיָדִי וְאָסִירָה אֶת־אֲבִימֶלֶךְ וַיֹּאמֶר לַאֲבִימֶלֶךְ רַבֶּה צְבָאֲךָ וָצֵאָה׃

9:29   וּמִי יִתֵּן

Twice   בֹ   Mp

Num 11:29; Judg 9:29

		Mm	וּמִי יִתֵּן *twice* וּמִי יִתֵּן

Num 11:2	כל עם יהוה נביאים
<u>Judg 9:29</u>	ואסירה את

Com.: The Masorah notes the *two* occurrences of this lemma with a וֹ cj., to distinguish them from its more numerous occurrences (19x) without a cj.

The Mp heading at Num 11:29 adds catchwords אֶת־הָעָם הַזֶּה (את העם הזה) to refer the reader to this verse.

9:29	וְאָסִירָה

Three times	גׄ	Mp

Judg 9:29; 2 Sam 16:9; Isa 1:25

Com.: The Masorah notes the *three* occurrences of this lemma with the cohortative ה, to distinguish them from its single occurrence without this cohortative ending (וְאָסִיר) at Isa 10:13.

9:29	רַבֵּה

Unique	לׄ	Mp

Com.: This lemma is featured in a Masoretic list of *hapax legomena* pairings from the same stem, *one* of which occurs in the Torah, *one* in the Prophets, and *one* in the Writings; see Frensdorff, *Ochlah*, §56, and Díaz-Esteban, *Sefer Oklah we-Oklah*, §57.

9:29	צְבָאֶךָ

Unique	לׄ	Mp

JUDGES 9:31

וַיִּשְׁלַח מַלְאָכִים אֶל־אֲבִימֶלֶךְ בְּתָרְמָה לֵאמֹר הִנֵּה גַעַל בֶּן־עֶבֶד וְאֶחָיו בָּאִים שְׁכֶמָה וְהִנָּם צָרִים אֶת־הָעִיר עָלֶיךָ:

9:31	בְּתָרְמָה

Unique	לׄ	Mp

9:31   שְׁכְמָה

Six times   ו   Mp

1–5   **Gen 37:14**; Josh 24:1; **Judg 9:1; 9:31; 21:19**
6   **2 Chr 10:1**

שְׁכְמָה *six times*   שכמה ו   Mm

1–5	Gen 37:14	חברון
	Josh 24:1	יהושע
	Judg 9:31	גַעל בן עבד
	Judg 9:1	אבימלך
	Judg 21:19	(בשילה) [בשלו]
6	רְחַבְעָם *of Chronicles* (2 Chr 10:1)	רחבעם דדברי הימים

Com.: The Masorah notes the *six* occurrences of this lemma with the locative ה, to distinguish them from its more numerous occurrences (50x) without this adverbial ending (שְׁכֶם).

This distinction is implied in the additional notation in the Mm *of Chronicles* to the 2 Chr 10:1 reference, which distinguishes it from its parallel passage in 1 Kgs 12:1, where the lemma occurs as שְׁכֶם.

9:31   וְהִנָּם צָרִים

Unique   ל   Mp

Com.: The Masorah notes the *sole* occurrence of צָרִים with וְהִנָּם, to distinguish it from its occurrence with וְהִנֵּה (וְהִנֵּה צָרִים) at 2 Kgs. 6:25.

JUDGES 9:32

וְעַתָּה קוּם לַיְלָה אַתָּה וְהָעָם אֲשֶׁר־אִתָּךְ וֶאֱרֹב בַּשָּׂדֶה׃

9:32   וֶאֱרֹב

Unique   ל   Mp

JUDGES 9:33

וְהָיָ֣ה בַבֹּ֗קֶר כִּזְרֹ֤חַ הַשֶּׁ֙מֶשׁ֙ תַּשְׁכִּ֣ים וּפָשַׁטְתָּ֣ עַל־הָעִ֔יר וְהִנֵּה־ה֥וּא וְהָעָ֖ם אֲשֶׁר־אִתּ֣וֹ יֹצְאִ֣ים אֵלֶ֑יךָ וְעָשִׂ֣יתָ לּ֔וֹ כַּאֲשֶׁ֖ר תִּמְצָ֥א יָדֶֽךָ׃ ס

9:33   וְהָיָ֣ה בַבֹּ֗קֶר

Twice   בׄ   Mp

Judg 9:33; Ruth 3:13

Com.: The Masorah notes the *two* occurrences of בַבֹּ֗קֶר with וְהָיָ֣ה, to distinguish them from its more numerous occurrences (8x) with וַיְהִי (וַיְהִ֣י בַבֹּ֗קֶר).

9:33   כִּזְרֹ֤חַ

Twice   בׄ   Mp

<u>**Judg 9:33**</u>; Jonah 4:8

כִּזְרֹ֤חַ *twice* and defective   כזרח בׄ וחס   Mm

<u>Judg 9:33</u>   והיה בבקר
Jonah 4:8   רוח קדים (חרשית) [חרישית]

Com.: By noting that this lemma occurs *twice* and written defective וֹ, the Masorah is also implying (correctly) that this lemma does not occur elsewhere written plene וֹ.

9:33   עַל־הָעִ֔יר

Seventeen times   יׄז   Mp

1–5   **Gen 34:25**; <u>Deut 20:20</u>; <u>**Judg 9:33**</u>; <u>2 Sam 12:28</u>; **1 Kgs 20:12**
6–10   <u>2 Kgs 6:14</u>; 10:5; <u>24:11</u>; 25:4; **Jer 22:8**
11–15   **Jer 26:20; 32:29; 37:8;** 52:7; Ezek 10:2
16–17   <u>**Neh 11:9**</u>; 13:18

עַל־הָעִיר *seventeen times*	עַל הָעִיר יּז	Mm

1–5	Gen 34:25	כאבים
	Deut 20:20	מצור
	Judg 9:33	כזרח
	2 Sam 12:28	וחנה
	1 Kgs 20:12	שימו
6–10	2 Kgs 6:14	(ויקיפו) [ויקפו]
	2 Kgs 10:5	ואשר
	2 Kgs 24:11	ויבא
	2 Kgs 25:4	ותבקע
	Jer 22:8	ועברו
11–15	Jer 37:8	ושבו
	Jer 32:29	הנלחמים
	Jer 26:20	וגם איש
	Jer 52:7	ותבקע
	Ezek 10:2	בינות
16–17	Neh 11:9	ויואל
	Neh 13:18	כה עשו

And likewise every instance of וְגַנּוֹתִי apart from *one*　　　וכל וגנותי דכות ב מ א

Com.: The Masorah notes the *seventeen* occurrences of the phrase עַל־הָעִיר, to distinguish them from its slightly more numerous occurrences (21x) with the prep. אֶל (אֶל־הָעִיר).

This distinction is implied in the additional notations to the Mp headings at Gen 34:25, 2 Sam 12:28 and Neh 11:9, and at the end of all the Mm notes, that the verbal form וְגַנּוֹתִי also occurs with the phrase עַל־הָעִיר with *one* exception, that of 2 Kgs 19:34, where it occurs with אֶל (וְגַנּוֹתִי אֶל הָעִיר).

9:33　　וְהִנֵּה־הוּא

Five times　　ה　　Mp

1–5　　**Gen 42:27**; Deut 22:17; **Judg 9:33; Jer 18:3** (*qərê*); **2 Chr 26:20**

Com.: The Masorah notes the *five* occurrences of this lemma in the masc., to distinguish them from its *single* occurrence in the fem. (וְהִנֵּה־הִוא) at Gen 29:25.

JUDGES 9:36

וַיַּרְא־גַּעַל אֶת־הָעָם וַיֹּאמֶר אֶל־זְבֻל הִנֵּה־עָם יוֹרֵד מֵרָאשֵׁי הֶהָרִים וַיֹּאמֶר אֵלָיו זְבֻל אֵת צֵל הֶהָרִים אַתָּה רֹאֶה כָּאֲנָשִׁים: ס

9:36   עָם

Seventeen times qameṣ and similarly every ʾaṭnaḥ, qabbalah (= ẕaqep) and sôp pasûq apart from two

Mp   יז קמצֿ וכל אתנ֯
וקבל וסופֿ פסוק דכות בֿ מֿ בֿ

1–5   Num 23:9; 23:24; Deut 4:33; **Judg 9:36**; 9:37
6–10   **2 Kgs 13:7**; **15:10**; Isa 42:6; Ezek 33:31; **Joel 2:16**
11–15   Ps 18:44; **62:9**; **72:4**; **Prov 14:28**; Job 34:20
16–17   **Esth 3:8**; **1 Chr 17:21**

Com.: The Masorah notes the *seventeen* occurrences of עָם with a *qameṣ*, to distinguish them from its more numerous (100+) occurrences with a *pataḥ* (עַם).

This distinction is implied in the additional notation that עָם is also found with the accents *ẕaqep*, *ʾaṭnaḥ* and *sôp pasûq*, apart from *two times* (at Ruth 2:11 and 2 Chr 1:9) when, with a *ẕaqep gaḏôl*, it occurs as עָֽם.

The headings of the Mp at 2 Kgs 15:10, Ps 62:9, Prov 14:28 and 1 Chr 17:21 incorrectly read *sixteen* instead of *seventeen* no doubt a graphic error of ו *six* for ז *seven*.

In the Mp heading here, the term *qabbalah* (קבל) appears in place of *ẕaqep*; for a discussion of this term, see *BHQ, Judges*, 21*.

JUDGES 9:37

וַיֹּסֶף עוֹד גַּעַל לְדַבֵּר וַיֹּאמֶר הִנֵּה־עָם יוֹרְדִים מֵעִם טַבּוּר הָאָרֶץ וְרֹאשׁ־אֶחָד בָּא מִדֶּרֶךְ אֵלוֹן מְעוֹנְנִים:

9:37   יוֹרְדִים

Twice plene   בֿ מל   Mp

Judg 9:37; 1 Sam 9:27

Com.: The Masorah notes the *two* occurrences of this lemma written plene ו, to distinguish them from its *three* occurrences written defective ו (יֹרְדִים).

9:37   מְעוֹנְנִים

Three times   גׄ   Mp

Deut 18:14 (מְעֹנְנִים); Judg 9:37; Mic 5:11 (וּמְעוֹנְנִים)

Mm   מעוננים גׄ בׄ מלׄ וחד חסׄ   מְעוֹנְנִים *three times, twice* plene *and once* defective

Judg 9:37   מדרך אלון
Mic 5:11   והכרתי כשפים
Deut 18:14   אל מעננים ואל קסמים

וחד ועננים כפלשתים   And *once* (וְעֹנְנִים): Isa 2:6

Com.: The Masorah notes the *three* occurrences of this lemma, with and without וcj., *twice* written plene ו (here and Mic 5:11), and *once* written defective ו (Deut 18:14).

The Mm has an additional note, adding to these *three* occurrences the parallel form וְעֹנְנִים at Isa 2:6.

JUDGES 9:38

וַיֹּאמֶר אֵלָיו זְבֻל אַיֵּה אֵפוֹא פִיךָ אֲשֶׁר תֹּאמַר מִי אֲבִימֶלֶךְ כִּי נַעַבְדֶנּוּ הֲלֹא זֶה הָעָם אֲשֶׁר מָאַסְתָּה בּוֹ צֵא־נָא עַתָּה וְהִלָּחֶם בּוֹ: ס

9:38   מָאַסְתָּה

Twice plene   בׄ מלׄ   Mp

Judg 9:38; 1 Sam 15:26

Com.: The Masorah notes the *two* occurrences of this lemma written plene ה, to distinguish them from its *four* occurrences written defective ה (מָאַסְתָּ).

JUDGES 9:41

וַיֵּשֶׁב אֲבִימֶלֶךְ בָּארוּמָה וַיְגָרֶשׁ זְבֻל אֶת־גַּעַל וְאֶת־אֶחָיו מִשֶּׁבֶת בִּשְׁכֶם:

9:41   בָּארוּמָה

Unique   לׄ   Mp

Com.: This lemma is featured in a Masoretic list of words where an א is written but not read; see the Mm to <u>Num 11:4</u> *sub* וְהָאסַפְסֻף, Frensdorff, *Ochlah*, §103, and Dí-az-Esteban, *Sefer Oklah we-Oklah*, §86.

9:41   וְאֶת־אֶחָיו

Five times   הֹ   Mp

1–5   **Gen 47:11**; 47:12; **Deut 33:9**; **Judg 9:41**; Jer 35:3

וְאֶת־אֶחָיו *five times*   ואת אחיו הֹ   Mm

1–5	Gen 47:12	ויכלכל יוסף את
	<u>Gen 47:11</u>	ויושב יוסף את אביו
	<u>Deut 33:9</u>	האמר לאביו ולאמו
	<u>Judg 9:41</u>	בארומה ויגרש
	Jer 35:3	את יאזניה

Com.: The Masorah notes the *five* occurrences of this lemma with a ו cj., to distinguish them from its more numerous occurrences (10x) without a cj., *two* of which are in vv. 5 and 24.

9:41   בִּשְׁכֶם

Six times   וֹ

1–5   Gen 37:12; 37:13; Josh 24:25; 24:32; Judg 8:31
6–8   Judg 9:6; 9:26; **9:41**

The Mp heading here of *six times* is inexact since, as listed above, there are *eight* occurrences of this lemma. The note more precisely should have read *six times in the Prophets*.

The Masorah notes the *eight* occurrences of this lemma with the prep. בּ, to distinguish it from its more numerous occurrences (48x) without this preposition, *twenty* of which occur in this chapter.

Neither M^C nor M^A has a note on this lemma here.

JUDGES 9:43

וַיִּקַּ֣ח אֶת־הָעָ֗ם וַיֶּחֱצֵם֙ לִשְׁלֹשָׁ֣ה רָאשִׁ֔ים וַיֶּאֱרֹ֖ב בַּשָּׂדֶ֑ה וַיַּ֗רְא וְהִנֵּ֤ה הָעָם֙ יֹצֵ֣א מִן־הָעִ֔יר וַיָּ֥קָם עֲלֵיהֶ֖ם וַיַּכֵּֽם׃

9:43   וַיֶּחֱצֵ֖ם

Unique   ל   Mp

JUDGES 9:44

וַאֲבִימֶ֗לֶךְ וְהָרָאשִׁים֙ אֲשֶׁ֣ר עִמּ֔וֹ פָּשְׁט֕וּ וַיַּ֣עַמְד֔וּ פֶּ֖תַח שַׁ֣עַר הָעִ֑יר וּשְׁנֵ֣י הָרָאשִׁ֗ים פָּשְׁט֛וּ עַל־כָּל־ אֲשֶׁ֥ר בַּשָּׂדֶ֖ה וַיַּכּֽוּם׃

9:44   וְהָרָאשִׁים֙

Unique   ל   Mp

Com.: The Masorah notes the *sole* occurrence of this lemma with a וֹ cj., to distinguish it from its occurrence without a cj. at **Judg 7:20** and this verse.

9:44   הָרָאשִׁ֗ים

Twice   בֿ   Mp

Com.: See **Judg 7:20**.

9:44   וַיַּכּֽוּם

Eleven times   יֽא   Mp

Com.: See **Josh 7:5**.

JUDGES 9:45

וַאֲבִימֶ֜לֶךְ נִלְחָ֣ם בָּעִ֗יר כֹּ֚ל הַיּ֣וֹם הַה֔וּא וַיִּלְכֹּד֙ אֶת־הָעִ֔יר וְאֶת־הָעָ֥ם אֲשֶׁר־בָּ֖הּ הָרָ֑ג וַיִּתֹּץ֙ אֶת־הָעִ֔יר וַיִּזְרָעֶ֖הָ מֶֽלַח׃ פ

9:45   וְאֶת־הָעָ֥ם

Twelve times   יֿב   Mp

Com.: See **Josh 6:10**.

JUDGES 9:46

וַיִּשְׁמְע֗וּ כָּל־בַּעֲלֵ֣י מִגְדַּל־שְׁכֶ֑ם וַיָּבֹ֔אוּ אֶל־צְרִ֖יחַ בֵּ֥ית אֵ֥ל בְּרִֽית׃

9:46 בֵּ֥ית אֵ֥ל

Unique with the accents (*ṭippḥâ* and *mêr°kâ*) ל בטע Mp

Com.: The Masorah notes the *sole* occurrence of this lemma with these accents (*ṭippḥâ* and *mêr°kâ*), to distinguish them from its more numerous occurrences (45x) with other accents.

JUDGES 9:48

וַיַּ֨עַל אֲבִימֶ֜לֶךְ הַר־צַלְמ֗וֹן הוּא֮ וְכָל־הָעָ֣ם אֲשֶׁר־אִתּוֹ֒ וַיִּקַּח֩ אֲבִימֶ֨לֶךְ אֶת־הַקַּרְדֻּמּוֹת֙ בְּיָד֔וֹ וַיִּכְרֹת֙ שׂוֹכַ֣ת עֵצִ֔ים וַיִּשָּׂאֶ֕הָ וַיָּ֖שֶׂם עַל־שִׁכְמ֑וֹ וַיֹּ֨אמֶר אֶל־הָעָ֤ם אֲשֶׁר־עִמּוֹ֙ מָ֣ה רְאִיתֶ֣ם עָשִׂ֔יתִי מַהֲר֖וּ עֲשׂ֥וּ כָמֽוֹנִי׃

9:48 שׂוֹכַ֣ת

Unique ל Mp

9:48 וַיִּשָּׂאֶ֕הָ

Unique ל Mp

Com.: The Masorah notes the *sole* occurrence of this lemma with the fem. sfx., to distinguish it from its occurrence with the masc. sfx. (וַיִּשָּׂאֵ֖הוּ) at 2 Kgs 4:20.

9:48 מַהֲר֖וּ

Four times ד Mp

Gen 45:9; Judg 9:48; 2 Sam 15:14; Esth 5:5

Com.: The Masorah notes the *four* occurrences of this lemma with a *pataḥ* under the מ, to distinguish them from its *three* occurrences of this lemma with a *ḥîreq* (מִהֲר֖וּ).

In addition to listing the above *four* references, the Mm to Esth 5:5 has an additional note listing the *three* occurrences of this lemma with a *ḥîreq* under the מ.

JUDGES 9:49

וַיִּכְרְתוּ גַם־כָּל־הָעָם אִישׁ שׂוֹכֹה וַיֵּלְכוּ אַחֲרֵי אֲבִימֶלֶךְ וַיָּשִׂימוּ עַל־הַצְּרִיחַ וַיַּצִּיתוּ עֲלֵיהֶם אֶת־
הַצְּרִיחַ בָּאֵשׁ וַיָּמֻתוּ גַּם כָּל־אַנְשֵׁי מִגְדַּל־שְׁכֶם כְּאֶלֶף אִישׁ וְאִשָּׁה׃ פ

9:49   כְּאֶלֶף

Unique   ל   Mp

Com.: This lemma is featured in a Masoretic list of words occurring only *once* with a כ
at the beginning of the word; see Frensdorff, *Ochlah*, §19, and Díaz-Esteban, *Sefer
Oklah we-Oklah*, §20.

JUDGES 9:50

וַיֵּלֶךְ אֲבִימֶלֶךְ אֶל־תֵּבֵץ וַיִּחַן בְּתֵבֵץ וַיִּלְכְּדָהּ׃

9:50   תֵּבֵץ

<*Unique*>   <ל>   Mp

Com.: The Masorah notes the *sole* occurrence of this lemma without the prep. ב, to
distinguish it from its *two* occurrences with this prep. (בְּתֵבֵץ) in this verse, and in 2
Sam 11:21; see the next entry.

In M^L this lemma has a circellus but no note but, since this word only occurs *once*, the
note most probably should be *unique*.

9:50   בְּתֵבֵץ

Unique   ל   Mp

1–2   **Judg 9:50**; 2 Sam 11:21

Com.: The Mp heading here of *unique* is incorrect since there are *two* occurrences of
this lemma.

The Masorah notes the *two* occurrences of this lemma with the prep. ב, to distinguish
it from its *sole* occurrence without this prep. in the same verse; see directly above.

Neither M^C nor M^A has a note on this lemma here.

JUDGES 9:51

וּמִגְדַּל־עֹז הָיָה בְתוֹךְ־הָעִיר וַיָּנֻסוּ שָׁמָּה כָּל־הָאֲנָשִׁים וְהַנָּשִׁים וְכֹל בַּעֲלֵי הָעִיר וַיִּסְגְּרוּ בַּעֲדָם וַיַּעֲלוּ עַל־גַּג הַמִּגְדָּל:

9:51   וּמִגְדַּל

Seven times   ז   Mp

Com.: See **Josh 15:37**.

9:51   וְכֹל בַּעֲלֵי

Unique   ל   Mp

JUDGES 9:52

וַיָּבֹא אֲבִימֶלֶךְ עַד־הַמִּגְדָּל וַיִּלָּחֶם בּוֹ וַיִּגַּשׁ עַד־פֶּתַח הַמִּגְדָּל לְשָׂרְפוֹ בָאֵשׁ:

9:52   לְשָׂרְפוֹ

Unique   ל   Mp

Com.: The Masorah notes the *sole* occurrence of this lemma with the prep. ל, to distinguish it from its occurrence without this prep. (שָׂרְפוֹ) at Amos 2:1.

JUDGES 9:53

וַתַּשְׁלֵךְ אִשָּׁה אַחַת פֶּלַח רֶכֶב עַל־רֹאשׁ אֲבִימֶלֶךְ וַתָּרִץ אֶת־גֻּלְגָּלְתּוֹ:

9:53   וַתַּשְׁלֵךְ

Three times   ג   Mp

Gen 21:15; Judg 9:53; Ps 50:17

Com.: The Masorah notes the *three* occurrences of this lemma with a ו consec., to distinguish them from its *single* occurrence with a ו cj. (וְתַשְׁלֵךְ) at Dan 8:12.

This distinction is affirmed in the Mp heading at Dan 8:12, which reads *unique rapê* (e.g., with a ו cj.), and *three times dageš* (e.g., with ו consec.).

9:53   וַתָּרִץ

Unique   ל   Mp

Com.: This lemma is featured in a Masoretic list of words that occur *twice*, *once* with a
ו cj. (here), and *once* without (תָּרִיץ) at Ps 68:32; see Frensdorff, *Ochlah*, §1, and Díaz-Esteban, *Sefer Oklah we-Oklah*, §1.

9:53   אֶת־גֻּלְגָּלְתּוֹ

Unique   ל   Mp

Com.: The Masorah notes the *sole* occurrence of this lemma without a ו cj., to distinguish it from its occurrence with a cj. (וְאֶת־גֻּלְגָּלְתּוֹ) at 1 Chr 10:10.

> **JUDGES 9:54**
>
> וַיִּקְרָא מְהֵרָה אֶל־הַנַּעַר | נֹשֵׂא כֵלָיו וַיֹּאמֶר לוֹ שְׁלֹף חַרְבְּךָ וּמוֹתְתֵנִי פֶּן־יֹאמְרוּ לִי אִשָּׁה הֲרָגָתְהוּ
> וַיִּדְקְרֵהוּ נַעֲרוֹ וַיָּמֹת׃

9:54   וּמוֹתְתֵנִי

Twice   בֿ   Mp

Judg 9:54; 2 Sam 1:9 (וּמֹתְתֵנִי)

וּמוֹתְתֵנִי *twice, once* defective *and once* plene   ומותתני בֿ חד חסֿ וחד מל   Mm

Judg 9:54   ויקרא מהרה אל הנער
2 Sam 1:9   ויאמר אלי עמד נא עלי

Com.: The Masorah notes the *two* occurrences of this lemma, to distinguish them
from the *sole* occurrence of a similar form מוֹתְתֵנִי at Jer 20:17.

9:54   יאמרו לי

Twice   בֿ   Mp

Judg 9:54; Job 34:34

Com.: The Masorah notes the *two* occurrences of לִי with יֹאמְרוּ, to distinguish them
from the *two* occurrences of לִי with וַיֹּאמְרוּ (וַיֹּאמְרוּ לִי) at Exod 32:23 and Neh 1:3.

9:54   הֲרַגְתָּהוּ

Unique   ל   Mp

9:54   וַיִּדְקְרֵהוּ

Unique   ל   Mp

JUDGES 9:55

וַיִּרְאוּ אִישׁ־יִשְׂרָאֵל כִּי מֵת אֲבִימֶלֶךְ וַיֵּלְכוּ אִישׁ לִמְקֹמוֹ:

9:55   לִמְקֹמוֹ

Three times defective   ג חס   Mp

Com.: See **Judg 7:7**.

JUDGES 9:56

וַיָּשֶׁב אֱלֹהִים אֵת רָעַת אֲבִימֶלֶךְ אֲשֶׁר עָשָׂה לְאָבִיו לַהֲרֹג אֶת־שִׁבְעִים אֶחָיו:

9:56   וַיָּשֶׁב אֱלֹהִים

Unique   ל   Mp

Com.: The Masorah notes the *sole* occurrence of וַיָּשֶׁב with אֱלֹהִים, to distinguish it from its *four* occurrences with יְהוָה (וַיָּשֶׁב יְהוָה).

JUDGES 9:57

וְאֵת כָּל־רָעַת אַנְשֵׁי שְׁכֶם הֵשִׁיב אֱלֹהִים בְּרֹאשָׁם וַתָּבֹא אֲלֵיהֶם קִלֲלַת יוֹתָם בֶּן־יְרֻבָּעַל: פ

9:57   וְאֵת כָּל־רָעַת

Unique   ל   Mp

Com.: The Masorah notes the *sole* occurrence of this lemma with כָּל, to distinguish it from its occurrence without כָּל (וְאֵת רָעַת) at 1 Sam 25:39.

9:57   הֵשִׁיב אֱלֹהִים

Unique   ל   Mp

9:57   וַתָּבֹא אֲלֵיהֶם

Twice   בֿ   Mp

Judg 9:57; Jer 2:3 (תָּבֹא אֲלֵיהֶם)

Com.: The Masorah notes the *two* occurrences of this lemma, *once* with a ו consec. (here), and *once* without (תָּבֹא אֲלֵיהֶם) in Jer 2:3.

9:57   קִלְלַת

קִלְלַת *three times*   קללת גֿ   Mm

Deut 21:23	כי קללת אלהים תלוי
<u>Judg 9:57</u>	קללת יותם בן ירבעל
Prov 26:2	כן קללת חנם לא (תבוא) [תבא]

Com.: The Masorah notes the *three* occurrences of this lemma in the cstr., to distinguish them from its more numerous occurrences (7x) in the absol. (קְלָלָה).

JUDGES 10:1

וַיָּקָם אַחֲרֵי אֲבִימֶלֶךְ לְהוֹשִׁיעַ אֶת־יִשְׂרָאֵל תּוֹלָע בֶּן־פּוּאָה בֶּן־דּוֹדוֹ אִישׁ יִשָּׂשכָר וְהוּא־יֹשֵׁב בְּשָׁמִיר בְּהַר אֶפְרָיִם:

10:1   דּוֹדוֹ

Five times plene   הֿ מל   Mp

1–5   **<u>Judg 10:1</u>; 1 Sam 10:16; Amos 6:10; <u>1 Chr 11:12</u>; 11:26**

דּוֹדוֹ *five times* plene   דודו הֿ מל   Mm

1–5	<u>Judg 10:1</u>	תולע בן פואה בן דודו
	1 Sam 10:16	ויאמר שאול
	Amos 6:10	ונשאו דודו
	<u>1 Chr 11:12</u>	ואחריו אלעזר
	1 Chr 11:26	וגבורי החילים

Com.: The Masorah notes the *five* occurrences of this lemma written plene first ו, to distinguish them from its *seven* occurrences written defective first ו (דֹּדוֹ).

JUDGES 10:2

וַיִּשְׁפֹּט אֶת־יִשְׂרָאֵל עֶשְׂרִים וְשָׁלֹשׁ שָׁנָה וַיָּמָת וַיִּקָּבֵר בְּשָׁמִיר: פ

10:2 וַיִּקָּבֵר בְּשָׁמִיר

Unique ל Mp

JUDGES 10:4

וַיְהִי־לוֹ שְׁלֹשִׁים בָּנִים רֹכְבִים עַל־שְׁלֹשִׁים עֲיָרִים וּשְׁלֹשִׁים עֲיָרִים לָהֶם לָהֶם יִקְרְאוּ | חַוֹּת יָאִיר
עַד הַיּוֹם הַזֶּה אֲשֶׁר בְּאֶרֶץ הַגִּלְעָד:

10:4 לָהֶם לָהֶם

Unique ל Mp

Com.: This lemma is featured in a Masoretic list of words occurring together only *once*; see Frensdorff, *Ochlah*, §72.

10:4 בְּאֶרֶץ הַגִּלְעָד

Twice ב Mp

Judg 10:4; 1 Chr 2:22

Com.: The Masorah notes the *two* occurrences of בְּאֶרֶץ with הַגִּלְעָד, to distinguish *them* from its *two* occurrences with גִּלְעָד (בְּאֶרֶץ גִּלְעָד) at 1Kgs 4:19 and 1 Chr 5:9.

JUDGES 10:5

וַיָּמָת יָאִיר וַיִּקָּבֵר בְּקָמוֹן: פ

10:5 בְּקָמוֹן

Unique ל Mp

JUDGES 10:6

וַיֹּסִ֣פוּ | בְּנֵ֣י יִשְׂרָאֵ֗ל לַעֲשׂ֣וֹת הָרַע֮ בְּעֵינֵ֣י יְהוָה֒ וַיַּעַבְד֣וּ אֶת־הַבְּעָלִ֣ים וְאֶת־הָעַשְׁתָּר֗וֹת וְאֶת־אֱלֹהֵ֤י
אֲרָם֙ וְאֶת־אֱלֹהֵ֣י צִיד֔וֹן וְאֵת֙ | אֱלֹהֵ֣י מוֹאָ֔ב וְאֵת֙ אֱלֹהֵ֣י בְנֵי־עַמּ֔וֹן וְאֵ֖ת אֱלֹהֵ֣י פְלִשְׁתִּ֑ים וַיַּעַזְב֥וּ אֶת־
יְהוָ֖ה וְלֹ֥א עֲבָדֽוּהוּ׃

10:6   וַיֹּ֣סִפוּ

Three times written like this*   ג כֹּת כֵן   Mp

Judg 10:6; 13:1; 1 Chr 14:13

וַיֹּסִפוּ *three times* written like this   ויספו ג כת כן   Mm

קָמוֹן *of* וַיֹּסִיפוּ (Judg 10:6)   ויספו דקמון
Judg 13:1   ויהי איש
וַיֹּסִ֣פוּ עוֹד פְּלִשְׁתִּים *of Chronicles*   (ויספו) [ויסיפו] עוד פלשתים
(1 Chr 14:13)   דדברי הימים

Com.: There are many problems with this Masorah which, as Breuer notes in *The Aleppo Codex*, 278–79, has no doubt suffered corruption in its transmission.

* M^L, contrary to M (וַיֹּסִיפוּ), writes the lemma here defective second י (וַיֹּסִפוּ); see Breuer, *The Biblical Text*, 61. However, the reading of M (וַיֹּסִיפוּ) fits the references listed in the Mm rather than וַיֹּסִפוּ. This is seen in the additional notation *of Chronicles* to the 1 Chr 14:13 reference, since the notation contrasts this reference, which has the form וַיֹּסִ֣פוּ, with a parallel passage in 2 Sam 5:22, where the lemma occurs as וַיֹּסִ֣פוּ.

The number *three* does not fit a וַיֹּסִ֣פוּ lemma, since M has *five* such forms (Judg 3:12; 4:1; 20:22; 2 Sam 3:34; 5:22), and M^L has *seven* (since it writes the forms here and at Judg 13:1 also as וַיֹּסִ֣פוּ); see Breuer, *The Biblical Text*, 61 and 62.

In the Mm, the addition *of* קָמוֹן to the Judg 10:6 reference alludes to the place mentioned in the previous verse, and the catchwords וַיְהִי אִישׁ given for the Judg 13:1 reference actually belong to the following verse (13:2).

Both M^C and M^A read וַיֹּסִיפוּ. M^A has a Mp note here reading *three times written like this*, but M^C has no note.

10:6   עֲבָדוּהוּ

Unique plene   ל מֹל   Mp

עֲבָדוּהוּ   *three times* plene in this and another form   ג מֹל בליש   Mm

Judg 10:6	[עֲבָדוּהוּ]	ויעזבו את יהוה ולא עבדוהו
Ezek 48:19	[יַעֲבְדוּהוּ]	(העבד) [והעבד] העיר
Ps 72:11	[יַעֲבְדוּהוּ]	כל גוים יעבדוהו

Com.: The Masorah notes the *three* occurrences of this lemma in various forms written plene first וֹ, to distinguish them from its *three* occurrences in various forms written defective first וֹ, such as עֲבָדֻהוּ in Jer 28:14.

The heading of the Mp here of *unique plene* reflects the *sole* occurrence of the lemma in this particular form (עֲבָדוּהוּ).

JUDGES 10:8

וַיִּרְעֲצוּ וַיְרֹצְצוּ אֶת־בְּנֵי יִשְׂרָאֵל בַּשָּׁנָה הַהִיא שְׁמֹנֶה עֶשְׂרֵה שָׁנָה אֶת־כָּל־בְּנֵי יִשְׂרָאֵל אֲשֶׁר בְּעֵבֶר הַיַּרְדֵּן בְּאֶרֶץ הָאֱמֹרִי אֲשֶׁר בַּגִּלְעָד:

10:8
Half of the book   חצי הספ   Mp

Com.: In Mᴸ there is no circellus for this note.

JUDGES 10:9

וַיַּעַבְרוּ בְנֵי־עַמּוֹן אֶת־הַיַּרְדֵּן לְהִלָּחֵם גַּם־בִּיהוּדָה וּבְבִנְיָמֵין וּבְבֵית אֶפְרָיִם וַתֵּצֶר לְיִשְׂרָאֵל מְאֹד:

10:9   וּבְבִנְיָמִן

Twice, once plene and *once* defective   ב חד מֹל והד חֹס   Mp

Judg 10:9; 2 Chr 11:10 (וּבְבִנְיָמִן)

Mm   ובבנימין בׄ חד מל והד חס   וּבְבִנְיָמִן *twice, once* plene *and once* defective

Judg 10:9	גם ביהודה
2 Chr 11:10	ואת צרעה

Com.: The Masorah notes the *two* forms of this lemma, *one* written plene second י (here), and *one* written defective second י (2 Chr 11:10).

JUDGES 10:10

וַיִּזְעֲקוּ֙ בְּנֵ֣י יִשְׂרָאֵ֔ל אֶל־יְהוָ֖ה לֵאמֹ֑ר חָטָ֣אנוּ לָ֔ךְ וְכִ֤י עָזַ֙בְנוּ֙ אֶת־אֱלֹהֵ֔ינוּ וַֽנַּעֲבֹ֖ד אֶת־הַבְּעָלִֽים׃ פ

10:10   וְכִ֤י עָזַ֙בְנוּ֙

Mp   לׄ   *Unique*

Com.: The Masorah notes the *sole* occurrence of this lemma with a ו cj., to distinguish it from its *three* occurrences without a cj. (כִּי עָזַבְנוּ).

JUDGES 10:11

וַיֹּ֤אמֶר יְהוָה֙ אֶל־בְּנֵ֣י יִשְׂרָאֵ֔ל הֲלֹ֥א מִמִּצְרַ֖יִם וּמִן־הָ֣אֱמֹרִ֔י וּמִן־בְּנֵ֥י עַמּ֖וֹן וּמִן־פְּלִשְׁתִּֽים׃

10:11   וּמִן־בְּנֵ֥י

Mp   דׄ   *Four times*

Lev 1:14 (מִן־בְּנֵ֣י); **14:30** (מִן־בְּנֵ֣י); **Judg 10:11;** Joel 1:12 (מִן־בְּנֵ֣י)

Mm   ומן בני דׄ   וּמִן־בְּנֵ֥י *four times*

Lev 1:14	היונה
Lev 14:30	היונה
Judg 10:11	(מצרים) [ממצרים]
Joel 1:12	הגפן

Com.: The Masorah notes the *four* occurrences of this lemma where the prep. מִן is not joined to בְּנֵי, to distinguish them from the more numerous occurrences (100+) where the prep. מִן is attached to בְּנֵי (מִבְּנֵי/וּמִבְּנֵי).

This enumeration does not include the occurrences of this lemma in Chronicles (38x) and the Aramaic sections of Daniel and Ezra (5x).

The headings of the Mp and the Mm at <u>Lev 1:14</u> are more expansive reading *four times and similarly all Chronicles apart from seven.*

The heading of the Mp at Lev 14:30 reads the same, but mistakenly has *apart from two* instead of *apart from seven.*

10:11   וּמִן־פְּלִשְׁתִּים

Twice   בּ   Mp

Judg 10:11; <u>2 Chr 17:11</u>

Com.: The Masorah notes the *two* occurrences of this lemma with the separable prep. מִן, to distinguish *them* from its *two* occurrences with the inseparable prep. מ (וּמִפְּלִשְׁתִּים) at 2 Sam 8:12 and 1 Chr 18:11.

JUDGES 10:12
וְצִידוֹנִים וַעֲמָלֵק וּמָעוֹן לָחֲצוּ אֶתְכֶם וַתִּצְעֲקוּ אֵלַי וָאוֹשִׁיעָה אֶתְכֶם מִיָּדָם׃

10:12   וְצִידוֹנִים

Unique and plene   ל וּמל   Mp

Com.: By noting that this lemma is *unique* and written plene י, the Masorah is also implying (correctly) that this lemma does not occur elsewhere written defective י.

10:12   וּמָעוֹן

Twice   בּ   Mp

Judg 10:12; <u>1 Chr 2:45</u>

The Masorah notes the *two* occurrences of this lemma with a ו cj., to distinguish them from its more numerous occurrences (9x) without a cj.

10:12   וַתִּצְעֲקוּ

Unique   ל   Mp

Com.: The Masorah notes the *sole* occurrence of this lemma with a ו consec., to distinguish it from its *sole* occurrence without a ו (תִּצְעֲקוּ) at Isa 65:14.

10:12   וָאוֹשִׁיעָה

Unique   ל   Mp

JUDGES 10:13

וְאַתֶּם עֲזַבְתֶּם אוֹתִי וַתַּעַבְדוּ אֱלֹהִים אֲחֵרִים לָכֵן לֹא־אוֹסִיף לְהוֹשִׁיעַ אֶתְכֶם׃

10:13   אוֹסִיף

Nineteen times   יט   Mp

1–5   **Gen 8:21**^{a} (אֹסֵף); 8:21^b (אֹסֵף); Exod 10:29 (אֹסֵף); Josh 7:12; Judg 2:21
6–10   **Judg 10:13**; 1 Kgs 12:11; **12:14** (אֹסִיף); **2 Kgs 21:8** (אֹסִיף); Hos 1:6
11–15   Amos 7:8; 8:2; Jonah 2:5; Prov 23:35; **Job 34:32** (אֹסִיף)
16–19   Job 40:5; **2 Chr 10:11** (אֹסִיף); **10:14** (אֹסִיף); 33:8 (אֹסִיף)*

Com.: The Masorah notes the *nineteen* occurrences of this lemma written in various ways (plene and defective ו, plene and defective י, and doubly defective).

All the other Mp headings highlighted above restrict their notes to various books or particular writings.

Gen 8:21^a (אֹסֵף)	*Three times defective*, enumerating the *three* doubly defective occurrences at Gen 8:21^a, 8:21^b and Exod 10:29.
1 Kgs 12:14 (אֹסִיף)	*Twice written like this in the book*, refers to the *two* occurrences of this form in the book of Kings; here and at 2 Kgs 21:8.
2 Kgs 21:8 (אֹסִיף)	*Six times written like this*, refers to all *six* occurrences of this form.
Job 34:32 (אֹסִיף)	*Unique in the book*, refers to the *sole* occurrence of this form in Job.
2 Chr 10:11 (אֹסִיף)	*Six defective*, refers to all *six* occurrences of this form.
2 Chr 10:14 (אֹסִיף)	*Three times written (like this) in the book*, refers to the *three* occurrences of אֹסִיף in Chronicles.

* M^L, contrary to M (אָסִיף), reads 2 Chr 33:8 plene וֹ (אוֹסִיף); see Breuer, *The Biblical Text*, 338 and 393, and thus has only *five*, not *six* occurrences of the form אָסִיף. However, the enumeration inherent in the text of M is supported by the Mp headings at 2 Kgs 21:8 and at 2 Chr 10:11, which both read *six* times written defective (וֹ, e.g., אָסִיף), and by the Mp heading at 2 Chr 10:14, which reads *three times in the book* (thus assuming that 2 Chr 33:8 is written defective and not plene as in M^L).

JUDGES 10:14

לְכֹ֗וּ וְזַעֲקוּ֙ אֶל־הָ֣אֱלֹהִ֔ים אֲשֶׁ֥ר בְּחַרְתֶּ֖ם בָּ֑ם הֵ֧מָּה יוֹשִׁ֛יעוּ לָכֶ֖ם בְּעֵ֥ת צָרַתְכֶֽם׃

10:14   וְזַעֲקוּ

Three times with *pataḥ*   זַ֤   Mp

Judg 10:14; Jer 25:34; Joel 1:14

וְזַעֲקוּ *three times* with *pataḥ*   וזעקו ג פתח   Mm

Judg 10:14   לכו וזעקו אל האלהים
Jer 25:34   הילילו (הרועים) [הרעים]
Joel 1:14   קדשו צום

Com.: The Masorah notes the *three* occurrences of this lemma with *pataḥ* under the ז (imper.), to distinguish them from its *three* occurrences with *qameṣ* under the ז (וְזָעֲקוּ, perf.); see Ognibeni, *’Oklah*, §202, §295.

10:14   צָרַתְכֶם

Unique   ל   Mp

The Masorah notes the occurrence of this lemma with בְּעֵת with a sfx. (בְּעֵת צָרַתְכֶם), possibly to distinguish it from its *three* occurrences with בְּעֵת without a sfx. (בְּעֵת צָרָה).

JUDGES 10:15

וַיֹּאמְר֣וּ בְנֵֽי־יִשְׂרָאֵ֣ל אֶל־יְהוָה֮ חָטָאנוּ֒ עֲשֵׂה־אַתָּ֣ה לָ֗נוּ כְּכָל־הַטּ֣וֹב בְּעֵינֶ֑יךָ אַ֖ךְ הַצִּילֵ֥נוּ נָ֖א הַיּ֥וֹם
הַזֶּֽה׃

10:15   כְּכָל־הַטּ֣וֹב

Twice   בֿ   Mp

Judg 10:15; 1 Sam 11:10

Com.: The Masorah notes the *two* occurrences of this lemma with the prep. ב, to distinguish them from its *sole* occurrence with the prep. ב (בְּכָל־הַטּ֣וֹב) at Deut 26:11.

JUDGES 10:16

וַיָּסִ֜ירוּ אֶת־אֱלֹהֵ֤י הַנֵּכָר֙ מִקִּרְבָּ֔ם וַיַּֽעַבְד֖וּ אֶת־יְהוָ֑ה וַתִּקְצַ֥ר נַפְשׁ֖וֹ בַּעֲמַ֥ל יִשְׂרָאֵֽל׃ פ

10:16   וַתִּקְצַ֥ר

Four times   דֿ   Mp

Num 21:4; Judg 10:16; 16:16; Zech 11:8

Com.: The Masorah notes the *four* occurrences of this lemma with a ו consec., to distinguish *them* from its *sole* occurrence without a ו (תִּקְצַ֥ר) at Job 21:4.

10:16   בַּעֲמַ֥ל

Twice   בֿ   Mp

Judg 10:16; Ps 73:5

בַּעֲמַ֥ל *twice*, and their references   בעמל בֿ וסימנהון   Mm

Judg 10:16   ותקצר נפשו בעמל
Ps 73:5   בעמל אנוש (אינימו) [אינמו]

Com.: The Masorah notes the *two* occurrences of this lemma with the prep. ב, to distinguish them from its *three* occurrences without this prep. (עֲמַ֥ל).

JUDGES 10:17

וַיִּצָּעֲקוּ֙ בְּנֵ֣י עַמּ֔וֹן וַֽיַּחֲנ֖וּ בַּגִּלְעָ֑ד וַיֵּאָֽסְפוּ֙ בְּנֵ֣י יִשְׂרָאֵ֔ל וַֽיַּחֲנ֖וּ בַּמִּצְפָּֽה׃

10:17   וַיִּצָּעֲקוּ֙

Three times   גֿ   Mp

Judg 10:17; 1 Sam 13:4; 2 Kgs 3:21

Com.: The Masorah notes the *three* occurrences of this lemma in the *niphal*, to distinguish them from its more numerous occurrences (7x) in the *qal* (וַיִּצְעֲקוּ); see Ognibeni, *'Oklah*, §301.

10:17   וַיֵּאָסְפוּ֙

Twelve times   יֿב   Mp

Com.: See **Judg 9:6**.

JUDGES 10:18

וַיֹּאמְר֨וּ הָעָ֜ם שָׂרֵ֣י גִלְעָד֮ אִ֣ישׁ אֶל־רֵעֵהוּ֒ מִ֣י הָאִ֗ישׁ אֲשֶׁ֤ר יָחֵל֙ לְהִלָּחֵ֔ם בִּבְנֵ֖י עַמּ֑וֹן יִהְיֶ֣ה לְרֹ֔אשׁ לְכֹ֖ל יֹשְׁבֵ֥י גִלְעָֽד׃ פ

10:18   וַיֹּאמְר֨וּ הָעָ֜ם

Three times   גֿ   Mp

Com.: See **Josh 24:24**

In M^L the circellus has been placed only on הָעָ֜ם but, since this form occurs more than *three times*, the note must refer, with M^C and M^A, to the phrase וַיֹּאמְר֨וּ הָעָ֜ם.

10:18   אֲשֶׁ֤ר יָחֵל֙

Unique   לֿ   Mp

10:18   לְרֹ֔אשׁ

Twenty-four times   כֿד   Mp

Com.: See **Judg 5:30**.

JUDGES 11:1

וְיִפְתָּח הַגִּלְעָדִי הָיָה גִּבּוֹר חַיִל וְהוּא בֶּן־אִשָּׁה זוֹנָה וַיּוֹלֶד גִּלְעָד אֶת־יִפְתָּח:

11:1   וְיִפְתָּח

Three times   גׄ   Mp

Josh 15:43; Judg 11:1; Job 11:5 (וְיִפְתַּח)

וְיִפְתָּח *three times*, *twice* with *qameṣ* and *once* with *paṭaḥ*,   ויפתח גׄ בׄ קמץ וחד פתח   Mm
one is the name of a person, and *one* is the   חד שם בר נשא וחד
name of a town, and *one* means *to open*   שם קריה וחד לשון פתוחה

Com.: The Masorah notes the *three* occurrences of this lemma, with *qameṣ* and with *paṭaḥ*, in *three* different meanings. *One* as the name of a person *Jephthah* (here), *one* as the name of a town *Iphtah* (Josh 15:43), and *one* as a verbal form *and would open* (*his lips*, Job 11:5).

This lemma with *qameṣ* (Josh 15:43 and here) is featured in a Masoretic list of homonymous doublets; see Frensdorff, *Ochlah*, §59, and Díaz-Esteban, *Sefer Oklah we-Oklah*, §60.

It is also featured in a Masoretic list of *sixteen* verses in which the initial word with a וֹ cj. and the last word (without a וֹ cj.) of the verse are the same see **1 Kgs 22:48**.

11:1   וַיּוֹלֶד גִּלְעָד

Unique   לׄ   Mp

JUDGES 11:2

וַתֵּלֶד אֵשֶׁת־גִּלְעָד לוֹ בָּנִים וַיִּגְדְּלוּ בְנֵי־הָאִשָּׁה וַיְגָרְשׁוּ אֶת־יִפְתָּח וַיֹּאמְרוּ לוֹ לֹא־תִנְחַל בְּבֵית־
אָבִינוּ כִּי בֶּן־אִשָּׁה אַחֶרֶת אָתָּה:

11:2   בְּבֵית־אָבִינוּ

Twice   בׄ   Mp

Gen 31:14; Judg 11:2

בְּבֵית־אָבִינוּ *twice* ב בית אבינו Mm

Gen 31:14 העוד לנו חלק
<u>Judg 11:2</u> ויגרש את יפתח

Com.: The Mp heading at Gen 31:14 adds catchwords לֹא תִנְחַל) לא תנחל) to refer the reader to this verse.

JUDGES 11:3

וַיִּבְרַ֤ח יִפְתָּח֙ מִפְּנֵ֣י אֶחָ֔יו וַיֵּ֖שֶׁב בְּאֶ֣רֶץ ט֑וֹב וַיִּֽתְלַקְּט֤וּ אֶל־יִפְתָּח֙ אֲנָשִׁ֣ים רֵיקִ֔ים וַיֵּצְא֖וּ עִמּֽוֹ׃ פ

11:3 וַיִּבְרַ֤ח יִפְתָּח֙

Unique ל Mp

11:3 בְּאֶ֣רֶץ ט֑וֹב

Unique ל Mp

Com.: The Masorah notes the *sole* occurrence of this lemma with the prep. בּ, to distinguish it from its occurrence with the prep. מ (מֵאֶ֣רֶץ ט֑וֹב) in v. 5; see directly below.

11:3 וַיִּֽתְלַקְּט֤וּ

Unique ל Mp

JUDGES 11:4

וַיְהִ֖י מִיָּמִ֑ים וַיִּלָּחֲמ֥וּ בְנֵי־עַמּ֖וֹן עִם־יִשְׂרָאֵֽל׃

11:4 וַיְהִ֖י מִיָּמִ֑ים

Three times ג Mp

Com.: See <u>Josh 23:1</u>.

JUDGES 11:5

וַיְהִ֗י כַּאֲשֶׁר־נִלְחֲמ֥וּ בְנֵֽי־עַמּ֖וֹן עִם־יִשְׂרָאֵ֑ל וַיֵּֽלְכוּ֙ זִקְנֵ֣י גִלְעָ֔ד לָקַ֥חַת אֶת־יִפְתָּ֖ח מֵאֶ֥רֶץ טֽוֹב׃

וַיְהִ֗י　11:5

Twice with the accent (*zaqep gadôl*) in the book　　ב בטע בסיפֿ　　Mp

Judg 6:7; 11:5

וַיְהִ֗י *twice* with the accent (*zaqep gadôl*) in the book　　ויהי ב בטע בסיפֿ　　Mm

Judg 6:7　　כי זעקו
Judg 11:5　　כאשר נלחמו

Com.: The Masorah notes the *two* occurrences of this lemma in the book with the accent *zaqep gadôl*.

מֵאֶ֥רֶץ טֽוֹב　11:5

Unique　ל　Mp

Com.: The Masorah notes the *sole* occurrence of this lemma with the prep. מ, to distinguish it from its occurrence with the prep. ב (בְּאֶ֥רֶץ טֽוֹב) in v. 3; see directly above.

Com.: In M[L] above the ל there is a Mp note of י, which has no associated circellus and does not match any of the immediate words in its vicinity.

JUDGES 11:6

וַיֹּאמְר֣וּ לְיִפְתָּ֗ח וְהָיִ֙יתָה֙ לָּ֔בָה וְהָיִ֤יתָה לָּ֙נוּ֙ לְקָצִ֔ין וְנִלְחֲמָ֖ה בִּבְנֵ֥י עַמּֽוֹן׃

וְהָיִ֤יתָה　11:6

Twice plene　ב מל　Mp

Judg 11:6; 2 Sam 5:2 (הָיִ֥יתָה)

Com.: The Masorah notes the *two* occurrences of this lemma written plene second י, to distinguish them from its *sole* occurrence written defective second י (וְהָיִ֖תָה) at 2 Sam 10:11.

11:6 וְנִלְחֲמָה

Four times דֹ Mp

Com.: See **Judg 1:3**.

> ### JUDGES 11:7
>
> וַיֹּאמֶר יִפְתָּח לְזִקְנֵי גִלְעָד הֲלֹא אַתֶּם שְׂנֵאתֶם אוֹתִי וַתְּגָרְשׁוּנִי מִבֵּית אָבִי וּמַדּוּעַ בָּאתֶם אֵלַי
> עַתָּה כַּאֲשֶׁר צַר לָכֶם:

11:7 וַתְּגָרְשׁוּנִי

Twice בֹ Mp

Com.: The Mp heading here of *twice* is incorrect since this is this lemma's only occurrence. M^A correctly reads *unique*, and M^C reads *unique and plene* (ו).

11:7 וּמַדּוּעַ

Ten times יֹ Mp

1–5   **Num 12:8; 16:3; Judg 9:28; 11:7; 11:26**
6–10 **1 Sam 20:2; 2 Sam 18:11; 19:44; 1 Kgs 1:13; 2:43**

וּמַדּוּעַ *ten times* מדוע י Mm

1–5	Num 12:8	לא יראתם
	Num 16:3	ומדוע תתנשאו על קהל
	Judg 9:28	ומדוע נעבדנו
	Judg 11:7	ומדוע באתם
	Judg 11:26	לא הצלתם
6–10	1 Sam 20:2	ומדוע יסתיר אבי
	2 Sam 18:11	לא (הכיהו) [הכיתו] שם
	2 Sam 19:44	ומדוע הקלתני
	1 Kgs 1:13	(אדניה) [אדניהו]
	1 Kgs 2:43	לא שמרת

Com.: The Masorah notes the *ten* occurrences of this lemma with a ו cj., to distinguish
them from its more numerous occurrences (61x) without a cj.

JUDGES 11:8

וַיֹּאמְרוּ זִקְנֵי גִלְעָד אֶל־יִפְתָּח לָכֵן עַתָּה שַׁבְנוּ אֵלֶיךָ וְהָלַכְתָּ עִמָּנוּ וְנִלְחַמְתָּ בִּבְנֵי עַמּוֹן וְהָיִיתָ לָּנוּ
לְרֹאשׁ לְכֹל יֹשְׁבֵי גִלְעָד:

11:8   לְרֹאשׁ

Five times in the book   ה בסיפ   Mp

1–5   **Judg 5:30**; **10:18**; **11:8**; **11:9**; 11:11

Com.: The Mp heading here notes the *five* occurrences of this lemma in the book, to distinguish them from its more numerous occurrences (19x) in other books; see directly below at v. 9.

The Mp headings at Judg 10:18 and 11:9 note all *twenty-four* occurrences of this lemma throughout the Bible. However, the Mp heading at Judg 5:30 mistakenly reads *twenty-one* instead of *twenty-four*.

JUDGES 11:9

וַיֹּאמֶר יִפְתָּח אֶל־זִקְנֵי גִלְעָד אִם־מְשִׁיבִים אַתֶּם אוֹתִי לְהִלָּחֵם בִּבְנֵי עַמּוֹן וְנָתַן יְהוָה אוֹתָם לְפָנָי
אָנֹכִי אֶהְיֶה לָכֶם לְרֹאשׁ:

11:9   מְשִׁיבִים

Unique   ל   Mp

11:9   לְרֹאשׁ

Twenty-four times   כֹּד   Mp

Com.: See **Judg 5:30**.

JUDGES 11:10

וַיֹּאמְרוּ זִקְנֵי־גִלְעָד אֶל־יִפְתָּח יְהוָה יִהְיֶה שֹׁמֵעַ בֵּינוֹתֵינוּ אִם־לֹא כִדְבָרְךָ כֵּן נַעֲשֶׂה:

11:10   בֵּינוֹתֵינוּ

Three times   ג   Mp

Com.: See **Josh 22:34**.

JUDGES 11:11

וַיֵּ֨לֶךְ יִפְתָּ֜ח עִם־זִקְנֵ֣י גִלְעָ֗ד וַיָּשִׂ֨ימוּ הָעָ֥ם אוֹת֛וֹ עֲלֵיהֶ֖ם לְרֹ֣אשׁ וּלְקָצִ֑ין וַיְדַבֵּ֨ר יִפְתָּ֧ח אֶת־כָּל־דְּבָרָ֛יו
לִפְנֵ֥י יְהוָ֖ה בַּמִּצְפָּֽה׃ פ

11:11 וּלְקָצִין

Unique ל Mp

Com.: The Masorah notes the *sole* occurrence of this lemma with a ו cj., to distinguish it from its *sole* occurrence without a cj. in v. 6.

11:11 אֶת־כָּל־דְּבָרָיו

Twice ב Mp

Judg 11:11; Amos 7:10

Com.: The Masorah notes the *two* occurrences of this lemma with כָּל, to distinguish them from its *five* occurrences without כָּל (אֶת דְּבָרָיו).

JUDGES 11:12

וַיִּשְׁלַ֤ח יִפְתָּח֙ מַלְאָכִ֔ים אֶל־מֶ֥לֶךְ בְּנֵֽי־עַמּ֖וֹן לֵאמֹ֑ר מַה־לִּ֣י וָלָ֔ךְ כִּֽי־בָ֥אתָ אֵלַ֖י לְהִלָּ֥חֵ֖ם בְּאַרְצִֽי׃

11:12 לִּי וָלָךְ

Four times ד Mp

Judg 11:12; 1 Kgs 17:18; 2 Kgs 3:13; **2 Chr 35:21**

Com.: The Masorah notes the *four* occurrences of this lemma with a *qameṣ* under the ו, to distinguish them from its *sole* occurrence with a *šəwâ* under the ו (לִי וְלָךְ) at 1 Kgs 17:13.

JUDGES 11:13

וַיֹּ֣אמֶר מֶלֶךְ֩ בְּנֵֽי־עַמּ֨וֹן אֶל־מַלְאֲכֵ֣י יִפְתָּ֗ח כִּֽי־לָקַ֨ח יִשְׂרָאֵ֤ל אֶת־אַרְצִי֙ בַּעֲלוֹת֣וֹ מִמִּצְרַ֔יִם מֵֽאַרְנ֥וֹן
וְעַד־הַיַּבֹּ֖ק וְעַד־הַיַּרְדֵּ֑ן וְעַתָּ֛ה הָשִׁ֥יבָה אֶתְהֶ֖ן בְּשָׁלֽוֹם׃

11:13 אֶל־מַלְאֲכֵי

Unique ל Mp

Com.: This lemma is featured in a Masoretic list of words occurring *once* with a preceding אֶל (here), and *once* with a preceding עַל (**1 Sam 19:20**); see Frensdorff, *Ochlah*, §2, and Díaz-Esteban, *Sefer Oklah we-Oklah*, §2.

11:13   בַּעֲלוֹתוֹ

Three times   גׄ   Mp

Judg 11:13; 1 Sam 15:2 (בַּעֲלֹתוֹ); **Isa 11:16** (עֲלֹתוֹ)

Com.: The Masorah notes the *three* occurrences of this lemma, with and without the prep. בַּ, *twice* written defective וֹ (1 Sam 15:2 and Isa 11:16), and *once* written plene וֹ (here).

11:13   וְעַד־הַיַּבֹּק

Twice   בׄ   Mp

Judg 11:13; 11:22

Com.: The Masorah notes the *two* occurrences of וְעַד with הַיַּבֹּק, to distinguish them from its *two* occurrences with יַבֹּק (וְעַד יַבֹּק) at Deut 3:16 and Josh 12:2.

11:13   וְעַד־הַיַּרְדֵּן

Twice   בׄ   Mp

Judg 11:13; 11:22

Com.: The Masorah notes the *two* occurrences of this lemma with a וֹ cj., to distinguish them from its *five* occurrences without a cj.

In M^L this lemma has no circellus.

11:13   הָשִׁיבָה

Three times   גׄ   Mp

Judg 11:13; Ps 35:17; 51:14

הַשִׁיבָה *three times*, and their references   השיבה ג׳ וסימנהון   Mm

Judg 11:13   השיבה אתהן בשלום
Ps 35:17   השיבה נפשי משאיהם
Ps 51:14   השיבה לי ששון (יש׳) [ישעד]

Com.: The Masorah notes the *three* occurrences of this lemma with the lengthened imper., to distinguish them from its more numerous occurrences (14x) with the regular imper. (הָשֵׁב).

JUDGES 11:14

וַיּ֣וֹסֶף ע֤וֹד יִפְתָּח֙ וַיִּשְׁלַ֣ח מַלְאָכִ֔ים אֶל־מֶ֖לֶךְ בְּנֵ֥י עַמּֽוֹן׃

11:14   וַיּ֣וֹסֶף

Seven times plene   ז׳ מל׳   Mp

1–5   **Num 22:26; Judg 11:14; 1 Sam 20:17; 23:4; 1 Kgs 16:33**
6–7   **Isa 7:10; 2 Chr 28:22**

Com.: The Masorah notes the *seven* occurrences of this lemma written plene וֹ, to distinguish them from its more numerous occurrences (22x) written defective וֹ (וַיֹּסֶף); see **1 Sam 9:8**.

JUDGES 11:16

כִּ֖י בַּעֲלוֹתָ֣ם מִמִּצְרָ֑יִם וַיֵּ֨לֶךְ יִשְׂרָאֵ֤ל בַּמִּדְבָּר֙ עַד־יַם־ס֔וּף וַיָּבֹ֖א קָדֵֽשָׁה׃

11:16   קָדֵֽשָׁה

Twice   ב׳   Mp

Num 13:26; **Judg 11:16**

קָדֵשָׁה *twice*   קדשה ב׳   Mm

Num 13:26   (מלכו) וילכו ויבאו
Judg 11:16   וילך ישראל

Com.: The Masorah notes the *two* occurrences of this lemma with the locative ה, to distinguish them from its more numerous occurrences (13x) without this adverbial ending (קָדֵשׁ).

JUDGES 11:17

וַיִּשְׁלַ֣ח יִשְׂרָאֵ֣ל מַלְאָכִ֣ים ׀ אֶל־מֶ֣לֶךְ אֱד֗וֹם ׀ לֵאמֹר֙ אֶעְבְּרָה־נָּ֣א בְאַרְצֶ֔ךָ וְלֹ֤א שָׁמַע֙ מֶ֣לֶךְ אֱד֔וֹם וְגַ֨ם אֶל־מֶ֤לֶךְ מוֹאָב֙ שָׁלַ֔ח וְלֹ֖א אָבָ֑ה וַיֵּ֖שֶׁב יִשְׂרָאֵ֥ל בְּקָדֵֽשׁ׃

11:17   שָׁלַח וְלֹא

Unique   ל   Mp

JUDGES 11:18

וַיֵּ֣לֶךְ בַּמִּדְבָּ֗ר וַיָּ֜סָב אֶת־אֶ֤רֶץ אֱדוֹם֙ וְאֶת־אֶ֣רֶץ מוֹאָ֔ב וַיָּבֹ֤א מִמִּזְרַח־שֶׁ֙מֶשׁ֙ לְאֶ֣רֶץ מוֹאָ֔ב וַֽיַּחֲנ֖וּן בְּעֵ֣בֶר אַרְנ֑וֹן וְלֹא־בָ֙אוּ֙ בִּגְב֣וּל מוֹאָ֔ב כִּ֥י אַרְנ֖וֹן גְּב֥וּל מוֹאָֽב׃

11:18   וַיָּסָב

Unique   ל   Mp

Com.: The Masorah notes the *sole* occurrence of this lemma (*qal* of סָבַב), to distinguish it from the *nine* occurrences in its more usual form וַיִּסֹּב.

11:18   לְאֶרֶץ מוֹאָב

Unique   ל   Mp

Com.: The Masorah notes the *sole* occurrence of this lemma with the prep. ל, to distinguish it from its *three* occurrences without this prep. (אֶרֶץ מוֹאָב), *one* of which occurs in this verse, and *one* in v. 15.

11:18   וַיַּחֲנוּן

Unique   ל   Mp

Com.: The Masorah notes the *sole* occurrence of this lemma with a paragogic נ, to distinguish it from more numerous occurrences (81x) without this נ (וַיַּחֲנוּ).

This lemma is featured in a Masoretic list of words occurring only *once* with a final נ; see Frensdorff, *Ochlah,* §75, and Ognibeni, *'Oklah,* §72.

11:18   וְלֹא־בָאוּ

Unique   ל   Mp

Com.: The Masorah notes the *sole* occurrence of this lemma with a ו cj., to distinguish it from its *three* occurrences without a cj.

JUDGES 11:20

וְלֹא־הֶאֱמִין סִיחוֹן אֶת־יִשְׂרָאֵל עֲבֹר בִּגְבֻלוֹ וַיֶּאֱסֹף סִיחוֹן אֶת־כָּל־עַמּוֹ וַיַּחֲנוּ בְּיָהְצָה וַיִּלָּחֶם עִם־
יִשְׂרָאֵל:

11:20   בִּגְבֻלוֹ

Five times defective   ה חסֹ   Mp

1–5   **Gen 23:17** (גְבֻלוֹ); **Num 20:21; 21:23; Judg 11:20**; Ezek 43:12 (גְבֻלֽוֹ)

Com.: The Masorah notes the *five* occurrences of this lemma in various forms written defective ו, to distinguish them from its *four* occurrences written plene ו (גְבוּלוֹ).

11:20   וַיִּלָּחֶם עִם־יִשְׂרָאֵל

Twice   בֹ   Mp

Exod 17:8; **Judg 11:20**

Com.: The Masorah notes the *two* occurrences of this lemma with the prep. עִם, to distinguish them from its *three* occurrences with the prep. ב (וַיִּלָּחֶם בְּיִשְׂרָאֵל).

JUDGES 11:21

וַיִּתֵּן יְהֹוָה אֱלֹהֵי־יִשְׂרָאֵל אֶת־סִיחוֹן וְאֶת־כָּל־עַמּוֹ בְּיַד יִשְׂרָאֵל וַיַּכּוּם וַיִּירַשׁ יִשְׂרָאֵל אֵת כָּל־אֶרֶץ
הָאֱמֹרִי יוֹשֵׁב הָאָרֶץ הַהִיא:

11:21   וַיַּכּוּם

Eleven times   יאֹ   Mp

Com.: See **Josh 7:5.**

11:21   יוֹשֵׁב

Four times plene in the book   ד מל בס   Mp

Com.: See **Judg 1:9.**

JUDGES 11:22

וַיִּירְשׁוּ אֵת כָּל־גְּבוּל הָאֱמֹרִי מֵאַרְנוֹן וְעַד־הַיַּבֹּק וּמִן־הַמִּדְבָּר וְעַד־הַיַּרְדֵּן׃

11:22   וְעַד־הַיַּבֹּק

Twice   בׄ   Mp

Com.: See directly above at **Judg 11:13.**

11:22   וְעַד־הַיַּרְדֵּן

Twice   בׄ   Mp

Com.: See directly above at **Judg 11:13.**

JUDGES 11:24

הֲלֹא אֵת אֲשֶׁר יוֹרִישְׁךָ כְּמוֹשׁ אֱלֹהֶיךָ אוֹתוֹ תִירָשׁ וְאֵת כָּל־אֲשֶׁר הוֹרִישׁ יְהוָה אֱלֹהֵינוּ מִפָּנֵינוּ אוֹתוֹ נִירָשׁ׃

11:24   יוֹרִישְׁךָ

Unique   לׄ   Mp

11:24   תִירָשׁ

Unique   לׄ   Mp

Com.: The Masorah notes the *sole* occurrence of this lemma with a *qameṣ* under the ר, to distinguish it from its *sole* occurrence with a *paṭaḥ* (תִירַשׁ) at Prov 30:23.

JUDGES 11:25

וְעַתָּה הֲטוֹב טוֹב אַתָּה מִבָּלָק בֶּן־צִפּוֹר מֶלֶךְ מוֹאָב הֲרוֹב רָב עִם־יִשְׂרָאֵל אִם־נִלְחֹם נִלְחַם בָּם:

11:25   הֲטוֹב

Four times   דֿ   Mp

Judg 11:25; **18:19**; Job 10:3; 13:9

הֲטוֹב *four times*, and their references   הטוב דֿ וסימנהון   Mm

Judg 11:25	מבלק
Judg 18:19	היותך
Job 13:9	יחקר
Job 10:3	תעשק

Com.: The Masorah notes the *four* occurrences of this lemma with the interrog. ה, to distinguish them from its more numerous occurrences (46x) with the def. article (הַטּוֹב); see Ognibeni, *'Oklah*, §15E.

11:25   מִבָּלָק

Unique   לֿ   Mp

Com.: The Masorah notes the *sole* occurrence of this lemma with the prep. מ, to distinguish it from its more numerous occurrences (40x) without this preposition.

11:25   הֲרוֹב

Three times   גֿ   Mp

Judg 11:25; **Job 11:2** (הֲרֹב); **40:2** (הֲרֹב)

Com.: The Masorah notes the *three* occurrences of this lemma, *twice* written defective ו (Job 11:2 and 40:2), and *once* written plene ו (here).

11:25   נִלְחֹם

Unique   לֹ   Mp

Com.: The Masorah notes the *sole* occurrence of this lemma with a *ḥolem* (infin. absol.), to distinguish it from its more numerous occurrences (12x) with a *pataḥ* (נִלְחַם, perf.), *one* of which is in the same verse, and from its more numerous occurrences (11x) with a *qameṣ* (נִלְחָם, ptcp.).

Com.: In M^L there are two circelli on this lemma.

11:25   נִלְחַם

Twelve times   יֹב   Mp

Com.: See **Judg 9:17**.

> ### JUDGES 11:26
>
> בְּשֶׁ֣בֶת יִ֠שְׂרָאֵל בְּחֶשְׁבּ֨וֹן וּבִבְנוֹתֶ֜יהָ וּבְעַרְע֣וֹר וּבִבְנוֹתֶ֗יהָ וּבְכָל־הֶֽעָרִים֙ אֲשֶׁר֙ עַל־יְדֵ֣י אַרְנ֔וֹן שְׁלֹ֥שׁ מֵא֖וֹת שָׁנָ֑ה וּמַדּ֛וּעַ לֹֽא־הִצַּלְתֶּ֖ם בָּעֵ֥ת הַהִֽיא׃

11:26   בְּשֶׁבֶת

בְּשֶׁבֶת *twice*   בשבת בֹ   Mm^1

Judg 11:26   בשבת ישראל בחשבון
Ezek 38:14   בשבת עמי ישראל

And *once* (כְּשֶׁבֶת): Esth 1:2   [אחשורוש] (אחשורש) וחד כשבת המלך

בְּשֶׁבֶת *twice*   בשבת בֹ   Mm^2

Judg 11:26   ישראל בחשבון
Ezek 38:14   עמי ישראל

Com.: The Masorah notes the *two* occurrences of this lemma with the prep. בְּ, and *one* occurrence with the prep. כְּ (כְּשֶׁבֶת) at Esth 1:2.

This note occurs twice on the same folio, the first one at the upper left of fol. 141r, and the second at the bottom right of this folio.

11:26   בְּחֶשְׁבּוֹן וּבִבְנוֹתֶיהָ

Unique   ל   Mp

Com.: In M^L the circellus has been placed only on וּבִבְנוֹתֶיהָ but, since this lemma occurs *four times* written plene and defective ו (and *twice* in this verse), it is most likely that the note refers to the combined phrase בְּחֶשְׁבּוֹן וּבִבְנוֹתֶיהָ, which only occurs *once* here.

11:26   וּמַדּוּעַ

Ten times   י   Mp

Com.: See directly above at **Judg 11:7**.

> ### JUDGES 11:27
>
> וְאָנֹכִי לֹא־חָטָאתִי לָךְ וְאַתָּה עֹשֶׂה אִתִּי רָעָה לְהִלָּחֶם בִּי יִשְׁפֹּט יְהוָה הַשֹּׁפֵט הַיּוֹם בֵּין בְּנֵי יִשְׂרָאֵל וּבֵין בְּנֵי עַמּוֹן׃

11:27   וְאָנֹכִי

Nine times at the beginning of a verse   ט ראש פסוק וכל תרי עשׂר דכו   Mp
and similarly *all* The Twelve

1–5   **Deut 10:10; 31:18; Judg 11:27; 2 Sam 3:39**; Isa 51:15
6–9   **Isa 66:18; Jer 2:21; 3:19**; Ps 22:7

וְאָנֹכִי *nine times* at the beginning of a verse,   ואנכי ט ראש פסוק וסימנהון   Mm
and their references

1–5	Deut 10:10	עמדתי בהר
	Deut 31:18	הסתר אסתיר פני
	Judg 11:27	לא חטאתי
	2 Sam 3:39	ואנכי היום רך
	Isa 66:18	מעשיהם ומחשבתיהם
6–9	Ps 22:7	תולעת ולא איש
	Jer 2:21	נטעתיך שרק (כלו) [כלה] זרע
	Jer 3:19	אשיתך
	Isa 51:15	רגע הים

And similarly *all* The Twelve   וכל תרי עשׂר דכותהון

Com.: The Masorah notes the *nine* occurrences of this lemma at the beginning of a verse with a י cj., to distinguish them from its more numerous occurrences (17x) at the beginning of a verse without a cj.

The Masorah also notes that this lemma at the beginning of a verse also occurs (5x) in The Twelve.

All the Mp headings highlighted above read *nine* times, apart from the one at Isa 66:18, which mistakenly reads *ten* times.

JUDGES 11:29

וַתְּהִי עַל־יִפְתָּח רוּחַ יְהֹוָה וַיַּעֲבֹר אֶת־הַגִּלְעָד וְאֶת־מְנַשֶּׁה וַיַּעֲבֹר אֶת־מִצְפֵּה גִלְעָד וּמִמִּצְפֵּה גִלְעָד עָבַר בְּנֵי עַמּוֹן׃

11:29		עַל־יִפְתָּח
Unique	ל	Mp

Com.: The Masorah notes the *sole* occurrence of this lemma with the prep. עַל, to distinguish it from its *three* occurrences with אֶל (אֶל יִפְתָּח) in vv. 3, 8, and 10.

This lemma is featured in a Masoretic list of words that only occur *once* preceded by the prep. עַל; see Frensdorff, *Ochlah*, §76, and Díaz-Esteban, *Sefer Oklah we-Oklah*, §155

11:29		וְאֶת־מְנַשֶּׁה
Twice	בֿ	Mp

Gen 48:13; <u>Judg 11:29</u>

וְאֶת־מְנַשֶּׁה	*twice*	ואת מנשה בֿ		Mm
Gen 48:13		ואת מנשה בשמאלו		
<u>Judg 11:29</u>		ויעבר את הגלעד		

Com.: The Masorah notes the *two* occurrences of this lemma with a י cj., to distinguish them from its *four* occurrences without a cj.

11:29		עָבַר בְּנֵי עַמּוֹן
Unique	ל	Mp

JUDGES 11:30

וַיִּדַּר יִפְתָּח נֶדֶר לַיהוָה וַיֹּאמַר אִם־נָתוֹן תִּתֵּן אֶת־בְּנֵי עַמּוֹן בְּיָדִי:

11:30   וַיִּדַּר

Three times   גׄ   Mp

Gen 28:20; Num 21:2; Judg 11:30

וַיִּדַּר *three times*   ג ׄ וידר   Mm

Gen 28:20   וידר יעקב
Num 21:2   וידר ישראל נדר
Judg 11:30   וידר יפתח נדר (לייי) [ליהוה]

Com.: The Masorah notes the *three* occurrences of this lemma with the וֹ consec., to distinguish it from its *three* occurrences without a וֹ (יִדֹּר).

11:30   נָתוֹן

Five times plene   הׄ מלׄ   Mp

1–4   **Gen 41:43** (וְנָתוֹן); Deut 15:10; Judg 8:25; **11:30**;
5   *All* the Writings (**Qoh 8:9** [וְנָתוֹן]; **Esth 2:3**; **6:9**)

Com.: The Masorah notes the *five* occurrences of this lemma in various forms written plene וֹ, to distinguish them from its *six* occurrences in various forms written defective וֹ (נָתֹן/וְנָתֹן).

The Mp heading here of *five times* plene is taking *all* the Writings as *one* reference, but the Mp headings at Gen 41:43, Esth 2:3 and 6:9, that read *seven* times, take these *three* references in the Writings as separate entries.

The Mp heading at Qoh 8:9 mistakenly reads *seventeen times* for *seven times*.

JUDGES 11:31

וְהָיָה הַיּוֹצֵא אֲשֶׁר יֵצֵא מִדַּלְתֵי בֵיתִי לִקְרָאתִי בְּשׁוּבִי בְשָׁלוֹם מִבְּנֵי עַמּוֹן וְהָיָה לַיהוָה וְהַעֲלִיתִהוּ
עוֹלָה: פ

11:31   הַיּוֹצֵא

Four times plene in the Prophets   ד֭ מל בנב֭   Mp

Judg 11:31; **Jer 5:6**; **21:9** (וְהַיּוֹצֵא); **Ezek 33:30**

הַיּוֹצֵא *four times* plene in the Prophets   היוצא ד מל בנביא   Mm

Judg 11:31	והיה היוצא אשר יצא
Jer 5:6	כל היוצא מהנה
The *first* occurrence of וְהַיּוֹצֵא (Jer 21:9)	והיוצא {מהנה} קדמ֭
Ezek 33:30	מה הדבר היוצא מאת יהוה

And similarly *all* the Writings   וכל כתיבייה דכותהון

Com.: The Masorah notes the *four* occurrences of this lemma in various forms in the
Prophets written plene וֹ, to distinguish them from its *five* occurrences in various
forms in the Prophets written defective ו (הַיֹּצֵא).

This distinction is implied in the additional notation in the Mm of the *first* occurrence
to the catchword וְהַיּוֹצֵא in the Jer 21:9 reference, which distinguishes the lemma in
that verse from its *second* occurrence at Jer 38:2, where it is written defective ו as וְהַיֹּצֵא.

The Masorah also notes that in the Writings the plene form (הַיּוֹצֵא) is the *only* one that
occurs.

11:31   וְהַעֲלִיתִהוּ

Unique   ל֭   Mp

Com.: Both M^C and M^A read here plene second י (וְהַעֲלִיתִיהוּ), and both these mss.
have Mp notes that read *unique and plene* (second י).

JUDGES 11:33

וַיַּכֵּם מֵעֲרוֹעֵר וְעַד־בּוֹאֲךָ מִנִּית עֶשְׂרִים עִיר וְעַד אָבֵל כְּרָמִים מַכָּה גְדוֹלָה מְאֹד וַיִּכָּנְעוּ בְּנֵי עַמּוֹן מִפְּנֵי בְּנֵי יִשְׂרָאֵל: פ

11:33	מֵעֲרוֹעֵר וְעַד־בּוֹאֲךָ
Unique	ל Mp

11:33	וְעַד אָבֵל
Twice	בֿ Mp

Judg 11:33; 1 Sam 6:18

Com.: The Masorah notes the *two* occurrences of this lemma with a ו cj., to distinguish them from its *two* occurrences without a cj. (עַד אָבֵל) at Num 33:49 and 1 Kgs 4:12.

11:33	מַכָּה גְדוֹלָה מְאֹד
Three times	גֿ Mp

(הַמַּכָּה גְדוֹלָה מְאֹד) Josh 10:20; **Judg 11:33**; 1 Sam 4:10

Com.: The Masorah notes the *three* occurrences of this lemma, *twice* without the def. article on מַכָּה (Josh 10:20 and here), and *once* written with the def. article on מַכָּה (הַמַּכָּה גְדוֹלָה מְאֹד, 1 Sam 4:10).

JUDGES 11:34

וַיָּבֹא יִפְתָּח הַמִּצְפָּה אֶל־בֵּיתוֹ וְהִנֵּה בִתּוֹ יֹצֵאת לִקְרָאתוֹ בְתֻפִּים וּבִמְחֹלוֹת וְרַק הִיא יְחִידָה אֵין־לוֹ מִמֶּנּוּ בֵּן אוֹ־בַת:

11:34	וְהִנֵּה בִתּוֹ
Unique	ל Mp

11:34   וּבְמְחֹלוֹת

Twice   בֿ   Mp

Exod 15:20 (וּבִמְחֹלֹת); Judg 11:34

Com.: The Masorah notes the *two* occurrences of this lemma, *one* written plene second ו (here) and *one* written defective second ו (Exod 15:20).

The Mp heading at Exod 15:20 adds catchwords וְהִנֵּה בָתוֹ) והנה בתו יצאת לקראתו יָצֵאת לִקְרָאתוֹ) to refer the reader to this verse.

This lemma is featured in a Masoretic list of doublets that commence with וב; see Frensdorff, *Ochlah*, §62, and Díaz-Esteban, *Sefer Oklah we-Oklah*, §63.

11:34   וְרַק

Twice   בֿ   Mp

Com.: See **Josh 6:18**.

11:34   יְחִידָה

Unique   לֿ   Mp

Com.: The Masorah notes the *sole* occurrence of this lemma in the fem., to distinguish it from its *three* occurrences in the masc. (יָחִיד).

JUDGES 11:35

וַיְהִי֩ כִרְאוֹת֨וֹ אוֹתָ֜הּ וַיִּקְרַ֣ע אֶת־בְּגָדָ֗יו וַיֹּאמֶר֮ אֲהָ֣הּ בִּתִּי֙ הַכְרֵ֣עַ הִכְרַעְתִּ֔נִי וְאַ֖תְּ הָיִ֣יתְ בְּעֹכְרָ֑י וְאָנֹכִ֗י פָּצִ֤יתִי־פִי֙ אֶל־יְהֹוָ֔ה וְלֹ֥א אוּכַ֖ל לָשֽׁוּב׃

11:35   הַכְרֵעַ

Unique   לֿ   Mp

11:35   הִכְרַעְתִּנִי

Unique   לֿ   Mp

11:35   בְּעֹכְרָי

Unique   ל   Mp

Com.: In M^L this lemma does not have a circellus.

11:35   וְלֹא אוּכַל

Three times   גׄ   Mp

Judg 11:35; Jer 20:9; <u>Neh 6:3</u>

Com.: The Masorah notes the *three* occurrences of this lemma with a ו cj., to distinguish them from its more numerous occurrences (22x) without a cj.

JUDGES 11:36

וַתֹּאמֶר אֵלָיו אָבִי פָּצִיתָה אֶת־פִּיךָ אֶל־יְהוָה עֲשֵׂה לִי כַּאֲשֶׁר יָצָא מִפִּיךָ אַחֲרֵי אֲשֶׁר עָשָׂה לְךָ
יְהוָה נְקָמוֹת מֵאֹיְבֶיךָ מִבְּנֵי עַמּוֹן׃

11:36   פָּצִיתָה

Unique   ל   Mp

JUDGES 11:37

וַתֹּאמֶר אֶל־אָבִיהָ יֵעָשֶׂה לִּי הַדָּבָר הַזֶּה הַרְפֵּה מִמֶּנִּי שְׁנַיִם חֳדָשִׁים וְאֵלְכָה וְיָרַדְתִּי עַל־הֶהָרִים
וְאֶבְכֶּה עַל־בְּתוּלַי אָנֹכִי וְרֵעוֹתָי׃

11:37   יֵעָשֶׂה

Thirty-six times   לֻׄ   Mp

1–5	<u>Gen 29:26</u>; **34:7**; **Exod 2:4**; **12:16**ᵃ; 12:16ᵇ
6–10	**Exod 21:31**; 31:15; **Lev 2:8**; **7:24**; 11:32
11–15	**Lev 13:51**; 24:19; **Num 4:26**; 6:4; 15:11
16–20	**Num 15:34; 28:15; 28:24**; Deut 25:9; **Judg 11:37**
21–25	**1 Sam 11:7; 17:26; 17:27**; 2 Sam 13:12; **2 Kgs 12:14**
26–30	Isa 3:11; Jer 3:16; 5:13; Ezek 12:11; 15:5
31–35	Ezek 44:14; Obad 15; **Esth 2:11; 6:9; 6:11;**
36	**Ezra 10:3**

Com.: The Masorah notes the *thirty-six* occurrences of this lemma in the *niphal*, to distinguish them from its more numerous occurrences (123x) in the *qal* (יַעֲשֶׂה); see Ognibeni, *'Oklah*, §13A.

11:37   הֶרְפֵּה

Twice   ב   Mp

Judg 11:37; 2 Kgs 4:27

Com.: The Masorah notes the *two* occurrences of this lemma, to distinguish them from the more numerous occurrences (6x) of its parallel form הֶרֶף; see **1 Sam 11:3**.

11:37   שְׁנַיִם חֳדָשִׁים

Unique   ל   Mp

1–3   **Judg 11:37**; 11:39; 1 Kgs 5:28

Com.: The Mp heading here of *unique* is incorrect since there are *three* occurrences of this lemma.

The Masorah notes the *three* occurrences of חֳדָשִׁים with שְׁנַיִם, to distinguish it from its *sole* occurrence with שְׁנֵי (שְׁנֵי חֳדָשִׁים) in v. 38.

Neither M^C nor M^A has a note on this lemma here.

11:37   וְאֶבְכֶּה

Twice   ב   Mp

Judg 11:37; Jer 8:23

Com.: The Masorah notes the *two* occurrences of this lemma with a ו cj., to distinguish them from its *three* occurrences with a ו consec. (וָאֶבְכֶּה); see **2 Sam 12:22**.

11:37   וְרֵעִיתִי

Read וְרֵעוֹתָי   ורעותי קרי   Mp

Com.: The *kətîb* (ורעיתי), and the *qərê* (וְרֵעוֹתָי) represent miscellaneous variations in nouns; see Gordis, *The Biblical Text*, 124.

This lemma is featured in a Masoretic list of words that has a ‏י‎ written in the middle of a word that is read as ‏ו‎; see the Mm at <u>Num 1:16</u> *sub* ‏קריא‎, Frensdorff, *Ochlah*, 80, and Díaz-Esteban, *Sefer Oklah we-Oklah*, §71.

In M[L] this lemma has no circellus.

JUDGES 11:38

וַיֹּ֣אמֶר לֵ֔כִי וַיִּשְׁלַ֥ח אוֹתָ֖הּ שְׁנֵ֣י חֳדָשִׁ֑ים וַתֵּ֤לֶךְ הִיא֙ וְרֵ֣עוֹתֶ֔יהָ וַתֵּ֥בְךְּ עַל־בְּתוּלֶ֖יהָ עַל־הֶהָרִֽים׃

11:38   וְרֵעוֹתֶ֔יהָ

Unique   ל   Mp

JUDGES 11:39

וַיְהִ֞י מִקֵּ֣ץ ׀ שְׁנַ֣יִם חֳדָשִׁ֗ים וַתָּ֙שָׁב֙ אֶל־אָבִ֔יהָ וַיַּ֣עַשׂ לָ֔הּ אֶת־נִדְר֖וֹ אֲשֶׁ֣ר נָדָ֑ר וְהִיא֙ לֹא־יָדְעָ֣ה אִ֔ישׁ וַתְּהִי־חֹ֖ק בְּיִשְׂרָאֵֽל׃

11:39   אֶת־נִדְר֖וֹ

Unique   ל   Mp

Com.: The Masorah notes the *sole* occurrence of this lemma without a ‏ו‎ cj., to distinguish it from its occurrence with a cj. at 1 Sam 1:21.

11:39   וַתְּהִי־חֹק בְּיִשְׂרָאֵל

Unique   ל   Mp

JUDGES 11:40

מִיָּמִ֣ים ׀ יָמִ֗ימָה תֵּלַ֙כְנָה֙ בְּנ֣וֹת יִשְׂרָאֵ֔ל לְתַנּ֕וֹת לְבַת־יִפְתָּ֖ח הַגִּלְעָדִ֑י אַרְבַּ֥עַת יָמִ֖ים בַּשָּׁנָֽה׃ ס

11:40   מִיָּמִים ׀ יָמִימָה

Five times   ה   Mp

1–5   **<u>Exod 13:10</u>; Judg 11:40; 21:19; 1 Sam 1:3; 2:19**

Com.: The Masorah notes the *five* occurrences of this lemma, to distinguish them from the more numerous occurrences (11x) of its parallel phrase ‏שָׁנָה בְּשָׁנָה‎ also meaning *yearly*; see Ginsburg, 4, ‏י‎, §257.

11:40   לְתַנּוֹת

Twice   בֿ   Mp

Judg 11:40; Mal 1:3

Com.: This lemma is featured in a Masoretic list of homonyms; see Frensdorff, *Ochlah*, §59, and Díaz-Esteban, *Sefer Oklah we-Oklah*, §60. Here the meaning is *to celebrate*, whereas in Mal 1:3 the meaning is *for jackals*.

JUDGES 12:1

וַיִּצָּעֵק֙ אִ֣ישׁ אֶפְרַ֔יִם וַֽיַּעֲבֹ֖ר צָפ֑וֹנָה וַיֹּאמְר֣וּ לְיִפְתָּ֗ח מַדּ֜וּעַ ׀ עָבַ֣רְתָּ ׀ לְהִלָּחֵ֣ם בִּבְנֵֽי־עַמּ֗וֹן וְלָ֙נוּ֙ לֹ֣א קָרָ֔אתָ לָלֶ֖כֶת עִמָּ֑ךְ בֵּיתְךָ֗ נִשְׂרֹ֥ף עָלֶ֖יךָ בָּאֵֽשׁ׃

12:1   וַיִּצָּעֵק

Three times   גֿ   Mp

Com.: See **Judg 7:23**.

12:1   וְלָנוּ

Three times   גֿ   Mp

Judg 12:1; 1 Sam 23:20; Dan 9:7

וְלָנוּ *three times*, and their references   ולנו גֿ וסימנהון   Mm

Judg 12:1	ולנו לא קראת ללכת
1 Sam 23:20	ולנו הסגירו
Dan 9:7	ולנו בשת הפנים

And *once* (וְלָנוּ): Ezra 4:3   וחד לא לכם ולנו

Com.: The Masorah notes the *three* occurrences of this lemma with a *šĕwâ* under the ו cj., and the Mm has an additional note that this lemma occurs with a *qameṣ* under the cj. (וְלָנוּ) at Ezra 4:3.

JUDGES 12:2

וַיֹּ֤אמֶר יִפְתָּח֙ אֲלֵיהֶ֔ם אִ֣ישׁ רִ֗יב הָיִ֜יתִי אֲנִ֛י וְעַמִּ֥י וּבְנֵֽי־עַמּ֖וֹן מְאֹ֑ד וָאֶזְעַ֣ק אֶתְכֶ֗ם וְלֹֽא־הֹושַׁעְתֶּ֥ם
אֹותִ֖י מִיָּדָֽם׃

12:2   וְעַמִּ֥י

Eleven times   יֹא   Mp

1–5   Exod 9:27; **Judg 12:2; Jer 2:11**; 2:32; **5:31**
6–10   Jer 8:7; **31:14**; Hos 11:7; **Esth 7:3; 7:4**
11   **1 Chr 28:2**

Com.: The Masorah notes the *eleven* occurrences of this lemma with a ו cj., to distinguish them from its more numerous occurrences (100+) without a cj.

12:2   וָאֶזְעַ֣ק אֶתְכֶ֗ם

Unique   ל   Mp

JUDGES 12:3

וָאֶרְאֶ֞ה כִּֽי־אֵינְךָ֣ מֹושִׁ֗יעַ וָאָשִׂ֨ימָה נַפְשִׁ֤י בְכַפִּי֙ וָאֶעְבְּרָה֙ אֶל־בְּנֵ֣י עַמֹּ֔ון וַיִּתְּנֵ֥ם יְהוָ֖ה בְּיָדִ֑י וְלָמָ֞ה
עֲלִיתֶ֥ם אֵלַ֛י הַיֹּ֥ום הַזֶּ֖ה לְהִלָּ֥חֶם בִּֽי׃

12:3   וָאָשִׂ֨ימָה

Twice   ב   Mp

Judg 12:3; Ezra 8:17

Com.: The Masorah notes the *two* occurrences of this lemma with the cohortative ה,
to distinguish them from its *four* occurrences without this cohortative ending.

12:3   בְּכַפִּי

בְּכַפִּי *nine times* in this and a related form	בכפי ט בלשנׁ	Mm

1–5	<u>Exod 33:22</u>	ושכתי כפי עליך
	Exod 33:23	והסרתי את כפי
	<u>Judg 12:3</u>	ואשימה נפשי
	1 Sam 28:21	ואשים נפשי
	Ezek 22:13	והנה הכיתי
6–9	<u>Ezek 21:22</u>[a]	וגם אני אכה כפי אל כפי
	Twice in the verse (Ezek 22:22[b])	שנים בפסוקה
	Ps 119:109	נפשי בכפי
	Job 13:14	ונפשי אשים

Com.: The Masorah notes the *nine* occurrences of this lemma in related forms in the sg., to distinguish them from its *eight* occurrences in related forms בּ in the pl. (כַּפַּי/בְּכַפַּי); see Ognibeni, *'Oklah*, §220.

> ## JUDGES 12:4
>
> וַיִּקְבֹּץ יִפְתָּח אֶת־כָּל־אַנְשֵׁי גִלְעָד וַיִּלָּחֶם אֶת־אֶפְרָיִם וַיַּכּוּ אַנְשֵׁי גִלְעָד אֶת־אֶפְרַיִם כִּי אָמְרוּ פְּלִיטֵי אֶפְרַיִם אַתֶּם גִּלְעָד בְּתוֹךְ אֶפְרַיִם בְּתוֹךְ מְנַשֶּׁה׃

12:4   בְּתוֹךְ

Two verses in which there is the sequence בְּתוֹךְ...בְּתוֹךְ	בׁ פסוק אית בהון בתוך בתוך	Mp

<u>Judg 12:4</u>; Ezek 9:4

Two verses in which there is the sequence בְּתוֹךְ...בְּתוֹךְ	בׁ פסוק איתה בהון בתוך בתוך	Mm

<u>Judg 12:4</u>	גלעד בתוך אפרים בתוך מנשה
Ezek 9:4	בתוך (העם) [העיר] בתוך ירושלם

Com.: The Masorah notes the *two* verses in which there is the sequence of the prepositional phrases בְּתוֹךְ...בְּתוֹךְ.

Com.: In M[L] there is no circellus for this lemma.

JUDGES 12:5

וַיִּלְכֹּד גִּלְעָד אֶת־מַעְבְּרוֹת הַיַּרְדֵּן לְאֶפְרָיִם וְהָיָה כִּי יֹאמְרוּ פְּלִיטֵי אֶפְרַיִם אֶעֱבֹרָה וַיֹּאמְרוּ לוֹ אַנְשֵׁי־גִלְעָד הַאֶפְרָתִי אַתָּה וַיֹּאמֶר | לֹא׃

12:5   אֶת־מַעְבְּרוֹת הַיַּרְדֵּן

Twice   בֿ   Mp

Judg 3:28; **12:5**

Com.: In M^{L} two circelli have been placed on the words גִּלְעָד אֶת and הַיַּרְדֵּן מַעְבְּרוֹת making a lemma the four-word phrase גִּלְעָד אֶת־מַעְבְּרוֹת הַיַּרְדֵּן. But since this phrase occurs only *once*, it is most likely that the intended note was only for אֶת־מַעְבְּרוֹת הַיַּרְדֵּן.

12:5   הַאֶפְרָתִי

Three times   גֿ   Mp

Com.: The Mp heading here of *three times* is incorrect since this is the *only* occurrence of this lemma. Both M^{C} and M^{A} correctly read here *unique*.

JUDGES 12:6

וַיֹּאמְרוּ לוֹ אֱמָר־נָא שִׁבֹּלֶת וַיֹּאמֶר סִבֹּלֶת וְלֹא יָכִין לְדַבֵּר כֵּן וַיֹּאחֲזוּ אוֹתוֹ וַיִּשְׁחָטוּהוּ אֶל־מַעְבְּרוֹת הַיַּרְדֵּן וַיִּפֹּל בָּעֵת הַהִיא מֵאֶפְרַיִם אַרְבָּעִים וּשְׁנַיִם אָלֶף׃

12:6   סִבֹּלֶת

Unique   ל   Mp

Com.: The Masorah notes the *sole* occurrence of this lemma with a ס, to distinguish it from its *three* occurrences with a שׁ (שִׁבֹּלֶת), *one* of which is in this verse.

12:6   וַיִּשְׁחָטוּהוּ

Unique   ל   Mp

12:6   וַיִּשְׁחָטוּהוּ אֶל

<*Five times*>   <הֹ>   Mp

1–5   **Judg 12:6**; <u>2 Kgs 10:14</u> (וַיִּשְׁחָטוּם); Jer 41:7 (וַיִּשְׁחָטֵם); Ezek 40:39 (לִשְׁחוֹט);
             40:41 (יִשְׁחָטוּ)

Com.: The Masorah notes the *five* occurrences of forms of the verb שָׁחַט together with
אֶל, to distinguish them from occurrences of forms of this verb with עַל, such as at
Exod 34:25; Lev 1:11; and 14:6; see Dotan/Reich, *Masora Thesaurus, ad loc.*

In M^L there is a circellus on this lemma but no note, and neither M^C nor M^A has a
note here.

JUDGES 12:8

וַיִּשְׁפֹּט אַחֲרָיו אֶת־יִשְׂרָאֵל אִבְצָן מִבֵּית לָחֶם:

12:8   אִבְצָן

Twice   בֹ   Mp

Judg 12:8; 12:10

JUDGES 12:9

וַיְהִי־לוֹ שְׁלֹשִׁים בָּנִים וּשְׁלֹשִׁים בָּנוֹת שִׁלַּח הַחוּצָה וּשְׁלֹשִׁים בָּנוֹת הֵבִיא לְבָנָיו מִן־הַחוּץ וַיִּשְׁפֹּט
אֶת־יִשְׂרָאֵל שֶׁבַע שָׁנִים:

12:9   הַחוּצָה

Sixteen times   יוֹ   Mp

1–5   Gen 15:5; **19:17**; **24:29**; <u>**39:12**</u>; 39:13
6–10   Gen 39:15; **39:18**; Deut 24:11; **25:5**; Josh 2:19
11–15   **<u>Judg 12:9</u>**; <u>1 Sam 9:26</u>; 2 Sam 13:17; 1 Kgs 8:8; **Ezek 34:21**
16   **2 Chr 5:9**

הַחוּצָה *sixteen times*, and their references	החוצה יֹ וסימנהון	Mm

1–5	Gen 15:5	ויוצא
	Gen 19:17	כהוציאם
	Gen 24:29	ולרבקה
	Gen 39:12	ותתפשהו
	Gen 39:18	כהרימי קולי
6–10	Gen 39:13	(כראתו) [כראותה]
	Gen 39:15	כשמעו
	Deut 24:11	העבוט החוצה
	Deut 25:5	אחים
	Josh 2:19	מדלתי ביתך החוצה
11–15	Judg 12:9	שלח
	1 Sam 9:26	הוא (ושמו) [ושמואל]
	2 Sam 13:17	משרתו
	1 Kgs 8:8	(ויאריכו) [ויארכו]
	And its companion (2 Chr 5:9)	וחביר
16	Ezek 34:21	אותנה

Com.: The Masorah notes the *sixteen* occurrences of this lemma with the locative ה, to distinguish them from its *seven* forms without this adverbial ending.

All the Mp references highlighted above read *sixteen times* except the one at Ezek 34:21, which mistakenly reads *twelve times*.

JUDGES 12:10

וַיָּמָת אִבְצָן וַיִּקָּבֵר בְּבֵית לָחֶם: פ

12:10	אִבְצָן

Twice	בֹ	Mp

Judg 12:8; 12:10

12:10	בְּבֵית לָחֶם

Three times	גֹ	Mp

Judg 12:10; Ruth 4:11; 1 Chr 11:16

בְּבֵית לָחֶם *three times*	בבית לחם גֿ		Mm

Judg 12:10	אבצן ויקבר
וּנְצִיב *of Chronicles* (1 Chr 11:16)	ונציב דדברי הימים
Ruth 4:11	(ויקרא) [וקרא] שם בבית

Com.: The Masorah notes the *three* occurrences of this lemma with the prep. בְּ, to distinguish them from its more numerous occurrences (11x) without this preposition.

This distinction is implied in the additional notation in the Mm *of Chronicles* to the 1 Chr 11:16 reference, which distinguishes the lemma in that verse from its form it has in the parallel verse in 2 Sam 23:14, where it is written without the prep. בְּ (בֵּית לָחֶם).

The Mp heading of 1 Chr 11:16 mistakenly reads *twice*, but the Mm there correctly lists the *three* references.

JUDGES 12:11

וַיִּשְׁפֹּט אַחֲרָיו אֶת־יִשְׂרָאֵל אֵילוֹן הַזְּבוּלֹנִי וַיִּשְׁפֹּט אֶת־יִשְׂרָאֵל עֶשֶׂר שָׁנִים:

12:11   הַזְּבוּלֹנִי

Three times   גֿ   Mp

Num 26:27; **Judg 12:11**; **12:12**

JUDGES 12:12

וַיָּמָת אֵלוֹן הַזְּבוּלֹנִי וַיִּקָּבֵר בְּאַיָּלוֹן בְּאֶרֶץ זְבוּלֻן: פ

12:12   הַזְּבוּלֹנִי

Three times   גֿ   Mp

Com.: See directly above at **Judg 12:11**.

JUDGES 12:13

וַיִּשְׁפֹּט אַחֲרָיו אֶת־יִשְׂרָאֵל עַבְדּוֹן בֶּן־הִלֵּל הַפִּרְעָתוֹנִי:

12:13   וַיִּשְׁפֹּט אַחֲרָיו

Unique with the accents (*mêrḵâ* and *ṭipḥa*)   ל בטע   Mp

Com.: The Masorah notes the *sole* occurrence of this lemma with the accents (*mêrḵâ* and *ṭipḥa*), to distinguish them from its *two* other occurrences with the accents *mahpak* and *paštâ* (וַיִּשְׁפֹּט אַחֲרָיו) in vv. 8 and 11.

JUDGES 12:14

וַיְהִי־ל֞וֹ אַרְבָּעִ֣ים בָּנִ֗ים וּשְׁלֹשִׁים֙ בְּנֵ֣י בָנִ֔ים רֹכְבִ֖ים עַל־שִׁבְעִ֣ים עֲיָרִ֑ם וַיִּשְׁפֹּ֥ט אֶת־יִשְׂרָאֵ֖ל שְׁמֹנֶ֥ה שָׁנִֽים:

12:14   עֲיָרִם

Twice defective   ב חס   Mp

Gen 32:16 (וַעְיָרִם); **Judg 12:14**

Com.: The Masorah notes the *two* occurrences of this lemma written defective second י, to distinguish them from its *three* occurrences written plene second י (עֲיָרִים).

JUDGES 12:15

וַיָּ֤מָת עַבְדּוֹן֙ בֶּן־הִלֵּ֣ל הַפִּרְעָתוֹנִ֔י וַיִּקָּבֵ֥ר בְּפִרְעָת֖וֹן בְּאֶ֣רֶץ אֶפְרָ֑יִם בְּהַ֖ר הָעֲמָלֵקִֽי: פ

12:15   בְּפִרְעָתוֹן

Unique   ל   Mp

JUDGES 13:1

וַיֹּסִ֙פוּ֙ בְּנֵ֣י יִשְׂרָאֵ֔ל לַעֲשׂ֥וֹת הָרַ֖ע בְּעֵינֵ֣י יְהוָ֑ה וַיִּתְּנֵ֧ם יְהוָ֛ה בְּיַד־פְּלִשְׁתִּ֖ים אַרְבָּעִ֥ים שָׁנָֽה: פ

13:1   וַיֹּסִפוּ

Three times written like this   ג כת כן   Mp

Com.: On this problematic note, see **Judg 10:6**.

JUDGES 13:2

וַיְהִי֩ אִ֨ישׁ אֶחָ֧ד מִצׇּרְעָ֛ה מִמִּשְׁפַּ֥חַת הַדָּנִ֖י וּשְׁמ֣וֹ מָנ֑וֹחַ וְאִשְׁתּ֥וֹ עֲקָרָ֖ה וְלֹ֥א יָלָֽדָה׃

13:2   וַיְהִי אִישׁ אֶחָד

Twice   בׄ   Mp

Judg 13:2; 1 Sam 1:1

Com.: The Masorah notes the *two* occurrences of וַיְהִי אִישׁ with אֶחָד, to distinguish them from its more numerous occurrences (6x) without אֶחָד (וַיְהִי אִישׁ).

13:2   וְלֹא יָלָדָה

Unique   לׄ   Mp

Com.: The Masorah notes the *sole* occurrence of this lemma with a ו cj., to distinguish it from its occurrence without a cj. at Isa 54:1.

JUDGES 13:3

וַיֵּרָ֥א מַלְאַךְ־יְהֹוָ֖ה אֶל־הָאִשָּׁ֑ה וַיֹּ֣אמֶר אֵלֶ֗יהָ הִנֵּה־נָ֤א אַתְּ־עֲקָרָה֙ וְלֹ֣א יָלַ֔דְתְּ וְהָרִ֖ית וְיָלַ֥דְתְּ בֵּֽן׃

13:3   יָלַדְתְּ

Twice   בׄ   Mp

Judg 13:3; <u>Ezek 16:20</u>

Com.: The Masorah notes the *two* occurrences of this lemma with a *paṭaḥ* under the ל, to distinguish them from its *sole* occurrence with a *qameṣ* (יָלָדְתְּ) at 1 Sam 4:20.

The Mp heading and the Mm heading at <u>**Ezek 16:20**</u> reads *three times*, and the Mm lists all *three* forms, *two* with a *paṭaḥ* under the ל and *one* (1 Sam 4:20) with a *qameṣ* under the ל.

13:3   וְהָרִית

Unique   לׄ   Mp

JUDGES 13:4

וְעַתָּה֙ הִשָּׁ֣מְרִי נָ֔א וְאַל־תִּשְׁתִּ֖י יַ֣יִן וְשֵׁכָ֑ר וְאַל־תֹּאכְלִ֖י כָּל־טָמֵֽא׃

13:4   הִשָּׁ֣מְרִי נָ֔א

Unique   ל   Mp

Com.: The Masorah notes the *sole* occurrence of this lemma in the fem., to distinguish it from its *sole* occurrence in the masc. (הִשָּׁ֣מֶר נָ֔א) at 1 Sam 19:2.

13:4   כָּל־טָמֵֽא

Unique   ל   Mp

Com.: The Masorah notes the *sole* occurrence of this lemma without a ו cj., to distinguish it from its occurrence with a cj. at Num 5:2.

JUDGES 13:5

כִּי֩ הִנָּ֨ךְ הָרָ֜ה וְיֹלַ֣דְתְּ בֵּ֗ן וּמוֹרָה֙ לֹא־יַעֲלֶ֣ה עַל־רֹאשׁ֔וֹ כִּי־נְזִ֧יר אֱלֹהִ֛ים יִהְיֶ֥ה הַנַּ֖עַר מִן־הַבָּ֑טֶן וְה֗וּא יָחֵ֛ל לְהוֹשִׁ֥יעַ אֶת־יִשְׂרָאֵ֖ל מִיַּ֥ד פְּלִשְׁתִּֽים׃

13:5   וְיֹלַ֣דְתְּ

Three times   ג֗   Mp

Gen 16:11; <u>Judg 13:5</u>; 13:7

וְיֹלַ֣דְתְּ *three times* defective, and their references   וילדת ג֗ חסירין וסימנהון   Mm

Gen 16:11	ישמעאל
<u>Judg 13:5</u>	הנך
Judg 13:7	הנך

And *once* (וְיָלַ֣דְתְּ): 1 Sam 4:20   וחד אל תיראי

Com.: The Masorah notes the *three* occurrences of this lemma, to distinguish them from the *two* occurrences of its parallel form וְיֹלֶ֣דֶת at Isa 7:14 and Jer 31:8; see Ognibeni, *'Oklah*, §313.

The heading of the Mm of *three times defective* (ו) is inexact since there are no examples of this form written plene ו. Possibly it may refer to the fact that the form being a fem. sg. ptcpl. is without its expected *səġōls*; cf., the description of Joüon/Muraoka (*Grammar*, §89j), "forms (that) lack the expected segholisation."

M^C correctly reads here *three times and defective*, whereas M^A, as M^L, just reads *three times*.

The additional note at the end of the Mm note of *and once* יָלְדְתְּ (1 Sam 4:20) seems to be misplaced, and more likely belongs with the note on יָלָדְתְּ; see directly above in v. 3; and Dotan/Reich, *Masora Thesaurus, ad loc.*

This lemma occurs in the ms. in folio 144v but the Mm note appears on the top of the following folio 145r.

JUDGES 13:6

וַתָּבֹא הָאִשָּׁה וַתֹּאמֶר לְאִישָׁהּ לֵאמֹר אִישׁ הָאֱלֹהִים בָּא אֵלַי וּמַרְאֵהוּ כְּמַרְאֵה מַלְאַךְ הָאֱלֹהִים נוֹרָא מְאֹד וְלֹא שְׁאִלְתִּיהוּ אֵי־מִזֶּה הוּא וְאֶת־שְׁמוֹ לֹא־הִגִּיד לִי׃

13:6   וּמַרְאֵהוּ

Twice   בֿ   Mp

Lev 13:34; **Judg 13:6**

Com.: The Masorah notes the *two* occurrences of this lemma with a ו cj., to distinguish them from its more numerous occurrences (8x) without a cj.

13:6   מַלְאַךְ הָאֱלֹהִים

Eight times   חֿ   Mp

Com.: See **Judg 6:20**.

13:6   שְׁאִלְתִּיהוּ

Unique   לֿ   Mp

Com.: The Masorah notes the *sole* occurrence of this lemma with the sfx. הו, to distinguish it from its occurrence with the alternate sfx. ו (שְׁאִלְתִּיו) at 1 Sam 1:20.

This lemma is featured in a Masoretic list of words occurring twice, *once* with a ה at the beginning (1 Sam 1:28), and *once* without (here); see Frensdorff, *Ochlah*, §8, and Díaz-Esteban, *Sefer Oklah we-Oklah*, §8.

JUDGES 13:7

וַיֹּ֣אמֶר לִ֗י הִנָּ֤ךְ הָרָה֙ וְיֹלַ֣דְתְּ בֵּ֔ן וְעַתָּ֞ה אַל־תִּשְׁתִּ֣י | יַ֣יִן וְשֵׁכָ֗ר וְאַל־תֹּֽאכְלִי֙ כָּל־טֻמְאָ֔ה כִּֽי־נְזִ֤יר
אֱלֹהִים֙ יִהְיֶ֣ה הַנַּ֔עַר מִן־הַבֶּ֖טֶן עַד־יֹ֥ום מֹותֹֽו׃ פ

13:7   וַיֹּ֣אמֶר לִ֗י

Eight times   ח֞   Mp

1–5   **Judg 13:7**; **2 Sam 1:8**; **Isa 49:3**; **Prov 4:4**; Neh 2:2
6–8   **Neh 2:4**; 2:6; **1 Chr 28:6**

וַיֹּ֣אמֶר לִ֗י *eight times*, and their references   ויאמר לי ח וסימנהון   Mm

1–5   Judg 13:7   הנך הרה
         2 Sam 1:8   מי אתה
         Isa 49:3   עבדי אתה
         Neh 2:4   על מה זה
         Neh 2:2   מדוע פניך רעים
6–8   Neh 2:6   והשגל יושבת
         1 Chr 28:6   שלמה בנך הוא
         Prov 4:4   וירני ויאמר לי

Com.: The Masorah notes the *eight* occurrences of וַיֹּ֣אמֶר with לִי, to distinguish them
from its more numerous occurrences (59x) with אֶל (וַיֹּ֣אמֶר אֵלַי).

The Mp heading at 1 Chr 28:6 correctly reads *unique in the book*, and the Mp reading at
Neh 2:4 of *five times*, if not a graphic error of ה *five* or ח *eight*, may represent the number
of occurrences in the Writings.

13:7   וְיֹלַ֣דְתְּ

Three times   ג֞   Mp

Com.: See directly above at **Judg 13:5**.

13:7   וְאַל־תֹּֽאכְלִי

Unique   ל֞   Mp

1–2   Judg 13:4; **13:7**

Com.: The Mp heading here of *unique* is incorrect since there are *two* occurrences of this lemma.

The Masorah notes the *two* occurrences of this lemma with וְאֵל, to distinguish it from its *two* occurrences with לֹא (לֹא תֹאכְלִי) at 1 Sam 1:8 and Ezek 36:14.

M^A correctly reads here *twice*, but M^C has no note.

JUDGES 13:8

וַיֶּעְתַּר מָנוֹחַ אֶל־יְהוָה וַיֹּאמַר בִּי אֲדוֹנָי אִישׁ הָאֱלֹהִים אֲשֶׁר שָׁלַחְתָּ יָבוֹא־נָא עוֹד אֵלֵינוּ וְיוֹרֵנוּ מַה־נַּעֲשֶׂה לַנַּעַר הַיּוּלָּד׃

13:8   וַיֶּעְתַּר

Four times   ד   Mp

Gen 25:21; **Exod 8:26**; **10:18**; **Judg 13:8**

Com.: The Masorah notes the *four* occurrences of this lemma and, as indicated in the headings of the Mm to Gen 25:21 and Exod 8:26, *two* of these occurrences are at the beginning of a verse (Gen 25:21 and Judg 13:8), and *two* are in the middle of a verse (Exod 8:26 and 10:18).

13:8   בִּי אֲדוֹנָי

Five times   ה   Mp

Com.: See **Josh 7:8**.

13:8   אֲדוֹנָי

Unique plene   ל מל   Mp

Com.: The Masorah notes the *sole* occurrence of this lemma written plene וֹ, to distinguish them from its more numerous occurrences (400+) written defective וֹ (אֲדֹנָי); see **Judg 19:26** *sub* אֲדוֹנֶיהָ.

13:8   וְיוֹרֵנוּ

Three times   ג   Mp

Judg 13:8; Isa 2:3 (וְיֹרֵנוּ); **Mic 4:2**

וְיוֹרֵנוּ *three times*, *twice* plene and *once*   ויורנו ג̇ ב̇ מל̇ וחד חסיר וסימנהון   Mm
defective, and their references

Judg 13:8   מה נעשה לנער
וְיֹרֵנוּ מִדְּרָכָיו *of Isaiah* (Isa 2:3)   וירנו מדרכיו דישעיה
And its companion *in The Twelve* (Mic 4:2)   וחביר דתר̇ עשר̇

Com.: The Masorah notes the *three* occurrences of this lemma, *twice* written plene וֹ
(here and Mic 4:2), and *once* written defective וֹ (Isa 2:3).

The additional notations *of Isaiah* to the Isa 2:3 reference, and *of in The Twelve* to the
Mic 4:2 reference, are purely for reference purposes to distinguish both references in
parallel texts from each other.

13:8   הַיּוּלָד

Unique and plene   ל̇ ומל̇   Mp

Com.: By noting that this lemma is *unique* and written plene וֹ, the Masorah is also
implying (correctly) that this lemma does not occur elsewhere written defective וֹ.

┌───┐
│   **JUDGES 13:9**   │
│ וַיִּשְׁמַע הָאֱלֹהִים בְּקוֹל מָנוֹחַ וַיָּבֹא מַלְאַךְ הָאֱלֹהִים עוֹד אֶל־הָאִשָּׁה וְהִיא יוֹשֶׁבֶת בַּשָּׂדֶה וּמָנוֹחַ │
│   אִישָׁהּ אֵין עִמָּהּ:   │
└───┘

13:9   וַיִּשְׁמַע הָאֱלֹהִים

Unique   ל̇   Mp

Com.: The Masorah notes the *sole* occurrence of וַיִּשְׁמַע with הָאֱלֹהִים, to distinguish it
from its *three* occurrences with אֱלֹהִים (וַיִּשְׁמַע אֱלֹהִים).

This lemma is featured in a Masoretic list of phrases occurring only *once*, where the
second element of the phrase has a def. article; see Frensdorff, *Ochlah*, §189.

13:9   מַלְאַךְ הָאֱלֹהִים

Eight times   ח̇   Mp

Com.: See **Judg 6:20**.

JUDGES 13:10

וַתְּמַהֵר֙ הָֽאִשָּׁ֔ה וַתָּ֖רׇץ וַתַּגֵּ֣ד לְאִישָׁ֑הּ וַתֹּ֣אמֶר אֵלָ֔יו הִנֵּ֨ה נִרְאָ֤ה אֵלַי֙ הָאִ֔ישׁ אֲשֶׁר־בָּ֥א בַיּ֖וֹם אֵלָֽי׃

13:10   אֵלָ֔יו

Seven times with the accent *zaqep* in the book   ז בטע זקף בסיפֿ   Mp

1–5   Judg 3:13; 6:12; 6:17; **13:10**; 16:9
6   Judg 16:14

Com.: The Mp heading here of *seven times* is incorrect since there are only *six* occurrences of this lemma in the book. The Masorah notes the *six* occurrences of this lemma in the book with the *zaqep* accent, to distinguish them from its more numerous occurrences (26x) in the book with other accents.

Neither M^C nor M^A has a note on this lemma here.

In M^L the circellus has been placed between וַתֹּ֣אמֶר אֵלָ֔יו, but since this phrase with *zaqep* (on אֵלָ֔יו) occurs only *three* times in the book (13:10, 16:9 and 14) it is most likely that the note refers solely to אֵלָ֔יו which does occur *six* times in the book.

13:10   נִרְאָ֤ה אֵלַי הָאִ֔ישׁ

Unique   ל   Mp

In M^L only one circellus has been placed between אֵלַי and הָאִ֔ישׁ but, since the phrase אֵלַי הָאִ֔ישׁ occurs *three times*, it is most likely that the note should include the preceding word נִרְאָ֤ה since the full phrase נִרְאָ֤ה אֵלַי הָאִ֔ישׁ only occurs this once; see also Dotan/Reich, *Masora Thesaurus*, *ad loc.*

JUDGES 13:12

וַיֹּ֣אמֶר מָנ֔וֹחַ עַתָּ֖ה יָבֹ֣א דְבָרֶ֑יךָ מַה־יִּֽהְיֶ֥ה מִשְׁפַּט־הַנַּ֖עַר וּמַעֲשֵֽׂהוּ׃

13:12   וּמַעֲשֵֽׂהוּ

Three times   ג   Mp

Judg 13:12; 1 Sam 25:2; Ps 64:10

Com.: The Masorah notes the *three* occurrences of this lemma with a ו cj., to distinguish them from its more numerous occurrences (11x) without a cj.

JUDGES 13:13

וַיֹּאמֶר מַלְאַךְ יְהוָה אֶל־מָנוֹחַ מִכֹּל אֲשֶׁר־אָמַרְתִּי אֶל־הָאִשָּׁה תִּשָּׁמֵר׃

13:13   הָאִשָּׁה תִּשָּׁמֵר

Unique   ל   Mp

JUDGES 13:14

מִכֹּל אֲשֶׁר־יֵצֵא מִגֶּפֶן הַיַּיִן לֹא תֹאכַל וְיַיִן וְשֵׁכָר אַל־תֵּשְׁתְּ וְכָל־טֻמְאָה אַל־תֹּאכַל כֹּל אֲשֶׁר־צִוִּיתִיהָ תִּשְׁמֹר׃

13:14   וְיַיִן וְשֵׁכָר

Three times   ג   Mp

Deut 29:5; Judg 13:14; 1 Sam 1:15

וְיַיִן וְשֵׁכָר *three times*, and their references   וויין ושכר ג וסימנהון   Mm

Deut 29:5   לחם לא אכלתם
Judg 13:14   אל תשת וכל טמאה
1 Sam 1:15   לא שתיתי

Com.: The Masorah notes the *three* occurrences of this lemma with an initial ו cj., to distinguish them from its *three* occurrences without this initial cj. (יַיִן וְשֵׁכָר).

JUDGES 13:15

וַיֹּאמֶר מָנוֹחַ אֶל־מַלְאַךְ יְהוָה נַעְצְרָה־נָּא אוֹתָךְ וְנַעֲשֶׂה לְפָנֶיךָ גְּדִי עִזִּים׃

13:15   נַעְצְרָה

Unique   ל   Mp

Com.: The Masorah notes the *sole* occurrence of this lemma with the cohortative ה, to distinguish it from its occurrence without this cohortative ending at 1 Chr 29:14 (נַעְצֹר).

13:15   אוֹתְךָ

Four times one is liable to err   ד מטע   Mp

Judg 13:15; Jer 12:1 (אֹתָךְ)*; 49:16 (אֹתָךְ); Prov 6:22 (אֹתָךְ)

Com.: The Masorah notes the *four* occurrences of this lemma where, because of its pointing, one might erroneously think that this is a fem. form; see Ginsburg 4, א, §1427.

This enumeration does not include the *five* occurrences of this lemma in Ezekiel, nor the *two* occurrences with a *sôp pasûq* at 1 Kgs 22:24 and Jer 19:10.

This lemma is featured in a Mm at <u>Jer 19:10</u> *sub* אוֹתְךָ listing the *nine* occurrences of forms this lemma written plene ו that are masculine; see **1 Kgs 22:24**.

* M[L], contrary to M (אֹתָךְ), reads Jer 12:1 plene as אוֹתְךָ; see Breuer, *The Biblical Text*, 172.

JUDGES 13:16

וַיֹּאמֶר מַלְאַךְ יְהוָה אֶל־מָנוֹחַ אִם־תַּעְצְרֵנִי לֹא־אֹכַל בְּלַחְמֶךָ וְאִם־תַּעֲשֶׂה עֹלָה לַיהוָה תַּעֲלֶנָּה כִּי לֹא־יָדַע מָנוֹחַ כִּי־מַלְאַךְ יְהוָה הוּא׃

13:16   תַּעְצְרֵנִי

Unique   ל   Mp

13:16   וְאִם־תַּעֲשֶׂה

Unique   ל   Mp

Com.: The Masorah notes the *sole* occurrence of this lemma with a ו cj., to distinguish it from its occurrence without a cj. at Gen 30:31.

13:16   תַּעֲלֶנָּה

Unique   ל   Mp

Com.: This lemma is featured in a Masoretic list of words that occur *twice*, once with a ו cj. (Dan 8:8), and *once* without (here); see Frensdorff, *Ochlah*, §1, and Díaz-Esteban, *Sefer Oklah we-Oklah*, §1.

JUDGES 13:17

וַיֹּאמֶר מָנוֹחַ אֶל־מַלְאַךְ יְהוָה מִי שְׁמֶךָ כִּי־יָבֹא דְבָרְךָ וְכִבַּדְנוּךָ׃

13:17   מִי שְׁמֶךָ

Unique   ל   Mp

Com.: The Masorah notes the *sole* occurrence of שְׁמֶךָ with מִי, to distinguish it from its *sole* occurrence with מַה (מַה שְׁמֶךָ) at Gen 32:28.

13:17   דְבָרְךָ

Read דְּבָרְךָ   דברך ק   Mp

Com.: The *kɔṯîḇ* (דבריך), and the *qɔrê* (דְבָרְךָ) are examples of *kɔṯîḇ/qɔrê* variations in the sing. and pl.; see Gordis, *The Biblical Text*, 136–37.

This lemma is one of *eight* occurrences where forms of דְבָרְךָ are written with a superfluous י; see the Mm at 1 Kgs 8:26, Frensdorff, *Ochlah*, §131, and Díaz-Esteban, *Sefer Oklah we-Oklah*, §115.

In M[L] this lemma has no circellus.

JUDGES 13:18

וַיֹּאמֶר לוֹ מַלְאַךְ יְהוָה לָמָּה זֶּה תִּשְׁאַל לִשְׁמִי וְהוּא־פֶלִאי׃ ס

13:18   פֶלִאי

Unique   ל   Mp

JUDGES 13:19

וַיִּקַּח מָנוֹחַ אֶת־גְּדִי הָעִזִּים וְאֶת־הַמִּנְחָה וַיַּעַל עַל־הַצּוּר לַיהוָה וּמַפְלִא לַעֲשׂוֹת וּמָנוֹחַ וְאִשְׁתּוֹ רֹאִים׃

13:19   וְאֶת־הַמִּנְחָה

Eight times   ח   Mp

1–5   **Exod 40:29; Lev 14:20; Judg 13:19; 1 Kgs 8:64ᵃ; 8:64ᵇ**
6–8   **Ezek 45:17; 46:15; 2 Chr 7:7**

Com.: The Masorah notes the *eight* occurrences of this lemma with a וֹ cj., to distinguish them from its more numerous occurrences (14x) without a cj.

13:19   וּמַפְלִא

Four times defective   ד חס   Mp

Lev 27:2 (יַפְלִא); **Num 6:2** (יַפְלִא); **Judg 13:19;** Isa 28:29 (הַפְלִא)*

Com.: The Masorah notes the *four* occurrences of this lemma in varied forms written defective י, to distinguish them from its *four* occurrences in varied forms written plene י (הִפְלִיא/לְהַפְלִיא).

* M^L, contrary to M (הִפְלִא), has only *three* occurrences of this lemma since it writes the form at Isa 28:29 plene (הִפְלִיא); see Breuer, *The Biblical Text,* 146 and 397. However, the Mp heading here of *four times defective* supports the enumeration inherent in the text of M.

The Mp headings at Lev 27:2 and Num 6:2 of *twice defective* refer to the *twofold* occurrence of the form יַפְלִא, that only occur at these references.

This lemma is featured in a Masoretic list of *hapax legomena* that start with וּמ; see Frensdorff, *Ochlah,* §18, and Díaz-Esteban, *Sefer Oklah we-Oklah,* §19.

13:19   וּמָנוֹחַ וְאִשְׁתּוֹ

Twice   ב   Mp

Judg 13:19; 13:20

Com.: The Masorah notes the *two* occurrences of וְאִשְׁתּוֹ with וּמָנוֹחַ, to distinguish them from its occurrence with מָנוֹחַ (מָנוֹחַ וְאִשְׁתּוֹ) in v. 2.

┌───┐
│   **JUDGES 13:20**   │
│ וַיְהִי בַעֲלוֹת הַלַּהַב מֵעַל הַמִּזְבֵּחַ הַשָּׁמַיְמָה וַיַּעַל מַלְאַךְ־יְהוָה בְּלַהַב הַמִּזְבֵּחַ וּמָנוֹחַ וְאִשְׁתּוֹ רֹאִים │
│   וַיִּפְּלוּ עַל־פְּנֵיהֶם אָרְצָה: │
└───┘

13:20   בַעֲלוֹת

Five times   ה   Mp

1–5   **Judg 13:20; 1 Kgs 11:15; 18:36; Jer 35:11; Jonah 4:7**

Com.: The Masorah notes the *five* occurrences of this lemma with the prep. בְּ, to distinguish them from its *six* occurrences with the prep. כְּ (כְּעָלוֹת); see Ognibeni, *'Oklah*, §8E.

This distinction is implied in the Mm of 1 Kgs 11:15 in the additional notation *of Elijah* to the 1 Kgs 18:36 reference, which distinguishes it from its passage in 2 Kgs 3:20 that refers to Elisha, and where the lemma occurs as כְּעָלוֹת.

13:20   הַשָּׁמַיְמָה

Eleven times   יֹא   Mp

Com.: See **Josh 8:20**.

13:20   וּמָנוֹחַ וְאִשְׁתּוֹ

Twice   בֿ   Mp

Com.: See directly above at **Judg 13:19**.

JUDGES 13:21
וְלֹא־יָסַף עוֹד מַלְאַךְ יְהוָה לְהֵרָאֹה אֶל־מָנוֹחַ וְאֶל־אִשְׁתּוֹ אָז יָדַע מָנוֹחַ כִּי־מַלְאַךְ יְהוָה הוּא׃

13:21   לְהֵרָאֹה

Twice   בֿ   Mp

Judg 13:21; 1 Sam 3:21

Com.: The Masorah notes the *two* occurrences of this lemma ending in אֹה, to distinguish them from its *three* occurrences ending in וֹת (לְהֵרָאוֹת); see **2 Sam 17:17.**

JUDGES 13:22
וַיֹּאמֶר מָנוֹחַ אֶל־אִשְׁתּוֹ מוֹת נָמוּת כִּי אֱלֹהִים רָאִינוּ׃

13:22   אֱלֹהִים רָאִינוּ

Unique   לֿ   Mp

Com.: The Masorah notes the *sole* occurrence of אֱלֹהִים with רָאִינוּ, to distinguish it from its *sole* occurrence with רָאִיתִי (אֱלֹהִים רָאִיתִי) in 1 Sam 28:13.

JUDGES 13:23

וַתֹּאמֶר לוֹ אִשְׁתּוֹ לוּ חָפֵץ יְהוָה לַהֲמִיתֵנוּ לֹא־לָקַח מִיָּדֵנוּ עֹלָה וּמִנְחָה וְלֹא הֶרְאָנוּ אֶת־כָּל־אֵלֶּה
וְכָעֵת לֹא הִשְׁמִיעָנוּ כָּזֹאת:

13:23 לוּ

Twenty-two times כֹּב Mp

1–5 Gen 17:18; **23:13**; 30:34; **50:15**; **Num 14:2**ª
6–10 Num 14:2ᵇ; **20:3** (וְלוּ); **22:29**; **Deut 32:29**; **Josh 7:7** (וְלוּ)
11–15 <u>Judg 8:19</u>; **13:23**; **1 Sam 14:30** (לוּא); **2 Sam 18:12** (וְלוּא, *qərê*); **19:7** (*qərê*)
16–20 **Isa 48:18** (לוּא); **63:19** (לוּא); **Ezek 14:15**; **Mic 2:11**; **Ps 81:14**
21–21 **Job 6:2**; **16:4**

Com.: The Masorah notes the *twenty-two* occurrences of this lemma in varied forms
pointed with a *šûreq*, to distinguish them from its more numerous occurrences
pointed with a *ḥolem* (לוֹ); see the Mm at <u>Judg 8:19</u>.

Notes on the Mp headings highlighted above

1 *Seven* of the Mp headings highlighted above read *twenty-two times* (Gen 23:13,
  50:15, Num 22:29, Judg 13:23, Ezek 14:15, Mic 2:11 and Job 16:4).

2 The Mp heading at Gen 50:15 has *two* notes for this lemma. *One* reads *twenty-two*
  times, and the other בֹ דמטע, that is, there are *two* instances in this list where one
  might mistakenly err (and read the neg. לֹא instead of לוּ). These instances are at
  2 Sam 18:12 and 19:7, where both forms have *kə̄tîb* and *qərê* forms. The *kə̄tîb*
  forms are written as negatives וְלֹא and לֹא but are read as wishes וְלוּ and לוּ.
  So the reader is cautioned not to err in these two cases by reading the neg. form
  לֹא instead of the wish form לוּ.

3 The reading of *twelve times* at Num 14:2ª is simply an error for *twenty-two*.

4 The headings at Num 20:3 and Josh 7:7 read *three times* for occurrences of this
  lemma with a ו cj. (וְלוּ/וְלוּא), the *third* reference being 2 Sam 18:12.

5 *Three* of the headings (Deut 32:29; Ps 81:14 and Job 6:2) note the fact that this
  lemma occurs *six times* at the beginning of a verse (the other *three* being Isa
  48:18, Ezek 14:15, and Mic 2:11).

6 The headings at 1 Sam 14:30, Isa 48:18 and 63:19 note the fact that at these *three*
  verses the lemma is written plene (א) as לוּא.

13:23   הֶרְאָנוּ

Twice   בֿ   Mp

Deut 5:24; **Judg 13:23**

13:23   וּכָעֵת

Unique   ל   Mp

Com.: The Masorah notes the *sole* occurrence of this lemma in the absol., to distinguish it from its *two* occurrences in the cstr. (וּכְעֵת) at **1 Sam 4:20** and 2 Chr 21:19.

13:23   הִשְׁמִיעָנוּ

Unique   ל   Mp

+---+
| **JUDGES 13:24** |
| |
| וַתֵּלֶד הָאִשָּׁה בֵּן וַתִּקְרָא אֶת־שְׁמוֹ שִׁמְשׁוֹן וַיִּגְדַּל הַנַּעַר וַיְבָרְכֵהוּ יְהוָה׃ |
+---+

13:24   וַתִּקְרָא אֶת־שְׁמוֹ

וַתִּקְרָא אֶת־שְׁמוֹ *ten times*, and their references   ותקרא את שמו י וסימנהון   Mm

1–5	Gen 4:25	שת
	Gen 30:11	גד
	Gen 30:13	אשר
	Gen 38:5	שלה
	1 Sam 1:20	שמואל
6–10	Gen 30:20	(זבולן) [זבלון]
	Gen 30:24	יוסף
	Gen 38:4	אונן
	Judg 13:24	שמשון
	2 Sam 12:24	שלמה

Com.: The Masorah notes the *ten* occurrences of this lemma with אֶת, to distinguish them from its *nine* occurrences without אֶת (וַתִּקְרָא שְׁמוֹ); see Ognibeni, *'Oklah*, §35A.

JUDGES 13:25

וַתָּ֙חֶל֙ ר֣וּחַ יְהוָ֔ה לְפַעֲמ֑וֹ בְּמַחֲנֵה־דָ֖ן בֵּ֥ין צָרְעָ֖ה וּבֵ֥ין אֶשְׁתָּאֹֽל׃ פ

13:25   לְפַעֲמ֑וֹ

Unique   ל   Mp

13:25   אֶשְׁתָּאֹל

Three times   ג̇   Mp

Josh 15:33 (אֶשְׁתָּאֹ֑ול); Judg 13:25; 16:31

Com.: The Masorah notes the *three* occurrences of this lemma, *twice* written defective
ֹ (here and Judg 16:31), and *once* written plene ֹו (Josh 15:33).

JUDGES 14:3

וַיֹּ֣אמֶר ל֣וֹ אָבִ֣יו וְאִמּ֡וֹ הַאֵין֩ בִּבְנ֙וֹת אַחֶ֜יךָ וּבְכָל־עַמִּ֣י אִשָּׁ֗ה כִּֽי־אַתָּ֤ה הוֹלֵךְ֙ לָקַ֣חַת אִשָּׁ֔ה מִפְּלִשְׁתִּ֖ים
הָעֲרֵלִ֑ים וַיֹּ֙אמֶר שִׁמְשׁ֤וֹן אֶל־אָבִיו֙ אוֹתָ֣הּ קַֽח־לִ֔י כִּֽי־הִ֖יא יָשְׁרָ֥ה בְעֵינָֽי׃

14:3   בִּבְנ֙וֹת

Twice   ב̇   Mp

Gen 34:1; Judg 14:3

Com.: The Masorah notes the *two* occurrences of this lemma with the prep. בְּ, to
distinguish them from its occurrences (18x) with the prep. מ, two of which are in vv.
1 and 2.

The Mp note at Gen 34:1 adds the catchwords האין בבנות אחיך (הַאֵ֥ין בִּבְנ֣וֹת אַחֶ֖יךָ),
which refer the reader to this verse.

14:3   הֹולֵךְ

Twenty-nine times plene   כֹּט מל   Mp

1–5	**Gen 15:2; 25:32; 28:20; Exod 19:19; Lev 11:27**
6–10	**Lev 11:42ᵃ**; 11:42ᵇ; <u>**Num 17:11**</u> (וְהֹולֵךְ); **22:22; 24:14**
11–15	**Josh 23:14;** <u>**Judg 4:9**</u>**; 14:3**; 2 Sam 15:12; 15:20ᵃ
16–20	<u>**2 Sam 15:20ᵇ**</u>**; 1 Kgs 20:36;** Isa 30:29 (כַּהֹלֵךְ); **Jonah 1:11**; 1:13
20–25	Mic 2:7; **Hab 1:6** (הַהֹלֵךְ); Ps 15:2; 78:39; Cant 7:10
26–27	**Esth 9:4ᵃ**; 9:4ᵇ

Com.: The Mp heading here of *twenty-nine times plene* is incorrect since there are only *twenty-seven* occurrences of this lemma.

The Masorah notes the *twenty-seven* occurrences of this lemma in various forms written plene ‍ו, to distinguish them from its more numerous occurrences (60x) in various forms written defective ‍ו.

This enumeration does not include the *seventeen* occurrences of this lemma in Proverbs and Qoheleth.

Both Mᶜ and Mᴬ correctly read here *twice plene in the book.*

The question of whether the form at Mic 2:7 was plene or defective was a matter of debate among the Masoretes; see Breuer, *The Biblical Text*, 102, n. 4*, and 235, n. 7.

Notes on the highlighted forms

Gen 15:2	*Seventeen times plene in the Torah.* Error for *nine* or for *ten* if the form with a ‍ו cj. (וְהֹולֵךְ) at Num 17:11 is included.
Gen 25:32; Exod 19:19;	*Nine times plene in the Torah.* Does not include the form Num 22:22; 24:14 with a ‍ו cj. (וְהֹולֵךְ) at Num 17:11.
Gen 28:20	*Ten times plene in the Torah.* Includes the form with a ‍ו cj. (וְהֹולֵךְ) at Num 17:11.
Lev 11:27; 11:42ᵃ	*Three times plene in the book* (of Leviticus, Lev 11:27; 11:42ᵃ; 11:42ᵇ).
Num 17:11	The Mp and Mm read *nine times plene in the Torah.* The Mm list includes Num 17:11, but excludes Gen 28:20.
Josh 23:14	*Unique plene in the book* (of Joshua).

Judg 4:9	The Mp and Mm read *twice plene in the book* (of Judges, Judg 4:9; 14:3).
Judg 14:3	*Twenty-nine times plene.* Error for *twenty-seven.*
2 Sam 15:20[b]	Mp and Mm read *twenty-seven times plene.*
1 Kgs 20:36	*Twenty-seven times* plene.
Jonah 1:11	*Three times plene in the book* (of The Twelve): Jonah 1:11; 1:13; Mic 2:7). Not including the form with the def. article at Hab 1:6 (הַהֹלֵךְ).
Hab 1:6	*Unique plene.* Refers to the *sole* occurrence here of the form הַהֹלֵךְ.
Esth 9:4[a]	*Twice plene in the book* (Esth 9:4[a]; 9:4[b]).

14:3   יְשָׁרָה

Twice   בֿ   Mp

Judg 14:3; Hab 2:4

Com.: The Masorah notes the *two* occurrences of this lemma pointed as a perf., to distinguish *them* from its *three* occurrences pointed as a fem. adj. (יְשָׁרָה).

JUDGES 14:4

וְאָבִיו וְאִמּוֹ לֹא יָדְעוּ כִּי מֵיהוָה הִיא כִּי־תֹאֲנָה הוּא־מְבַקֵּשׁ מִפְּלִשְׁתִּים וּבָעֵת הַהִיא פְּלִשְׁתִּים מֹשְׁלִים בְּיִשְׂרָאֵל: פ

14:4   וְאָבִיו וְאִמּוֹ

Eight times written   חֿ כתֿ   Mp

Judg 14:4; 14:5

Com.: The Mp heading here of *eight times written* is incorrect since there are only *two* occurrences of this lemma; here and in v. 5, and the addition of *written* is not applicable to this lemma.

The Masorah notes the *two* occurrences of this lemma with a וֹ cj., to distinguish them from its more numerous occurrences (9x) without a cj. (אָבִיו וְאִמּוֹ).

Neither M^C nor M^A has a note on this lemma here, but M^A has a note at Judg 14:5 that reads *twice*.

14:4   תְאֵנָה

Unique   ל   Mp

14:4   וּבָעֵת הַהִיא

Eight times   חֹ   Mp

1–5   **Judg 14:4**; **Jer 33:15**; 50:4; 50:20; **Joel 4:1**
6–8   **Dan 12:1ᵃ; 12:1ᵇ; 2 Chr 16:7**

בָעֵת הַהִיא	*eight times*	ובעת ההיא חֹ	Mm

1–5	Judg 14:4	פלשתים
	Jer 33:15	אצמיח לדוד
	Jer 50:20	יבקש את עון
	Joel 4:1	בימים ההמה
	Jer 50:4	יבאו בני (קהת) [ישראל]
6–8	2 Chr 16:7	בא חנני הראה
	Dan 12:1ᵃ	יעמד מיכאל השר הגדול
	Twice in the verse (Dan 12:1ᵇ)	בֹ בפסוק

Com.: The Masorah notes the *eight* occurrences of this lemma with a וֹ cj., to distinguish them from its more numerous occurrences (42x) without a cj.

JUDGES 14:6

וַתִּצְלַח עָלָיו רוּחַ יְהֹוָה וַיְשַׁסְּעֵהוּ כְּשַׁסַּע הַגְּדִי וּמְאוּמָה אֵין בְּיָדוֹ וְלֹא הִגִּיד לְאָבִיו וּלְאִמּוֹ אֵת אֲשֶׁר עָשָׂה:

14:6   וַיְשַׁסְּעֵהוּ

Unique   ל   Mp

14:6 וּמְאוּמָה

Twice בׄ Mp

Judg 14:6; Qoh 5:14

Com.: The Masorah notes the *two* occurrences of this lemma with a ו cj., to distinguish them from its more numerous occurrences (28x) without a cj.

JUDGES 14:7

וַיֵּרֶד וַיְדַבֵּר לָאִשָּׁה וַתִּישַׁר בְּעֵינֵי שִׁמְשׁוֹן:

14:7 לָאִשָּׁה

Five times הׄ Mp

Gen 3:13; **Num 5:21**; **Judg 14:7**; 2 Sam 11:3; **2 Kgs 8:6**

לָאִשָּׁה *five times*, and their references   לאשה הׄ וסימנׄ   Mm

Gen 3:13	ויאמר יהוה
Num 5:21	והשביע (אתה) [הכהן]
Judg 14:7	וירד
2 Sam 11:3	דוד וידרש
2 Kgs 8:6	וישאל המלך

And *once* (וְלָאִשָּׁה): 1 Sam 28:24   וחד ולאשה עגל מרבק בבית

Com.: The Masorah notes the *five* occurrences of this lemma with the def. prep. לְ, to distinguish them from its more numerous occurrences (53x) with the indef. prep. לְ (לְאִשָּׁה).

The Mm has an additional note that this lemma also occurs with a ו cj. (וְלָאִשָּׁה) at 1 Sam 28:24.

In M^L the circellus has mistakenly been placed on וַיְדַבֵּר לָאִשָּׁה, which only occurs this *once*.

14:7 וַתִּישַׁר

Unique לׄ Mp

JUDGES 14:8

וַיָּ֤שָׁב מִיָּמִים֙ לְקַחְתָּ֔הּ וַיָּ֣סַר לִרְאוֹת֙ אֵ֚ת מַפֶּ֣לֶת הָאַרְיֵ֔ה וְהִנֵּ֞ה עֲדַ֧ת דְּבוֹרִ֛ים בִּגְוִיַּ֥ת הָאַרְיֵ֖ה וּדְבָֽשׁ׃

14:8   מַפֶּ֣לֶת

Unique   ל   Mp

14:8   דְּבוֹרִ֛ים

Unique   ל   Mp

Com.: This lemma is featured in a Masoretic list of words occurring *twice*, *once* with a ה at the beginning (Deut 1:44), and *once* without (here); see Frensdorff, *Ochlah*, §8, and Díaz-Esteban, *Sefer Oklah we-Oklah*, §8. In this *Ochlah* list this lemma is written defective ו as דְּבֹרִים.

JUDGES 14:9

וַיִּרְדֵּ֣הוּ אֶל־כַּפָּ֗יו וַיֵּ֤לֶךְ הָלוֹךְ֙ וְאָכֹ֔ל וַיֵּ֙לֶךְ֙ אֶל־אָבִ֣יו וְאֶל־אִמּ֔וֹ וַיִּתֵּ֥ן לָהֶ֖ם וַיֹּאכֵ֑לוּ וְלֹֽא־הִגִּ֣יד לָהֶ֔ם כִּ֛י מִגְוִיַּ֥ת הָאַרְיֵ֖ה רָדָ֥ה הַדְּבָֽשׁ׃

14:9   וַיִּרְדֵּ֣הוּ

Unique   ל   Mp

14:9   אֶל־כַּפָּ֗יו

Unique   ל   Mp

Com.: This lemma is featured in a Masoretic list of words that only occur once with the prep. אֶל; see Frensdorff, *Ochlah*, §77, and Díaz-Esteban, *Sefer Oklah we-Oklah*, §156A

14:9   מִגְוִיַּ֥ת

Unique   ל   Mp

Com.: The Masorah notes the *sole* occurrence of this lemma with the prep. מ, to distinguish it from its occurrence with the prep. ב (בִּגְוִיַּת) in the previous verse.

14:9   רָדָה

Unique   ל   Mp

Com.: The Masorah notes the *sole* occurrence of this lemma with a *qameṣ* under the ר (3rd masc. sg. perf. from רָדָה), to distinguish it from its *two* occurrences with a *šĕwâ* (רְדָה, lengthened imper. from יָרַד) at Gen 45:9 and Ezek 32:19.

14:9   הַדְּבָשׁ

Twice   בֿ   Mp

Judg 14:9; 1 Sam 14:27

Com.: The Masorah notes the *two* occurrences of this lemma with the def. article, to distinguish them from its *sole* occurrence without this def. article (דְּבָשׁ) at 1 Sam 14:26.

> ## JUDGES 14:10
>
> וַיֵּרֶד אָבִיהוּ אֶל־הָאִשָּׁה וַיַּעַשׂ שָׁם שִׁמְשׁוֹן מִשְׁתֶּה כִּי כֵּן יַעֲשׂוּ הַבַּחוּרִים:

14:10   אָבִיהוּ

Seven times and plene   ז ומל   Mp

1–5   **Judg 14:10; 14:19; 16:31; 1 Kgs 5:15; Zech 13:3**
6–7   **1 Chr 26:10**; 2 Chr 3:1

אָבִיהוּ *seven times*   אביהו ז   Mm

1–5	Judg 14:10	(= הָאִשָּׁה)	אתתה
	Judg 14:19	(= וַיִּחַר אַפּוֹ)	רגזת
	Judg 16:31	(= בֵּית)	מן ביתה
	1 Kgs 5:15	(= מֶלֶךְ)	מלכה
	2 Chr 3:1	(= נִרְאָה)	חזיה
6–7	Zech 13:3	(= וּדְקָרֻהוּ)	ודקרה
	1 Chr 26:10	(= לְרֹאשׁ)	בראשה

The Masorah notes the *seven* occurrences of this lemma with the 3rd masc. sg. sfx. הו, to distinguish them from its more numerous (100+) occurrences with the sfx. ו (אָבִיו); see Ognibeni, *'Oklah,* §223.

The catchwords are given here, and in the Mm at <u>Zech 13:3</u>, in the form of an Aramaic mnemonic: "A woman angrily (rushed) from her house, the king saw her and pierced her head"; see Marcus, *Scribal Wit*, 64–65, 115.

JUDGES 14:11

וַיְהִ֤י כִּרְאוֹתָם֙ אוֹת֔וֹ וַיִּקְחוּ֙ שְׁלֹשִׁ֣ים מֵֽרֵעִ֔ים וַיִּהְי֖וּ אִתּֽוֹ׃

14:11 מֵֽרֵעִים

Unique ל Mp

Com.: The Masorah notes the *sole* occurrence of this lemma pointed this way (רֵעִים *companions* with the inseparable prep. מִן *from*), to distinguish it from its more numerous occurrences (15x) pointed as מְרֵעִים (masc. pl. *hiphil* ptcp. from רעע, *evildoers*).

JUDGES 14:12

וַיֹּ֤אמֶר לָהֶם֙ שִׁמְשׁ֔וֹן אָחֽוּדָה־נָּ֥א לָכֶ֖ם חִידָ֑ה אִם־הַגֵּ֣ד תַּגִּ֩ידוּ֩ אוֹתָ֨הּ לִ֜י שִׁבְעַ֨ת יְמֵ֤י הַמִּשְׁתֶּה֙ וּמְצָאתֶ֔ם וְנָתַתִּ֤י לָכֶם֙ שְׁלֹשִׁ֣ים סְדִינִ֔ים וּשְׁלֹשִׁ֖ים חֲלִפֹ֥ת בְּגָדִֽים׃

14:12 וַיֹּ֤אמֶר לָהֶם

Thirty times כֹ׳ Mp

Com.: See **Josh 4:5**.

14:12 אָחֽוּדָה־

Unique ל Mp

Com.: This lemma is featured in a Masoretic list of *hapax legomena* that are accented *mil'êl*; see Frensdorff, *Ochlah*, §32.

14:12 יְמֵי הַמִּשְׁתֶּה

Twice ב׳ Mp

Judg 14:12; Job 1:5

Com.: The Masorah notes the *two* occurrences of this lemma with the def. article on מִשְׁתֶּה, to distinguish them from its *sole* occurrence without this def. article (יְמֵי מִשְׁתֶּה) at Esth 9:22.

The Mp at Job 1:5 adds catchwords אחודה נא לכם (אֲחוּדָה־נָּא לָכֶם) to refer the reader to this verse.

14:12   חֲלִפֹת

Twice defective   בֹּ חסֹ   Mp

Gen 45:22ᵇ; Judg 14:12

Com.: The Masorah notes the *two* occurrences of this lemma written doubly defective (of the י and the ו), to distinguish them from its *five* occurrences written plene י and plene ו (חֲלִיפוֹת), and from its *three* occurrences written just defective י (חֲלִפוֹת).

JUDGES 14:13

וְאִם־לֹא תוּכְלוּ לְהַגִּיד לִי וּנְתַתֶּם אַתֶּם לִי שְׁלֹשִׁים סְדִינִים וּשְׁלֹשִׁים חֲלִיפֹת בְּגָדִים וַיֹּאמְרוּ לוֹ חוּדָה חִידָתְךָ וְנִשְׁמָעֶנָּה:

14:13   סְדִינִים

Twice   בֹּ   Mp

Judg 14:12; **14:13**

Com.: The Masorah notes the *two* occurrences of this lemma without any prefixes, to distinguish them from its *sole* occurrence with a ו cj. and the def. article (וְהַסְּדִינִים) at Isa 3:23.

14:13   חוּדָה

Unique   ל   Mp

Com.: The Masorah notes the *sole* occurrence of this lemma with the lengthened imper., to distinguish it from its occurrence with the regular imper. חוּד at Ezek 17:2.

14:13   וְנִשְׁמָעֶנָּה

Unique   ל   Mp

JUDGES 14:14

וַיֹּאמֶר לָהֶם מֵהָאֹכֵל יָצָא מַאֲכָל וּמֵעַז יָצָא מָתוֹק וְלֹא יָכְלוּ לְהַגִּיד הַחִידָה שְׁלֹשֶׁת יָמִים:

14:14   מֵהָאֹכֵל

Unique   ל   Mp

Com.: The Masorah notes the *sole* occurrence of this lemma with the prep. מ, to distinguish it from its more numerous occurrences (7x) without this preposition.

14:14   וּמֵעַז

Unique   ל   Mp

14:14   יָצָא מָתוֹק

Unique   ל   Mp

14:14   וְלֹא יָכְלוּ

<Twenty times>   <כ>   Mp

Com.: In Mᴸ this lemma has a circellus but no note. The lemma occurs *twenty times*, *two* of which are in the book (Judg 2:14 and here), but there are no Mp notes at any of its occurrences. Neither Mᶜ nor Mᴬ has a note here.

It is possible that the purpose of this note was to distinguish this lemma, which is written with a *šəwâ* under the כ, from its *three* occurrences with a *ḥolem* on the כ (וְלֹא יְכֹלוּ); see **2 Kgs 3:26**.

JUDGES 14:15

וַיְהִי | בַּיּוֹם הַשְּׁבִיעִי וַיֹּאמְרוּ לְאֵשֶׁת־שִׁמְשׁוֹן פַּתִּי אֶת־אִישֵׁךְ וְיַגֶּד־לָנוּ אֶת־הַחִידָה פֶּן־נִשְׂרֹף אוֹתָךְ וְאֶת־בֵּית אָבִיךְ בָּאֵשׁ הַלְיָרְשֵׁנוּ קְרָאתֶם לָנוּ הֲלֹא:

14:15   פַּתִּי

Twice   בֿ   Mp

Judg 14:15; 16:5

Com.: The Masorah notes the *two* occurrences of this lemma with a *paṭaḥ* under the פ,
to distinguish them from its more numerous occurrences (6x) with a *sᵊḡôl* (פֶּתִי).

This distinction is implied in the Mp heading at Judg 16:5, which reads *twice with a
paṭaḥ*, indicating a contrast with a form with a different vowel, which is most probably
a *sᵊḡôl*.

14:15   וַיַּגֵּד

Four times   דֿ   Mp

Judg 14:15; Jer 42:3; Job 11:6; 12:7

וַיַּגֵּד | וְיַגֵּד *four times*   ויגד דֿ   Mm

Judg 14:15   החידה
Jer 42:3   את הדרך
Job 11:6   (תעלומות) [תעלמות]
Job 12:7   בהמות

Com.: The Masorah notes the *four* occurrences of this lemma with a ו cj., to distinguish
them from its more numerous occurrences (45x) with a ו consec. (וַיַּגֵּד); see Ognibeni,
'*Oklah*, §37B.

The Mp heading at Job 11:6 mistakenly reads *three times*, a possible confusion with
another word וְיִפְתַּח in the previous verse, but on the same line in the ms., that
actually occurs *three times*; see **Josh 15:43**, and Dotan/Reich, *Masora Thesaurus, ad loc.*

14:15   אוֹתָךְ

Seventeen times indicating a fem.   יֿז בלש נק   Mp

1–5   **Gen 39:9**; **Num 5:21**; **Judg 14:15**; Jer 2:35; 11:17
6–10   Jer 30:14; Ezek 16:4*; 16:39^b; 16:40; 16:57
11–15   Ezek 16:59; 16:60; 22:14; 22:15; 23:25
16   **Ezek 23:29**

Com.: The Mp headings here, and at Gen 39:9, Num 5:21, Judg 14:15 and Ezek 23:29,
of *seventeen*, are incorrect since there are only *sixteen* occurrences of this lemma as
indicated in the Mm lists at Gen 39:9 and Ezek 23:29. The mistake is probably a
graphic one of writing יֿז *seventeen* instead of יֿו *sixteen*.

The Masorah notes the *sixteen* occurrences of this lemma indicating a fem. written plene וֹ, to distinguish them from its *ten* occurrences written defective וֹ (אֹתָךְ).

This distinction is implied in the Mp headings at Gen 39:9, Num 5:21 and Ezek 23:29 and in the Mm headings at <u>Gen 39:9</u> and <u>Ezek 23:29</u>, all of which read *seventeen times plene in this* (fem.) *meaning.*

* M[L], contrary to M (אֹתָךְ), writes Ezek 16:4 defective וֹ (אֹתָךְ); see Breuer, *The Biblical Text*, 204. On the other hand, M[L], contrary to M (אֹתָךְ), writes Ezek 16:39[a] plene (אוֹתָךְ); see Breuer, ibid, 206.

Neither M[C] nor M[A] has a note on this lemma here.

14:15	הֲלְיָרְשֵׁנוּ		
Unique		ל	Mp

> ### JUDGES 14:16
>
> וַתֵּבְךְּ אֵשֶׁת שִׁמְשׁוֹן עָלָיו וַתֹּאמֶר רַק־שְׂנֵאתַנִי וְלֹא אֲהַבְתָּנִי הַחִידָה חַדְתָּ לִבְנֵי עַמִּי וְלִי לֹא הִגַּדְתָּה וַיֹּאמֶר לָהּ הִנֵּה לְאָבִי וּלְאִמִּי לֹא הִגַּדְתִּי וְלָךְ אַגִּיד:

14:16	שְׂנֵאתַנִי		
Unique		ל	Mp

14:16	אֲהַבְתָּנִי		
Unique		ל	Mp

14:16	חַדְתָּ		
Unique		ל	Mp

14:16	וְלִי		
Eight times		ח֗	Mp

1–5   **<u>Judg 14:16</u>**; <u>1 Sam 18:8</u>; 1 Kgs 1:26; <u>Hag 2:8</u>; Ps 60:9
6–8   Ps 116:6; <u>139:17</u>; <u>Dan 4:33</u>

וְלִי *eight times* ולי ח֗ Mm

1–5	Judg 14:16	שמשון
	1 Sam 18:8	ולי נתנו האלפים
	1 Kgs 1:26	ולי אני עבדך
	The *first* occurrence of לִי גִלְעָד וְלִי מְנַשֶּׁה (Ps 60:9)	לי גלעד ולי מנשה קדמ׳
	Hag 2:8	לי הכסף
6–8	Ps 116:6	דלותי
	Ps 139:17	ולי מה יקרו
	Dan 4:33	ולי הדברי

Com.: The Masorah notes the *eight* occurrences of this lemma with a ו cj., to distinguish them from its more numerous occurrences (700+) without a cj.

The mention of the *first* occurrence of the phrase לִי גִלְעָד וְלִי מְנַשֶּׁה at the Ps 60:9 reference is to distinguish that phrase from its second occurrence at Ps 108:9, which reads לִי גִלְעָד לִי מְנַשֶּׁה, that is, it does not have the lemma וְלִי.

The Mp heading at 1 Kgs 1:26 mistakenly writes *five* for *eight*, a graphic error of ה *five* for ח *eight*.

14:16 הִגַּדְתָּה

Unique plene ל֗ מל Mp

Com.: The Masorah notes the *sole* occurrence of this lemma written plene ה, to distinguish them from its more numerous occurrences (7x) written defective ה (הִגַּדְתָּ).

JUDGES 14:17

וַתֵּבְךְּ עָלָיו֙ שִׁבְעַ֣ת הַיָּמִ֔ים אֲשֶׁר־הָיָ֥ה לָהֶ֖ם הַמִּשְׁתֶּ֑ה וַיְהִ֣י ׀ בַּיּ֣וֹם הַשְּׁבִיעִ֗י וַיַּגֶּד־לָהּ֙ כִּ֣י הֱצִיקַ֔תְהוּ וַתַּגֵּ֥ד הַחִידָ֖ה לִבְנֵ֥י עַמָּֽהּ׃

14:17 שִׁבְעַת הַיָּמִים

Eight times ח֗ Mp

1–5 **Gen 7:10** (לְשִׁבְעַת הַיָּמִים); **Exod 13:7; Judg 14:7; Isa 30:26; Ezek 45:23**
6–8 **Ezek 45:25**; 1 Chr 9:25 (לְשִׁבְעַת הַיָּמִים); **2 Chr 30:22**

Com.: The Masorah notes the *eight* occurrences of this lemma in various forms with the def. article on יָמִים, to distinguish them from its more numerous occurrences (81x) without this def. article (שִׁבְעַת יָמִים); see Ognibeni, *'Oklah*, §237.

All the Mp headings highlighted above read *eight times* except for that at Gen 7:10, which reads *twice* enumerating the *two* forms of לְשִׁבְעַת הַיָּמִים there, and at 1 Chr 9:25.

In M^L the Mp note in the margin is very faint.

14:17   הֱצִיקַתְהוּ

Unique   ל   Mp

JUDGES 14:18

וַיֹּאמְרוּ לֹוֹ אַנְשֵׁי הָעִיר בַּיֹּום הַשְּׁבִיעִי בְּטֶרֶם יָבֹא הַחַרְסָה מַה־מָּתֹוק מִדְּבַשׁ וּמֶה עַז מֵאֲרִי
וַיֹּאמֶר לָהֶם לוּלֵא חֲרַשְׁתֶּם בְּעֶגְלָתִי לֹא מְצָאתֶם חִידָתִי׃

14:18   הַחַרְסָה

Unique   ל   Mp

14:18   מַה־מָּתֹוק

Unique   ל   Mp

Com.: In M^L the circellus has been placed on מָתֹוק but, since this word occurs *six times*, it is more likely that the note refers to the phrase מַה־מָּתֹוק, which only occurs this *once*.

14:18   לוּלֵא

Four times written (with א)   ד כת   Mp

Gen 43:10; Judg 14:18; 2 Sam 2:27; Ps 27:13 (לוּלֵ֠א)

Com.: The Masorah notes the *four* occurrences of this lemma written with an א, to distinguish them from its more numerous occurrences (10x) written with a י (לוּלֵי).

The Mp heading at Ps 27:13 notes the dots that are above and below the first, third and fourth letters, and reads: *unique pointed above and below apart from* ו, that is, this form is unique in having the *three* letters other than the ו pointed with dots above and below them.

14:18   חֲרַשְׁתֶּם

Twice   בֿ   Mp

Judg 14:18; Hos 10:13

Com.: This lemma is featured in two contradictory Masoretic lists. One in a list of doublets with the same meaning; see Frensdorff, *Ochlah*, §70, and Díaz-Esteban, *Sefer Oklah we-Oklah*, §13.

The other is in a list homonymous doublets; see Frensdorff, *Ochlah*, §59, and Díaz-Esteban, *Sefer Oklah we-Oklah*, §60. But the meaning of both forms here, and at Hos 10:13 is the same: *you have plowed.*

JUDGES 14:19

וַתִּצְלַח עָלָיו רוּחַ יְהוָה וַיֵּרֶד אַשְׁקְלוֹן וַיַּךְ מֵהֶם ׀ שְׁלֹשִׁים אִישׁ וַיִּקַּח אֶת־חֲלִיצוֹתָם וַיִּתֵּן הַחֲלִיפוֹת לְמַגִּידֵי הַחִידָה וַיִּחַר אַפּוֹ וַיַּעַל בֵּית אָבִיהוּ׃ פ

14:19   חֲלִיצוֹתָם

Unique   לֿ   Mp

Com.: This lemma is featured in a Masoretic list on words that occur *once* with a *ḥolem* (here), and *once* with a *šureq* (עֲלִיצָתָם, Hab 3:14); see Frensdorff, *Ochlah*, §55, and Díaz-Esteban, *Sefer Oklah we-Oklah*, §56.

14:19   לְמַגִּידֵי

Unique   לֿ   Mp

14:19   אָבִיהוּ

Seven times   זֿ   Mp

Com.: See directly above at **Judg 14:10**.

JUDGES 14:20

וַתְּהִי אֵשֶׁת שִׁמְשׁוֹן לְמֵרֵעֵהוּ אֲשֶׁר רֵעָה לְוֹ:

14:20   לְמֵרֵעֵהוּ

Twice   בֿ   Mp

Judg 14:20; 15:6

Com.: The Masorah notes the *sole* occurrence of this lemma with the prep. לֹ, to distinguish it from its more numerous occurrences (8x) without this prep. (מֵרֵעֵהוּ).

14:20   רֵעָה

Unique   לֹ   Mp

Com.: The Masorah notes the *sole* occurrence of this lemma with a *qames* under the ע, to distinguish it from its *three* occurrences with a *segôl* (רֵעֶה).

JUDGES 15:1

וַיְהִי מִיָּמִים בִּימֵי קְצִיר־חִטִּים וַיִּפְקֹד שִׁמְשׁוֹן אֶת־אִשְׁתּוֹ בִּגְדִי עִזִּים וַיֹּאמֶר אָבֹאָה אֶל־אִשְׁתִּי
הֶחָדְרָה וְלֹא־נְתָנוֹ אָבִיהָ לָבוֹא:

15:1   וַיְהִי מִיָּמִים

Three times   גֿ   Mp

Com.: See **Josh 23:1**.

15:1   אָבֹאָה

Unique and defective   לֹ וחס   Mp

Com.: By noting that this lemma is *unique* and written defective וֹ, the Masorah is also implying (correctly) that this lemma does not occur elsewhere written plene וֹ.

This lemma is featured in a Masoretic list of words that occur *five* times, *four* times with a וֹ cj., and *once* (here) without a וֹ cj.; see **2 Kgs 19:23**.

15:1   הֶחָדְרָה

הֶחָדְרָה *twice*   החדרה בֿ   Mm

2 Sam 13:10   ותקח תמר את הלבבות
Judg 15:1   אבאה אל אשתי החדרה

Com.: The Masorah notes the *two* occurrences of this lemma with this pointing, to distinguish them from its *two* occurrences with a different pointing (הַחַדְרָה) at Gen 43:30 and 1 Kgs 1:15.

15:1   נְתָנוּ

Five times   הֿ   Mp

Com.: See **Judg 1:34.**

JUDGES 15:2

וַיֹּאמֶר אָבִיהָ אָמֹר אָמַרְתִּי כִּי־שָׂנֹא שְׂנֵאתָהּ וָאֶתְּנֶנָּה לְמֵרֵעֶךָ הֲלֹא אֲחֹתָהּ הַקְּטַנָּה טוֹבָה מִמֶּנָּה תְּהִי־נָא לְךָ תַּחְתֶּיהָ:

15:2   אָמֹר

Three times defective   גֿ חסֿ   Mp

Exod 21:5; **Judg 15:2**; 1 Sam 20:21

אָמֹר *three time*s defective, and (their) references   אמר גֿ חסֿ וסימֿ   Mm

Exod 21:5   ואם אמר יאמר העבד אהבתי
Judg 15:2   ויאמר אביה אמר
1 Sam 20:21   והנה אשלח את הנער לך

Com.: The Masorah notes the *three* occurrences of this lemma written defective וֹ, to distinguish them from its *three* occurrences written plene וֹ (אָמוֹר).

JUDGES 15:4

וַיֵּ֣לֶךְ שִׁמְשׁ֔וֹן וַיִּלְכֹּ֖ד שְׁלֹשׁ־מֵא֣וֹת שׁוּעָלִ֑ים וַיִּקַּ֣ח לַפִּדִ֗ים וַיֶּ֤פֶן זָנָב֙ אֶל־זָנָ֔ב וַיָּ֨שֶׂם לַפִּ֥יד אֶחָ֛ד בֵּין־שְׁנֵ֥י הַזְּנָב֖וֹת בַּתָּֽוֶךְ׃

15:4   שׁוּעָלִים

Twice plene   ב מל   Mp

Judg 15:4; Lam 5:18

Com.: The Masorah notes the *two* occurrences of this lemma written plene וּ, to distinguish them from its *three* occurrences written defective וּ (שֻׁעָלִים).

M[L], contrary to M (שֻׁעָלִים), has *two* more occurrences of this lemma at Cant 2:15[a] and Cant 2:15[b] since it writes both these forms plene וּ (שׁוּעָלִים); see Breuer, *The Biblical Text*, 304. However, the Mp heading highlighted above supports the enumeration inherent in the text of M.

15:4   בַּתָּוֶךְ

Five times   ה   Mp

Com.: See **Josh 8:22**.

JUDGES 15:5

וַיַּבְעֶר־אֵשׁ֙ בַּלַּפִּידִ֔ים וַיְשַׁלַּ֖ח בְּקָמ֣וֹת פְּלִשְׁתִּ֑ים וַיַּבְעֵ֛ר מִגָּדִ֥ישׁ וְעַד־קָמָ֖ה וְעַד־כֶּ֥רֶם זָֽיִת׃

15:5   וַיַּבְעֶר

Unique   ל   Mp

Com.: The Masorah notes the *sole* occurrence of this lemma with a *səḡôl* under the ע, to distinguish it from its *two* occurrences with a *ṣerê* under the ע (וַיַּבְעֵר), *one* of which occurs in this same verse, and the *other* in 2 Chr 28:3.

JUDGES 15:6

וַיֹּאמְר֣וּ פְלִשְׁתִּים֮ מִ֣י עָ֣שָׂה זֹאת֒ וַיֹּאמְר֗וּ שִׁמְשׁוֹן֙ חֲתַ֣ן הַתִּמְנִ֔י כִּ֤י לָקַח֙ אֶת־אִשְׁתּ֔וֹ וַֽיִּתְּנָ֖הּ לְמֵרֵעֵ֑הוּ וַיַּעֲל֣וּ פְלִשְׁתִּ֗ים וַיִּשְׂרְפ֥וּ אוֹתָ֛הּ וְאֶת־אָבִ֖יהָ בָּאֵֽשׁ׃

15:6   חֲתַן

Four times   דֹ   Mp

Exod 4:25; 4:26; Judg 15:6; 2 Kgs 8:27

חֲתַן *four times*   חתן דֹ   Mm

Exod 4:25	דמים
Exod 4:26	דמים
Judg 15:6	התמני כי לקח את אשתו
2 Kgs 8:27	בית אחאב

Com.: The Masorah notes the *four* occurrences of this lemma written with a *pataḥ*, to distinguish them from its more numerous occurrences written with a *qameṣ* (חָתָן).

This lemma is featured in a Masoretic list of words that occur *five times*, *four times* without a ו cj., and *once* with a cj. (**1 Sam 22:14**); see Frensdorff, *Ochlah*, §17, and Díaz-Esteban, *Sefer Oklah we-Oklah*, §18.

15:6   הַתִּמְנִי

Unique   לֹ   Mp

15:6   וְאֶת־אָבִיהָ

Twice   בֹ   Mp

Josh 6:23; Judg 15:6

וְאֶת־אָבִיהָ	*twice*	ואת אביה בֿ	Mm

<u>Josh 6:23</u>   ויבאו הנערים
<u>Judg 15:6</u>   וישרפו אותה

Com.: The Masorah notes the *two* occurrences of this lemma with a וֹ cj., to distinguish them from its *three* occurrences without a cj.

JUDGES 15:7

וַיֹּאמֶר לָהֶם שִׁמְשׁוֹן אִם־תַּעֲשׂוּן כָּזֹאת כִּי אִם־נִקַּמְתִּי בָכֶם וְאַחַר אֶחְדָּל:

15:7   תַּעֲשׂוּן

Fourteen times   יֹד   Mp

Com.: See **Judg 7:17**.

JUDGES 15:8

וַיַּךְ אוֹתָם שׁוֹק עַל־יָרֵךְ מַכָּה גְדוֹלָה וַיֵּרֶד וַיֵּשֶׁב בִּסְעִיף סֶלַע עֵיטָם: ס

15:8   אוֹתָם שׁוֹק

Unique   לֿ   Mp

15:8   בִּסְעִיף

Unique   לֿ   Mp

Com.: The Masorah notes the *sole* occurrence of this lemma with the prep. בְ, to distinguish it from its occurrence without this prep. in v. 11.

JUDGES 15:9

וַיַּעֲלוּ פְלִשְׁתִּים וַיַּחֲנוּ בִּיהוּדָה וַיִּנָּטְשׁוּ בַּלֶּחִי:

15:9   וַיִּנָּטְשׁוּ

Three times   גֿ   Mp

Judg 15:9; 2 Sam 5:18; **5:22**

JUDGES 15:10

וַיֹּאמְרוּ אִישׁ יְהוּדָה לָמָה עֲלִיתֶם עָלֵינוּ וַיֹּאמְרוּ לֶאֱסוֹר אֶת־שִׁמְשׁוֹן עָלִינוּ לַעֲשׂוֹת לוֹ כַּאֲשֶׁר
עָשָׂה לָנוּ׃

15:10   לָמָה עֲלִיתֶם

Unique   ל   Mp

Com.: The Masorah notes the *sole* occurrence of עֲלִיתֶם with לָמָה, to distinguish it from
its *sole* occurrence with וְלָמָה (וְלָמָה עֲלִיתֶם) at Judg 12:3.

15:10   לֶאֱסוֹר

Unique plene   ל מל   Mp

Com.: The Masorah notes the *sole* occurrence of this lemma written plene וֹ, to distinguish them from its *three* occurrences written defective וֹ (לֶאֱסֹר).

15:10   עָלִינוּ

Four times   ד   Mp

Gen 44:24; <u>Num 14:40</u> (וְעָלִינוּ); Judg 15:10; <u>1 Sam 14:10</u> (וְעָלִינוּ)

Com.: The Masorah notes the *four* occurrences of this lemma, *twice* with a וֹ cj. (Num
14:40 and 1 Sam 14:10), and *twice* without a cj. (Gen 44:24 and here).

The Mp headings at Gen 44:24 and Num 14:40 read *twice*, correctly enumerating their
particular forms, whereas the headings here, and at 1 Sam 14:10 read *four times*
enumerating all *four* forms, with and without a cj.

The Mp heading at Gen 44:24 adds the catchwords לֶאֱסוֹר אֶת־ (לאסור את שמשון
שִׁמְשׁוֹן) to refer the reader to this verse.

JUDGES 15:11

וַיֵּרְדוּ שְׁלֹשֶׁת אֲלָפִים אִישׁ מִיהוּדָה אֶל־סְעִיף סֶלַע עֵיטָם וַיֹּאמְרוּ לְשִׁמְשׁוֹן הֲלֹא יָדַעְתָּ כִּי־
מֹשְׁלִים בָּנוּ פְּלִשְׁתִּים וּמַה־זֹּאת עָשִׂיתָ לָּנוּ וַיֹּאמֶר לָהֶם כַּאֲשֶׁר עָשׂוּ לִי כֵּן עָשִׂיתִי לָהֶם׃

15:11   וּמַה־זֹּאת

Unique   ל   Mp

Com.: This lemma is featured in a Masoretic list of words which occur only *once* with a preceding וּמָה; see Frensdorff, *Ochlah*, §256.

JUDGES 15:12

וַיֹּאמְרוּ לוֹ לֶאֱסָרְךָ יָרַדְנוּ לְתִתְּךָ בְּיַד־פְּלִשְׁתִּים וַיֹּאמֶר לָהֶם שִׁמְשׁוֹן הִשָּׁבְעוּ לִי פֶּן־תִּפְגְּעוּן בִּי אַתֶּם:

15:12   תִּפְגְּעוּן

Unique   לֹ   Mp

JUDGES 15:13

וַיֹּאמְרוּ לוֹ לֵאמֹר לֹא כִּי־אָסֹר נֶאֱסָרְךָ וּנְתַנּוּךָ בְיָדָם וְהָמֵת לֹא נְמִיתֶךָ וַיַּאַסְרֻהוּ בִּשְׁנַיִם עֲבֹתִים חֲדָשִׁים וַיַּעֲלוּהוּ מִן־הַסָּלַע:

15:13   אָסֹר

Twice   בֿ   Mp

Judg 15:13; 16:11 (אָסוֹר)

Com.: The Masorah notes the *two* occurrences of this lemma, *one* written plene וֹ (Judg 16:11), and *one* written defective וֹ (here).

The Mp heading at Judg 16:11 of *four times plene* is incorrect since the form there is the *only* occurrence of this lemma written plene.

15:13   נֶאֱסָרְךָ

Unique   לֹ   Mp

15:13   וּנְתַנּוּךָ

Unique   לֹ   Mp

Com.: This lemma is featured in a list of Masoretic words that occur *once* with a וֹ cj. (here), and *once* without (2 Chr 25:16); see Frensdorff, *Ochlah*, §1, and Díaz-Esteban, *Sefer Oklah we-Oklah*, §1.

15:13   לֹא נְמִיתֶ֑ךָ

Unique   ל   Mp

Com.: The Masorah notes the *sole* occurrence of this lemma without a ו cj., to distinguish it from its *sole* occurrence with a cj. at Jer38:25.

15:13   וַיַּאַסְרֻ֖הוּ

Three times   ג̇   Mp

Judg 15:13; 16:21 (וַיַּאַסְרוּהוּ); **2 Chr 33:11**

Com.: The Masorah notes the *three* occurrences of this lemma in the pl., to distinguish them from its more numerous occurrences (6x) in the sg. (וַיַּאַסְרֵהוּ); see Ognibeni, *'Oklah*, §312.

> ## JUDGES 15:14
>
> הוּא־בָ֣א עַד־לֶ֗חִי וּפְלִשְׁתִּים֙ הֵרִ֣יעוּ לִקְרָאתֹ֔ו וַתִּצְלַ֤ח עָלָיו֙ ר֣וּחַ יְהוָ֔ה וַתִּהְיֶ֤ינָה הָעֲבֹתִים֙ אֲשֶׁ֣ר עַל־ זְרֹועֹותָ֗יו כַּפִּשְׁתִּים֙ אֲשֶׁ֣ר בָּעֲר֣וּ בָאֵ֔שׁ וַיִּמַּ֥סּוּ אֱסוּרָ֖יו מֵעַ֥ל יָדָֽיו׃

15:14   זְרֹועֹותָ֗יו

Unique plene   ל מל   Mp

Com.: The Masorah notes the *sole* occurrence of this lemma written plene second ו, to distinguish it from its *sole* occurrence written defective second ו (זְרֹעֹתָיו) at Hos 11:3.

15:14   כַּפִּשְׁתִּים

Unique   ל   Mp

Com.: This lemma is featured in two Masoretic lists. One is in a list of *hapax legomena* beginning with a כ; see Frensdorff, *Ochlah*, §19, and Díaz-Esteban, *Sefer Oklah we-Oklah*, §20.

The other is in a list of words that occur only *once* with a ב (Lev 13:52), and *once* with a כ (here); see Frensdorff, *Ochlah*, §4, and Díaz-Esteban, *Sefer Oklah we-Oklah*, §4.

JUDGES 15:15

וַיִּמְצָא לְחִי־חֲמוֹר טְרִיָּה וַיִּשְׁלַח יָדוֹ וַיִּקָּחֶהָ וַיַּךְ־בָּהּ אֶלֶף אִישׁ׃

15:15   טְרִיָּה

Twice   בׄ   Mp

Judg 15:15; <u>Isa 1:6</u>

Com.: This lemma is featured in a Masoretic list of homonyms; see Frensdorff, *Ochlah*, §59, and Díaz-Esteban, *Sefer Oklah we-Oklah*, §60. Here the meaning is *fresh*, in Isa 1:6 the meaning is *festering*.

JUDGES 15:16

וַיֹּאמֶר שִׁמְשׁוֹן בִּלְחִי הַחֲמוֹר חֲמוֹר חֲמֹרָתָיִם בִּלְחִי הַחֲמוֹר הִכֵּיתִי אֶלֶף אִישׁ׃

15:16   חֲמֹרָתָיִם

Unique   לׄ   Mp

JUDGES 15:17

וַיְהִי כְּכַלֹּתוֹ לְדַבֵּר וַיַּשְׁלֵךְ הַלְּחִי מִיָּדוֹ וַיִּקְרָא לַמָּקוֹם הַהוּא רָמַת לֶחִי׃

15:17   וַיְהִי֙

Six times with the accent (*pašṭâ*) in the book   ו בטע בסיפׄ   Mp

1–5   Judg 1:28; 3:18; 7:9; 9:42; **15:17**
6–10   Judg 16:4; 16:25; 19:1; 19:5; 21:4

Com.: The Mp heading here of *six times* is incorrect since there are *ten* occurrences of this lemma in the book. The Masorah notes the *ten* occurrences of this lemma in the book with the accent *pašṭâ*, to distinguish them from its more numerous occurrences in the book with different accents.

Neither M^C nor M^A has a note on this lemma here.

15:17   רָמַת לֶחִי

Unique   לׄ   Mp

JUDGES 15:18

וַיִּצְמָא֮ מְאֹד֒ וַיִּקְרָ֤א אֶל־יְהוָה֙ וַיֹּאמַ֔ר אַתָּ֤ה נָתַ֙תָּ֙ בְיַד־עַבְדְּךָ֔ אֶת־הַתְּשׁוּעָ֥ה הַגְּדֹלָ֖ה הַזֹּ֑את וְעַתָּ֗ה
אָמ֣וּת בַּצָּמָ֔א וְנָפַלְתִּ֖י בְּיַ֥ד הָעֲרֵלִֽים׃

15:18   נָתַתָּ

Twenty-five times defective   כה חס   Mp

1–5	**Gen 40:13**; Exod 25:16; 25:21; 25:26; **25:30**
6–10	**Exod 26:34**; 28:23; 28:30; 29:3; **29:6**
11–15	Exod 29:17; **30:16**; 30:18ᵃ; 30:18ᵇ; <u>40:7ᵃ</u>
16–20	Exod 40:7ᵇ; **40:8**; **Lev 2:15**; **24:7**; **Judg 15:18**
21–25	**1 Kgs 3:9**; 8:34; 8:39; **Ps 61:6**; **Dan 10:12**
26–28	Neh 9:20ᵃ; 9:35ᵃ; **9:35ᵇ**

Com.: The Mp heading here, and at Gen 40:13, of *twenty-five* is incorrect since there are *twenty-eight* occurrences of this lemma. The error may be ascribed to graphic confusion of ה *five* and ח *eight*.

The Masorah notes the *twenty-eight* occurrences of this lemma in various forms written defective ה, to distinguish them from its more numerous occurrences (65x) in various forms written plene ה (נָתַתָּה/וְנָתַתָּה).

The correct number of *twenty-eight* is given in the Mp headings at 1 Kgs 3:9 and Ps 61:6.

All the other Mp headings highlighted above list the number of this lemma as *twenty-nine* because they include either Neh 9:15 (not in the above list) or Neh 9:20ᵇ (not in the above list), which are in dispute; see Breuer, *The Biblical Text*, 353. The dispute can be seen, for example, in M^L in the Mm to <u>Exod 40:7</u>, since the form at Neh 9:15 is included as defective in the Mm list, but M^L writes this form plene in its text.

M^C reads here *twenty-nine times defective* including Neh 9:15; see Castro, *El codice*, 1:200, while M^A reads here *unique defective in the book* (of Judges).

15:18   הַגְּדֹלָה

Eight times defective   ח חס   Mp

1–5	<u>**Judg 15:18**</u>; Jer 11:16 (גְדֹלָה); Ezra 9:7 (גְדֹלָה); 9:13; Neh 1:3 (גְדֹלָה)
6–8	Neh 2:10 (גְדֹלָה); **7:4** (*וּגְדֹלָה); 9:37 (*גְדֹלָה)

הַגְדֻלָה *eight times* defective in the   הגדלה חֹ חסֹ בנביא ובכתיב   Mm
Prophets and Writings

1–5	<u>Judg 15:18</u>	ויצמא מאד
	Jer 11:16	לקול המולה
	Ezra 9:7	מימי (אבותינו) [אבתינו]
	Ezra 9:13	(ובאשמתינו) [ובאשמתנו] הגדלה
	Neh 1:3	ברעה
6–8	Neh 2:10	וירע להם רעה
	Neh 7:4	והעיר רחבת
	Neh 9:37	ובצרה (גדלה) [גדולה]

And similarly *all* Daniel apart from   וכל דניאל דכות בֹ מֹ אֹ והקרן הגדולה
one (הַגְדוֹלָה): Dan 8:21

And *all* (cases in) the Torah are defective   וכל אוריתא חסירין בר מן דֹ
apart from *four*

Com.: The Masorah notes the *eight* occurrences in the Prophets and Writings of this lemma in various forms written defective ו, to distinguish them from its more numerous occurrences (100+) in the Prophets and Writings in various forms written plene ו (גְדוֹלָה).

The Mm has *two* additional notes. The first is that this lemma is also the norm (5x) in Daniel, apart from *one* case when it is written plene ו (הַגְדוֹלָה) at Dan 8:21.

The *second* is that this lemma written defective ו is also the norm in the Torah (18x), apart from *four* cases. The *four* plene writings are at Num 22:18, Deut 4:36, 25:13 and 25:14, see the Mm to <u>Deut 25:13</u> *sub* גְדוֹלָה.

* M[L], contrary to M (וּגְדֻלָה and גְדֻלָה), has only *six* occurrences of this lemma since it writes the forms at Neh 7:4 and 9:37 plene ו (וּגְדוֹלָה and גְדוֹלָה); see Breuer, *The Biblical Text*, 350 and 353. However, the Mp heading highlighted above reads *eight times*, thus supporting the enumeration inherent in the text of M.

Furthermore M[L], contrary to M (הַגְדֻלָה), has *two* exceptions in Daniel since, in addition to Dan 8:21, it writes the form at Dan 8:8 plene ו (הַגְדוֹלָה). Nevertheless, the Mp note at Dan 8:21 reads *unique plene in the book*.

The Mp heading at Neh 7:4 (וּגְדֻלָה) reads *twice, once plene* (ו) enumerating the *two* forms of this form with a ו cj., *one* there (defective ו), and *one* at Qoh 9:13 (plene ו).

JUDGES 15:19

וַיִּבְקַע אֱלֹהִים אֶת־הַמַּכְתֵּשׁ אֲשֶׁר־בַּלֶּחִי וַיֵּצְאוּ מִמֶּנּוּ מַיִם וַיֵּשְׁתְּ וַתָּשָׁב רוּחוֹ וַיֶּחִי עַל־כֵּן | קָרָא
שְׁמָהּ עֵין הַקּוֹרֵא אֲשֶׁר בַּלֶּחִי עַד הַיּוֹם הַזֶּה:

15:19   וַיִּבְקַע אֱלֹהִים

Unique   לֹ   Mp

15:19   הַמַּכְתֵּשׁ

Twice   בֹ   Mp

Judg 15:19; Zeph 1:11

15:19   הַקּוֹרֵא

Ten times plene   י מלֹ   Mp

1–5   **Judg 15:19**; Isa 6:4; **40:3** (קוֹרֵא); 45:3; **64:6** (קוֹרֵא)
6–10   **Amos 5:8**; **Hab 2:2** (קוֹרֵא); **Ps 42:8** (קוֹרֵא); **1 Chr 9:19** (קוֹרֵא);
         2 Chr 31:14 (וְקוֹרֵא)

Com.: The Masorah notes the *ten* occurrences of this lemma in various forms written
plene ו, to distinguish them from its more numerous occurrences (17x) in various
forms written defective ֹ.

JUDGES 16:1

וַיֵּלֶךְ שִׁמְשׁוֹן עַזָּתָה וַיַּרְא־שָׁם אִשָּׁה זוֹנָה וַיָּבֹא אֵלֶיהָ:

16:1   עַזָּתָה

Twice   בֹ   Mp

Judg 16:1; 16:21

Com.: The Masorah notes the *two* occurrences of this lemma with the locative ה, to
distinguish them from its more numerous occurrences (17x) without this adverbial
ending (עַזָּה).

JUDGES 16:2

לַעֲזָּתִים | לֵאמֹר בָּא שִׁמְשׁוֹן הֵנָּה וַיָּסֹבּוּ וַיֶּאֶרְבוּ־לֹו כָל־הַלַּיְלָה בְּשַׁעַר הָעִיר וַיִּתְחָרְשׁוּ כָל־הַלַּיְלָה לֵאמֹר עַד־אֹור הַבֹּקֶר וַהֲרְגְנֻהוּ:

16:2   לַעֲזָּתִים

Unique   ל   Mp

16:2   וַיִּתְחָרְשׁוּ

Unique   ל   Mp

16:2   אֹור הַבֹּקֶר

Six times   ו   Mp

1–5   **Judg 16:2; 1 Sam 14:36; 25:34; 25:36; 2 Sam 17:22**
6   **2 Kgs 7:9**

אֹור הַבֹּקֶר   *six times*   אור הבקר ו   Mm

1–5   Judg 16:2   ויתחרשו כל הלילה
       1 Sam 14:36   ונבזה בהם
       1 Sam 25:34   כי אם נותר לנבל
       1 Sam 25:36   הגידה
       2 Sam 17:22   נעדר
6   2 Kgs 7:9   מחשים

Com.: The Masorah notes the *six* occurrences of this lemma which occur with the prep. עַד (עַד אֹור הַבֹּקֶר), possibly to avoid confusion with the *twelve* occurrences of the parallel phrase עַד הַבֹּקֶר. For example, some mss. read עַד הַבֹּקֶר at 1 Sam 25:22 as עַד אֹור הַבֹּקֶר (see Ginsburg, 4, א, §211, and *BHS ad loc.*).

JUDGES 16:3

וַיִּשְׁכַּ֣ב שִׁמְשׁוֹן֮ עַד־חֲצִ֣י הַלַּיְלָה֒ וַיָּ֣קׇם ׀ בַּחֲצִ֣י הַלַּ֗יְלָה וַיֶּאֱחֹ֞ז בְּדַלְת֣וֹת שַֽׁעַר־הָעִ֗יר וּבִשְׁתֵּ֤י הַמְּזוּזֹת֙
וַיִּסָּעֵם֙ עִֽם־הַבְּרִ֔יחַ וַיָּ֣שֶׂם עַל־כְּתֵפָ֑יו וַֽיַּעֲלֵם֙ אֶל־רֹ֣אשׁ הָהָ֔ר אֲשֶׁ֖ר עַל־פְּנֵ֥י חֶבְרֽוֹן׃ פ

16:3   בַּחֲצִ֣י הַלַּיְלָה

Three times   גׄ   Mp

Exod 12:29; Judg 16:3; Ruth 3:8

Com.: The Masorah notes the *three* occurrences of this lemma with the prep. בּ, to distinguish them from its *sole* occurrence without this prep. (חֲצִי הַלַּיְלָה) also in this verse.

The Mp heading at Ruth 3:8 extends the lemma to וַיְהִי בַּחֲצִי הַלַּיְלָה, and reads *twice* for the *two* occurrences of this phrase there, and at Exod 12:29. However, the Mm at <u>Ruth 3:8</u> limits the lemma to בַּחֲצִי הַלַּיְלָה, and lists these *three* ocurrences.

16:3   וַיִּסָּעֵם

Unique   לׄ   Mp

JUDGES 16:5

וַיַּעֲל֨וּ אֵלֶ֜יהָ סַרְנֵ֣י פְלִשְׁתִּ֗ים וַיֹּ֨אמְרוּ לָ֜הּ פַּתִּ֣י אוֹת֗וֹ וּרְאִי֙ בַּמֶּה֙ כֹּח֣וֹ גָד֔וֹל וּבַמֶּ֖ה נ֣וּכַל ל֑וֹ וַאֲסַרְנֻ֙הוּ֙
לְעַנּוֹת֔וֹ וַאֲנַ֗חְנוּ נִתַּן־לָ֙ךְ֙ אִ֣ישׁ אֶ֔לֶף וּמֵאָ֖ה כָּֽסֶף׃

16:5   פַּתִּי

Twice with *paṭaḥ*   ב פתח   Mp

Com.: See **Judg 14:15**.

16:5   וַאֲסַרְנֻהוּ

Unique   לׄ   Mp

16:5   לְעַנּוֹתוֹ

Three times   ג   Mp

Judg 16:5 (לְעַנּוֹתוֹ)*; 16:19 (לְעַנּוֹתוֹ); **2 Sam 7:10** (לְעַנּוֹתוֹ)

Com.: The Masorah notes the *three* occurrences of this lemma with the prep. לְ, to distinguish them from its *two* occurrences without this prep. (עַנּתוֹ) at Exod 1:11 and **2 Sam 13:32**.

* M^L, contrary to M (לְעַנּוֹתוֹ), writes the lemma here defective וֹ; see Breuer, *The Biblical Text*, 64.

M^A reads לְעַנּוֹתוֹ, and also has note of *three times*. M^C, as does M^L, reads לְעַנּתוֹ, and has no note.

16:5   נָתַן

Twenty-one times   כֹּא   Mp

Com.: See **Josh 24:33**

JUDGES 16:7

וַיֹּאמֶר אֵלֶיהָ שִׁמְשׁוֹן אִם־יַאַסְרֻנִי בְּשִׁבְעָה יְתָרִים לַחִים אֲשֶׁר לֹא־חֹרָבוּ וְחָלִיתִי וְהָיִיתִי כְּאַחַד הָאָדָם:

16:7   יַאַסְרֻנִי

יַאַסְרֻנִי *twice, once* defective *and once* plene   יאסרני ב̇ חד חסיר וחד מליין   Mm

Judg 16:7   בשבעה יתרים לחים
Judg 16:11   אסור יאסרוני (בעבותים) [בעבתים]

Com.: The Masorah notes the *two* occurrences of this lemma, *one* written plene וֹ (Judg 16:11), and *one* written defective וֹ (here).

This lemma is featured in a Masoretic list of doublets commencing with יְ; see Frensdorff, *Ochlah*, §66, and Díaz-Esteban, *Sefer Oklah we-Oklah*, §67.

16:7   חׇרְבוּ

Twice   בׄ   Mp

Judg 16:7; 16:8

Com.: The Masorah notes the *two* occurrences of this lemma in the *pual* to distinguish them from its *sole* occurrence in the *qal* (חׇרְבוּ) at Gen 8:13; see Ginsburg, 4, ח, §380.

16:7   כְּאַחַד

Twelve times   יבׄ   Mp

1–5	**Gen 3:22**; **49:16**; **Judg 16:7**; **16:11**; 17:11
6–10	**1 Sam 17:36**; 2 Sam 2:18; **9:11**; **13:13**; **Ezek 48:8**
11–12	**Obad 11**; **2 Chr 18:12**

כְּאַחַד *twelve times*   כאחד יבׄ   Mm

1–5	Gen 3:22	הן (האחד) [האדם]
	Gen 49:16	שבטי ישראל
	Judg 16:7	וחליתי והייתי
	Judg 16:11	וחליתי והייתי
	Judg 17:11	כאחד מבניו
6–10	1 Sam 17:36	(ומהם מבני) [כאחד מהם]
	2 Sam 13:13	הנבלים
	Ezek 48:8	כאחד החלקים
	2 Sam 2:18	כאחד הצבים
	2 Sam 9:11	מבני
11–12	Obad 11	ונכרים באו
	of Chronicles (2 Chr 18:12) לְמִיכׇיְהוּ	למיכיהו דדברי הימים

And *once* (וּכְאַחַד): Ps 82:7   וחד וכאחד השרים תפלו

Com.: The Masorah notes the *twelve* occurrences of this lemma with the prep. כ, to distinguish them from its more numerous occurrences (25x) without this preposition.

This distinction is implied in the additional notation in the Mm *of Chronicles* to the 2 Chr 18:12 reference, which distinguishes it from its parallel passage in 1 Kgs 22:13, where the lemma occurs as אׇחׇד.

The Mm has an additional note that this lemma also occurs with a ו cj. (וּכְאַחַד) at Ps 82:7.

JUDGES 16:8

וַיַּעֲלוּ־לָהּ סַרְנֵי פְלִשְׁתִּים שִׁבְעָה יְתָרִים לַחִים אֲשֶׁר לֹא־חֹרָבוּ וַתַּאַסְרֵהוּ בָּהֶם׃

16:8   חֹרָבוּ

Twice   בֹ   Mp

Com.: See directly above at **Judg 16:7**.

JUDGES 16:9

וְהָאֹרֵב יֹשֵׁב לָהּ בַּחֶדֶר וַתֹּאמֶר אֵלָיו פְּלִשְׁתִּים עָלֶיךָ שִׁמְשׁוֹן וַיְנַתֵּק אֶת־הַיְתָרִים כַּאֲשֶׁר יִנָּתֵק פְּתִיל־הַנְּעֹרֶת בַּהֲרִיחוֹ אֵשׁ וְלֹא נוֹדַע כֹּחוֹ׃

16:9   וַיְנַתֵּק

Unique   ל   Mp

16:9   יִנָּתֵק

Three times   גֹ   Mp

Judg 16:9; Job 18:14; Qoh 4:12

Com.: The Masorah notes the *three* occurrences of this lemma in the *niphal*, to distinguish them from its *two* occurrences in the *piel* (יְנַתֵּק) at Ezek 17:9 and Ps 107:14.

16:9   בַּהֲרִיחוֹ

Unique   ל   Mp

JUDGES 16:11

וַיֹּאמֶר אֵלֶיהָ אִם־אָסוֹר יַאַסְרוּנִי בַּעֲבֹתִים חֲדָשִׁים אֲשֶׁר לֹא־נַעֲשָׂה בָהֶם מְלָאכָה וְחָלִיתִי וְהָיִיתִי כְּאַחַד הָאָדָם׃

16:11   אָסוֹר

Four times plene   ד מל   Mp

Com.: The Mp heading here of *four times plene* is incorrect since this is the only occurrence of this form written plene וֹ. Both M^C and M^A read here *unique plene*.

For a suggestion as to how the *four times* might be accounted for as *four* plene forms of the verb אָסַר, see Dotan/Reich, *Masora Thesaurus, ad loc.*

16:11   יַאַסְרוּנִי

Twice, once plene and *once* defective   בׄ חד מל וחד חסׄ   Mp

Judg 16:7 (וַיַּאַסְרֻנִי); **16:11**

Com.: See directly above at Judg 16:7.

16:11   כְּאַחַד

Twelve times   יׄב   Mp

Com.: See **Judg 16:7**.

JUDGES 16:12
וַתִּקַּח דְּלִילָה עֲבֹתִים חֲדָשִׁים וַתַּאַסְרֵהוּ בָהֶם וַתֹּאמֶר אֵלָיו פְּלִשְׁתִּים עָלֶיךָ שִׁמְשׁוֹן וְהָאֹרֵב יֹשֵׁב בֶּחָדֶר וַיְנַתְּקֵם מֵעַל זְרֹעֹתָיו כַּחוּט:

16:12   וַיְנַתְּקֵם

Unique   לׄ   Mp

16:12   כַּחוּט

Unique   לׄ   Mp

Com.: This lemma is featured in a Masoretic list of words that occur *once* with a prefix כְּ (Cant 4:3), and *once* with a prefix כַּ (here); see Frensdorff, *Ochlah*, §11, and Díaz-Esteban, *Sefer Oklah we-Oklah*, §11.

JUDGES 16:13
וַתֹּאמֶר דְּלִילָה אֶל־שִׁמְשׁוֹן עַד־הֵנָּה הֵתַלְתָּ בִּי וַתְּדַבֵּר אֵלַי כְּזָבִים הַגִּידָה לִּי בַּמֶּה תֵּאָסֵר וַיֹּאמֶר אֵלֶיהָ אִם־תַּאַרְגִי אֶת־שֶׁבַע מַחְלְפוֹת רֹאשִׁי עִם־הַמַּסָּכֶת:

16:13   תַּאַרְגִי

Unique   לׄ   Mp

16:13   מַחְלְפוֹת

Twice   בׄ   Mp

Judg 16:13; 16:19

16:13   הַמַּסָּכֶת

Twice   בׄ   Mp

Judg 16:13; 16:14

JUDGES 16:14

וַתִּתְקַע בַּיָּתֵד וַתֹּאמֶר אֵלָיו פְּלִשְׁתִּים עָלֶיךָ שִׁמְשׁוֹן וַיִּיקַץ מִשְּׁנָתוֹ וַיִּסַּע אֶת־הַיְתַד הָאֶרֶג וְאֶת־הַמַּסָּכֶת:

16:14   וְאֶת־הַמַּסָּכֶת

Unique   לׄ   Mp

Com.: The Masorah notes the *sole* occurrence of הַמַּסָּכֶת with וְאֶת, to distinguish it from its *sole* occurrence with עם (עִם־הַמַּסָּכֶת) in the preceding verse.

JUDGES 16:15

וַתֹּאמֶר אֵלָיו אֵיךְ תֹּאמַר אֲהַבְתִּיךְ וְלִבְּךָ אֵין אִתִּי זֶה שָׁלֹשׁ פְּעָמִים הֵתַלְתָּ בִּי וְלֹא־הִגַּדְתָּ לִּי בַּמֶּה כֹּחֲךָ גָדוֹל:

16:15   אֲהַבְתִּיךְ

Twice   בׄ   Mp

Judg 16:15; Jer 31:3

אֲהַבְתִּיךְ *twice*, and their references   אהבתיך בׄ וסימנהון   Mm

Judg 16:15   איך תאמר אהבתיך
Jer 31:3   ואהבת עולם

Com.: The Masorah notes the *two* occurrences of this lemma with the fem. sfx., to distinguish them from its occurrence with the masc. sfx. אֲהַבְתִּיךָ at Isa 43:4.

16:15   וְלִבְּךָ

Five times   הֹ   Mp

1–5   **Judg 16:15**; Jer 22:17; Prov 22:17; 23:33; **Qoh 5:1**

וְלִבְּךָ *five times*   ולבד הֹ   Mm

1–5   Judg 16:15   איך תאמר אהבתיך
               Prov 22:17   ולבד תשית לדעתי
               Jer 22:17   כי אין עיניך ולבד
               Qoh 5:1   אל תבהל על פיך ולבד
               Prov 23:33   עיניך יראו זרות

Com.: The Masorah notes the *five* occurrences of this lemma with a ו cj., to distinguish them from its more numerous occurrences (45x) without a cj.

16:15   וְלֹא־הִגַּדְתָּ

Twice   בֹ   Mp

Gen 31:27; **Judg 16:15**

Com.: The Masorah notes the *two* occurrences of this lemma with a ו cj., to distinguish them from its *two* occurrences without a cj. at Gen 12:18 and 21:26.

JUDGES 16:16

וַיְהִי כִּי־הֵצִיקָה לּוֹ בִדְבָרֶיהָ כָּל־הַיָּמִים וַתְּאַלֲצֵהוּ וַתִּקְצַר נַפְשׁוֹ לָמוּת:

16:16   הֵצִיקָה

Unique   לֹ   Mp

16:16   וַתְּאַלֲצֵהוּ

Unique   לֹ   Mp

Com.: In M^L there is no circellus on this lemma.

16:16   וַתִּקְצַר

וַתִּקְצַר *four times*, and their references   ותקצר ד וסימנהון   Mm

Num 21:4	ותקצר נפש העם (מאד) [בדרך]
Judg 10:16	נפשו
Judg 16:16	נפשו
Zech 11:8	נפשי

Com.: The Masorah notes the *four* occurrences of this lemma with a ו consec., to distinguish them from its *sole* occurrence without a ו (תִּקְצַר) at Job 21:4.

JUDGES 16:17

וַיַּגֶּד־לָהּ אֶת־כָּל־לִבּוֹ וַיֹּאמֶר לָהּ מוֹרָה לֹא־עָלָה עַל־רֹאשִׁי כִּי־נְזִיר אֱלֹהִים אֲנִי מִבֶּטֶן אִמִּי אִם־גֻּלַּחְתִּי וְסָר מִמֶּנִּי כֹחִי וְחָלִיתִי וְהָיִיתִי כְּכָל־הָאָדָם:

16:17   רֹאשִׁי

Twenty-six times   כֹו   Mp

1–5	Gen 40:16; 40:17; Judg 16:13; **16:17**; 2 Kgs 4:19[a]
6–10	2 Kgs 4:19[b]; 6:32; Jer 8:23; Ezek 8:3; Ps 3:4
11–15	Ps 23:5; 27:6; 38:5; 40:13; 60:9
16–20	Ps 69:5; 108:9; 141:5; Job 10:15; 16:4
21–25	Job 19:9; 29:3; Cant 8:3; Lam 3:54; Dan 1:10
26	Ezra 9:3

Com.: The Masorah notes the *twenty-six* occurrences of this lemma with a *holem* on the ר, to distinguish them from its *four* occurrences with a *ṣere* under the ר (רֵאשִׁי).

16:17   גֻּלַּחְתִּי

Unique   ל   Mp

16:17   כְּכָל־הָאָדָם

Unique   ל   Mp

Com.: The Masorah notes the *sole* occurrence of this lemma with the prep. כ, to distinguish it from its more numerous occurrences (12x) without this prep. (כָּל־הָאָדָם).

JUDGES 16:18

וַתֵּ֣רֶא דְלִילָ֗ה כִּֽי־הִגִּ֣יד לָהּ֮ אֶת־כָּל־לִבּוֹ֒ וַתִּשְׁלַ֡ח וַתִּקְרָא֩ לְסַרְנֵ֨י פְלִשְׁתִּ֜ים לֵאמֹ֗ר עֲל֤וּ הַפַּ֙עַם֙ כִּֽי־
הִגִּ֥יד לָ֖הּ אֶת־כָּל־לִבּ֑וֹ וְעָל֤וּ אֵלֶ֙יהָ֙ סַרְנֵ֣י פְלִשְׁתִּ֔ים וַיַּעֲל֛וּ הַכֶּ֖סֶף בְּיָדָֽם׃

16:18   לָהּ

Read לִי   לִי קֹ   Mp

Com.: The *kətîb* (לה, *to her*), and the *qərê* (לי, *to me*) represent variant forms where the
qərê is preferable to the *kətîb*; see Gordis, *The Biblical Text*, 152.

JUDGES 16:19

וַתְּיַשְּׁנֵ֙הוּ֙ עַל־בִּרְכֶּ֔יהָ וַתִּקְרָ֣א לָאִ֗ישׁ וַתְּגַלַּ֛ח אֶת־שֶׁ֥בַע מַחְלְפ֖וֹת רֹאשׁ֑וֹ וַתָּ֙חֶל֙ לְעַנּוֹת֔וֹ וַיָּ֥סַר כֹּח֖וֹ
מֵעָלָֽיו׃

16:19   וַתְּיַשְּׁנֵהוּ

Unique   ל   Mp

16:19   רֹאשׁוֹ

Five times in the Prophets   ה בנביא   Mp

1–5	Judg 5:26; 13:5; **16:19**; 16:22; **1 Sam 1:11**
6–10	1 Sam 4:12; 10:1; 14:45; 17:5; 17:38
11–15	1 Sam 17:51; 31:9; 2 Sam 1:2; 1:10; 4:7ª
16–20	2 Sam 4:7ᵇ; 12:30; 14:26ª; 14:26ᵇ; 15:30
21–25	2 Sam 15:32; 16:9; 18:9; 20:21; 1 Kgs 2:32
26–30	2 Kgs 9:3; **9:6**; Isa 58:5; Jonah 4:6; Zech 2:4
31–32	Zech 3:5ª; 3:5ᵇ

Com.: The Mp heading here of *five times in the Prophets* is incorrect since there are
thirty-two occurrences of this lemma in the Prophets as correctly indicated in the Mp
heading at 2 Kgs 9:6.

The Masorah notes these *thirty-two* occurrences, to distinguish them from its *thir-
ty-three* occurrences in the rest of the Bible.

The Mp heading at 1 Sam 1:11 correctly reads *twenty times in the book* (of Samuel).

Neither M^C nor M^A has a note on this lemma here.

JUDGES 16:20

וַתֹּאמֶר פְּלִשְׁתִּים עָלֶיךָ שִׁמְשׁוֹן וַיִּקַץ מִשְּׁנָתוֹ וַיֹּאמֶר אֵצֵא כְּפַעַם בְּפַעַם וְאִנָּעֵר וְהוּא לֹא יָדַע כִּי יְהוָה סָר מֵעָלָיו׃

16:20   וְאִנָּעֵר

Unique   ל   Mp

JUDGES 16:21

וַיֹּאחֲזוּהוּ פְלִשְׁתִּים וַיְנַקְּרוּ אֶת־עֵינָיו וַיּוֹרִידוּ אוֹתוֹ עַזָּתָה וַיַּאַסְרוּהוּ בַּנְחֻשְׁתַּיִם וַיְהִי טוֹחֵן בְּבֵית הָאֲסִירִים׃

16:21   וַיֹּאחֲזוּהוּ

Unique   ל   Mp

Com.: The Masorah notes the *sole* occurrence of this lemma with a sfx. הו, to distinguish it from its *two* occurrences with אותו (וַיֹּאחֲזוּ אוֹתוֹ) at Judg 1:6 and 12:6

16:21   וַיְנַקְּרוּ

Unique   ל   Mp

16:21   וַיּוֹרִידוּ

Twice plene   ב מל   Mp

Num 1:51 (יוֹרִידוּ); **Judg 16:21**

וַיּוֹרִידוּ   *twice* plene   ויורידו ב מל   Mm

Num 1:51   ובנסע המשכן יורידו
Judg 16:21   ויורידו (אתו) [אותו] עזתה

And *once* doubly defective יֻרְדוּ (1 Kgs 5:23)   וחד חסיר דחסיר עבדי ירדו מן הלבנון

Com.: The Masorah notes the *two* occurrences of this lemma in various forms written both plene first ו and second י, to distinguish them from forms written defective first ו (e.g., וַיֹּרִדוּ, Josh 8:29 and 2 Kgs 11:19), or defective second י (e.g., וַיּוֹרִדוּ, Gen 44:11 and Deut 1:25).

The Mm additionally notes this lemma's *sole* occurrence written doubly defective
(יְרֽדוּ) at **1 Kgs 5:23**.

The Mp heading at Num 1:51 (יוֹרִידוּ) reads *unique plene*, to distinguish it from the
form יְרֽדוּ (1 Kgs 5:23), which is written doubly defective.

16:21   עַזָּ֑תָה

Twice   בֿ   Mp

Com.: See directly above at **Judg 16:1.**

16:21   וַיַּאַסְר֖וּהוּ

Three times   גֿ   Mp

Com.: See **Judg 15:13.**

16:21   טוֹחֵ֥ן

Unique   לֿ   Mp

Com.: This lemma is featured in two Masoretic lists. One is in a list of words occurring
only *once* in which their first and last letters are in reverse alphabetical order (אתבש);
see Frensdorff, *Ochlah*, §38, and Díaz-Esteban, *Sefer Oklah we-Oklah*, §39.

The other is in a list of *hapax legomena* pairings from its same stem, *one* of which occurs
in the Torah, *one* in the Prophets, and *one* in the Writings; see Frensdorff, *Ochlah*, §56,
and Díaz-Esteban, *Sefer Oklah we-Oklah*, §57.

16:21   הָאֲסִירִים

Read הָאֲסוּרִים   הָאֲסוּרִים קֿ   האסירים   Mp

Com.: The *kǝṯîb* (האסירים), and the *qǝrê* (הָאֲסוּרִים) represent noun variants of the
qāṭîl/qāṭûl type; see Gordis, *The Biblical Text*, 118.

This lemma is featured in a Masoretic list of words that occur *twice* in which a י is
written, but which is read as a ו; see Frensdorff, *Ochlah*, §138, and Díaz-Esteban, *Sefer
Oklah we-Oklah*, §122.

JUDGES 16:22

וַיָּ֧חֶל שְׂעַר־רֹאשׁ֛וֹ לְצַמֵּ֖חַ כַּאֲשֶׁ֥ר גֻּלָּֽח׃ פ

16:22   גֻּלָּח

Unique   ל   Mp

JUDGES 16:23

וְסַרְנֵ֣י פְלִשְׁתִּ֗ים נֶֽאֱסְפוּ֙ לִזְבֹּ֧חַ זֶֽבַח־גָּד֛וֹל לְדָג֥וֹן אֱלֹהֵיהֶ֖ם וּלְשִׂמְחָ֑ה וַיֹּ֣אמְר֔וּ נָתַ֤ן אֱלֹהֵ֙ינוּ֙ בְּיָדֵ֔נוּ אֵ֖ת
שִׁמְשׁ֥וֹן אוֹיְבֵֽינוּ׃

16:23   וּלְשִׂמְחָה

Three times   גׄ   Mp

Judg 16:23; Zech 8:19; Qoh 2:2

וּלְשִׂמְחָה *three times*   ולשמחה גׄ   Mm

Judg 16:23	לדגון אלהיהם ולשמחה
Zech 8:19	יהיה לבית יהודה לששון
Qoh 2:2	ולשמחה מה זה עשה

Com.: The Masorah notes the *three* occurrences of this lemma with a ו cj., to distinguish them from its *three* occurrences without a cj.

JUDGES 16:24

וַיִּרְא֤וּ אֹתוֹ֙ הָעָ֔ם וַֽיְהַלְל֖וּ אֶת־אֱלֹהֵיהֶ֑ם כִּ֣י אָמְר֗וּ נָתַ֨ן אֱלֹהֵ֤ינוּ בְיָדֵ֙נוּ֙ אֶת־אֽוֹיְבֵ֔נוּ וְאֵת֙ מַחֲרִ֣יב
אַרְצֵ֔נוּ וַאֲשֶׁ֥ר הִרְבָּ֖ה אֶת־חֲלָלֵֽינוּ׃

16:24   אֹתוֹ

Twice defective in the book   בׄ חס בסׄ   Mp

Judg 16:24; 16:31

Com.: The Masorah notes the *two* occurrences of this lemma in the book written defective ו, to distinguish them from its more numerous occurrences (17x) in the book written plene ו (אוֹתוֹ).

16:24   וַיְהַלְלוּ

Mm   ויהללו ד וסימנהון   וַיְהַלְלוּ *four times*, and their references

<u>Gen 12:15</u>	אל פרעה
<u>Judg 16:24</u>	אלהיהם
<u>2 Chr 29:30</u>	עד לשמחה
<u>Neh 5:13</u>	גם חצני

Com.: The Masorah notes the *four* occurrences of this lemma with a ו consec., to distinguish them from its more numerous occurrences (7x) without a ו (יְהַלְלוּ).

16:24   אוֹיְבֵנוּ

Mp[1]   ב֞ חס֞ י   *Twice* defective י

Judg 16:23*; **16:24**

Mp[2]   למד מל֞   To the Easterners (it is) plene

Com.: There are *two* Mp notes here. In the first, the Masorah notes the *two* occurrences of this lemma written defective second י, to distinguish them from its *three* occurrences of this lemma written plene second י (אוֹיְבֵינוּ).

* However, M^L, contrary to M (אוֹיְבֵנוּ), only has *one* occurrence of this lemma since it writes the form at Judg 16:23 plene second י (אוֹיְבֵינוּ); see Breuer, *The Biblical Text*, 64.

In the second Mp note, the Masorah records the Eastern tradition that the form here is plene, and M^L may have once had the Eastern writing because it is clear from the ms. that the second י was originally written and then was erased, but the י is still very visible.

> ### Judges 16:25
>
> וַיְהִי֙ כִּי־ט֣וֹב לִבָּ֔ם וַיֹּאמְר֔וּ קִרְא֥וּ לְשִׁמְשׁ֖וֹן וִישַֽׂחֶק־לָ֑נוּ וַיִּקְרְא֨וּ לְשִׁמְשׁ֜וֹן מִבֵּ֣ית הָאֲסוּרִ֗ים וַיְצַחֵק֙ לִפְנֵיהֶ֔ם וַיַּעֲמִ֥ידוּ אוֹת֖וֹ בֵּ֥ין הָעַמּוּדִֽים׃

16:25   כִּי טוֹב

Mp   כטוב ק   כְּטוֹב Read

Com.: The *katib* (כי טוב), and the *qərê* (כְּטוֹב) represent variants of equal value; see Gordis, *The Biblical Text*, 151.

This lemma is featured in a Masoretic list of words written as *two* words, but which should be read as *one* word; see the Mm at <u>Gen 30:11</u> *sub* בגד, Frensdorff, *Ochlah*, §100, and Díaz-Esteban, *Sefer Oklah we-Oklah*, §83.

It is also featured in a list of *four* occurrences of כְּטוֹב; see the Mm at **2 Sam 13:28**.

In M^L there is no circellus on this lemma.

16:25   וַיִּשָׂחֶק

Unique   לֹ   Mp

16:25   הָאֲסִירִים

Read הָאֲסוּרִים   האסורים קרי   Mp

Com.: The *kətîb* (האסירים), and the *qərê* (הָאֲסוּרִים) represent noun variants of the *qātîl/qātûl* type; see Gordis, *The Biblical Text*, 118.

This lemma is featured in a Masoretic list of words that occur *twice* in which a י is written, but is read as a ו; see Frensdorff, *Ochlah*, §138, and Díaz-Esteban, *Sefer Oklah we-Oklah*, §122.

In M^L there is no circellus on this lemma.

┌───┐
│   **JUDGES 16:26**   │
│ וַיֹּאמֶר שִׁמְשׁוֹן אֶל־הַנַּעַר הַמַּחֲזִיק בְּיָדוֹ הַנִּיחָה אוֹתִי וַהֲימִשֵׁנִי אֶת־הָעַמֻּדִים אֲשֶׁר הַבַּיִת נָכוֹן │
│   עֲלֵיהֶם וְאֶשָּׁעֵן עֲלֵיהֶם: │
└───┘

16:26   הַנִּיחָה

Twice   בֿ   Mp

Exod 32:10; Judg 16:26

Com.: The Mp heading at Exod 32:10 adds the catchwords וַיֹּאמֶר) ויאמר שמשון שִׁמְשׁוֹן) to refer the reader to this verse.

16:26   וַהֲימִשֵׁנִי

Read וַהֲמִשֵׁנִי   והמשני ק   Mp

Com.: The *kətîb* (והימשני), and the *qərê* (וַהֲמִשֵׁנִי) represents examples where consonants have been transposed; see Gordis, *The Biblical Text*, 116.

This form is featured in a Masoretic list of words in which two letters are written one way but are read transposed (presumably וְהַמִישְׁנִי); see Frensdorff, *Ochlah*, §91, and Díaz-Esteban, *Sefer Oklah we-Oklah*, §73.

16:26   הָעֹמְדִים

Eleven times defective   **יֹא חֹס**   Mp

1–5   **Exod 27:10**; **27:11**; **38:12**; **38:17** (לָעֹמְדִים); **Judg 16:26**
6–10   **1 Kgs 7:6**ᵇ (וְעֹמֵדִים); **7:21**; **7:41** (עֹמֵדִים); Jer 27:19; **Ezek 40:49** (וְעֹמֵדִים)
11   **2 Chr 3:16**

Com.: The Masorah notes the *eleven* occurrences of this lemma in various forms written defective וֹ, to distinguish them from its more numerous occurrences (11x) in various forms written plene וּ (עַמּוּדִים).

M^L, contrary to M (הָעַמּוּדִים), has *two* more occurrences of this lemma since it writes the forms at Exod 38:10 and 1 Kgs 7:41ᵃ defective וֹ (הָעֹמְדִים); see Breuer, *The Biblical Text*, 17 and 108. However, neither of these *two* forms are listed in the Mm of M^L at Exod 27:10 and 1 Kgs 7:21, and all the Mp headings, apart from *one*, highlighted above read *eleven times*, thus supporting the enumeration inherent in the text of M.

The one Mp heading that reads other than *eleven times defective* is Exod 38:17, which alone has the form לָעֹמְדִים, and reads *twice, once defective and once plene*. The plene occurrence of this form (לָעֹמוּדִים) is at Exod 38:28.

JUDGES 16:27

וְהַבַּ֜יִת מָלֵ֣א הָאֲנָשִׁים֮ וְהַנָּשִׁים֒ וְשָׁ֕מָּה כֹּ֖ל סַרְנֵ֣י פְלִשְׁתִּ֑ים וְעַל־הַגָּ֗ג כִּשְׁלֹ֤שֶׁת אֲלָפִים֙ אִ֣ישׁ וְאִשָּׁ֔ה הָרֹאִ֖ים בִּשְׂחֹ֥וק שִׁמְשֹֽׁון׃

16:27   בִּשְׂחוֹק

Twice plene in the Prophets   **ב מל בנב**   Mp

Judg 16:27; **Jer 20:7** (לִשְׂחוֹק)

Com.: The Masorah notes the *two* occurrences of this lemma in the Prophets in various forms written plene וֹ, to distinguish them from its *two* occurrences in the Prophets written defective וֹ (לִשְׂחֹק) at Jer 48:26 and Jer 48:39.

JUDGES 16:28

וַיִּקְרָ֧א שִׁמְשׁ֛וֹן אֶל־יְהוָ֖ה וַיֹּאמַ֑ר אֲדֹנָ֣י יֱהֹוִ֡ה זָכְרֵ֣נִי נָא֩ וְחַזְּקֵ֨נִי נָ֜א אַ֣ךְ הַפַּ֤עַם הַזֶּה֙ הָאֱלֹהִ֔ים וְאִנָּקְמָ֧ה נְקַם־אַחַ֛ת מִשְּׁתֵ֥י עֵינַ֖י מִפְּלִשְׁתִּֽים׃

16:28   וְאִנָּקְמָה

Twice   ב̇   Mp

Judg 16:28; Isa 1:24

16:28   נְקַם

Twice   ב̇   Mp

Lev 26:25; Judg 16:28

Com.: The Mp heading at Lev 26:25 adds the catchword ואנקמה (וְאִנָּקְמָה) to refer the reader to this verse.

This form is featured in a Masoretic list of words of two syllables that only occur *twice*; see Frendsdorff, *Ochlah*, §41, and Díaz-Esteban, *Sefer Oklah we-Oklah*, §42.

JUDGES 16:29

וַיִּלְפֹּ֨ת שִׁמְשׁ֜וֹן אֶת־שְׁנֵ֣י ׀ עַמּוּדֵ֣י הַתָּ֗וֶךְ אֲשֶׁ֤ר הַבַּ֙יִת֙ נָכ֣וֹן עֲלֵיהֶ֔ם וַיִּסָּמֵ֖ךְ עֲלֵיהֶ֑ם אֶחָ֥ד בִּימִינ֖וֹ וְאֶחָ֥ד בִּשְׂמֹאלֽוֹ׃

16:29   וַיִּלְפֹּת

Unique   ל̇   Mp

16:29   הַתָּוֶךְ

Twice   ב̇   Mp

Judg 16:29; Jer 39:3

Com.: The Masorah notes the *two* occurrences of this lemma with the def. article, to distinguish them from its more numerous occurrences (5x) with the def. prep. בַּ (בַּתָּוֶךְ).

16:29   וַיִּסְמֵךְ

Unique   ל   Mp

Com.: The Masorah notes the *sole* occurrence of this lemma with a ו consec., to distinguish it from its *two* occurrences without this ו (יִסְמֵךְ) at 2 Kgs 18:21 and Isa 36:6; see the Mm at <u>Isa 36:6</u> *sub* יִסְמֵךְ.

JUDGES 16:30

וַיֹּאמֶר שִׁמְשׁוֹן תָּמוֹת נַפְשִׁי עִם־פְּלִשְׁתִּים וַיֵּט בְּכֹחַ וַיִּפֹּל הַבַּיִת עַל־הַסְּרָנִים וְעַל־כָּל־הָעָם אֲשֶׁר־
בּוֹ וַיִּהְיוּ הַמֵּתִים אֲשֶׁר הֵמִית בְּמוֹתוֹ רַבִּים מֵאֲשֶׁר הֵמִית בְּחַיָּיו:

16:30   תָּמוֹת

Three times   ג̇   Mp

Num 23:10 (תָּמֹת); **Judg 16:30**; <u>**Job 36:14**</u> (תָּמֹת)

Com.: The Masorah notes the *three* occurrences of this lemma, written plene and defective ו, with a *ḥolem*, to distinguish them from its more numerous occurrences (33x) with a *šûreq* (תָּמוּת).

This word is featured in a Masoretic list of groups of words that occur *four times*, *three times* without a ו cj., and *once* with a ו cj. (Judg 20:5); see Frensdorff, *Ochlah*, §15, and Díaz-Esteban, *Sefer Oklah we-Oklah*, §16.

16:30   וַיֵּט בְּכֹחַ

Unique   ל   Mp

Com.: The Masorah notes the *sole* occurrence of וַיֵּט with בְּכֹחַ, possibly to distinguish it from its more numerous occurrences (26x) without בְּכֹחַ.

16:30   וְעַל־כָּל־הָעָם

Twice   ב̇   Mp

Judg 16:30; Jer 44:20

Com.: The Masorah notes the *two* occurrences of this lemma with a ו cj., to distinguish them from its *sole* occurrence with the prep. מִן (מֵעַל־כָּל־הָעָם) at Neh 8:5.

JUDGES 16:31

וַיֵּרְד֣וּ אֶחָיו֩ וְכָל־בֵּ֨ית אָבִ֤יהוּ וַיִּשְׂא֣וּ אֹתוֹ֙ וַֽיַּעֲל֔וּ | וַיִּקְבְּר֣וּ אוֹת֗וֹ בֵּ֤ין צָרְעָה֙ וּבֵ֣ין אֶשְׁתָּאֹ֔ל בְּקֶ֖בֶר מָנ֣וֹחַ אָבִ֑יו וְה֛וּא שָׁפַ֥ט אֶת־יִשְׂרָאֵ֖ל עֶשְׂרִ֥ים שָׁנָֽה׃ פ

16:31   וְכָל־בֵּ֨ית

Twelve times   יֹ֫ב   Mp

1–5   Gen 50:8; <u>Judg 9:6</u>; **16:31; 1 Sam 22:1; 22:16**
6–10   **2 Sam 6:5; 6:15; 1 Kgs 4:12; Jer 9:25; Ezek 11:15**
11–12   **Ezek 12:10; 37:16**

Com.: The Masorah notes the *twelve* occurrences of this lemma with a ו cj., to distinguish them from its more numerous occurrences (34x) without a cj.

All the highlighted Mp headings read *twelve times* apart from 2 Sam 6:5, which mistakenly writes *two* (ב) instead of *twelve* (יֹ֫ב).

16:31   אָבִ֤יהוּ

Seven times   ז   Mp

Com.: See **Judg 14:10**.

16:31   אֹתוֹ֙

Twice defective in the book   ב חס בס   Mp

Com.: See **Judg 16:24**.

16:31   אֶשְׁתָּאֹ֔ל

Three times   ג   Mp

Com.: See **Judg 13:25**.

JUDGES 17:1

וַיְהִי־אִ֤ישׁ מֵהַר־אֶפְרַ֙יִם֙ וּשְׁמ֣וֹ מִיכָ֔יְהוּ׃

17:1   אֶפְרַיִם

Four times with *qameṣ*. And similarly every *ʾaṭnaḥ* and *sôp pasûq*   ד קמץֹ וכל אתנֹ וסוֹף דכות   Mp

Num 13:8; Judg 17:1; Hos 4:17; 13:12

אֶפְרַיִם *four times* with *qameṣ*, and their references   אפרים ד קמץֹ וסימנהון   Mm

Num 13:8	(= לְמַטֵּה)	חוטרה
Judg 17:1	(= מִיכָיְהוּ)	דמיכיהו
Hos 13:12	(= צָרוּר)	צרור
Hos 4:17	(= חֲבוּר)	ומתקן

And similarly every *ʾaṭnaḥ* and *sôp pasûq*   וכל אתנחה וסוף פסוק דכותהון

Com.: The Masorah notes the *four* occurrences of this lemma with a *qameṣ* under the ר, to distinguish them from its more numerous occurrences (100+) with a *pataḥ* (אֶפְרַיִם).

The Masorah also notes that this lemma is written with a *qameṣ* with the accents *ʾaṭnaḥ* and *sôp pasûq*.

The catchwords are given in the form of an Aramaic mnemonic "The rod of Micah is tied up and established"; see Marcus, *Scribal Wit*, 66–67.

17:1   מִיכָיְהוּ

Four times   ד   Mp

Judg 17:1; 17:4; **Jer 36:11** (מִכָיְהוּ); **36:13** (מִכָיְהוּ)

מִיכָיְהוּ *four times*   מיכיהו ד̇   Mm

Judg 17:1   [מהר] (אחד) ויהי איש
Judg 17:4   וישב את הכסף
Jer 36:11   וישמע
Jer 36:13   [מכיהו] (מיכיהו) ויגד להם

And *all* Kings. And from 2 Chr 17:19   וכל מלכים ומן אלה המשרתים את המלך
to the end of the book,   עד סוף דסיפֿ בֿ מֿ בֿ מיכה
apart from *two* with מִיכָה

2 Chr 18:14   ויבא אל המלך
2 Chr 34:20   [חלקיהו] (חלקיה) את <המלך> ויצו

Com.: The Masorah notes the *four* occurrences of this lemma with the ending יְהוּ, to distinguish them from its more numerous occurrences (31x) with a ה ending (מִיכָה).

The Mm has an additional note that this lemma with the ending יְהוּ is also the norm (9x) in Kings, and in parts of Chronicles from 2 Chr 17:19 to the end of the book (7x), apart from *two* cases when it is written מִיכָה at 18:14 and 34:20.

The Mp heading at Jer 36:13 reads *twice defective* (בׄ) enumerating the *two* defective forms there, and at Jer 36:11, though the Mp heading at Jer 36:11 enumerates all *four* forms.

In Mᴸ the circellus has mistakenly been placed on the preceding word וּשְׁמוֹ, which occurs many more than *four* times. Thus it is more likely, as Mᴬ reads, that the note should be on מִיכָיְהוּ which only occurs *four* times. Mᶜ has no note here.

JUDGES 17:2

וַיֹּאמֶר לְאִמּוֹ אֶלֶף וּמֵאָה הַכֶּסֶף אֲשֶׁר לֻקַּח־לָךְ וְאַתְּ אָלִית וְגַם אָמַרְתְּ בְּאָזְנַי הִנֵּה־הַכֶּסֶף אִתִּי אֲנִי לְקַחְתִּיו וַתֹּאמֶר אִמּוֹ בָּרוּךְ בְּנִי לַיהוָה:

17:2   לֻקַּח

Five times   הׄ   Mp

1–5   **Gen 3:23**; **Judg 17:2**; 2 Kgs 2:10 (לֻקַּח); **Isa 52:5**; 53:8 (לֻקַּח)

לְקַח *five times*　　לקח הֹ　　Mm

1–5	Gen 3:23	וישלחהו
	<u>Judg 17:2</u>	[ויאמר] (לאמר)
	<u>Isa 52:5</u>	מה לי
	Isa 53:8	מעצר
	2 Kgs 2:10	הקשית

And *once* (וְלָקַח): Jer 29:22　　וחד ולקח מהם קללה

Com.: The Masorah notes the *five* occurrences of this lemma in the *pual*, to distinguish them from its more numerous occurrences (55x) in the *qal* (לְקַח/לָקַח).

The Mm has an additional note that this lemma also occurs with a ו cj. (וְלָקַח) at Jer 29:22.

All the Mp headings highlighted above read *five times*, but the Mp at 2 Kgs 2:10 incorrectly reads *five times with qames* (הֹ). The note should have read like the other Mp headings just *five times* or, like M^C at 2 Kgs 2:10, *twice* with *qames*.

17:2　　וְאַתִּי

Read וְאַתְּ　　ואת קֹ　　Mp

Com.: The *kǝtîb* (ואתי) represents the older 2nd pers. fem. sg. form of the pron. אַתִּי, whereas the *qǝrê* (וְאַתְּ) represents the regular form; see Gordis, *The Biblical Text*, 102.

This lemma is featured in a Masoretic list of words that are written at the end with a י, but which is not read; see Frensdorff, *Ochlah*, §127, and Díaz-Esteban, *Sefer Oklah we-Oklah*, §111.

This lemma is one of *seven* occurrences where אתי, with and without ו cj., is written but אַתְּ is read; see the Mm to <u>2 Kgs 8:1</u>.

JUDGES 17:3

וַיָּ֣שֶׁב אֶת־אֶֽלֶף־וּמֵאָ֣ה הַכֶּסֶף֮ לְאִמּוֹ֒ וַתֹּ֣אמֶר אִמּ֗וֹ הַקְדֵּ֣שׁ הִקְדַּ֣שְׁתִּי אֶת־הַכֶּ֣סֶף לַֽיהוָה֮ מִיָּדִ֣י לִבְנִי֒ לַעֲשׂוֹת֙ פֶּ֣סֶל וּמַסֵּכָ֔ה וְעַתָּ֖ה אֲשִׁיבֶ֥נּוּ לָֽךְ׃

17:3   וַיָּ֣שֶׁב

Twenty-five times   כֹּה   Mp

1–5   **Gen 14:16; 20:14**; 40:21; **Exod 4:7**; 15:19
6–10   **Exod 19:8**; Judg 9:56; **17:3**; 17:4; 1 Sam 14:27
11–15   **1 Sam 25:21; 2 Sam 15:29; 22:25; 1 Kgs 2:30**; 2 Kgs 13:25
16–20   **2 Kgs 17:3; 20:11; 22:9; Ezek 44:1; Ps 18:25**
21–25   **Ps 94:23; Prov 20:26; Job 33:26**; 1 Chr 21:27; 2 Chr 34:16

Com.: The Masorah notes the *twenty-five* occurrences of this lemma in the *hiphil*, to distinguish them from its more numerous occurrences (81x) in the *qal* (וַיֵּשֶׁב).

This distinction is implied in the Mp headings at Exod 19:8 and Ps 18:25, which read *twenty-five times with səḡôl* (כֹּה) thereby contrasting this form with one not having *səḡôl*, that is, וַיֵּשֶׁב.

17:3   הִקְדַּ֣שְׁתִּי

Six times   ו   Mp

1–5   Num 3:13; 8:17; **Judg 17:3**; 1 Kgs 9:3; 9:7
6   **2 Chr 7:20**

Com.: The Masorah notes the *six* occurrences of this lemma without a prefixed ו, to distinguish them from its *sole* occurrence with a ו consec. (וְהִקְדַּשְׁתִּי) at 2 Chr 7:16.

JUDGES 17:4

וַיָּ֤שֶׁב אֶת־הַכֶּ֙סֶף֙ לְאִמּ֔וֹ וַתִּקַּ֣ח אִמּ֞וֹ מָאתַ֣יִם כֶּ֗סֶף וַתִּתְּנֵ֙הוּ֙ לַצּוֹרֵ֔ף וַֽיַּעֲשֵׂ֙הוּ֙ פֶּ֣סֶל וּמַסֵּכָ֔ה וַיְהִ֖י בְּבֵ֥ית מִיכָֽיְהוּ׃

17:4   לַצּוֹרֵ֔ף

Twice, once plene and *once* defective   ב חד מל וחד חס   Mp

Judg 17:4; Prov 25:4 (לַצֹּרֵף)

Com.: The Masorah notes the *two* occurrences of this lemma, *one* written plene וֹ (here) and *one* written defective וֹ (Prov 25:4).

The Mp heading at Prov 25:4 simply writes *twice*.

JUDGES 17:5

וְהָאִישׁ מִיכָה לוֹ בֵּית אֱלֹהֶים וַיַּעַשׂ אֵפוֹד וּתְרָפִים וַיְמַלֵּא אֶת־יַד אַחַד מִבָּנָיו וַיְהִי־לוֹ לְכֹהֵן:

17:5   וַיְמַלֵּא

Nine times   ט   Mp

1–5   **Gen 29:28; Exod 35:31; Lev 9:17; Num 14:24; Judg 17:5**
6–9   Judg 17:12; **2 Kgs 23:14**; 24:4; **Nah 2:13**

Com.: The Masorah notes the *nine* occurrences of this lemma in the *piel*, to distinguish them from its *eight* occurrences in the *niphal* (וַיִּמָּלֵא).

The Mp heading at Num 14:24 reads *unique* indicating the lemma's *sole* occurrence in that book.

JUDGES 17:7

וַיְהִי־נַעַר מִבֵּית לֶחֶם יְהוּדָה מִמִּשְׁפַּחַת יְהוּדָה וְהוּא לֵוִי וְהוּא גֵר־שָׁם:

17:7   וְהוּא

Seven verses that have the sequence וְהוּא...וְהוּא   ז פסוק והוא והוא   Mp

1–5   **Judg 17:7**; 1 Kgs 2:8; 19:19; Isa 8:13; Hos 7:9
6–7   **Zech 6:13**; 1 Chr 2:21

Com.: The Masorah notes the *seven* verses that have the sequence וְהוּא...וְהוּא; see Frensdorff, *Ochlah*, §340.

In M^L there is no circellus on this lemma.

17:7   גֵּר־שָׁם

Four times   דֹ   Mp

Gen 35:27; Deut 18:6; **Judg 17:7**; **Ezra 1:4**

Com.: The Masorah notes the *four* occurrences of this lemma in the sg., to distinguish them from its *sole* occurrence in the pl. (גֵּרִים שָׁם) at Jer 35:7.

JUDGES 17:9

וַיֹּאמֶר־לֹו מִיכָה מֵאַיִן תָּבֹוא וַיֹּאמֶר אֵלָיו לֵוִי אָנֹכִי מִבֵּית לֶחֶם יְהוּדָה וְאָנֹכִי הֹלֵךְ לָגוּר בַּאֲשֶׁר אֶמְצָא:

17:9   אָנֹכִי

Eight times accented (*mil'êl*), and similarly all   חֹ בטע וכל

zaqep (*qatan*), *'atnah* and *sôp pasûq* apart from *one* אֹ   זקף ואתֹן וסוף פסוק דכות בֹ מֹ אֹ

1–5   Gen 3:10 (אָנֹכִי); **Exod 4:10**; **Judg 17:9**; <u>1 Sam 9:21</u> (אָנֹכִי); **30:13**

6–8   2 Sam 3:8 (אָנֹכִֿי); **Amos 7:14**ᶜ (אָנֹכִי); **Ruth 3:13** (אָנֹכִי)

Com.: The Masorah notes the *eight* occurrences of this lemma that are accented *mil'êl*, to distinguish them from its more numerous occurrences (11x) accented *milra'*.

The Masorah also notes that this lemma is accented *mil'êl* with the accents *'atnah*, *sôp pasûq*, and *zaqep qatan* apart from *one* (אָנֹכִי, Job 33:9), which is accented *milra'*.

The Mm note at <u>1 Sam 9:21</u> expressly mentions that this lemma with a *zaqep qatan* (זקפתא) is accented *mil'êl* because, by contrast, this lemma with a *zaqep gadôl* is accented *milra'* (Gen 26:24; Judg 11:9; 2 Sam 20:19; 1 Kgs 2:18); see Dotan/Reich, *Masora Thesaurus, ad loc.*

The Mp heading at <u>1 Sam 30:13</u> mistakenly reads *twice accented etc.* instead of *eight times accented etc.*

JUDGES 17:11

וַיּ֥וֹאֶל הַלֵּוִ֖י לָשֶׁ֣בֶת אֶת־הָאִ֑ישׁ וַיְהִ֤י הַנַּ֙עַר֙ ל֔וֹ כְּאַחַ֖ד מִבָּנָֽיו׃

17:11 וַיּוֹאֶל

Seven times ז֗ Mp

Com.: See **Josh 17:12**.

JUDGES 18:1

בַּיָּמִ֣ים הָהֵ֔ם אֵ֥ין מֶ֖לֶךְ בְּיִשְׂרָאֵ֑ל וּבַיָּמִ֣ים הָהֵ֗ם שֵׁ֣בֶט הַדָּנִ֞י מְבַקֶּשׁ־ל֤וֹ נַחֲלָה֙ לָשֶׁ֔בֶת כִּ֡י לֹא־נָ֫פְלָה לּ֜וֹ
עַד־הַיּ֥וֹם הַה֛וּא בְּתוֹךְ־שִׁבְטֵ֥י יִשְׂרָאֵ֖ל בְּנַחֲלָֽה׃ ס

18:1 וּבַיָּמִים הָהֵם

Unique ל֗ Mp

Com.: The Masorah notes the *sole* occurrence of this lemma with a ו cj., to distinguish it from its *sole* occurrence without a cj. in the same verse.

18:1 עַד־הַיּוֹם הַהוּא

Twice ב֗ Mp

Judg 18:1; **<u>Neh 8:17</u>**

Com.: The Masorah notes the *two* occurrences of עַד־הַיּוֹם with הַהוּא, to distinguish it from its more numerous occurrences (76x) with הַזֶּה (עַד־הַיּוֹם הַזֶּה), *one* of which occurs in v. 12.

In M^L the circellus has been placed only on עַד־הַיּוֹם, but since this phrase occurs many more than *two* times, the note most likely refers, as both M^C and M^A read, to the three-fold phrase עַד־הַיּוֹם הַהוּא that occurs only *twice*.

JUDGES 18:2

וַיִּשְׁלְח֣וּ בְנֵי־דָ֣ן | מִֽמִּשְׁפַּחְתָּ֡ם חֲמִשָּׁ֣ה אֲנָשִׁים֩ מִקְצוֹתָ֨ם אֲנָשִׁ֜ים בְּנֵי־חַ֗יִל מִצָּרְעָ֣ה וּמֵֽאֶשְׁתָּאֹ֒ל לְרַגֵּ֣ל אֶת־הָאָ֘רֶץ֮ וּלְחָקְרָהּ֒ וַיֹּאמְר֣וּ אֲלֵהֶ֗ם לְכ֨וּ חִקְר֜וּ אֶת־הָאָ֗רֶץ וַיָּבֹ֛אוּ הַר־אֶפְרַ֖יִם עַד־בֵּ֣ית מִיכָ֑ה וַיָּלִ֖ינוּ שָֽׁם:

18:2   מִֽמִּשְׁפַּחְתָּ֡ם

Unique   ל   Mp

Com.: This lemma is featured in a Masoretic list of words that occur *once* with a ו cj. (Lev 25:45), and *once* without (here); see Frensdorff, *Ochlah*, §1, and Díaz-Esteban, *Sefer Oklah we-Oklah*, §1.

At 1 Chr 4:27 this lemma occurs without the inseparable prep. מ (מִשְׁפַּחְתָּם) and the Mp heading there reads *unique and once* מִֽמִּשְׁפַּחְתָּם.

18:2   וּלְחָקְרָהּ

Unique   ל   Mp

18:2   לְכ֨וּ חִקְר֜וּ

Seven times   ז   Mp

Com.: The Mp heading here of *seven times* is incorrect since this is the *only* occurrence of this lemma. Both M^C and M^A correctly read here *unique*.

JUDGES 18:3

הֵ֚מָּה עִם־בֵּ֣ית מִיכָ֔ה וְהֵ֙מָּה֙ הִכִּ֔ירוּ אֶת־ק֥וֹל הַנַּ֖עַר הַלֵּוִ֑י וַיָּס֣וּרוּ שָׁ֗ם וַיֹּ֤אמְרוּ לוֹ֙ מִֽי־הֱבִיאֲךָ֣ הֲלֹ֔ם וּמָֽה־אַתָּ֥ה עֹשֶׂ֛ה בָּזֶ֖ה וּמַה־לְּךָ֥ פֹֽה:

18:3   הֵ֚מָּה

Nineteen times at the beginning of a verse   יט ראש פסוק   Mp

1–5	Gen 7:14; **Num 20:13**; <u>Judg 18:3</u>; 18:22; **19:22**
6–10	**1 Sam 9:5**; **9:11**; 9:27; Isa 24:14; **Ezek 23:10**
11–15	Ezek 27:24; **44:16**; **Job 24:13**; **Ps 20:9**; 48:6
16–19	**Ps 59:16**; **102:27**; **107:24**; 1 Chr 4:23

הֵמָּה *nineteen times* at the beginning of a verse　　המה יֹט ראש פסוק　　Mm

1–5	Gen 7:14	וכל החיה למינה
	Num 20:13	מי מריבה
	<u>Judg 18:3</u>	בית מיכה
	Judg 18:22	המה הרחיקו
	1 Sam 9:11	עלים
6–10	1 Sam 9:27	יורדים
	1 Sam 9:5	בארץ צוף
	Ezek 23:10	ערותה
	Isa 24:14	(נתצו) [ישאו] קולם
	Job 24:13	במרדי אור
	{1 Sam 9:11}	{במעלה}
11–15	1 Chr 4:23	היוצרים
	Ezek 44:16	המה (יבואו) [יבאו]
	Judg 19:22	מיטיבים את לבם
	Ezek 27:24	המה רכליך
	Ps 59:16	יניעון לאכל
16–19	Ps 107:24	ראו מעשי
	Ps 102:27	יאבדו
	Ps 20:9	המה כרעו ונפלו
	<Ps 48:6>	

Com.: The Masorah notes the *nineteen* occurrences of this lemma at the beginning of a verse, to distinguish them from the *ten* occurrences of this lemma at the beginning of a verse with a ו cj. (וְהֵמָּה); see **Josh 2:8**.

In the Mm list, two sets of catchwords are written for 1 Sam 9:11 (עלים and במעלה), whereas the catchword for Ps 48:6 is missing.

18:3　　וַיָּסֻרוּ

Twice plene　　ב מל　　Mp

Judg 18:3; 18:15

Com.: The Masorah notes the *two* occurrences of this lemma written plene ו, to distinguish them from its *three* occurrences written defective ו (וַיָּסְרוּ).

18:3　　וּמָה־אַתָּה

Unique　　ל　　Mp

Com.: The Masorah notes the *sole* occurrence of this lemma with a ו cj., to distinguish it from its more numerous occurrences (10x) without a cj.

18:3   וּמַה־לְּךָ

Unique   ל   Mp

Com.: The Masorah notes the *sole* occurrence of this lemma with a וֹ cj., to distinguish it from its more numerous occurrences (9x) without a cj., *one* of which occurs in v. 23.

This lemma is featured in a Masoretic list of words that occur once with a preceding וּמַה; see Frensdorff, *Ochlah*, §256.

JUDGES 18:4

וַיֹּאמֶר אֲלֵהֶם כָּזֶה וְכָזֶה עָשָׂה לִי מִיכָה וַיִּשְׂכְּרֵנִי וָאֱהִי־לוֹ לְכֹהֵן:

18:4   כָּזֶה וְכָזֶה

Three times   גֿ   Mp

Judg 18:4; 2 Sam 11:25; 1 Kgs 14:5

Com.: The Masorah notes the *three* occurrences of this lemma, to distinguish them from its *three* occurrences of the parallel phrase כָּזֹאת וְכָזֹאת; see Ginsburg, 4, ז, §42.

18:4   וַיִּשְׂכְּרֵנִי

Unique   ל   Mp

JUDGES 18:5

וַיֹּאמְרוּ לוֹ שְׁאַל־נָא בֵאלֹהִים וְנֵדְעָה הֲתַצְלִיחַ דַּרְכֵּנוּ אֲשֶׁר אֲנַחְנוּ הֹלְכִים עָלֶיהָ:

18:5   שְׁאַל־נָא

Three times   גֿ   Mp

1–5   Deut 4:32; **Judg 18:5**; Hag 2:11; Job 8:8; 12:7

The Mp heading here of *three times* is inexact since there are *five* occurrences of this lemma. The note more precisely should have read *three times in the Torah and Prophets*.

The Masorah notes the occurrences of שָׁאַל with נָא, to distinguish it from its more numerous occurrences (8x) without נָא.

Neither Mᶜ nor Mᴬ has a note on this lemma here.

JUDGES 18:7

וַיֵּלְכוּ֩ חֲמֵ֨שֶׁת הָאֲנָשִׁ֜ים וַיָּבֹ֣אוּ לַ֗יְשָׁה וַיִּרְא֣וּ אֶת־הָעָ֣ם אֲשֶׁר־בְּקִרְבָּ֣הּ יוֹשֶֽׁבֶת־לָבֶ֩טַח֩ כְּמִשְׁפַּ֨ט צִדֹנִ֤ים
שֹׁקֵ֣ט | וּבֹטֵ֗חַ וְאֵין־מַכְלִ֨ים דָּבָ֜ר בָּאָ֗רֶץ יוֹרֵ֣שׁ עֶ֔צֶר וּרְחֹקִ֥ים הֵ֙מָּה֙ מִצִּ֣דֹנִ֔ים וְדָבָ֥ר אֵין־לָהֶ֖ם עִם־
אָדָֽם׃

18:7   לַ֗יְשָׁה

Twice, once with *qameṣ* and *once* with *pataḥ*   ב֛ חד קמ֗ וחד פת֯   Mp

Judg 18:7; Isa 10:30 (לַ֗יְשָׁה)

Com.: The Masorah notes the *two* occurrences of this lemma in various forms with the locative ה, to distinguish them from its more numerous occurrences (7x) without this adverbial ending (לִישׁ).

This lemma is featured in a Masoretic list of words that occur *once* with a *qameṣ* (here), and *once* with a *pataḥ* (Isa 10:30); see Frensdorff, *Ochlah*, §23, and Díaz-Esteban, *Sefer Oklah we-Oklah*, §24.

18:7   כְּמִשְׁפַּ֨ט

Five times   ה֛   Mp

1–5   **Exod 21:9; Judg 18:7; 2 Kgs 17:33; Ezra 3:4; 2 Chr 8:14**

Com.: The Masorah notes the *five* occurrences of this lemma in the cstr., to distinguish them from its *two* occurrences in the absol. (כְּמִשְׁפָּט) at Ps 119:132 and 1 Chr 23:31.

The Mp headings at Exod 21:9 and Ezra 3:4 read *five times with pataḥ* (ה֯) as do the Mm headings at Exod 21:9, Ezra 3:4 and 2 Chr 8:14.

18:7   צִדֹנִ֤ים

Five times defective   ה֛ חס֗   Mp

1–5   **Judg 18:7**; 1 Kgs 5:20 (לְצִדֹנִים); 11:5; 11:33 (צִדֹנִין); **Ezra 3:7** (לַצִּדֹנִים)

Com.: The Masorah notes the *five* occurrences of this lemma in various forms written defective י, to distinguish them from its *seven* occurrences in various forms written plene י (צִידֹנִים).

The Mp heading at 1 Kgs 11:33 reads *unique and defective* pointing to the special form of צִדֹנִין, and also noting that this form does not occur elsewhere written plene first י.

18:7 וְאִין

Six verses in which there is the sequence וְאֵין...אֵין   ו פסוק אית בהון ואין אין

1–5   **Judg 18:7; 18:28; Isa 45:5**; Ps 142:5; Job 5:9
6   **Neh 4:17**

Com.: The Masorah notes the *six* verses in which there is the sequence וְאֵין...אֵין; see Frensdorff, *Ochlah*, §333, and Jobin, *Concordance*, 1–2.

In M^L this lemma has no circellus.

JUDGES 18:9

וַיֹּאמְרוּ קוּמָה וְנַעֲלֶה עֲלֵיהֶם כִּי רָאִינוּ אֶת־הָאָרֶץ וְהִנֵּה טוֹבָה מְאֹד וְאַתֶּם מַחְשִׁים אַל־תֵּעָצְלוּ
לָלֶכֶת לָבֹא לָרֶשֶׁת אֶת־הָאָרֶץ:

18:9   קוּמָה וְנַעֲלֶה

Unique   ל   Mp

Com.: The Masorah notes the *sole* occurrence of וְנַעֲלֶה with קוּמָה, to distinguish it from its *three* occurrences with קוּמוּ (קוּמוּ וְנַעֲלֶה).

18:9   מַחְשִׁים

Four times   דֿ   Mp

Judg 18:9; **1 Kgs 22:3**; 2 Kgs 7:9; **Neh 8:11**

מַחְשִׁים *four times*   מחשים דֿ   Mm

Judg 18:9	(ואת) [ואתם] מחשים
1 Kgs 22:3	ואנחנו מחשים
And its companion (2 Kgs 7:9)	(וחבֹ) [וחבירו]
Neh 8:11	והלוים מחשים

18:9   תֵּעָצְלוּ

Unique   ל   Mp

18:9　　לְבֹא

Nine times defective　　ט חס　　Mp

1–5　　<u>Gen 48:7</u>; Exod 12:23; Num 13:21 (לְבֹא); 34:8 (לְבֹא); Deut 9:1
6–9　　Deut 11:31; 20:19; Judg 18:9; Jer 42:15

Com.: The Masorah notes the *nine* occurrences of this lemma in various forms written defective ו, to distinguish them from its more numerous occurrences (82x) in various forms written plene ו (לְבוֹא/לְבוֹא).

M^L, contrary to M (לְבוֹא), has a tenth occurrence of this lemma since it writes Deut 30:18 defective ו; see Breuer, *The Biblical Text*, 41. Nevertheless all the headings above support the enumeration of M reading *nine times defective* (ו).

JUDGES 18:10

כְּבֹאֲכֶם תָּבֹאוּ ׀ אֶל־עַם בֹּטֵחַ וְהָאָרֶץ רַחֲבַת יָדַיִם כִּי־נְתָנָהּ אֱלֹהִים בְּיֶדְכֶם מָקוֹם אֲשֶׁר אֵין־שָׁם מַחְסוֹר כָּל־דָּבָר אֲשֶׁר בָּאָרֶץ׃

18:10　　כְּבֹאֲכֶם

כְּבֹאֲכֶם *three times*　　כבאכם ג　　Mm

<u>Josh 3:8</u>　　עד קצה מי הירדן
<u>Judg 18:10</u>　　תבאו אל עם בטח
1 Sam 9:13　　כבאכם העיר

Com.: The Masorah notes the *three* occurrences of this lemma with the prep. כ, to distinguish them from its *three* occurrences with the prep. ב (בְּבֹאֲכֶם).

18:10　　נְתָנָהּ אֱלֹהִים

Unique　　ל　　Mp

Com.: The Masorah notes the *sole* occurrence of אֱלֹהִים with נְתָנָהּ, to distinguish it from its *two* occurrences with נָתְנוּ (נָתְנוּ אֱלֹהִים) at Gen 31:7 and 1 Sam 23:14.

JUDGES 18:12

וַיַּעֲלוּ וַיַּחֲנוּ בְּקִרְיַת יְעָרִים בִּיהוּדָה עַל־כֵּן קָרְאוּ לַמָּקוֹם הַהוּא מַחֲנֵה־דָן עַד הַיּוֹם הַזֶּה הִנֵּה
אַחֲרֵי קִרְיַת יְעָרִים׃

18:12   בְּקִרְיַת יְעָרִים

Unique   ל   Mp

1–2   **Judg 18:12;** 1 Sam 7:2

Com.: The Mp heading here *of unique* is inexact since there are *two* occurrences of this
lemma. The note more precisely should have read *unique in the book.*

The Masorah notes the occurrences of this lemma with the prep. בּ, to distinguish
them from its more numerous occurrences (12x) without this prep., *one* of which
occurs in the same verse.

Neither M^C nor M^A has a note on this lemma here.

JUDGES 18:14

וַיַּעֲנוּ חֲמֵשֶׁת הָאֲנָשִׁים הַהֹלְכִים לְרַגֵּל אֶת־הָאָרֶץ לַיִשׁ וַיֹּאמְרוּ אֶל־אֲחֵיהֶם הַיְדַעְתֶּם כִּי יֵשׁ
בַּבָּתִּים הָאֵלֶּה אֵפוֹד וּתְרָפִים וּפֶסֶל וּמַסֵּכָה וְעַתָּה דְּעוּ מַה־תַּעֲשׂוּ׃

18:14   הַיְדַעְתֶּם

Three times   ג̇   Mp

Gen 29:5; <u>Judg 18:14</u>; <u>1 Kgs 22:3</u>

הַיְדַעְתֶּם *three times*   הידעתם ג̇   Mm

Gen 29:5   את לבן
<u>Judg 18:14</u>   יש בבתים
<u>1 Kgs 22:3</u>   רמת גלעד

Com.: The Masorah notes the *three* occurrences of this lemma with the interrog. ה, to
distinguish them from its more numerous occurrences (15x) without this interrogative.

JUDGES 18:15

וַיָּסוּרוּ שָׁמָּה וַיָּבֹאוּ אֶל־בֵּית־הַנַּעַר הַלֵּוִי בֵּית מִיכָה וַיִּשְׁאֲלוּ־לֹו לְשָׁלֹום׃

18:15   וַיָּסוּרוּ

Twice plene   ב מל   Mp

Com.: See **Judg 18:3**.

JUDGES 18:16

וְשֵׁשׁ־מֵאֹות אִישׁ חֲגוּרִים֙ כְּלֵי מִלְחַמְתָּם נִצָּבִים פֶּתַח הַשָּׁעַר אֲשֶׁר מִבְּנֵי־דָן׃

18:16   וְשֵׁשׁ

Three times at the beginning of a verse   ג ראש פסו   Mp

Exod 23:10; Judg 18:16; 2 Chr 9:18

Com.: The Masorah notes the *three* occurrences of this lemma at the beginning of a verse with a ו cj., to distinguish them from its *three* occurrences at the beginning of a verse without a cj.

This lemma is featured in a Masoretic list of words that occur *three times* at the beginning of a verse with a preceding ו, but which otherwise in the Bible occurs at the beginning of a verse without this ו; see Frensdorff, *Ochlah*, §173, and Ognibeni, *'Oklah*, §97.

18:16   חֲגוּרִים

Three times   ג   Mp

Exod 12:11 (חֲגֻרִים); **Judg 18:16; Dan 10:5** (חֲגוּרִים)

Com.: The Masorah notes the *three* occurrences of this lemma in various forms in the pl., to distinguish them from its *six* occurrences in various forms in the sg., *one* of which occurs in v. 11 (חָגוֹר), and *another* in v. 17 (הֶחָגוּר).

18:16   כְּלֵי מִלְחַמְתָּם

Unique   ל   Mp

Com.: The Masorah notes the *sole* occurrence of this lemma with a sfx., to distinguish it from its *six* occurrences without a sfx. (כְּלֵי מִלְחָמָה/כְּלֵי הַמִּלְחָמָה), *two* of which occur in vv. 11 and 17.

18:16   אֲשֶׁר מִבְּנֵי

Unique   ל   Mp

JUDGES 18:17

וַיַּעֲל֞וּ חֲמֵ֣שֶׁת הָאֲנָשִׁ֗ים הַהֹלְכִים֮ לְרַגֵּ֣ל אֶת־הָאָרֶץ֒ בָּ֣אוּ שָׁ֔מָּה לָקְח֗וּ אֶת־הַפֶּ֙סֶל֙ וְאֶת־הָאֵפוֹד֙ וְאֶת־הַתְּרָפִ֖ים וְאֶת־הַמַּסֵּכָ֑ה וְהַכֹּהֵ֗ן נִצָּב֙ פֶּ֣תַח הַשַּׁ֔עַר וְשֵׁשׁ־מֵא֣וֹת הָאִ֔ישׁ הֶחָג֖וּר כְּלֵ֥י הַמִּלְחָמָֽה׃

18:17   וְאֶת־הָאֵפ֖וֹד

Twice   ב   Mp

Exod 29:5 (וְאֶת־הָאֵפֹד); **Judg 18:17**

Com.: The Masorah notes the *two* occurrences of this lemma in various forms with a ו cj., to distinguish them from its *five* occurrences in various forms without a cj.

18:17   הָאִישׁ הֶחָגוּר

Unique   ל   Mp

Com.: The Masorah notes the *sole* occurrence of this lemma as a def., to distinguish it from its *sole* occurrence as an indef. (אִישׁ חָגוּר) in v. 11.

This phrase is featured in a Masoretic list of two-word phrases that only occur *once*, in which *both* words of the phrase have the def. article; see Frensdorff, *Ochlah*, §371.

JUDGES 18:18

וְאֵ֜לֶּה בָּ֗אוּ בֵּ֤ית מִיכָה֙ וַיִּקְחוּ֙ אֶת־פֶּ֣סֶל הָאֵפ֔וֹד וְאֶת־הַתְּרָפִ֖ים וְאֶת־הַמַּסֵּכָ֑ה וַיֹּ֤אמֶר אֲלֵיהֶם֙ הַכֹּהֵ֔ן מָ֥ה אַתֶּ֖ם עֹשִֽׂים׃

18:18   פֶּסֶל הָאֵפוֹד

Unique   ל   Mp

JUDGES 18:19

וַיֹּאמְרוּ לוֹ הַחֲרֵשׁ שִׂים־יָדְךָ עַל־פִּיךָ וְלֵךְ עִמָּנוּ וֶהְיֵה־לָנוּ לְאָב וּלְכֹהֵן הֲטוֹב ׀ הֱיוֹתְךָ כֹהֵן לְבֵית
אִישׁ אֶחָד אוֹ הֱיוֹתְךָ כֹהֵן לְשֵׁבֶט וּלְמִשְׁפָּחָה בְּיִשְׂרָאֵל׃

18:19   וְלֵךְ

Eleven times   יֹא   Mp

1–5   Gen 22:2 (וְלֶךְ); **27:13**; <u>Judg 18:19</u>; **1 Sam 16:1**; **29:7**
6–10   **2 Sam 14:21**; 2 Kgs 6:3; 8:8; **<u>9:1</u>**; **Ezek 3:1**
11   Ezek 3:11

וְלֵךְ *eleven times*   ולך יֹא   Mm

1–5   Gen 22:2   המריה והעלהו
         Gen 27:13   [שמע] (שוב)
         <u>Judg 18:19</u>   החרש
         <u>1 Sam 16:1</u>   מתאבל
         <u>1 Sam 29:7</u>   שוב
6–10   2 Sam 14:21   השב
         <u>2 Kgs 9:1</u>   רמת
         2 Kgs 6:3   הואל
         2 Kgs 8:8   [חזהאל] (חזאל)
         Ezek 3:11   בא
11   Ezek 3:1   דבר

Com.: The Masorah notes the *eleven* occurrences of this lemma with the וּ cj. pointed with a *šwâ*, to distinguish them from its *five* occurrences with the וּ cj. pointed with a *qameṣ* (וָלֵךְ).

18:19   וּלְכֹהֵן

Three times   גׄ   Mp

Exod 2:16; Judg 17:10; **18:19**

Com.: The Masorah notes the *three* occurrences of this lemma with a וּ cj., to distinguish them from its *six* occurrences without a cj.

18:19   הַטּוֹב

Four times   דֿ   Mp

Judg 11:25; 18:19; Job 10:3; 13:9

הַטּוֹב *four times*   הטוב דֿ   Mm

Judg 11:25   מבלק
Judg 18:19   היותך
Job 13:9   יחקר
Job 10:3   תעשק

Com.: The Masorah notes the *four* occurrences of this lemma with an interrog. ה, to distinguish them from its more numerous occurrences (46x) with a def. article (הַטּוֹב); see Ognibeni, *'Oklah*, §15E.

JUDGES 18:20
וַיִּיטַב לֵב הַכֹּהֵן וַיִּקַּח אֶת־הָאֵפוֹד וְאֶת־הַתְּרָפִים וְאֶת־הַפָּסֶל וַיָּבֹא בְּקֶרֶב הָעָם:

18:20   וַיִּיטַב לֵב

Unique   לֿ   Mp

Com.: The Masorah notes the *sole* occurrence of this lemma with a ו consec., to distinguish it from its occurrence without this ו (יִּיטַב לֵב).

18:20   וְאֶת־הַפָּסֶל

Unique   לֿ   Mp

Com.: The Masorah notes the *sole* occurrence of this lemma with a ו cj., to distinguish it from its *sole* occurrence without a cj. in v. 30.

JUDGES 18:21

וַיִּפְנוּ וַיֵּלֵכוּ וַיָּשִׂימוּ אֶת־הַטַּף וְאֶת־הַמִּקְנֶה וְאֶת־הַכְּבוּדָּה לִפְנֵיהֶם׃

18:21   הַכְּבוּדָּה

Three times and plene   ג׳ ומל׳   Mp

Judg 18:21; **Ezek 23:41** (כְּבוּדָּה); **Ps 45:14** (כְּבוּדָּה)

הַכְּבוּדָּה   *three times* and plene   הכבודה ג׳ ומל׳   Mm

Judg 18:21	את הטף ואת המקנה
Ps 45:14	כל כבודה בת מלך פנימה
Ezek 23:41	וישבת על מטה כבודה

Com.: The Masorah notes the *three* occurrences of this lemma, with and without the def. article, written plene ו.

The Mp headings here, and at Ezek 23:41, read *three times and plene* (ו), thus implying (correctly) that this lemma does not occur elsewhere written defective ו.

The Mp heading at Ps 45:14 mistakenly reads *unique plene*, but the form is not *unique* nor does it occur elsewhere in a defective form.

JUDGES 18:22

הֵמָּה הִרְחִיקוּ מִבֵּית מִיכָה וְהָאֲנָשִׁים אֲשֶׁר בַּבָּתִּים אֲשֶׁר עִם־בֵּית מִיכָה נִזְעֲקוּ וַיַּדְבִּיקוּ אֶת־בְּנֵי־
דָן׃

18:22   נִזְעֲקוּ

Unique   ל   Mp

18:22   וַיַּדְבִּיקוּ

Twice   ב׳   Mp

Judg 18:22; 20:45

וַיִּדְבִּיקוּ *twice*, and (their) references   וידביקו ב וסימנْ   Mm

Judg 20:45	וידביקו אחריו
Judg 18:22	נזעקו

Com.: The Masorah notes the *two* occurrences of this lemma written plene יֹ, to distinguish them from the *three* occurrences of its alternate form וַיִּדְבְּקוּ; see **1 Sam 14:22**.

JUDGES 18:23

וַיִּקְרְאוּ אֶל־בְּנֵי־דָן וַיַּסֵּבּוּ פְּנֵיהֶם וַיֹּאמְרוּ לְמִיכָה מַה־לְּךָ כִּי נִזְעָקְתָּ:

18:23   וַיַּסֵּבּוּ

Three times   גֵ   Mp

Judg 18:23; 1 Sam 5:8; 2 Chr 29:6

וַיַּסֵּבּוּ *three times*, and their references   ויסבו ג וסימנהון   Mm

2 Chr 29:6	פניהם ממשכן יהוה ויתנו
1 Sam 5:8	את ארון (אלהים) [אלהי]
Judg 18:23	ויאמרו למיכה

Com.: The Masorah notes the *three* occurrences of this lemma in the *hiphil*, to distinguish them from its more numerous occurrences (11x) in the *qal* (וַיִּסֹּבּוּ).

JUDGES 18:24

וַיֹּאמֶר אֶת־אֱלֹהַי אֲשֶׁר־עָשִׂיתִי לְקַחְתֶּם וְאֶת־הַכֹּהֵן וַתֵּלְכוּ וּמַה־לִּי עוֹד וּמַה־זֶּה תֹּאמְרוּ אֵלַי מַה־לָּךְ:

18:24   וְאֶת־הַכֹּהֵן

Twice   בֵ   Mp

Judg 18:24; 18:27

Com.: The Masorah notes the *two* occurrences of this lemma with a ו cj., to distinguish it from its *two* occurrence without a cj. at Lev 13:49 and 1 Sam 21:6

18:24 וּמַה־לִּי

Unique ל Mp

Com.: The Masorah notes the *sole* occurrence of this lemma with a ו cj., to distinguish it from its more numerous occurrences (8x) without a cj.

This lemma is featured in a Masoretic list of words that occur once with a preceding וּמַה; see Frensdorff, *Ochlah*, §256.

18:24 וּמַה־זֶּה

Unique ל Mp

Com.: The Masorah notes the *sole* occurrence of this lemma with a ו cj., to distinguish it from its more numerous occurrences (9x) without a cj.

This lemma is featured in a Masoretic list of words that occur once with a preceding וּמַה; see Frensdorff, *Ochlah*, §256.

> ## JUDGES 18:25
>
> וַיֹּאמְרוּ אֵלָיו בְּנֵי־דָן אַל־תַּשְׁמַע קוֹלְךָ עִמָּנוּ פֶּן־יִפְגְּעוּ בָכֶם אֲנָשִׁים מָרֵי נֶפֶשׁ וְאָסַפְתָּה נַפְשְׁךָ וְנֶפֶשׁ בֵּיתֶךָ׃

18:25 תַּשְׁמַע

Unique with *paṭaḥ* לֹ Mp

Com.: The Masorah notes the *sole* occurrence of this lemma written with a *paṭaḥ* under the ת (*hiphil*), to distinguish it from its more numerous occurrences (43x) with a *ḥireq* (תִּשְׁמַע, *qal*).

This lemma is featured in a Masoretic list of *hapax legomena* from the root שָׁמַע; see Ognibeni, *'Oklah*, §12G.

18:25 וְאָסַפְתָּה

Unique plene ל מל Mp

Com.: The Masorah notes the *sole* occurrence of this lemma written plene ה, to distinguish it from its *five* occurrences written defective ה (וְאָסַפְתָּ).

This lemma is one of *twenty* such forms that are written plene ה at the end of their words; see **2 Sam 2:26** *sub* יָדַעְתָּה.

JUDGES 18:26

וַיֵּלְכ֥וּ בְנֵי־דָ֖ן לְדַרְכָּ֑ם וַיַּ֣רְא מִיכָ֗ה כִּי־חֲזָקִ֤ים הֵ֙מָּה֙ מִמֶּ֔נּוּ וַיִּ֖פֶן וַיָּ֥שָׁב אֶל־בֵּיתֽוֹ׃

18:26   כִּי־חֲזָקִים

Unique   ל   Mp

The circellus has been placed only on חֲזָקִים but since this word occurs *three times*, it is more likely that the note refers to the phrase כִּי־חֲזָקִים, which only occurs this *once*.

JUDGES 18:27

וְהֵ֡מָּה לָקְח֣וּ אֵ֣ת אֲשֶׁר־עָשָׂ֣ה מִיכָ֡ה וְאֶת־הַכֹּהֵן֩ אֲשֶׁ֨ר הָיָה־ל֜וֹ וַיָּבֹ֣אוּ עַל־לַ֗יִשׁ עַל־עַ֤ם שֹׁקֵט֙ וּבֹטֵ֔חַ וַיַּכּ֥וּ אוֹתָ֖ם לְפִי־חָ֑רֶב וְאֶת־הָעִ֖יר שָׂרְפ֥וּ בָאֵֽשׁ׃

18:27   וְהֵמָּה

Ten times at the beginning of a verse   י ראֹ פסוק   Mp

Com.: See **Josh 2:8**.

18:27   וְאֶת־הָעִיר

Eight times   ח   Mp

Com.: See **Judg 1:8**.

JUDGES 18:28

וְאֵ֣ין מַצִּ֗יל כִּ֤י רְחֽוֹקָה־הִיא֙ מִצִּיד֔וֹן וְדָבָ֥ר אֵין־לָהֶ֖ם עִם־אָדָ֑ם וְהִ֣יא בָּעֵ֗מֶק אֲשֶׁ֣ר לְבֵית־רְח֔וֹב וַיִּבְנ֥וּ אֶת־הָעִ֖יר וַיֵּ֥שְׁבוּ בָֽהּ׃

18:28   וְאֵין

Six verses in which there is the sequence וְאֵין...אֵין   ו פסוק אית בהון ואין אין   Mp

Com.: See directly above at **Judg 18:7**.

In M^L this lemma has no circellus. The first part of this note (ו פסוק אית בהון) was written by the scribe three lines above the start of this verse. He then repeated the full note adjacent to this verse.

18:28 רְחוֹב

Twice plene as a city ב מל בקר֯ Mp

Judg 18:28; 2 Sam 10:6

Com.: The Masorah notes the *two* occurrences of this lemma, indicating the the name of a city, written plene וֹ, to distinguish them from its *four* occurrences indicating the name of a city, written defective וֹ (רְחֹב).

The Mp heading at 2 Sam 10:6 (and M^A here) reads *three times plene* to include the form with a וֹ cj. (וּרְחוֹב) at 2 Sam 10:8.

JUDGES 18:29

וַיִּקְרְא֤וּ שֵׁם־הָעִיר֙ דָּ֔ן בְּשֵׁם֙ דָּ֣ן אֲבִיהֶ֔ם אֲשֶׁ֥ר יוּלַּ֖ד לְיִשְׂרָאֵ֑ל וְאוּלָ֛ם לַ֥יִשׁ שֵׁם־הָעִ֖יר לָרִאשֹׁנָֽה׃

18:29 יוּלַּד

Twice plene ב מל Mp

Judg 18:29; Job 5:7 (יוּלָּד)

יוּלַּד *twice* plene, and (their) references יולד ב מל וסימ֮ Mm

Judg 18:29 לישראל
Job 5:7 לעמל יולד

Com.: The Masorah notes the *two* occurrences of this lemma written plene וֹ, to distinguish them from its more numerous occurrences (15x) written defective וֹ (יִלֵּד).

The Mp heading at Job 5:7 reads *unique with qames* (לָ) thereby noting that this is the *sole* occurrence of this form with a *qames*.

18:29 לָרִאשֹׁנָה

לָרִאשֹׁנָה *twice* לראשנה ב Mm

Gen 28:19 ואולם לוז שם העיר
Judg 18:29 ליש שם העיר

Com.: The Masorah notes the *two* occurrences of this lemma with the prep. לָ, to distinguish them from its more numerous occurrences (6x) without this preposition.

JUDGES 18:30

וַיָּקִימוּ לָהֶם בְּנֵי־דָן אֶת־הַפָּסֶל וִיהוֹנָתָן בֶּן־גֵּרְשֹׁם בֶּן־מְנַשֶּׁה הוּא וּבָנָיו הָיוּ כֹהֲנִים לְשֵׁבֶט הַדָּנִי עַד־יוֹם גְּלוֹת הָאָרֶץ׃

18:30   מְנַשֶּׁה

Four times elevated   ד תלוים   Mp

(מֵרְשָׁ֜עִים); Job 38:13 (רְשָׁ֜עִים); **38:15** (מִיָּ֜ר); Job 38:13 (רְשָׁ֜עִים); **Judg 18:30; Ps 80:14**

Com.: The Masorah notes the *four* raised letters that occur in the *four* words listed above; see Frensdorff, *Ochlah*, §160, and Díaz-Esteban, *Sefer Oklah we-Oklah*, §146.

JUDGES 18:31

וַיָּשִׂימוּ לָהֶם אֶת־פֶּסֶל מִיכָה אֲשֶׁר עָשָׂה כָּל־יְמֵי הֱיוֹת בֵּית־הָאֱלֹהִים בְּשִׁלֹה׃ פ

18:31   בֵּית־הָאֱלֹהִים

Forty-eight times   מֹח   Mp

1–5   **Judg 18:31**; Qoh 4:17; Dan 1:2; Ezra 1:4 (לְבֵית הָאֱלֹהִים); 2:68 (לְבֵית הָאֱלֹהִים)
6–10   Ezra 3:8; 6:22; 8:36; 10:1; 10:6
11–15   Ezra 10:9; Neh 6:10; 8:16; 11:11; 11:16 (לְבֵית הָאֱלֹהִים)
16–20   Neh 11:22; 13:7; 13:9; 13:11; 1 Chr 6:33
21–25   1 Chr. 9:11; 9:13; 9:26; 9:27; 22:2
26–30   1 Chr 23:28; 25:6; 26:20; 28:12; 28:21
31–35   1 Chr 29:7; 2 Chr 3:3; 4:19; 5:1; 5:14
36–40   2 Chr 7:5; 15:18; 23:9; 24:7; 24:13
41–45   2 Chr 24:27; 28:24[a]; 28:24[b]; 31:13; 31:21
46–48   2 Chr 35:8; 36:18; 36:19

Com.: The Masorah notes the *forty-eight* occurrences of בֵּית/לְבֵית with הָאֱלֹהִים, to distinguish them from the more numerous occurrences (100+) of בֵּית/לְבֵית with יְהוָה (בֵּית יְהוָה/לְבֵית יְהוָה); see Ginsburg, 4, ב, §252.

M^A reads here *unique in the Prophets* for the *sole* occurrence in the Prophets of this lemma at this reference.

JUDGES 19:2

וַתִּזְנֶה עָלָיו פִּילַגְשׁוֹ וַתֵּלֶךְ מֵאִתּוֹ אֶל־בֵּית אָבִיהָ אֶל־בֵּית לֶחֶם יְהוּדָה וַתְּהִי־שָׁם יָמִים אַרְבָּעָה חֳדָשִׁים׃

19:2   וַתִּזְנֶה

Twice, once at the beginning of a verse, and   ב֜ חד ראש פסו וחד סוף פסו   Mp
once at the end of a verse

Judg 19:2; <u>Isa 57:3</u>

Com.: The Masorah notes the *two* occurrences of this lemma, *one* at the beginning of a verse (here), and *one* at the end of a verse (Isa 57:3).

The Mp heading at Isa 57:3 inexactly reads *unique*. It should have read *unique in the book* or *unique at the end of a verse*.

This lemma is featured in a Masoretic list of words that occur *once* at the beginning and *once* at the end of a verse; see Frensdorff, *Ochlah*, §90, and Ognibeni, *'Oklah*, §109.

JUDGES 19:3

וַיָּקָם אִישָׁהּ וַיֵּלֶךְ אַחֲרֶיהָ לְדַבֵּר עַל־לִבָּהּ לַהֲשִׁיבוֹ וְנַעֲרוֹ עִמּוֹ וְצֶמֶד חֲמֹרִים וַתְּבִיאֵהוּ בֵּית אָבִיהָ וַיִּרְאֵהוּ אֲבִי הַנַּעֲרָה וַיִּשְׂמַח לִקְרָאתוֹ׃

19:3   אִישָׁהּ

Twenty-five times   כֹּה   Mp

1–5   Gen 16:3; Num 5:13; 5:29; 30:8; 30:9
6–10   Num 30:11; 30:12; 30:13[a]; 30:13[b]; 30:14
11–15   Num 30:15; Deut 25:11; Judg 13:9; <u>19:3</u>; 1 Sam 1:8
16–20   **1 Sam 1:23**; 2:19; **2 Sam 3:16**; **11:26**; **2 Kgs 4:9**
21–25   **2 Kgs 4:22**; Ezek 16:32; 16:45; Hos 2:4; Ruth 1:9

אִישָׁהּ *twenty-five times*   אישה כֹה   Mm

1–5	Gen 16:3	ותקח שרי
	Num 5:13	ושכב איש
	Num 5:29	הקנאת
	Num 30:8	ושמע
	Num 30:9	ואם ביום שמע
6–10	Num 30:11	ואם בית אישה
	Num 30:12	ושמע
	Num 30:13ᵃ	ואם הפר
	Twice in the verse (Num 30:13ᵇ)	שנים בפסוקה
	Num 30:14	כל נדר וכל
11–15	Num 30:15	ואם החרש
	Deut 25:11	כי ינצו אנשים
	Judg 13:9	וישמע (האל׳) [האלהים] בקול
	<u>Judg 19:3</u>	ויקם אישה
	1 Sam 1:8	ויאמר לה
16–20	1 Sam 1:23	אלקנה
	1 Sam 2:19	ומעיל קטן
	2 Sam 3:16	וילך אתה
	2 Sam 11:26	אשת אוריה
	2 Kgs 4:9	ותאמר אל אישה
21–25	2 Kgs 4:22	ותקרא אל אישה
	Ezek 16:32	המנאפת
	Ezek 16:45	בת אמך את
	Hos 2:4	ריבו באמכם
	Ruth 1:9	ומצאן מנוחה

Com.: The Masorah notes the *twenty-five* occurrences of this lemma with a fem. sfx. *her husband*, to distinguish them from the more numerous occurrences (100+) of the common word אִשָּׁה *woman*.

The Mp headings here, and at 2 Sam 11:26, read *twenty-five*. The heading at 2 Sam 3:16 of *twenty-eight* is no doubt a simple graphic error of ח *eight* and ה *five*.

The headings at 1 Sam 1:23, 2 Kgs 4:9 and 2 Kgs 4:22 read *twenty-one*, quite possibly taking the *five* Samuel references as *one* reference; see Dotan/Reich, *Masora Thesaurus*, *ad loc.*

19:3   לַהֲשִׁיבֽוּ

Read   לַהֲשִׁיבָה   להשיבה קׄ   Mp

Com.: This lemma is featured in a Masoretic list of words that occur with a ו at the end of a word, but which are read as a ה; see the Mm at <u>Dan 5:5</u> *sub* נפקו, Frensdorff, *Ochlah*, §115, and Díaz-Esteban, *Sefer Oklah we-Oklah*, §97.

In M^L this lemma has no circellus.

19:3   וַתְּבִיאֵהוּ

Unique plene   ל מל   Mp

Com.: The Masorah notes the *sole* occurrence of this lemma written plene י, to distinguish them from its *two* occurrences written defective י (וַתְּבִאֵהוּ) at Exod 2:10 and **1 Sam 1:24**.

JUDGES 19:5
וַיְהִי בַּיּוֹם הָרְבִיעִי וַיַּשְׁכִּימוּ בַבֹּקֶר וַיָּקָם לָלֶכֶת וַיֹּאמֶר אֲבִי הַנַּעֲרָה אֶל־חֲתָנוֹ סְעָד לִבְּךָ פַּת־לֶחֶם וְאַחַר תֵּלֵכוּ:

19:5   חֲתָנֽוֹ

Twice   בׄ   Mp

Com.: The Mp heading here of *twice* is incorrect since this is the *only* occurrence of this lemma. M^A correctly reads here *unique*, but M^C has no note.

JUDGES 19:6
וַיֵּשְׁבוּ וַיֹּאכְלוּ שְׁנֵיהֶם יַחְדָּו וַיִּשְׁתּוּ וַיֹּאמֶר אֲבִי הַנַּעֲרָה אֶל־הָאִישׁ הוֹאֶל־נָא וְלִין וְיִטַב לִבֶּךָ:

19:6   וַיֵּשְׁבוּ וַיֹּאכְלֽוּ

Unique   לׄ   Mp

19:6   הוֹאֶל

Five times   הֹ   Mp

1–4   **Judg 19:6; 2 Sam 7:29** (הוֹאֶל)**; 2 Kgs 5:23** (הוֹאֶל)**;** 6:3

Com.: The Mp heading here of *five times* is incorrect since there are only *four* occurrences of this lemma. The correct number is given in the Mp headings at 2 Sam 7:29 and 2 Kgs 5:23.

The Masorah notes the *four* occurrences of this lemma, written with *ṣerê* and *sᵊḡôl*, to distinguish them from the *three* occurrences of a similar form הוֹאִיל.

Neither M^C nor M^A has a note on this lemma here.

JUDGES 19:7
וַיָּ֤קָם הָאִישׁ֙ לָלֶ֔כֶת וַיִּפְצַר־בּוֹ֙ חֹתְנ֔וֹ וַיָּ֖שָׁב וַיָּ֥לֶן שָֽׁם׃

19:7   וַיִּפְצַר

Four times   דֹ   Mp

Gen 19:3; 33:11; Judg 19:7; 2 Kgs 5:16

Com.: The Masorah notes the *four* occurrences of this lemma from פָּצַר, to distinguish them from the more numerous occurrences (9x) of its by-form פָּרַץ (וַיִּפְרֹץ; see *HALOT*, 2: 954, 972). For the interchange of the צ and פ with the pl. of this form in another Masoretic list, see Ognibeni, 'Oklah, §176.

The Mp headings at Gen 19:3 and Gen 33:11 read *four times with paṭaḥ* (דֹ).

JUDGES 19:8
וַיַּשְׁכֵּ֨ם בַּבֹּ֜קֶר בַּיּ֣וֹם הַחֲמִישִׁי֮ לָלֶכֶת֒ וַיֹּ֗אמֶר אֲבִ֤י הַֽנַּעֲרָה֙ סְעָד־נָ֣א לְבָבְךָ֔ וְהִֽתְמַהְמְה֖וּ עַד־נְט֣וֹת הַיּ֑וֹם וַיֹּאכְל֖וּ שְׁנֵיהֶֽם׃

19:8   סְעָד

Twice   בֹ   Mp

Judg 19:5; **19:8**

19:8   וְהִתְמַהְמְהוּ

Unique   ל   Mp

Com.: The Masorah notes the *sole* occurrence of this lemma with a ו cj., to distinguish it from its *sole* occurrence without a cj. at Isa 29:9.

JUDGES 19:9

וַיָּקׇם הָאִישׁ לָלֶכֶת הוּא וּפִילַגְשׁוֹ וְנַעֲרוֹ וַיֹּאמֶר לוֹ חֹתְנוֹ אֲבִי הַנַּעֲרָה הִנֵּה נָא רָפָה הַיּוֹם לַעֲרֹב
לִינוּ־נָא הִנֵּה חֲנוֹת הַיּוֹם לֵין פֹּה וְיִיטַב לְבָבֶךָ וְהִשְׁכַּמְתֶּם מָחָר לְדַרְכְּכֶם וְהָלַכְתָּ לְאֹהָלֶךָ:

19:9   רָפָה

Twice written with   ה   ג כת ה   Mp

Judg 19:9; 1 Chr 8:37

Com.: The Masorah notes that these two forms, which are homonyms (רָפָה here is a verbal form *is waning*, whereas רָפָה in 1 Chr 8:37 is a name *Raphah*), are written with ה.

Another similar form רְפָה *heal!* is written both ways, *once* with ה at Ps 60:4 (רְפָה) and *once* with א at Num 12:13 (רְפָא).

19:9   לַעֲרֹב

Twice   ב   Mp

Judg 19:9 (לַעֲרוֹב)*; Ezek 27:9

Com.: The Masorah notes the *two* occurrences of this lemma with the prep. ל, to distinguish them from its *sole* occurrence without this prep. at Ps 119:122.

* M^L, contrary to M (לַעֲרוֹב), writes the lemma here defective ו; see Breuer, *The Biblical Text*, 657). M^C and M^A both write the lemma here as לַעֲרוֹב. The Mp of M^A reads *twice*, but the Mp of M^C reads *unique plene* (ו).

At Ezek 27:9 the Mp of M^L reads *twice*, the Mp of M^A, in accord with M, reads *twice*, *once defective and once plene*, while M^C has no Mp note there.

In M^L the circellus has been placed on לַעֲרֹב לִינוּ but, since this phrase only occurs *once*, it is most likely that, with M^A, the note should just be on לַעֲרֹב, that does occur *twice*.

19:9   וְהִשְׁכַּמְתֶּם

Three times   גׄ   Mp

Gen 19:2; Judg 19:9; 1 Sam 29:10

וְהִשְׁכַּמְתֶּם *three times*, and their references   והשכמתם גׄ וסימנהון   Mm

Gen 19:2   והלכתם לדרככם
Judg 19:9   מחר
1 Sam 29:10   ואור לכם

19:9   לְאֹהֳלֶךָ

Unique defective   ל חסׄ   Mp

Com.: The Masorah notes the *sole* occurrence of this lemma written defective יׄ (sg.), to distinguish it from its *three* occurrences written plene יׄ (לְאֹהָלֶיךָ, pl.).

In Mᴸ the erasure of an original יׄ to conform to the Mp note, is clearly apparent.

┌───┐

JUDGES 19:10

וְלֹא־אָבָה הָאִישׁ לָלוּן וַיָּקָם וַיֵּלֶךְ וַיָּבֹא עַד־נֹכַח יְבוּס הִיא יְרוּשָׁלָ͏ִם וְעִמּוֹ צֶמֶד חֲמוֹרִים חֲבוּשִׁים
וּפִילַגְשׁוֹ עִמּוֹ׃

└───┘

19:10   חֲמוֹרִים

Six times plene   ו מלׄ   Mp

1–5   **Judg 19:10; 19:21** (לַחֲמוֹרִים); **2 Sam 16:2** (הַחֲמוֹרִים); **Ezek 23:20;**
       1 Chr 5:21 (וַחֲמוֹרִים)
6   **1 Chr 12:41** (בַּחֲמוֹרִים)

	חֲמוֹרִים	*six times* plene, and their references	חמורים ו מל וסימנהון Mm

1–5	<u>Judg 19:21</u>	ויביאהו לביתו (ויבל) [ויבול]
	Judg 19:10	ולא אבה האיש
	לְבֵית־הַמֶּלֶךְ לִרְכֹּב *of Ziba* (2 Sam 16:2)	לבית המלך לרכב (דציבאות) [דציבא]
	<u>Ezek 23:20</u>	ותעגבה על
	1 Chr 5:21	מקניהם
6	1 Chr 12:41	וגם הקרובים אליהם

Com.: The Masorah notes the *six* occurrences of this lemma in various forms written plene וֹ, to distinguish them from its more numerous occurrences (20x) in various forms written defective וֹ (חֲמֹרִים).

In the Mm, the addition *of Ziba* to the 2 Sam 16:2 reference specifies that the verse occurs in the passage concerns Ziba, servant of Mephibosheth.

The first two letters (ות) of the first catchword of the Ezek 23:20 (וֹתעגבה) reference have mistakenly been repeated and attached to the previous word (דציבא) as דציבאות.

19:10	חֲבוּשִׁים

Unique plene	ל מל	Mp

Com.: The Masorah notes the *sole* occurrence of this lemma written plene וֹ, to distinguish it from its *two* occurrences written defective וֹ (חֲבֻשִׁים) at 2 Sam 16:1 and Ezek 27:24.

> ### JUDGES 19:11
>
> הֵם עִם־יְב֔וּס וְהַיּ֖וֹם רַ֣ד מְאֹ֑ד וַיֹּ֨אמֶר הַנַּ֜עַר אֶל־אֲדֹנָ֗יו לְכָה־נָּ֛א וְנָס֛וּרָה אֶל־עִיר־הַיְבוּסִ֥י הַזֹּ֖את וְנָלִ֥ין בָּֽהּ׃

19:11	רַד

Unique with *paṭaḥ*	ל	Mp

Com.: The Masorah notes the *sole* occurrence of this lemma written with a *paṭaḥ*, to distinguish it from its more numerous occurrences (12x) written with a *ṣerê* (רֵד), and from its *sole* occurrence written with a *qameṣ* (רָד) at Hos 12:1.

This lemma is featured in a Masoretic list of words that occur *once* with a *paṭaḥ*, and *once* with a *qameṣ*; see Frensdorff, *Ochlah*, §23, and Díaz-Esteban, *Sefer Oklah we-Oklah*, §24.

JUDGES 19:12

וַיֹּאמֶר אֵלָיו אֲדֹנָיו לֹא נָסוּר אֶל־עִיר נָכְרִי אֲשֶׁר לֹא־מִבְּנֵי יִשְׂרָאֵל הֵנָּה וְעָבַרְנוּ עַד־גִּבְעָה:

19:12   לֹא נָסוּר

Unique   ל   Mp

Com.: The Masorah notes the *sole* occurrence of this lemma without a ו cj., to distinguish it from its occurrence with a cj. (וְלֹא נָסוּר) at Judg 20:8.

19:12   יִשְׂרָאֵל הֵנָּה

Twice   בֿ   Mp

Exod 39:14; **Judg 19:12**

Com.: The Masorah notes the *two* occurrences of יִשְׂרָאֵל with הֵנָּה, to distinguish them from its *two* occurrences with הֵנֵּה (יִשְׂרָאֵל הֵנֵּה) at Judg 6:15 and 1 Sam 12:1.

JUDGES 19:13

וַיֹּאמֶר לְנַעֲרֹו לֵךְ וְנִקְרְבָה בְּאַחַד הַמְּקֹמֹות וְלַנּוּ בַגִּבְעָה אֹו בָרָמָה:

19:13   לֵךְ

Three times defective (in sense of) going   גֿ חסֿ בהליכה   Mp

Num 23:13 (*kǝtîb*); **Judg 19:13**; <u>2 Chr 25:17</u> (*kǝtîb*)

Com.: The Masorah notes the *three* occurrences of this lemma in the sense of going, written defective ה, to distinguish them from its more numerous occurrences (28x), in the sense of going, written plene ה (לְכָה); see the Mm at <u>Isa 3:6</u> *sub* לְכָה.

This distinction is implied in the Mm to <u>2 Chr 25:17</u> in the additional notation *of Chronicles* to the 2 Chr 25:17 reference, which distinguishes it from its parallel passage in 2 Kgs 14:8, where the lemma occurs as לְכָה.

At the Num 23:13 and 2 Chr 25:17 references, the form לֵךְ is the *kǝtîb* whereas the form לְכָה is the *qǝrê*.

19:13   וְלַנּוּ

Unique   ל   Mp

JUDGES 19:15

וַיָּסֻרוּ שָׁם לָבוֹא לָלוּן בַּגִּבְעָה וַיָּבֹא וַיֵּשֶׁב בִּרְחוֹב הָעִיר וְאֵין אִישׁ מְאַסֵּף־אוֹתָם הַבַּיְתָה לָלוּן׃

19:15   וְאֵין אִישׁ

Seven times   ז̇   Mp

1–5   **Gen 39:11**; **Judg 19:15**; **19:18**; **1 Sam 9:2**; Isa 41:28
6–7   Isa 50:2; 57:1

Com.: The Masorah notes the *seven* occurrences of this lemma with a ו cj., to distinguish them from its *seven* occurrences without a cj.

19:15   מְאַסֵּף

Four times   ד̇   Mp

Num 10:25; **Judg 19:15**; **19:18**; Jer 9:21

19:15   הַבַּיְתָה

Nineteen times   יט̇   Mp

Com.: See **Josh 2:18.**

JUDGES 19:16

וְהִנֵּה | אִישׁ זָקֵן בָּא מִן־מַעֲשֵׂהוּ מִן־הַשָּׂדֶה בָּעֶרֶב וְהָאִישׁ מֵהַר אֶפְרַיִם וְהוּא־גָר בַּגִּבְעָה וְאַנְשֵׁי הַמָּקוֹם בְּנֵי יְמִינִי׃

19:16   וְהִנֵּה

Twice at the beginning of a verse in the book   ב רא פס בסיפ   Mp

Com.: See **Judg 4:22.**

JUDGES 19:17

וַיִּשָּׂא עֵינָיו וַיַּרְא אֶת־הָאִישׁ הָאֹרֵחַ בִּרְחֹב הָעִיר וַיֹּאמֶר הָאִישׁ הַזָּקֵן אָנָה תֵלֵךְ וּמֵאַיִן תָּבוֹא׃

19:17   וַיִּשָּׂא עֵינָיו

Five times   הֹ   Mp

Com.: See **Josh 5:13**.

19:17   בִּרְחֹב

Unique defective   ל חֹס   Mp

Com.: The Masorah notes the *sole* occurrence of this lemma written defective וֹ, to distinguish it from its more numerous occurrences (8x) written plene ו (בִּרְחוֹב).

19:17   וַיֹּאמֶר הָאִישׁ הַזָּקֵן

Twice   בֹ   Mp

Judg 19:17; 19:20

19:17   וּמֵאַיִן

Five times   הֹ   Mp

1–5   **Josh 9:8**; **Judg 19:17**; 2 Kgs 20:14; Isa 39:3; Jonah 1:8.

Com.: The Masorah notes the *five* occurrences of this lemma with a ו cj., to distinguish them from its more numerous occurrences (14x) without a cj.

JUDGES 19:18

וַיֹּאמֶר אֵלָיו עֹבְרִים אֲנַחְנוּ מִבֵּית־לֶחֶם יְהוּדָה עַד־יַרְכְּתֵי הַר־אֶפְרַיִם מִשָּׁם אָנֹכִי וָאֵלֵךְ עַד־בֵּית לֶחֶם יְהוּדָה וְאֶת־בֵּית יְהוָה אֲנִי הֹלֵךְ וְאֵין אִישׁ מְאַסֵּף אוֹתִי הַבָּיְתָה׃

19:18   אֲנִי הֹלֵךְ

Four times   דֹ   Mp

Judg 19:18; 2 Sam 12:23; 15:20ᵃ (וַאֲנִי הוֹלֵךְ); **15:20ᵇ** (הוֹלֵךְ)

Com.: The Masorah notes the *four* occurrences of הֹלֵךְ in various forms with אֲנִי, to distinguish them from its more numerous occurrences (7x) in various forms with אָנֹכִי (אָנֹכִי הֹלֵךְ).

19:18　וְאֵין אִישׁ

Seven times　ז֟　Mp

Com.: See directly above at **Judg 19:15.**

19:18　מְאַסֵּף

Four times　ד֟　Mp

Num 10:25; **Judg 19:15; 19:18;** Jer 9:21

19:18　הַבָּיְתָה

Nineteen times　יט֟　Mp

Com.: See **Josh 2:18.**

> ### JUDGES 19:19
>
> וְגַם־תֶּבֶן גַּם־מִסְפּוֹא֙ יֵשׁ לַחֲמוֹרֵ֔ינוּ וְ֠גַם לֶ֣חֶם וָיַ֤יִן יֶשׁ־לִי֙ וְלַֽאֲמָתֶ֔ךָ וְלַנַּ֖עַר עִם־עֲבָדֶ֑יךָ אֵ֥ין מַחְס֖וֹר כָּל־דָּבָֽר׃

19:19　לַחֲמוֹרֵינוּ

Unique plene　ל מל֟　Mp

Com.: The Mp heading here, and in M[C], of *unique* plene (ו) is inexact since there is no occurrence of this lemma written defective ו. The note more precisely should have read *unique and plene.*

M[A] reads here *twice* to include the form of this lemma written defective ו and without the prep. ל (חֲמֹרֵינוּ) at Gen 43:18.

JUDGES 19:20

וַיֹּאמֶר הָאִישׁ הַזָּקֵן שָׁלוֹם לְךָ רַק כָּל־מַחְסוֹרְךָ עָלָי רַק בָּרְחוֹב אַל־תָּלַן׃

19:20   שָׁלוֹם לְךָ

Twice   בׄ   Mp

Judg 19:20; Dan 10:19

Com.: The Masorah notes the *two* occurrences of שָׁלוֹם with לְךָ, to distinguish them from its *three* occurrences with לָךְ (שָׁלוֹם לָךְ); see **Judg 6:23**.

19:20   מַחְסוֹרְךָ

Unique   לׄ   Mp

Com.: The Masorah notes the *sole* occurrence of this lemma without a ו cj., to distinguish it from its occurrence with a cj. (וּמַחְסֹרְךָ) at Prov 6:11.

19:20   בָּרְחוֹב

Four times   דׄ   Mp

Gen 19:2; **Judg 19:20**; <u>Isa 59:14</u>; Job 29:7

Com.: The Masorah notes the *four* occurrences of this lemma with the def. prep. בָּ, to distinguish them from its *four* occurrences with the indef. prep. בְּ (בִּרְחוֹב).

19:20   תָּלַן

Twice   בׄ   Mp

Judg 19:20; Job 17:2

Com.: The Masorah notes the *two* occurrences of this lemma with a *paṭaḥ* under the ל, to distinguish them from its *sole* occurrence with a *sǝḡôl* (תָּלֶן) at 2 Sam 17:16.

JUDGES 19:21

וַיְבִיאֵהוּ לְבֵיתוֹ וַיָּבָול לַחֲמוֹרִים וַיִּרְחֲצוּ רַגְלֵיהֶם וַיֹּאכְלוּ וַיִּשְׁתּוּ׃

19:21   וַיְבִיאֵהוּ

Five times plene   ה מל   Mp

1–5   **Gen 29:13; Judg 19:21; 1 Sam 16:12; 2 Kgs 4:20; Ezek 17:4**

Com.: The Masorah notes the *five* occurrences of this lemma written plene second י, to distinguish them from its *six* occurrences written defective second י (וַיְבִאֵהוּ).

This enumeration does not include the *two* occurrences of this lemma in the Writings at 2 Chr 25:23 and 36:4.

The Mp heading at 2 Kgs 4:20 reads *eight times*, no doubt a graphic error of ח *eight* for ה *five*.

The Mp headings at 2 Kgs 4:20 and Ezek 17:4, and the Mm at 1 Sam 16:12, add *and similarly all the Writings apart from one* (וַיְבִאֵהוּ, 2 Chr 36:10).

19:21   וַיָּבָול

Five times plene   ה מל   Mp

Com.: The Mp heading here of *five times* plene (ו) is incorrect since this is the *only* occurrence of this lemma. The note seems to be a duplication of the one for the previous lemma. What is expected here is either a *qərê* וַיָּבֶל (so *BHS*), or a note יתיר ו, as in M^C and M^A.

19:21   לַחֲמוֹרִים

Six times plene   ו מל   Mp

Com.: See directly above at **Judg 19:10**.

JUDGES 19:22

הֵ֣מָּה מֵיטִיבִ֣ים אֶת־לִבָּם֒ וְהִנֵּה֩ אַנְשֵׁ֨י הָעִ֜יר אַנְשֵׁ֣י בְנֵֽי־בְלִיַּ֗עַל נָסַ֨בּוּ֙ אֶת־הַבַּ֔יִת מִֽתְדַּפְּקִ֖ים עַל־
הַדָּ֑לֶת וַיֹּאמְר֗וּ אֶל־הָאִ֨ישׁ בַּ֤עַל הַבַּ֨יִת֙ הַזָּקֵ֣ן לֵאמֹ֔ר הוֹצֵ֗א אֶת־הָאִ֛ישׁ אֲשֶׁר־בָּ֥א אֶל־בֵּיתְךָ֖ וְנֵדָעֶֽנּוּ׃

19:22   הֵ֣מָּה

Nineteen times at the beginning of a verse   יֹט רא פֹס   Mp

Com.: See **Judg 18:3**.

In M^L this lemma has no circellus. However, the following word מֵיטִיבִ֣ים has a circellus but no note, so it would seem that the circellus has simply been misplaced.

19:22   מִֽתְדַּפְּקִ֖ים

Unique   ל   Mp

19:22   עַל־הַדָּ֑לֶת

Unique   ל   Mp

Com.: This lemma is featured in a Masoretic list of words that occur *once* with a preceding עַל (here), and *once* with a preceding אֶל (Exod 21:6); see Frensdorff, *Ochlah*, §2, and Díaz-Esteban, *Sefer Oklah we-Oklah*, §2.

19:22   בַּ֤עַל הַבַּ֨יִת הַזָּקֵ֣ן

Unique   ל   Mp

19:22   הוֹצֵ֗א

Five times   הֹ   Mp

Com.: See **Judg 6:30**.

19:22   וְנֵדָעֶֽנּוּ

Unique   ל   Mp

JUDGES 19:23

וַיֵּצֵא אֲלֵיהֶם הָאִישׁ בַּעַל הַבַּיִת וַיֹּאמֶר אֲלֵהֶם אַל־אַחַי אַל־תָּרֵעוּ נָא אַחֲרֵי אֲשֶׁר־בָּא הָאִישׁ הַזֶּה אֶל־בֵּיתִי אַל־תַּעֲשׂוּ אֶת־הַנְּבָלָה הַזֹּאת:

19:23   אֲלֵהֶם

Six times defective in the book   ו חס̇ בסיפֿ   Mp

1–5   **Judg 3:28**; **8:23**; 8:24; 18:2; 18:4
6   **Judg 19:23**

אֲלֵהֶם *six times* defective in the book,   אלהם ו חס̇ בסיפֿ וסימנהון   Mm
and their references

1–5   Judg 3:28   רדפו אחרי כי
        Judg 8:23   לא אמשל אני
        Judg 8:24   אשאלה מכם שאלה
        Judg 18:2   לכו חקרו
        Judg 18:4   וישכרני
6   Judg 19:23^b   אל תרעו

Com.: The Masorah notes the *six* occurrences of this lemma in the book written defective י, to distinguish them from its more numerous occurrences (10x) in the book written plene י (אֲלֵיהֶם).

The Mp heading at Judg 8:23 enumerates the *twenty-nine* occurrences of this lemma in the Prophets, for which there is a Mm at 1 Kgs 12:16 and Ezek 33:25.

19:23   אַל־תָּרֵעוּ

Three times   ג̇   Mp

Judg 19:23; Ps 105:15; 1 Chr 16:22

Com.: The Masorah notes the *three* occurrences of this lemma with אַל, to distinguish them from its *two* occurrences without אַל at Gen 19:7 and 1 Sam 12:25.

In M^L at the Ps 105:15 reference, the notes for this lemma and the preceding one וְלִנְבִיאַי have mistakenly been reversed. The heading for this lemma reads *unique* instead of *three times*, and the one for the preceding lemma וְלִנְבִיאַי reads *three times* instead of *unique*; see Dotan/Reich, *Masora Thesaurus, ad loc.*

19:23   אַל־תַּעֲשׂוּ

Three times   גֿ   Mp

Gen 19:8; **Judg 19:23; Jer 5:10**

Com.: The Masorah notes the *three* occurrences of this lemma with אַל, to distinguish them from its more numerous occurrences (31x) with לֹא (לֹא תַעֲשׂוּ).

JUDGES 19:24

הִנֵּה בִתִּי הַבְּתוּלָה וּפִילַגְשֵׁהוּ אוֹצִיאָה־נָּא אוֹתָם וְעַנּוּ אוֹתָם וַעֲשׂוּ לָהֶם הַטּוֹב בְּעֵינֵיכֶם וְלָאִישׁ הַזֶּה לֹא תַעֲשׂוּ דְּבַר הַנְּבָלָה הַזֹּאת:

19:24   וּפִילַגְשֵׁהוּ

Unique   לֿ   Mp

Com.: The Masorah notes the *sole* occurrence of this lemma with the sfx. הו, to distinguish it from its *four* occurrences with the sfx. וֹ (וּפִילַגְשׁוֹ), *two* of which occur in vv. 9 and 10 of this chapter.

19:24   אוֹצִיאָה

Twice   בֿ   Mp

Gen 19:8; **Judg 19:24**

Com.: The Masorah notes the *two* occurrences of this lemma with the cohortative ה, to distinguish them from its *two* occurrences without this cohortative ending (אוֹצִיא) at Exod 3:11 and Ezek 20:38.

19:24   וְעַנּוּ

Unique   לֿ   Mp

Com.: The Masorah notes the *sole* occurrence of this lemma with a ו cj., to distinguish it from its occurrence without a cj. at Isa 27:2.

19:24 וְלָאִישׁ

Unique לֹ Mp

Com.: The Masorah notes the *sole* occurrence of this lemma with a וֹ cj., to distinguish it from its more numerous occurrences (32x) without a cj.; see **1 Sam 2:15**.

JUDGES 19:25

וְלֹא־אָב֣וּ הָאֲנָשִׁים֮ לִשְׁמֹ֣עַ לוֹ֒ וַיַּחֲזֵ֤ק הָאִישׁ֙ בְּפִ֣ילַגְשׁ֔וֹ וַיֹּצֵ֥א אֲלֵיהֶ֖ם הַח֑וּץ וַיֵּדְע֣וּ א֠וֹתָהּ וַיִּֽתְעַלְּלוּ־
בָ֤הּ כָּל־הַלַּ֙יְלָה֙ עַד־הַבֹּ֔קֶר וַֽיְשַׁלְּח֖וּהָ בַּעֲל֥וֹת הַשָּֽׁחַר׃

19:25 וַיֹּצֵא

וַיֹּצֵא *thirteen times* defective ויצא יג חס Mm

1–5	Num 17:23	פרח
	Num 17:24	(המטות) [המטת]
	Judg 19:25	בפילגשו
	2 Sam 10:16	הדדעזר
	2 Sam 13:18	משרתו {מש}
6–10	2 Sam 22:20	למרחב
	2 Kgs 15:20	מנחם
	2 Kgs 23:6	האשרה
	2 Kgs 10:22	המלתחה
	Jer 20:3	פשחור
11–13	<Jer 52:31>	
	2 Chr 16:2	מאצרות
	Job 12:22	מגלח

Com.: The Masorah notes the *thirteen* occurrences of this lemma written defective וֹ, to distinguish them from its *twelve* occurrences written plene וֹ (וַיּוֹצֵא); see **Judg 6:19**.

M[L], contrary to M (וַיּוֹצֵא), has a *fourteenth* occurrence of this lemma since it writes the form at Jer 51:16 defective; see Breuer, *The Biblical Text*, 196.

19:25 וַיֹּצֵא אֲלֵיהֶם

Twice בֹ Mp

Gen 43:23 (וַיּוֹצֵא); **Judg 19:25**

וַיֵּצֵא אֲלֵיהֶם *twice*   ו", ב [אליהם] (אלהם) ויצא   Mm

Gen 43:23   את שמעון
<u>Judg 19:25</u>   ויחזק האיש

Com.: The Masorah notes the *two* occurrences of וַיֵּצֵא with אֲלֵיהֶם, to distinguish them from its *sole* occurrence with לָהֶם (וַיֵּצֵא לָהֶם) at 2 Kgs 10:22.

19:25   וַיֵּדְעוּ

Six times   וֹ   Mp

1–5   Gen 3:7; **Judg 19:25; 1 Sam 4:6;** 2 Sam 3:37; <u>**Zech 11:11**</u>
6   **Neh 6:16**

Com.: The Masorah notes the *six* occurrences of this lemma (an impf. consec.), to distinguish them from its more numerous occurrences (66x) with a perf. consec. (וְיָדְעוּ).

19:25   וַיִּשַׁלְּחוּהָ

Unique   ל   Mp

19:25   בְּעָלוֹת

Read כַּעֲלוֹת   כעלות קֿ   Mp

Com.: The *kǝṯîb* (בעלות), and the *qǝrê* (כַּעֲלוֹת) represent examples of interchanges between the letters בּ and כּ; see Gordis, *The Biblical Text*, 144.

This lemma is featured in a Masoretic list of words that are written with a בּ, but read as a כּ; see Frensdorff, *Ochlah*, §149, and Díaz-Esteban, *Sefer Oklah we-Oklah*, §137.

In M[L] this lemma has no circellus.

JUDGES 19:26
וַתָּבֹא הָאִשָּׁה לִפְנוֹת הַבֹּקֶר וַתִּפֹּל פֶּתַח בֵּית־הָאִישׁ אֲשֶׁר־אֲדוֹנֶיהָ שָּׁם עַד־הָאוֹר׃

19:26   לִפְנוֹת הַבֹּקֶר

Unique   ל   Mp

Com.: The Masorah notes the *sole* occurrence of לִפְנוֹת with הַבֹּקֶר, to distinguish it from its *two* occurrences with בֹּקֶר (לִפְנוֹת בֹּקֶר) at Exod 14:27 and Ps 46:6.

19:26   אֲדוֹנֶיהָ

Five times plene   ה מל׳   Mp

1–5   **Judg 13:8** (אֲדוֹנִי); **19:26**; **Mal 1:6** (אֲדוֹנִים); **Ps 123:2** (אֲדוֹנֵיהֶם); **147:5** (אֲדוֹנֵינוּ)
6   **2 Chr 17:8** (אֲדוֹנִיָּה)

Com.: The Mp heading here of *five times plene* is incorrect since there are *six* occurrences of this lemma. The Masorah notes the *six* occurrences of this lemma in various forms written plene וֹ, to distinguish them from its more numerous occurrences (700+) in various forms written defective וֹ (e.g., אֲדֹנִי).

Only *one* of the Mp headings highlighted above (Mal 1:6) reads *six times plene*, all the rest read *unique plene* indicating the exclusiveness of their particular forms.

Both M^C and M^A read here *unique plene* indicating the uniqueness of this particular lemma (אֲדוֹנֶיהָ).

JUDGES 19:27

וַיָּקָם אֲדֹנֶיהָ בַּבֹּקֶר וַיִּפְתַּח דַּלְתוֹת הַבַּיִת וַיֵּצֵא לָלֶכֶת לְדַרְכּוֹ וְהִנֵּה הָאִשָּׁה פִילַגְשׁוֹ נֹפֶלֶת פֶּתַח הַבַּיִת וְיָדֶיהָ עַל־הַסַּף׃

19:27   הָאִשָּׁה פִילַגְשׁוֹ

Unique   ל   Mp

19:27   וְיָדֶיהָ

Unique   ל   Mp

Judg 19:27; Prov 31:20

The Mp heading here of *unique* is inexact since there are *two* occurrences of this lemma. The note more precisely should have read *unique in the book*.

Neither M^C nor M^A has a note on this lemma here.

JUDGES 19:28

וַיֹּאמֶר אֵלֶיהָ קוּמִי וְנֵלֵכָה וְאֵין עֹנֶה וַיִּקָּחֶהָ עַל־הַחֲמֹור וַיָּקָם הָאִישׁ וַיֵּלֶךְ לִמְקֹמֹו׃

19:28   קוּמִי וְנֵלֵכָה

Unique   ל̇   Mp

Com.: In M[L] the circellus has been placed only on וְנֵלֵכָה but, since this form occurs more than *once*, it is most likely that the note should have been on these two words that only occur this *once*.

19:28   וְאֵין עֹנֶה

Five times   ה̇   Mp

1–5   **Judg 19:28**; 1 Kgs 18:26; 18:29; Isa 50:2 (עֹונֶה); 66:4 (עֹונֶה)

Com.: The Masorah notes the *five* occurrences of this lemma, *three times* written defective ו (Judg 19:28, 1 Kgs 18:26 and 29), and *twice* written plene ו (Isa 50:2 and 66:4).

19:28   לִמְקֹמֹו

Three times defective   ג̇ חס   Mp

Com.: See **Judg 7:7**.

JUDGES 19:29

וַיָּבֹא אֶל־בֵּיתֹו וַיִּקַּח אֶת־הַמַּאֲכֶלֶת וַיַּחֲזֵק בְּפִילַגְשֹׁו וַיְנַתְּחֶהָ לַעֲצָמֶיהָ לִשְׁנֵים עָשָׂר נְתָחִים
וַיְשַׁלְּחֶהָ בְּכֹל גְּבוּל יִשְׂרָאֵל׃

19:29   הַמַּאֲכֶלֶת

הַמַּאֲכֶלֶת *three times*, and their references   המאכלת ג̇ וסימנהון   Mm

Gen 22:6   ויקח אברהם
Gen 22:10   וישלח אברהם <את> ידו
Judg 19:29   ויבא אל

19:29   וַיְנַתְּחֶהָ

Twice   בֿ   Mp

Com.: The Mp heading here of *twice* is incorrect since this is the *only* occurrence of this lemma. M^C correctly reads here *unique*, but M^A has no note.

19:29   וַיְשַׁלְּחֶהָ

Twice   בֿ   Mp

Gen 21:14; **Judg 19:29**

> ## JUDGES 19:30
>
> וְהָיָה כָל־הָרֹאֶה וְאָמַר לֹא־נִהְיְתָה וְלֹא־נִרְאֲתָה כָּזֹאת לְמִיּוֹם עֲלוֹת בְּנֵי־יִשְׂרָאֵל מֵאֶרֶץ מִצְרַיִם עַד הַיּוֹם הַזֶּה שִׂימוּ־לָכֶם עָלֶיהָ עֻצוּ וְדַבֵּרוּ׃ פ

19:30   לְמִיּוֹם

Three times   גֿ   Mp

Judg 19:30; 2 Sam 7:6; Isa 7:17

לְמִיּוֹם *three times*   למיום גֿ   Mm

Judg 19:30	עלות
הֶעֱלֹתִי *of Samuel* (2 Sam 7:6)	(העלותי) [העלתי] דשמואל
Isa 7:17	סור אפרים

Com.: The Masorah notes the *three* occurrences of this lemma, to distinguish them from the more numerous occurrences (11x) of its alternate phrase מִן הַיּוֹם.

This distinction is implied in the Mm in the additional notation *of Samuel* to the 2 Sam 7:6 reference, which distinguishes it from its parallel passage in 1 Chr 17:5, where the lemma occurs as מִן הַיּוֹם.

In M^L the Mp for this lemma has erroneously been placed in the left margin instead of the right one.

19:30 עֲלוֹת

Unique and plene ל וּמל Mp

1–5 Gen 32:25; Exod 19:12; **Judg 19:30**; Amos 7:1; **2 Chr 36:16**

Com.: The Mp heading here *of unique and plene* is inexact since there are *four* more occurrences of this lemma. The note more precisely should have read *unique and plene in the book*.

By noting that this lemma is *unique* and written plene ו (in the book), the Masorah is also implying (correctly) that this lemma does not occur in the book written defective ו.

The Mp heading at 2 Chr 36:16 and of M^A here read *six times* to include the *five* forms listed above, and the form without a ו (עֲלֹת) at Neh 3:19. M^C has no note here.

In M^L the Mp for this lemma has erroneously been placed in the right margin instead of in the left one.

19:30 עצו

Twice and defective ב וחס Mp

Judg 19:30; Isa 8:10

עֲצוּ *twice* and defective עצו ב וחס Mm

Judg 19:30 ודברו
Isa 8:10 עצה ותפר

Com.: By noting that this lemma occurs *twice* and is written defective ו, the Masorah is also implying (correctly) that this lemma does not occur elsewhere written plene ו.

JUDGES 20:1

וַיֵּצְאוּ֩ כָּל־בְּנֵ֨י יִשְׂרָאֵ֜ל וַתִּקָּהֵ֣ל הָעֵדָ֗ה כְּאִ֣ישׁ אֶחָ֞ד לְמִדָּ֤ן וְעַד־בְּאֵ֤ר שֶׁ֙בַע֙ וְאֶ֣רֶץ הַגִּלְעָ֔ד אֶל־יְהוָ֖ה הַמִּצְפָּֽה׃

20:1   וַתִּקָּהֵ֣ל

Twice   ב֖   Mp

<u>Lev 8:4</u>; Judg 20:1

JUDGES 20:2

וַיִּֽתְיַצְּב֞וּ פִּנּ֣וֹת כָּל־הָעָ֗ם כֹּ֚ל שִׁבְטֵ֣י יִשְׂרָאֵ֔ל בִּקְהַ֖ל עַ֣ם הָאֱלֹהִ֑ים אַרְבַּ֨ע מֵא֥וֹת אֶ֛לֶף אִ֥ישׁ רַגְלִ֖י שֹׁ֥לֵֽף חָֽרֶב׃ פ

20:2   וַיִּֽתְיַצְּב֞וּ

Five times   ה֞   Mp

Com.: See **Josh 24:1**.

20:2   אִ֥ישׁ רַגְלִ֖י

Twice   ב֖   Mp

1–4   **Judg 20:2; <u>2 Sam 8:4</u>; 1 Chr 18:4; <u>19:18</u>**

Com.: The Mp heading here of *twice* is incorrect since there are *four* occurrences of this lemma. It is possible that the note only refers to occurrences in the Prophets, in which case the note should have read *twice in the Prophets*.

The Mp note in M^A reads here *four times*, as do all the Mp headings in M^L at the *three* other Mp notes highlighted above. M^C has no note here.

The Masorah notes the *four* occurrences of רַגְלִי with אִישׁ meaning *infantryman*, to distinguish them from its *seven* occurrences without אִישׁ also meaning *infantryman*, and from its *six* occurrences meaning *my foot*.

JUDGES 20:3

וַיִּשְׁמְעוּ בְּנֵי בִנְיָמִן כִּי־עָלוּ בְנֵי־יִשְׂרָאֵל הַמִּצְפָּה וַיֹּאמְרוּ בְּנֵי יִשְׂרָאֵל דַּבְּרוּ אֵיכָה נִהְיְתָה הָרָעָה
הַזֹּאת:

20:3   בְּנֵי־יִשְׂרָאֵל²

\<Twice in the verse\>   \<ב בפסוק\>   Mp

In M^L this lemma has a circellus here but no note. It may have been meant to indicate the occurrence of this lemma *twice* in this verse.

20:3   אֵיכָה

Seventeen times   יׄ   Mp

1–5   **Deut 1:12**; <u>7:17</u>; **12:30; 18:21; 32:30**
6–10   **Judg 20:3**; 2 Kgs 6:15; Isa 1:21; **Jer 8:8; 48:17**
11–15   Ps 73:11; **Cant 1:7ª**; 1:7ᵇ; **Lam 1:1; 2:1**
16–17   **Lam 4:1; 4:2**

Com.: The Masorah notes the *seventeen* occurrences of this lemma with a lenghtened ending, to distinguish them from its more numerous occurrences (43x) without this lenghtened ending (אֵיךְ).

Three of the Mp headings highlighted above (Deut 1:12, 12:30 and 18:21) read only *sixteen times*, and the Mm at <u>Deut 7:17</u> lists only *sixteen* omitting 2 Kgs 6:15.

JUDGES 20:4

וַיַּעַן הָאִישׁ הַלֵּוִי אִישׁ הָאִשָּׁה הַנִּרְצָחָה וַיֹּאמַר הַגִּבְעָתָה אֲשֶׁר לְבִנְיָמִן בָּאתִי אֲנִי וּפִילַגְשִׁי לָלוּן:

20:4   הָאִישׁ הַלֵּוִי

Unique   ל   Mp

Com.: This phrase is featured in a Masoretic list of two-word phrases that only occur *once*, in which both words of the phrase has the def. article; see Frensdorff, *Ochlah*, §371.

20:4   הָאִשָּׁה הַנִּרְצָחָה

Unique   ל   Mp

Com.: This phrase is featured in a Masoretic list of two-word phrases that *only* occur *once*, in which both words of the phrase has the def. article; see Frensdorff, *Ochlah*, §371.

JUDGES 20:5

וַיָּקֻמוּ עָלַי בַּעֲלֵי הַגִּבְעָה וַיָּסֹבּוּ עָלַי אֶת־הַבַּיִת לָיְלָה אוֹתִי דִּמּוּ לַהֲרֹג וְאֶת־פִּילַגְשִׁי עִנּוּ וַתָּמֹת:

20:5   דִּמּוּ

Unique   ל   Mp

20:5   פִּילַגְשִׁי

Unique   ל   Mp

Com.: The Masorah notes the *sole* occurrence of this lemma without a ו cj., to distinguish it from its *sole* occurrence with a ו cj. in v. 4.

20:5   וַתָּמֹת

Unique   ל   Mp

Com.: This word is featured in two Masoretic lists. One is in a list of words that occur *four times*, *three times* without a prefixed ו, and once with a prefixed ו (here); see Frensdorff, *Ochlah*, §15, and Díaz-Esteban, *Sefer Oklah we-Oklah*, §16.

The other is in a list of words that occur beginning with ות, *once* as a ו consec. (here), and *once* as a ו cj. (Isa 50:2); see Frensdorff, *Ochlah*, §50, and Díaz-Esteban, *Sefer Oklah we-Oklah*, §51.

JUDGES 20:6

וָאֹחֵ֤ז בְּפִֽילַגְשִׁי֙ וָֽאֲנַתְּחֶ֔הָ וָֽאֲשַׁלְּחֶ֔הָ בְּכָל־שְׂדֵ֖ה נַחֲלַ֣ת יִשְׂרָאֵ֑ל כִּ֥י עָשׂ֛וּ זִמָּ֥ה וּנְבָלָ֖ה בְּיִשְׂרָאֵֽל׃

20:6   וָאֹחֵ֤ז

Unique   ל   Mp

Com.: The Masorah notes the *sole* occurrence of this lemma with a ו consec. (*I took hold of*), to distinguish it from its *sole* occurrence without a ו (אֹחֵז, a ptcp. *holding*) at 2 Chr 25:5.

20:6   וָֽאֲנַתְּחֶ֔הָ

Unique   ל   Mp

20:6   וָֽאֲשַׁלְּחֶ֔הָ

Unique   ל   Mp

JUDGES 20:8

וַיָּ֙קָם֙ כָּל־הָעָ֜ם כְּאִ֣ישׁ אֶחָ֗ד לֵאמֹ֔ר לֹ֥א נֵלֵ֖ךְ אִ֣ישׁ לְאָהֳל֑וֹ וְלֹ֥א נָס֖וּר אִ֥ישׁ לְבֵיתֽוֹ׃

20:8   כְּאִ֣ישׁ

Twenty times   כ̇   Mp

1–5   **Num 14:15; Judg 6:16**; 20:1; <u>20:8</u>; **20:11**
6–10   **1 Sam 11:7**; <u>2 Sam 19:15</u>; **Isa 42:13**; <u>66:13</u>; Jer 6:23
11–15   **Jer 14:9; 23:9**; 50:42; **Zech 4:1; Ps 38:15**
16–20   Prov 6:11; 24:34; Ezra 3:1; **Neh 7:2; 8:1**

כְּאִישׁ *twenty times*	כאיש כֹּ	Mm

1–5	Num 14:15	והמתה את העם הזה
	Judg 6:16	(והבית) [והכית]
	Judg 20:1	ותקהל
	<u>Judg 20:8</u>	ויקם כל
	Judg 20:11	ויאסף
6–10	1 Sam 11:7	צמד
	<u>2 Sam 19:15</u>	(וישם) [ויט]
	Isa 42:13	(גבור) [כגבור] (יצוא) [יצא]
	<u>Isa 66:13</u>	אשר אמו תנחמנו
	Jer 6:23	קשת וכידון
11–15	Jer 14:9	כאיש נדהם
	Jer 23:9	(לנביאים) [לנבאים] נשבר לב בקרבי
	<Jer 50:42>	
	Zech 4:1	ויעירני כאיש אשר
	Ps 38:15	ואהי כאיש אשר
16–20	Prov 6:11	ובא כמהלך ראשך
	<Prov 24:34>	
	Ezra 3:1	ויגע החדש
	Neh 7:2	ואצוה את חנני
	Neh 8:1	ויאספו

Com.: The Masorah notes the *twenty* occurrences of this lemma with a *šəwâ* under the כ, possibly to distinguish them from its *sole* occurrence with a *qameṣ* (כָּאִישׁ) at **Judg 8:21**.

> ### JUDGES 20:9
>
> וְעַתָּ֕ה זֶ֣ה הַדָּבָ֔ר אֲשֶׁ֥ר נַעֲשֶׂ֖ה לַגִּבְעָ֑ה עָלֶ֖יהָ בְּגוֹרָֽל׃

20:9	בְּגוֹרָל

Four times	דֹ	Mp

Josh 14:2 (בְּגוֹרָל); 19:51; **Judg 20:9**; Mic 2:5

Com.: The Masorah notes the *four* occurrences, apart from Numbers, of this lemma with the indef. prep. בְּ to distinguish them from its *seven* occurrences with the def. prep. בַּ (בַּגּוֹרָל); see **Josh 21:6**.

JUDGES 20:10

וְלָקַחְנוּ עֲשָׂרָה֩ אֲנָשִׁ֨ים לַמֵּאָ֜ה לְכֹ֣ל ׀ שִׁבְטֵ֣י יִשְׂרָאֵ֗ל וּמֵאָ֤ה לָאֶ֙לֶף֙ וְאֶ֣לֶף לָרְבָבָ֔ה לָקַ֥חַת צֵדָ֖ה לָעָ֑ם
לַעֲשׂ֗וֹת לְבוֹאָם֙ לְגֶ֣בַע בִּנְיָמִ֔ן כְּכָל־הַנְּבָלָ֔ה אֲשֶׁ֥ר עָשָׂ֖ה בְּיִשְׂרָאֵֽל׃

20:10   לַמֵּאָה

Unique   ל   Mp

Com.: This lemma is featured in a Masoretic list of words beginning with a ל and vowel that only occur *once*; see Frensdorff, *Ochlah*, §26, and Díaz-Esteban, *Sefer Oklah we-Oklah*, §27.

20:10   לָאֶלֶף

Twice   בֿ   Mp

Judg 20:10; Isa 60:22

לָאֶלֶף *twice*, and their references   לאלף בֿ וסימנהון   Mm

Judg 20:10   ומאה לאלף ואלף לרבבה לקחת צדה
<Isa 60:22>

Com.: The Masorah notes the *two* occurrences of this lemma with the def. prep. לְ, to distinguish them from its *four* occurrences with the indef. prep. ל (לְאֶלֶף).

This lemma is featured in a Masoretic list of *doublets* that begin with ל and a vowel; see Frensdorff, *Ochlah*, §28, and Díaz-Esteban, *Sefer Oklah we-Oklah*, §29.

This lemma occurs in the ms. in folio 148v, but the Mm note appears on the bottom of the following folio 149r.

20:10   לָרְבָבָה

Unique   ל   Mp

Com.: This lemma is featured in a Masoretic list of words beginning with a ל and vowel that only occur *once*; see Frensdorff, *Ochlah*, §26, and Díaz-Esteban, *Sefer Oklah we-Oklah*, §27.

20:10   צֵדָה

Three times defective   ג̇ מל̇   Mp

Com.: See **Judg 7:8**.

20:10   לְבוֹאָם

Twice   ב̇   Mp

Judg 20:10; Ezra 3:8

20:10   לְגֶבַע בִּנְיָמִן

Unique   ל̇   Mp

Com.: The Masorah notes the *sole* occurrence of this lemma with the prep. ל, to distinguish it from its *sole* occurrence with the prep. ב (בְּגֶבַע בִּנְיָמִן) at 1 Sam 13:16.

> ## JUDGES 20:11
>
> וַיֵּאָסֵף כָּל־אִישׁ יִשְׂרָאֵל אֶל־הָעִיר כְּאִישׁ אֶחָד חֲבֵרִים׃ פ

20:11   וַיֵּאָסֵף

Three times   ג̇   Mp

1–2   **Num 11:30; Judg 20:11**

Com.: The Mp heading here of *three times* is incorrect since there are only *two* occurrences of this lemma as correctly noted here by M^C and M^A, and in M^L in the Mp heading at Num 11:30.

The Masorah notes the *two* occurrences of this lemma accented *milraʿ*, to distinguish them from its *five* occurrences accented *milʿēl* (e.g., וַיֵּאֱסֹף).

This lemma is featured in a Masoretic list of words only occurring *twice* that commence with וי; see Frensdorff, *Ochlah*, §68, and Díaz-Esteban, *Sefer Oklah we-Oklah*, §69.

20:11   כְּאִישׁ

Twenty times   כ   Mp

Com.: See directly above at **Judg 20:8**.

20:11   חֲבֵרִים

Twice: הַיּוֹשֶׁבֶת בַּגַּנִּים   ב היושבת בגנים   Mp

Judg 20:11; Cant 8:13

Com.: The Masorah notes the *two* occurrences of this lemma with a *ṣerê* under the ב, to distinguish them from its *two* occurrences with a *qameṣ* (חֲבָרִים of Ps 58:6, and חֲבָרִים of Job 40:30); see Ginsburg, 4, ח, §28.

The Mp heading here adds catchwords (הַיּוֹשֶׁבֶת בַּגַּנִּים) היושבת בגנים to refer the reader to Cant 8:13.

┌───┐

JUDGES 20:12

וַיִּשְׁלְח֞וּ שִׁבְטֵ֣י יִשְׂרָאֵ֗ל אֲנָשִׁים֙ בְּכָל־שִׁבְטֵ֣י בִנְיָמִ֔ן לֵאמֹ֕ר מָ֚ה הָרָעָ֣ה הַזֹּ֔את אֲשֶׁ֥ר נִהְיְתָ֖ה בָּכֶֽם׃

└───┘

20:12   שִׁבְטֵי בִנְיָמִן

Twice   ב   Mp

Judg 20:12; 1 Sam 9:21

שִׁבְטֵי בִנְיָמִן *twice*, and their references   שבטי בנימן ב וסימנהון   Mm

Judg 20:12   וישלחו שבטי ישראל
1 Sam 9:21   ומשפחתי הצערה

Com.: The Masorah notes the *two* occurrences of בִנְיָמִן with שִׁבְטֵי, to distinguish them from its *three* occurrences with שֵׁבֶט (שֵׁבֶט בִּנְיָמִן).

JUDGES 20:13

וְעַתָּ֡ה תְּנוּ֩ אֶת־הָאֲנָשִׁ֨ים בְּנֵֽי־בְלִיַּ֜עַל אֲשֶׁ֣ר בַּגִּבְעָ֗ה וּנְמִיתֵם֙ וּנְבַעֲרָ֤ה רָעָה֙ מִיִּשְׂרָאֵ֔ל
וְלֹ֤א אָבוּ֙ ֗ ֖ ֗ בְּנֵ֣י בִנְיָמִ֔ן לִשְׁמֹ֕עַ בְּק֖וֹל אֲחֵיהֶ֑ם בְּנֵֽי־יִשְׂרָאֵֽל׃

20:13   וּנְבַעֲרָה

Unique   ל   Mp

20:13   ֗ ֖ ֗

בְּנֵ֣י is read but not written   בני קׄ ולא כתׄ   Mp¹

Read   בְּנֵ֣י   בני קׄ   Mp²

Com.: There are two Mp notes here. One states that בְּנֵ֣י is read but not written. The other is a regular *qərê* directing a reading of בְּנֵ֣י.

In M^L the vowels, but not the consonants, of the word בְּנֵ֣י are written, and this is one of *ten* cases where words are read though not written; see the Mm to <u>Jer 50:29</u> *sub* לָהּ, the Mm to <u>Ruth 3:5</u> *sub* אֵלַי, Frensdorff, *Ochlah*, §97, and Díaz-Esteban, *Sefer Oklah we-Oklah*, §80.

There is also another tradition that knows of *eleven* cases of this phenomenon; see Martín-Contreras, "The Phenomenon," 77–87.

In M^L this lemma has no circellus.

JUDGES 20:14

וַיֵּאָסְפ֤וּ בְנֵֽי־בִנְיָמִן֙ מִן־הֶ֣עָרִ֔ים הַגִּבְעָ֑תָה לָצֵ֥את לַמִּלְחָמָ֖ה עִם־בְּנֵ֥י יִשְׂרָאֵֽל׃

20:14   מִן־הֶעָרִים

Three times   ג̇   Mp

Deut 4:42; **Judg 20:14**; <u>2 Chr 15:8</u> (וּמִן־הֶעָרִים)

Com.: The Masorah notes the *three* occurrences of הֶעָרִים with the separable prep. מִן, to distinguish them from its *four* occurrences with the inseparable prep. מ (מֵהֶעָרִים), *one* of which is in v. 15.

JUDGES 20:15

וַיִּתְפָּקְדוּ֩ בְנֵ֨י בִנְיָמִ֜ן בַּיּ֣וֹם הַה֗וּא מֵהֶעָרִים֙ עֶשְׂרִ֤ים וְשִׁשָּׁה֙ אֶ֔לֶף אִ֖ישׁ שֹׁ֣לֵֽף חָ֑רֶב לְבַ֗ד מִיֹּשְׁבֵ֤י הַגִּבְעָה֙ הִתְפָּֽקְד֔וּ שְׁבַ֥ע מֵא֖וֹת אִ֥ישׁ בָּחֽוּר׃

20:15   וַיִּתְפָּֽקְדוּ

Unique   ל   Mp

Com.: The Masorah notes the *sole* occurrence of this lemma in the pl., to distinguish it from its *sole* occurrence in the sg. (וַיִּתְפָּקֵד) at Judg 21:9.

20:15   מֵהֶעָרִים

Four times   ד   Mp

Josh 20:4; Judg 20:15; 20:42; Ezek 25:9

מֵהֶעָרִים *four times*, and their references   מהערים ד וסימנהון   Mm

Josh 20:4	ונס אל אחת
Judg 20:15	ויתפקדו
Judg 20:42	ואשר
Ezek 25:9	את כתף מואב

Com.: The Masorah notes the *four* occurrences of this lemma with the inseparable prep. מ, to distinguish them from its *two* occurrences with the separable prep. מִן (מִן־הֶעָרִים); see above at v. 14.

20:15   מִיֹּשְׁבֵי

Three times   ג   Mp

Judg 20:15; 21:9 (מִיֹּשְׁבֵי); 21:12 (מִיֹּושְׁבֵי)

Com.: The Masorah notes the *three* occurrences of this lemma, *twice* written plene ו (Judg 21:9 and 12), and *once* written defective ו (here).

20:15   הִתְפָּקְדוּ

Twice   בׄ   Mp

Judg 20:15; 20;17

Com.: The Masorah notes the *two* occurrences of this lemma with a *ḥireq* under the ה, to distinguish them from its *four* occurrences with a *qameṣ* (הָתְפָּקְדוּ); see **1 Kgs 20:27**.

The Mp heading at Judg 20:17 (see directly below) mistakenly reads *unique*.

JUDGES 20:16

מִכֹּל ׀ הָעָם הַזֶּה שְׁבַע מֵאוֹת אִישׁ בָּחוּר אִטֵּר יַד־יְמִינוֹ כָּל־זֶה קֹלֵעַ בָּאֶבֶן אֶל־הַשַּׂעֲרָה וְלֹא יַחֲטִא׃ פ

20:16   אִטֵּר

Twice   בׄ   Mp

Com.: See **Judg 3:15.**

20:16   קֹלֵעַ

Twice, once defective and *once* plene   בׄ חד חסׄ וחד מלׄ   Mp

Judg 20:16; Jer 10:18 (קוֹלֵעַ)

Com.: The Masorah notes the *two* occurrences of this lemma, *once* written defective ו (here), and *once* written plene ו (Jer 10:18).

JUDGES 20:17

וְאִישׁ יִשְׂרָאֵל הִתְפָּקְדוּ לְבַד מִבִּנְיָמִן אַרְבַּע מֵאוֹת אֶלֶף אִישׁ שֹׁלֵף חָרֶב כָּל־זֶה אִישׁ מִלְחָמָה׃

20:17   הִתְפָּקְדוּ

Unique   לׄ   Mp

Com.: The Mp heading here of *unique* is incorrect since there are *two* occurrences of this lemma; see directly above at **Judg 20:15.**

M^A correctly reads here *twice*, but M^C has no note.

JUDGES 20:18

וַיָּקֻמוּ וַיַּעֲלוּ בֵית־אֵל וַיִּשְׁאֲלוּ בֵאלֹהִים וַיֹּאמְרוּ בְּנֵי יִשְׂרָאֵל מִי יַעֲלֶה־לָּנוּ בַתְּחִלָּה לַמִּלְחָמָה עִם־
בְּנֵי בִנְיָמִן וַיֹּאמֶר יְהוָה יְהוּדָה בַתְּחִלָּה:

20:18   וַיִּשְׁאֲלוּ בֵאלֹהִים

Seven times   זֹ   Mp

1–5   Judg 18:5 (שְׁאַל נָא); **20:18; 1 Sam 14:37** (וַיִּשְׁאַל שָׁאוּל)
1 Sam 22:13 (לִשְׁאָל־לֹו); 22:15 (וְשָׁאוֹל לֹו)

6–7   (וַיִּשְׁאַל עוֹד דָּוִיד) 14:14; **1 Chr 14:10** (וַיִּשְׁאַל דָּוִיד)

Com.: The Masorah notes the *seven* occurrences of שָׁאַל in various forms with בֵאלֹהִים, to distinguish them from its more numerous occurrences (12x) with בַיהוָה, *one* of which is in v. 23 (וַיִּשְׁאֲלוּ בַיהוָה).

In Mᴸ the circellus has been placed only on בֵאלֹהִים but, since this form appears more than *seven times*, it is most likely that, as in Mᴬ, the note refers to this lemma, which only occurs *seven times*.

JUDGES 20:19

וַיָּקוּמוּ בְנֵי־יִשְׂרָאֵל בַּבֹּקֶר וַיַּחֲנוּ עַל־הַגִּבְעָה: פ

20:19   וַיָּקוּמוּ

Nine times plene   ט מל   Mp

1–5   **Gen 24:54; Num 22:14; Judg 20:19; 1 Sam 23:24; 31:12**
6–9   **2 Kgs 7:7; Ezra 1:5; Neh 9:3; 1 Chr 10:12**

Com.: The Masorah notes the *nine* occurrences of this lemma written first וֹ plene, to distinguish them from its more numerous occurrences (27x) written defective first וֹ (וַיָּקֻמוּ).

Mᴸ, contrary to M (וַיָּקֻמוּ), has a *tenth* occurrence of this lemma since it writes the form at 2 Kgs 7:5 plene; see Breuer, *The Biblical Text*, 123 and 398. Nevertheless, this verse is not included in the Mm lists in Mᴸ on this lemma at 1 Sam 23:24 and Ezra 1:5, and all the Mp headings highlighted above read *nine times*, thus supporting the enumeration inherent in the text of M.

20:19   עַל־הַגִּבְעָה

Twice   בֿ   Mp

Judg 20:19; Isa 30:17

Com.: The Masorah notes the *two* occurrences of הַגִּבְעָה with עַל, to distinguish them
from its *five* occurrences with אֶל (אֶל הַגִּבְעָה).

JUDGES 20:20

וַיֵּצֵא אִישׁ יִשְׂרָאֵל לַמִּלְחָמָה עִם־בִּנְיָמֵן וַיַּעַרְכוּ אִתָּם אִישׁ־יִשְׂרָאֵל מִלְחָמָה אֶל־הַגִּבְעָה:

20:20   אִתָּם

Thirty-six times   לֿו   Mp

1–5   Gen 7:13; 11:31; 14:8; 23:8; 34:8
6–10   Gen 40:4; 42:7; 43:16; Exod 6:4; 12:38
11–15   Exod 34:33; Lev 16:16; 26:39; 26:44; Num 22:20
16–20   Num 32:19; Deut 28:69; Josh 22:15; **Judg 20:20; 1 Sam 25:15**
21–25   2 Sam 12:17; **1 Kgs 20:23**; 2 Kgs 6:4; 17:35; 22:7
26–30   Isa 14:20; 30:8; 60:9; **65:23**; Jer. 27:18
31–35   **Ezek 30:5; 34:30**; 38:5; **Prov 1:15; 24:1**
36–37   **Dan 1:19**; 2 Chr. 22:12

Com.: The Mp heading here of *thirty-six times* is incorrect since there are *thirty-seven*
occurrences of this lemma as noted in all the other Mp headings highlighted above.

The Masorah notes the *thirty-seven* occurrences of this lemma with a *ḥireq* under the א
(a prep.), to distinguish them from its more numerous occurrences (200+) with a
ḥolem on the א (אֹתָם, an accusative marker).

Neither M^C nor M^A has a note on this lemma here.

JUDGES 20:22

וַיִּתְחַזֵּק הָעָם אִישׁ יִשְׂרָאֵל וַיֹּסִפוּ לַעֲרֹךְ מִלְחָמָה בַּמָּקוֹם אֲשֶׁר־עָרְכוּ שָׁם בַּיּוֹם הָרִאשׁוֹן:

20:22   וַיִּתְחַזֵּק

Eight times   חֿ   Mp

1–5   Gen 48:2; **Judg 20:22**; 1 Sam 30:6; 2 Chr 1:1; **12:13**
6–8   2 Chr 13:21; **<u>17:1</u>**; 27:6

Com.: The Masorah notes the *eight* occurrences of this lemma with a *ṣerê* under the וֹ, to distinguish them from its *two* occurrences with a *paṭaḥ* (וַיְּתְחַזֵּק) at 2 Chr 21:4 and 32:5.

This distinction is implied in the Mp headings at 2 Chr 12:13 and 17:1, which read *eight times with a ṣerê* (הֵ) assuming a contrast with another vowel, which can only be a *paṭaḥ*.

JUDGES 20:23

וַיַּעֲל֣וּ בְנֵֽי־יִשְׂרָאֵ֗ל וַיִּבְכּ֣וּ לִפְנֵֽי־יְהוָה֮ עַד־הָעֶרֶב֒ וַיִּשְׁאֲל֤וּ בַֽיהוָה֙ לֵאמֹ֔ר הַאוֹסִ֗יף לָגֶ֙שֶׁת֙ לַמִּלְחָמָ֔ה עִם־בְּנֵ֥י בִנְיָמִ֖ן אָחִ֑י וַיֹּ֧אמֶר יְהוָ֛ה עֲל֖וּ אֵלָֽיו׃ פ

20:23   הַאוֹסִ֗יף

Twice   בֿ   Mp

Judg 20:23; 20:28 (הַאוֹסִף)

Com.: The Masorah notes the *two* occurrences of this lemma written plene and defective י with the interrog. ה, to distinguish them from its more numerous occurrences (10x) without this interrogative.

This lemma is featured in a Masoretic list of doublets with an initial ה or הַ; see Frensdorff, *Ochlah*, §64, and Díaz-Esteban, *Sefer Oklah we-Oklah*, §65.

20:23   לָגֶ֙שֶׁת֙ לַמִּלְחָמָ֔ה

Unique   ל   Mp

JUDGES 20:25

וַיֵּצֵא֩ בִנְיָמִ֨ן ׀ לִקְרָאתָ֥ם ׀ מִן־הַגִּבְעָה֮ בַּיּ֣וֹם הַשֵּׁנִי֒ וַיַּשְׁחִ֩יתוּ֩ בִבְנֵ֨י יִשְׂרָאֵ֜ל ע֗וֹד שְׁמֹנַ֨ת עָשָׂ֥ר אֶ֛לֶף אִ֖ישׁ אָ֑רְצָה כָּל־אֵ֖לֶּה שֹׁ֥לְפֵי חָֽרֶב׃

20:25   שְׁמֹנַ֨ת עָשָׂ֥ר

Unique   ל   Mp

Com.: The Masorah notes the *sole* occurrence of עָשָׂר with שְׁמֹנַת (cstr.), to distinguish it from its more numerous occurrences (5x) with שְׁמֹנָה (absol. שְׁמֹנָה עָשָׂר), *one* of which is in v. 44.

20:25   שֹׁ֥לְפֵי חָֽרֶב

Unique   ל   Mp

JUDGES 20:26

וַיַּעֲלוּ כָל־בְּנֵי יִשְׂרָאֵל וְכָל־הָעָם וַיָּבֹאוּ בֵית־אֵל וַיִּבְכּוּ וַיֵּשְׁבוּ שָׁם לִפְנֵי יְהֹוָה וַיָּצוּמוּ בַיּוֹם־הַהוּא עַד־הָעָרֶב וַיַּעֲלוּ עֹלוֹת וּשְׁלָמִים לִפְנֵי יְהוָה:

20:26   וַיָּצוּמוּ

Three times plene   ג מל   Mp

Judg 20:26; **1 Sam 7:6**; 1 Chr 10:12

וַיָּצוּמוּ *three times* plene, and their references   ויצומו ג מל וסימנהון   Mm

Judg 20:26	ויעלו כל <בני> ישראל
1 Sam 7:6	ויקבצו המצפתה
וַיָּקוּמוּ כָּל־אִישׁ *of Chronicles* (1 Chr 10:12)	ויקומו כל איש דדבר ימים

Com.: The Masorah notes the *three* occurrences of this lemma written plene וֹ, to distinguish them from its *two* occurrences written defective וֹ (וַיָּצֻמוּ).

This distinction is implied in the additional notation in the Mm *of Chronicles* to the 1 Chr 10:12 reference, which distinguishes it from its parallel passage in 1 Sam 31:12–13, where the lemma occurs as וַיָּצֻמוּ.

JUDGES 20:27

וַיִּשְׁאֲלוּ בְנֵי־יִשְׂרָאֵל בַּיהוָה וְשָׁם אֲרוֹן בְּרִית הָאֱלֹהִים בַּיָּמִים הָהֵם:

20:27   אֲרוֹן בְּרִית הָאֱלֹהִים

Unique   ל   Mp

1–4   **Judg 20:27**; **1 Sam 4:4**; **2 Sam 15:24**; <u>**1 Chr 16:6**</u>

Com.: The Mp heading here of *unique* is inexact since there are *four* occurrences of this lemma as corrrectly indicated in M[A] here, in the Mp headings at 2 Sam 15:24 and 1 Chr 16:6, and in the heading and lists of the Mm of <u>1 Chr 16:6</u>. M[C] has no note here.

The note more precisely should have read *unique in the book*.

The Masorah notes the *four* occurrences of the phrase אֲרוֹן בְּרִית with הָאֱלֹהִים , to distinguish them from its more numerous occurrences (24x) with אֲרוֹן בְּרִית/ יְהֹוָה (יְהֹוָה).

The Mp heading at 1 Sam 4:4, which reads *three times*, is inexact. It should have read *three times in the Prophets*.

JUDGES 20:28

וּפִינְחָס בֶּן־אֶלְעָזָר בֶּן־אַהֲרֹן עֹמֵד | לְפָנָיו בַּיָּמִים הָהֵם לֵאמֹר הַאוֹסִף עוֹד לָצֵאת לַמִּלְחָמָה עִם־בְּנֵי־בִנְיָמִן אָחִי אִם־אֶחְדָּל וַיֹּאמֶר יְהֹוָה עֲלוּ כִּי מָחָר אֶתְּנֶנּוּ בְיָדֶךָ:

20:28   הַאוֹסִף

Twice   בֿ   Mp

Com.: See **Judg 20:23**.

JUDGES 20:31

וַיֵּצְאוּ בְנֵי־בִנְיָמִן לִקְרַאת הָעָם הָנְתְּקוּ מִן־הָעִיר וַיָּחֵלּוּ לְהַכּוֹת מֵהָעָם חֲלָלִים כְּפַעַם | בְּפַעַם בַּמְסִלּוֹת אֲשֶׁר אַחַת עֹלָה בֵית־אֵל וְאַחַת גִּבְעָתָה בַּשָּׂדֶה כִּשְׁלֹשִׁים אִישׁ בְּיִשְׂרָאֵל:

20:31   הָנְתְּקוּ

Unique   לֿ   Mp

20:31   וַיָּחֵלּוּ

Four times   דֿ   Mp

Judg 20:31; Ezek 9:6; **Hos 8:10**; 2 Chr 29:17

Com.: The Masorah notes the *four* occurrences of this lemma (*hiphil* of חָלַל) with the ו consec., to distinguish them from its *three* occurrences with a ו cj. (וַיְחֵלּוּ/וְיָחֵלּוּ, *piel* of יָחַל).

20:31 בַּמְסִלּוֹת

Twice בׄ Mp

Judg 20:31; 20:45

Com.: The Masorah notes the *two* occurrences of this lemma with the prep. בְּ, to distinguish them from its *three* occurrences without this prep. (מְסִלּוֹת).

20:31 גִּבְעָתָה

Twice בׄ Mp

Judg 20:31; 1 Sam 10:26

Com.: The Masorah notes the *two* occurrences of this lemma without the def. article, to distinguish them from its more numerous occurrences (5x) with the def. article, *two* of which occur in vv. 4 and 14.

20:31 כִּשְׁלֹשִׁים אִישׁ

Three times גׄ Mp

Judg 20:31; 20:39: 1 Sam 9:22 (כִּשְׁלֹשִׁם*)

Com.: The Masorah notes the *three* occurrences of this lemma in various forms with the prep. כְּ, to distinguish them from its *sole* occurrence without this prep. at Judg 14:19.

* M^L, contrary to M (כִּשְׁלֹשִׁם), writes the form at 1 Sam 9:22 plene י (כִּשְׁלֹשִׁים) despite the fact that the Mp heading there reads *unique defective* (י); see Breuer, *The Biblical Text*, 71.

JUDGES 20:32

וַיֹּאמְרוּ בְּנֵי בִנְיָמִן נִגָּפִים הֵם לְפָנֵינוּ כְּבָרִאשֹׁנָה וּבְנֵי יִשְׂרָאֵל אָמְרוּ נָנוּסָה וּנְתַקְּנֻהוּ מִן־הָעִיר אֶל־
הַמְסִלּוֹת:

20:32   כְּבָרִאשֹׁנָה

Five times   הֵ   Mp

Judg 20:32; <u>1 Kgs 13:6</u>; <u>Isa 1:26</u>; Jer 33:7; 33:11

Com.: The Masorah notes the *five* occurrences of this lemma with the prep. כְּ, to distinguish them from its more numerous occurrences (14x) without this preposition.

20:32   נָנוּסָה

Unique   ל   Mp

Com.: The Masorah notes the *sole* occurrence of this lemma with the cohortative הָ, to distinguish it from its *two* occurrences without this cohortative (נָנוּס) at 2 Sam 18:3 and Isa 30:16.

20:32   וּנְתַקְּנֻהוּ

Unique   ל   Mp

JUDGES 20:33

וְכֹל | אִישׁ יִשְׂרָאֵל קָמוּ מִמְּקוֹמוֹ וַיַּעַרְכוּ בְּבַעַל תָּמָר וְאֹרֵב יִשְׂרָאֵל מֵגִיחַ מִמְּקֹמוֹ מִמַּעֲרֵה־גָבַע:

20:33   וְכֹל | אִישׁ

Seventeen times   יֹז   Mp

1–5   Exod 35:22; 35:23; 36:1; **Judg 3:29; <u>20:33</u>**
6–10   **1 Sam 14:22; 17:19; 17:24;** 22:2ᵃ; 22:2ᵇ
11–15   **2 Sam 16:18; 17:14;** 17:24; 2 Kgs 23:2; **Ezek 39:20**
16   <u>2 Chr 34:30</u>

וְכֹל | אִישׁ *sixteen times*   [יֹז] (יֹז) וכל איש   Mm

1–5	Exod 35:22	אשר הניף
	Exod 35:23	אשר נמצא
	Exod 36:1	חכם
	Judg 3:29	כל שמן וכל
	Judg 20:33	קמו (ממקמו) [ממקומו]
6–10	2 Kgs 23:2	ויעל המלך
	And its companion (2 Chr 34:30)	וחבירו
	1 Sam 17:19	ושאול והמה
	1 Sam 14:22	המתחבאים בהר אפרים
	1 Sam 17:24	בראותם את
11–15	1 Sam 22:2[a]	ויתקבצו אליו
	Twice in the verse (1 Sam 22:2[b])	שנים בפסוק
	2 Sam 17:14	ויאמר אבשלום
	2 Sam 17:24	מחנימה
	2 Sam 16:18	ויאמר חושי
16	Ezek 39:20	ושבעתם

Com.: The Mp heading here of *seventeen* is incorrect since there are only *sixteen* oc-currences of this lemma. The error is probably a graphic one confusing ז *seven* with ו *six*.

The Masorah notes the *sixteen* occurrences of this lemma with a ו cj., to distinguish them from its more numerous occurrences (39x) without a cj.

Six of the Mp headings highlighted above, and the Mm heading here, read *seventeen times* (Judg 3:29, 20:33, 1 Sam 14:22, 17:19, 17:24 and 2 Sam 16:18), whereas only *three* Mp headings, and the Mm heading at 2 Chr 34:30 read *sixteen times* (2 Sam 17:14, Ezek 39:20 and 2 Chr 34:30).

M[A] correctly reads here *sixteen times*, but M[C] has no note.

20:33   מֵגִיחַ

Unique   ל   Mp

JUDGES 20:34

וַיָּבֹ֣אוּ מִנֶּ֣גֶד לַגִּבְעָ֩ה עֲשֶׂ֨רֶת אֲלָפִ֜ים אִ֤ישׁ בָּחוּר֙ מִכָּל־יִשְׂרָאֵ֔ל וְהַמִּלְחָמָ֖ה כָּבֵ֑דָה וְהֵם֙ לֹ֣א יָדְע֔וּ כִּי־ נֹגַ֥עַת עֲלֵיהֶ֖ם הָרָעָֽה: פ

וְהַמִּלְחָמָה 20:34

Mm   וְהמלחמה ג   *three times*   וְהַמִּלְחָמָה

Judg 20:34   כבדה והם לא
Judg 20:42   הדביקתהו
1 Sam 14:23   והמחמה (עֹב) [עברה]

Com.: The Masorah notes the *three* occurrences of this lemma with a וֹ cj., to distinguish them from its more numerous occurrences (69x) without a cj.

20:34   כָּבֵ֑דָה

Unique   ל   Mp

Com.: This lemma is featured in two Masoretic lists. One is in a list of *hapax legomena* that are accented *mil'êl*, see Frensdorff, *Ochlah*, §32, and Díaz-Esteban, *Sefer Oklah we-Oklah*, §33.

The other is in a list of *hapax legomena* pairings from its same stem, *one* of which occurs in the Torah, *one* in the Prophets, and *one* in the Writings; see Frensdorff, *Ochlah*, §56, and Díaz-Esteban, *Sefer Oklah we-Oklah*, §57.

JUDGES 20:36

וַיִּרְא֤וּ בְנֵֽי־בִנְיָמִן֙ כִּ֣י נִגָּ֔פוּ וַיִּתְּנ֤וּ אִֽישׁ־יִשְׂרָאֵל֙ מָק֣וֹם לְבִנְיָמִ֔ן כִּ֤י בָֽטְחוּ֙ אֶל־הָ֣אֹרֵ֔ב אֲשֶׁ֣ר שָׂ֔מוּ אֶל־ הַגִּבְעָֽה:

20:36   נִגָּ֔פוּ

Unique   ל   Mp

Com.: The Masorah notes the *sole* occurrence of this lemma with a *qameṣ* under the ג (pausal), to distinguish it from its *three* occurrences with a *šəwâ* (נִגְּפוּ, non-pausal).

20:36   בָּטְחוּ אֶל

Ten times   יֿ   Mp

1–5   **Judg 20:36**; 2 Kgs 18:22; 18:30; Isa 36:7; 36:15
6–10   Jer 7:4; Ps 4:6; 31:7; **Prov 3:5**; Qoh 9:4

Com.: The Masorah notes the *ten* occurrences of this lemma of the verb בָּטַח in various forms with אֶל, to distinguish them from the more numerous occurrences of this verb in various forms with עַל; see the Mm to M^A here, and *Mikra'ot Gedolot 'Haketer'*, *Joshua-Judges*, 174–75.

JUDGES 20:37

וְהָאֹרֵב הֵחִישׁוּ וַיִּפְשְׁטוּ אֶל־הַגִּבְעָה וַיִּמְשֹׁךְ הָאֹרֵב וַיַּךְ אֶת־כָּל־הָעִיר לְפִי־חָרֶב׃

20:37   הֵחִישׁוּ

Unique   לֿ   Mp

JUDGES 20:38

וְהַמּוֹעֵד הָיָה לְאִישׁ יִשְׂרָאֵל עִם־הָאֹרֵב הֶרֶב לְהַעֲלוֹתָם מַשְׂאַת הֶעָשָׁן מִן־הָעִיר׃

20:38   וְהַמּוֹעֵד

Unique   לֿ   Mp

Com.: The Masorah notes the *sole* occurrence of this lemma with a ו cj., to distinguish it from its *three* occurrences without a cj.

20:38   הֶרֶב

Twice   בֿ   Mp

Judg 20:38; Ps 51:4 (*qərê*)

הֶרֶב *twice*   הרב בֿ   Mm

<u>Judg 20:38</u>   העשן מן העיר

Ps 51:4   כבסני מעוני ומחטאתי

Com.: The Masorah notes the *two* occurrences of this lemma, to distinguish them from its more numerous occurrences (45x) of its longer form (הַרְבֵּה); see Ognibeni, *'Oklah*, §22F.

20:38   מַשְׂאַת

מַשְׂאַת *six times*   משאת וֿ   Mm

1–5	<u>Gen 43:34</u>	ותרב משאת בנימן
	<u>Judg 20:38</u>	הרב להעלותם משאת
	2 Sam 11:8	ותצא אחריו משאת
	2 Chr 24:9	ויתנו קול ביהודה
	<u>2 Chr 24:6</u>	ויקרא המלך
6	Ps 141:2	תכון תפלתי קטרת

And *once* (וּמַשְׂאַת): Amos 5:11   וחד ומשאת בר תקחו ממנו

Com.: The Masorah notes the *six* occurrences of this lemma with a *pataḥ* under the א, to distinguish them from its *three* occurrences with a *ṣerê* (מַשְׂאֵת).

The Mm has an additional note that this lemma also occurs with a ו cj. (וּמַשְׂאַת) at Amos 5:11.

JUDGES 20:39

וַיַּהֲפֹךְ אִישׁ־יִשְׂרָאֵל בַּמִּלְחָמָה וּבִנְיָמִן הֵחֵל לְהַכּוֹת חֲלָלִים בְּאִישׁ־יִשְׂרָאֵל כִּשְׁלֹשִׁים אִישׁ כִּי אָמְרוּ אַךְ נִגּוֹף נִגָּף הוּא לְפָנֵינוּ כַּמִּלְחָמָה הָרִאשֹׁנָה:

20:39   וּבִנְיָמִן

Nine exceptional cases   טֿ מיחד   Mp

1–5   **Gen 45:14**; **Exod 1:3**; **Judg 20:39**; **Obad 19**; Ps 80:3

6–9   1 Chr 7:10; **8:1**; 21:6; **2 Chr 34:32**

Com.: The Masorah notes the *nine* exceptional cases where the form וּבִנְיָמִן is not preceded by Judah nor Joseph.

Four of the Mp headings highlighted above elaborate on this note.

The Mp heading at 2 Chr 34:32 reads *nine exceptional cases and similarly all (cases with) Judah and Joseph*, whereas the Mp headings at Gen 45:14, Exod 1:3 leave out the term *exceptional* and just read *nine times and similarly all (cases with) Judah and Joseph*.

Most expansive is the Mp heading at 1 Chr 8:1, which reads *nine times, and similarly all (cases of) Judah and Benjamin, and Joseph and Benjamin*.

20:39   כִּשְׁלֹשִׁים אִישׁ

Three times   גֿ   Mp

Com.: See **Judg 20:31**.

20:39   נִגּוֹף

Unique   ל   Mp

20:39   נִגָּף

Three times   גֿ   Mp

Deut 28:25; Judg 20:39; 2 Sam 10:15 (נִגַּף)

Com.: The Masorah notes the *three* occurrences of this lemma, *twice* with a *qameṣ* under the גֿ (Deut 28:25 and here), and *once* with a *paṭaḥ* (2 Sam 10:15).

20:39   כַּמִּלְחָמָה

Unique   ל   Mp

Com.: This lemma is featured in a Masoretic list of *hapax legomena* beginning with a כ; see Frensdorff, *Ochlah*, §19, and Díaz-Esteban, *Sefer Oklah we-Oklah*, §20.

> ## JUDGES 20:40
>
> וְהַמַּשְׂאֵת הֵחֵלָּה לַעֲלוֹת מִן־הָעִיר עַמּוּד עָשָׁן וַיִּפֶן בִּנְיָמִן אַחֲרָיו וְהִנֵּה עָלָה כְלִיל־הָעִיר הַשָּׁמָיְמָה׃

20:40   וְהַמַּשְׂאֵת

Unique   ל   Mp

20:40   לַעֲלוֹת

לַעֲלוֹת *fourteen times*, and their references   לעלות יד וסימנהון   Mm

1–5	Judg 20:40	והמשאת
	1 Sam 2:28	ובחר
	2 Sam 5:22	פלשתים
	1 Sam 9:14	הבמה
	1 Kgs 18:29	המנחה
6–10	1 Kgs 12:18	במרכבה
	And its companion (2 Chr 10:18)	וחביר
	2 Kgs 12:18	חזאל
	Hab 3:16	יגודנו
	2 Chr 18:2	ויסיתהו
11–14	Ps 62:10	במאזנים
	Job 36:20	אל תשאף
	Ezra 1:5	העיר
	Ezra 7:28	הטה חסד

And similarly *all* the Torah and Joshua apart from *three*:   וכל אורית ויהושע דכות ב מ ג

Lev 24:2   צו
Exod 27:20   תצוה
Josh 22:23   לבנות

The Masorah also notes that this lemma occurs in the *qal* in the Torah (2x) and Joshua (3x), apart from the *three* listed cases when it occurs in the *hiphil* (לְהַעֲלוֹת).

20:40   הַשָּׁמַיְמָה

Eleven times   יא   Mp

Com.: See **Josh 8:20**.

JUDGES 20:41

וְאִישׁ יִשְׂרָאֵל הָפַךְ וַיִּבָּהֵל אִישׁ בִּנְיָמִן כִּי רָאָה כִּי־נָגְעָה עָלָיו הָרָעָה׃

20:41   וַיִּבָּהֵל

Unique   ל   Mp

JUDGES 20:42

וַיִּפְנ֞וּ לִפְנֵ֨י אִ֤ישׁ יִשְׂרָאֵל֙ אֶל־דֶּ֣רֶךְ הַמִּדְבָּ֔ר וְהַמִּלְחָמָ֖ה הִדְבִּיקָ֑תְהוּ וַאֲשֶׁר֙ מֵהֶ֣עָרִ֔ים מַשְׁחִיתִ֥ים אוֹת֖וֹ בְּתוֹכֽוֹ׃

20:42   וְהַמִּלְחָמָה

Three times   גׄ   Mp

Judg 20:34; **20:42; 1 Sam 14:23**

Com.: The Masorah notes the *three* occurrences of this lemma with a ו cj., to distinguish them from its more numerous occurrences (69x) without a cj.

20:42   הִדְבִּיקָתְהוּ

Unique   לׄ   Mp

20:42   מֵהֶעָרִים

Four times   דׄ   Mp

Com.: See directly above at **Judg 20:15**.

20:42   מַשְׁחִיתִים

Seven times   זׄ   Mp

1–5   **Gen 19:13** (מַשְׁחִתִים); **Judg 20:42; 2 Sam 20:15** (מַשְׁחִיתָם); **Isa 1:4; Jer 6:28**
6–7   **Jer 22:7** (מַשְׁחִתִים); **2 Chr 27:2**

Com.: The Masorah here (and at Jer 6:28, 22:7, and 2 Chr 27:2) notes the *seven* occurrences of this lemma. *Four* are written doubly plene י (מַשְׁחִיתִים, Judg 20:42, Isa 1:4, Jer 6:28, 2 Chr 27:2), *two* are written defective first י (מַשְׁחִתִים, Gen 19:13 and Jer 22:7), and *one* is written defective second י (מַשְׁחִיתָם, 2 Sam 20:15).

The Mp heading at Isa 1:4, which has a doubly plene form (מַשְׁחִיתִים), notes only these plene forms in its reading *four times plene* (Judg 20:42, Isa 1:4, Jer 6:28, 2 Chr 27:2).

Two of the Mp headings highlighted above (Gen 19:13 and 2 Sam 20:15) read *eight times*, presumably because, in addition to the *seven* forms listed above, they include the form at 1 Sam 6:5 with the def. article (הַמַּשְׁחִיתָם).

JUDGES 20:43

כִּתְּרוּ אֶת־בִּנְיָמִן הִרְדִיפֻהוּ מְנוּחָה הִדְרִיכֻהוּ עַד נֹכַח הַגִּבְעָה מִמִּזְרַח־שָׁמֶשׁ׃

20:43   הִדְרִיכֻהוּ

Twice   בֿ   Mp

Judg 20:43; **Job 28:8** (הִדְרִיכֻוהוּ*)

Mm   הדריכיהו בֿ חד חסיר וחד מלֿ וסימנהון   הִדְרִיכֻהוּ *twice, once* defective and *once* plene, and their references

Judg 20:43   מנוחה הדריכהו עד
Job 28:8   לא הדריכהו (בצי) [בני] שחץ

The *first one* is defective   קדמֿ חסֿ

Com.: The Masorah notes the *two* occurrences of this lemma, *one* written defective ו (here), and *one* written plene ו (Job 28:8).

* M¹, contrary to M (הִדְרִיכֻוהוּ), has *two* defective forms of this lemma since it writes the form at Job 28:8 defective (הִדְרִיכֻהוּ). But the Mm note of *twice, once defective and once plene* conforms to the text of M.

JUDGES 20:45

וַיִּפְנוּ וַיָּנֻסוּ הַמִּדְבָּרָה אֶל־סֶלַע הָרִמּוֹן וַיְעֹלְלֻהוּ בַּמְסִלּוֹת חֲמֵשֶׁת אֲלָפִים אִישׁ וַיַּדְבִּיקוּ אַחֲרָיו עַד־גִּדְעֹם וַיַּכּוּ מִמֶּנּוּ אַלְפַּיִם אִישׁ׃

20:45   הַמִּדְבָּרָה

Twelve times   יֿב   Mp

1–5   **Exod 4:27**; **Lev 16:10**; 16:21; **Num 21:23**; **33:8**
6–10   **Deut 1:40**; 2:1; **Judg 20:45**; 20:47; **1 Sam 13:18**
11–12   **1 Sam 26:3**; Ezek 29:5

Com.: The Masorah notes the *twelve* occurrences of this lemma with the locative ה, to distinguish them from its more numerous occurrences (39x) without this adverbial ending.

The Mp heading at Exod 4:27 reads *thirteen times* reflecting the Eastern reading that reads הַמִּדְבָּר of Judg 20:42 as הַמִּדְבָּרָה; see Breuer, *Masora Magna*, 284, n. 3.

20:45	וַיְעֹלְלֻהוּ
Unique	ל Mp

20:45	בַּמְסִלּוֹת
Twice	בֿ Mp

Judg 20:31; 20:45

20:45	גִּדְעֹם
Unique	ל Mp

Com.: This lemma is featured in a Masoretic list of *hapax legomena* pairings, *one* of which occurs in the Torah, *one* in the Prophets, and *one* in the Writings; see Frensdorff, *Ochlah*, §57, and Díaz-Esteban, *Sefer Oklah we-Oklah*, §58.

JUDGES 20:47

וַיִּפְנוּ וַיָּנֻסוּ הַמִּדְבָּרָה אֶל־סֶלַע הָרִמּוֹן שֵׁשׁ מֵאוֹת אִישׁ וַיֵּשְׁבוּ בְּסֶלַע רִמּוֹן אַרְבָּעָה חֳדָשִׁים:

20:47	הַמִּדְבָּרָה
Twelve times	יֿב Mp

Com.: See directly above at **Judg 20:45**.

JUDGES 20:48

וְאִישׁ יִשְׂרָאֵל שָׁבוּ אֶל־בְּנֵי בִנְיָמִן וַיַּכּוּם לְפִי־חֶרֶב מֵעִיר מְתֹם עַד־בְּהֵמָה עַד כָּל־הַנִּמְצָא גַּם כָּל־
הֶעָרִים הַנִּמְצָאוֹת שִׁלְּחוּ בָאֵשׁ: פ

20:48   וַיַּכּוּם

Eleven times   יֹא   Mp

Com.: See **Josh 7:5**.

20:48   מְתֹם

Four times   דֹ   Mp

Judg 20:48; Isa 1:6; Ps 38:4; **38:8**

Com.: The Masorah notes the *four* occurrences of this lemma with a *ḥolem*, to distinguish them from its *two* occurrences with a *ḥireq* (מְתִם) at Deut 2:34 and Deut 3:6.

20:48   הַנִּמְצָאוֹת

Four times plene   דֹ מל   Mp

1–2   Gen 19:15 (הַנִּמְצָאֹת); **Judg 20:48**

Com.: The Mp heading here of *four times plene* is incorrect since there are only *two* occurrences of this lemma, *one* written plene וֹ (here), and *one* written defective וֹ (הַנִּמְצָאֹת) at Gen 19:15.

M^A correctly reads here *twice, once plene and once defective*, but M^C has no note.

This lemma is featured in a Masoretic list of doublets with an initial הַ or הֶ; see Frensdorff, *Ochlah*, §64.

JUDGES 21:2

וַיָּבֹא הָעָם בֵּית־אֵל וַיֵּשְׁבוּ שָׁם עַד־הָעֶרֶב לִפְנֵי הָאֱלֹהִים וַיִּשְׂאוּ קוֹלָם וַיִּבְכּוּ בְּכִי גָדוֹל:

21:2   לִפְנֵי הָאֱלֹהִים

Six times, and similarly *all* Qoheleth   ו וכל קהלת   Mp

Com.: See **Josh 24:1**.

Judges 21:5

וַיֹּאמְרוּ֙ בְּנֵ֣י יִשְׂרָאֵ֔ל מִ֣י אֲשֶׁ֣ר לֹא־עָלָ֣ה בַקָּהָל֩ מִכָּל־שִׁבְטֵ֨י יִשְׂרָאֵ֜ל אֶל־יְהוָ֗ה כִּ֤י הַשְּׁבוּעָ֣ה הַגְּדוֹלָ֔ה הָיְתָ֗ה לַ֠אֲשֶׁר לֹא־עָלָ֥ה אֶל־יְהוָ֛ה הַמִּצְפָּ֖ה לֵאמֹ֑ר מ֥וֹת יוּמָֽת׃

21:5   בַקָּהָל֩

Four times   ד֜   Mp

Judg 21:5; Job 30:28; Lam 1:10; 2 Chr 30:17

Com.: The Masorah notes the *four* occurrences of this lemma with the def. prep. בַּ to distinguish them from the *four* occurrences with the indef. prep. בְ.

This distinction is implied in the the Mp headings to Job 30:28, Lam 1:10 and 2 Chr 30:17, and the Mm headings to Lam 1:10 and 2 Chr 30:17, that read *four times dages̆*, that is, with the def. prep. בַּ as opposed to the indef. prep. without a *dages̆*.

The catchwords in the Mm to 2 Chr 30:17 are given in the form of an Aramaic mnemonic "let us rise, and go up for I was commanded many things"; see Marcus, *Scribal Wit*, 155–56.

21:5   הַשְּׁבוּעָה הַגְּדוֹלָה

Unique   ל   Mp

Com.: This phrase is featured in a Masoretic list of two-word phrases that only occur *once*, in which both words of the phrase has the def. article; see Frensdorff, *Ochlah*, §371.

21:5   מוֹת יוּמָת

Twice in the Prophets   ב֯ בנב֯י   Mp

Judg 21:5; Ezek 18:13

Com.: The Masorah notes the *two* occurrences in the Prophets of מוֹת with יוּמָת to distinguish them from its *three* occurrences in the Prophets with יָמוּת (מוֹת יָמוּת); see the Mm at Num 26:65 *sub* מוֹת יָמֻתוּ.

JUDGES 21:6

וַיִּנָּחֲמוּ֙ בְּנֵ֣י יִשְׂרָאֵ֔ל אֶל־בִּנְיָמִ֖ן אָחִ֑יו וַיֹּ֣אמְר֔וּ נִגְדַּ֥ע הַיֹּ֛ום שֵׁ֥בֶט אֶחָ֖ד מִיִּשְׂרָאֵֽל׃

21:6   וַיִּנָּחֲמוּ֙

Twice   בֿ   Mp

Judg 21:6; Ezek 31:16

Com.: The Masorah notes the *two* occurrences of this lemma in the *niphal*, to distinguish them from its *sole* occurrence in the *piel* (וַיְנַחֲמוּ) at Job 42:11.

21:6   וַיִּנָּחֲמוּ...אֶל

Seven times   זֿ   Mp

1–5   **Judg 21:6**; 2 Sam 10:2 (לְנַחֲמוֹ...אֶל); 24:16 (וַיִּנָּחֶם...אֶל);
     Jer 26:3 (וְנִחַמְתִּי אֶל); 26:13 (וְיִנָּחֵם...אֶל)
6–7   Jer 26:19 (נִחַמְתִּי אֶל); 42:10 (וְנִחַמְתִּי...אֶל)

Com.: The Masorah notes the *seven* occurrences of forms of the verb נָחַם with אֶל (see Ginsburg, 2, נ, §186), to distinguish them from the more numerous occurrences (22x) of this verb with עַל.

In M^L the circellus has been placed on אֶל־בִּנְיָמִן, but this phrase occurs only *once* as is noted by M^C and M^A, both of which read here *unique*. It is most likely, as suggested by Dotan/Reich (*Masora Thesaurus, ad loc.*), that the lemma be extended to include וַיִּנָּחֲמוּ, since the phrase נָחַם...אֶל does occur *seven times.*

JUDGES 21:7

מַה־נַּעֲשֶׂ֥ה לָהֶ֛ם לַנֹּותָרִ֖ים לְנָשִׁ֑ים וַאֲנַ֙חְנוּ֙ נִשְׁבַּ֣עְנוּ בַֽיהוָ֔ה לְבִלְתִּ֛י תֵּת־לָהֶ֥ם מִבְּנֹותֵ֖ינוּ לְנָשִֽׁים׃

21:7   מִבְּנֹותֵ֖ינוּ

Four times plene   דֿ מל   Mp

Judg 21:7; 21:18; Ps 144:12 (בְּנֹותֵינוּ); **2 Chr 29:9** (וּבְנֹותֵינוּ)

Com.: The Masorah notes the *four* occurrences of this lemma in various forms written plene ו, to distinguish them from its more numerous occurrences (8x) in various forms written defective ו (בְּנֹתֵינוּ).

JUDGES 21:9

וַיִּתְפָּקֵד הָעָם וְהִנֵּה אֵין־שָׁם אִישׁ מִיּוֹשְׁבֵי יָבֵשׁ גִּלְעָד׃

21:9   וַיִּתְפָּקֵד

Unique   ל   Mp

Com.: The Masorah notes the *sole* occurrence of this lemma in the sg., to distinguish it from its *sole* occurrence in the pl. (וַיִּתְפָּקְדוּ) at Judg 20:15.

21:9   מִיּוֹשְׁבֵי

מיושבי ג̇ ב̇ מל וחד חסיר   Mm   מִיּוֹשְׁבֵי *three* times, *twice* plene and *once* defective

<u>Judg 20:15</u>	ויתפקדו בני בנימן
Judg 21:9	ויתפקד העם
Judg 21:12	וימצאו מיושבי (יבש) [יביש]

Com.: The Masorah notes the *three* occurrences of this lemma, *twice* written plene ו (here and Judg 21:12), and *once* written defective ו (מִישְׁבֵי, Judg 20:15).

This lemma occurs in the ms. in folio 150r, but the Mm note appears on the bottom of the preceding folio 149v.

JUDGES 21:10

וַיִּשְׁלְחוּ־שָׁם הָעֵדָה שְׁנֵים־עָשָׂר אֶלֶף אִישׁ מִבְּנֵי הֶחָיִל וַיְצַוּוּ אוֹתָם לֵאמֹר לְכוּ וְהִכִּיתֶם אֶת־יוֹשְׁבֵי
יָבֵשׁ גִּלְעָד לְפִי־חֶרֶב וְהַנָּשִׁים וְהַטָּף׃

21:10   וַיְצַוּוּ

Unique   ל   Mp

1–4   <u>Gen 50:16</u>: **Josh 3:3; Judg 21:10; 21:20** (*qərē*)

Com.: The Mp heading here of *unique* is inexact since there are *four* occurrences of this lemma, *two* in the book of Judges. However, since the *kətîb* form ויצו at Judg 21:20 is written defective second ו, the note may be taken to mean only plene forms of this lemma, of which there is only *one* in the book, so the note more precisely should have read *unique plene in the book.*

This interepretation is supported by the Mm of <u>Gen 50:16</u>, which reads *three times plene and once defective* (second וֹ). And the end of the note specifies that it is the Judg 21:20 that is written defective.

Both M^C and M^A correctly read here *four times* as does the heading at **Josh 3:3** in M^L.

21:10   יֹשְׁבֵי

Unique plene   ל מל   Mp

Com.: The Mp heading here of *unique* is incorrect since there are *thirty-four* occurrences of this lemma; see **Josh 15:63**. Most probably the number four דֹ was left out after the ל, since it should have read לדֹ.

M^A correctly reads here *thirty-four times plene*, but M^C has no note.

JUDGES 21:11

וְזֶה הַדָּבָר אֲשֶׁר תַּעֲשׂוּ כָּל־זָכָר וְכָל־אִשָּׁה יֹדַעַת מִשְׁכַּב־זָכָר תַּחֲרִימוּ׃

21:11   וְזֶה הַדָּבָר

Four times at the beginning of a verse   דֹ ראש פסו   Mp

<u>Exod 29:1</u>; <u>Josh 5:4</u>; <u>Judg 21:11</u>; 1 Kgs 11:27

וְזֶה הַדָּבָר *four times* at the beginning of a verse   וזה הדבר דֹ ראש פסוק   Mm

<u>Exod 29:1</u>	אשר תעשה
Josh 5:4	אשר מל יהושע
<u>Judg 21:11</u>	תעשו
<u>1 Kgs 11:27</u>	(את) [אשר] הרים

Com.: The Masorah notes the *four* occurrences of this lemma at the beginning of a verse, with a וֹ cj., to distinguish them from its *six* occurrences of this lemma at the beginning of a verse without a cj.

In M^L the circellus has been placed only on וְזֶה, but this form occurs many more than *four times* at the beginning of a verse so it is most likely, as indicated in the Mp headings in M^C and M^A and in the Mm here, that the note refers to the two words וְזֶה הַדָּבָר.

21:11 וְכָל־אִשָּׁה

Three times גׄ Mp

Exod 35:25; Num 31:17; **Judg 21:11**

Com.: The Masorah notes the *three* occurrences of וְכָל with אִשָּׁה, to distinguish them from its more numerous occurrences (16x) with אִישׁ (וְכָל־אִישׁ).

21:11 יֹדַעַת

Three times גׄ Mp

Num 31:17; **Judg 21:11**; <u>Ps 139:14</u>

Com.: The Masorah notes the *three* occurrences of this lemma pointed as a fem. ptcp., to distinguish them from its more numerous occurrences (55x) pointed as a 2nd pers. masc. perf. (יָדַעְתָּ); see Ognibeni, *'Oklah*, §7M, or from its *three* occurrences pointed as a 2nd pers. fem. perf. (יָדַעַתְּ).

JUDGES 21:12

וַיִּמְצְא֞וּ מִיּוֹשְׁבֵ֣י | יָבֵ֣ישׁ גִּלְעָ֗ד אַרְבַּ֤ע מֵאוֹת֙ נַעֲרָ֣ה בְתוּלָ֔ה אֲשֶׁ֧ר לֹֽא־יָדְעָ֛ה אִ֖ישׁ לְמִשְׁכַּ֣ב זָכָ֑ר וַיָּבִ֤יאוּ אוֹתָם֙ אֶל־הַֽמַּחֲנֶ֔ה שִׁלֹ֕ה אֲשֶׁ֖ר בְּאֶ֥רֶץ כְּנָֽעַן: ס

21:12 לְמִשְׁכַּב זָכָר

Twice בׄ Mp

Num 31:17; Judg 21:12

Com.: This lemma is featured in a Masoretic list of *hapax legomena* in a similar section where *one* has a prefixed ל (here), and the *other* does not have this ל (מִשְׁכַּב זָכָר at Judg 21:11); see Frensdorff, *Ochlah*, §245, and Ognibeni, *'Oklah*, §136.

JUDGES 21:14

וַיָּ֤שָׁב בִּנְיָמִן֙ בָּעֵ֣ת הַהִ֔יא וַיִּתְּנ֤וּ לָהֶם֙ הַנָּשִׁ֔ים אֲשֶׁ֣ר חִיּ֔וּ מִנְּשֵׁ֖י יָבֵ֣שׁ גִּלְעָ֑ד וְלֹֽא־מָצְא֥וּ לָהֶ֖ם כֵּֽן:

21:14 אֲשֶׁר חִיּוּ

Unique לׄ Mp

21:14   יָבֵשׁ

Six times defective   ו חס֙   Mp

1–5   Judg 21:9; 21:10; **21:14**; **2 Kgs 15:10**; 1 Chr 10:12 (בְּיָבֵשׁ)
6   All עֵץ יָבֵשׁ

Com.: The Masorah notes the *six* occurrences of this lemma, with and without prep. בְּ, written defective י. The occurrences include *five* cases of the lemma used as a name of a place or a person, and *one* case designated as עֵץ יָבֵשׁ, which consists of the *fourteen* occurrences of יָבֵשׁ used as a verb or adj.; see Breuer, *The Biblical Text*, 66.

M[L], contrary to M (יבישׁ), has a *seventh* occurrence since it writes this lemma (indicating a name of a place) defective י at 1 Sam 11:1[a]; see Breuer, *The Biblical Text*, 72. However, the Mp headings here of *six times* supports the enumeration inherent in the text of M.

In M[L] the חס֙ part of the note is not too clear.

JUDGES 21:17

וַיֹּאמְרוּ יְרֻשַּׁת פְּלֵיטָה לְבִנְיָמֶן וְלֹא־יִמָּחֶה שֵׁבֶט מִיִּשְׂרָאֵל:

21:17   יְרֻשַּׁת

Twice and defective   ב וחס֙   Mp

Judg 21:17; Ps 61:6

Com.: By noting that this lemma occurs *twice* and is written defective ו, the Masorah is also implying (correctly) that this lemma does not occur elsewhere written plene ו.

JUDGES 21:18

וַאֲנַחְנוּ לֹא נוּכַל לָתֵת־לָהֶם נָשִׁים מִבְּנוֹתֵינוּ כִּי־נִשְׁבְּעוּ בְנֵי־יִשְׂרָאֵל לֵאמֹר אָרוּר נֹתֵן אִשָּׁה לְבִנְיָמֶן: ס

21:18   מִבְּנוֹתֵינוּ

Four times plene   ד מל֙   Mp

Com.: See **Judg 21:7**.

21:18   אָר֨וּר

Eight times with the accent (*zaqep̄ gaḏôl*)   ח֨ בטע   Mp

1–5   Deut 27:16; 27:17; **27:18**; 27:21; 27:23
6–8   Deut 27:24; **Judg 21:18**

Com.: The Mp heading here of *eight times* is incorrect since there are only *seven* occurrences of this lemma with a *zaqep̄ gaḏôl* accent. The correct number *seven* is given in the Mp heading at Deut 27:18.

Neither M^C nor M^A has a note on this lemma here.

JUDGES 21:19

וַיֹּאמְר֡וּ הִנֵּה֩ חַג־יְהוָ֨ה בְּשִׁל֜וֹ מִיָּמִ֣ים | יָמִ֗ימָה אֲשֶׁ֞ר מִצְּפ֤וֹנָה לְבֵֽית־אֵל֙ מִזְרְחָ֣ה הַשֶּׁ֔מֶשׁ לִמְסִלָּ֔ה הָֽעֹלָ֛ה מִבֵּֽית־אֵ֖ל שְׁכֶ֑מָה וּמִנֶּ֖גֶב לִלְבוֹנָֽה׃

21:19   חַג־יְהוָה

Four times   ד֔   Mp

Exod 10:9; **Lev 23:39; Judg 21:19; Hos 9:5**

חַג־יְהֹוָה *four times*   חג יהוה ד֔   Mm

Exod 10:9	בנערינו (ובזקיננו) [ובזקנינו]
Lev 23:39	באספכם את תבואת
Judg 21:19	הנה חג יהוה (בשלה) [בשלו]
Hos 9:5	ליום מועד

Com.: The Masorah notes the *four* occurrences of חַג with יְהוָה, to distinguish them from its *five* occurrences with לַיהֹוָה (חג לַיהוָה).

21:19   בְּשִׁלוֹ

בְּשִׁלוֹ *eight times* defective   בשלו ח̇ חס̇   Mm

1–5	Judg 21:19	הנה חג יהוה (בשלה) [בשלו]
	1 Sam 1:24	ותבאהו בית יהוה
	1 Sam 3:21, the *second part of the verse*	כי נגלה יהוה תיניֿ דפסוק
	1 Sam 14:3	בן פינחס
	Jer 7:14	ועשיתי
6–8	Jer 26:9	מדוע נבית
	Jer 41:5	אנשים
	Ps 78:60	ויטש משכן שלו

Com.: The Masorah notes the *eight* occurrences of this lemma in various forms written defective י, to distinguish them from its *four* occurrences in various forms written plene י (בְּשִׁילוֹ); see directly below at **Judg 21:21**.

The additional note of the *second part of the verse* to the 1 Sam 3:21 reference distinguishes the second part of the verse from its first part, where the lemma occurs as בְּשִׁלה.

21:19   מִצְפוֹנָה

Unique   ל   Mp

Com.: The Masorah notes the *sole* occurrence of this lemma with a *šəwâ* under the צ, to distinguish it from its *sole* occurrence with a *qameṣ* (מִצְפוֹנָה) at Josh 15:10.

21:19   לִמְסִלָּה

Unique   ל   Mp

Com.: This lemma is featured in a Masoretic list of words that occur *once* with a indef. ל (here), but otherwise with a def. לַ (Jer 31:21 and 1 Chr 26:18); see Frensdorff, *Ochlah*, §27, Díaz-Esteban, *Sefer Oklah we-Oklah*, §28, and Ognibeni, *'Oklah*, §280, p. 428.

21:19   שְׁכֶמָה

Six times   ו̇   Mp

Com.: See **Judg 9:1**.

21:19   וּמִנֶּ֖גֶב

Unique   ל   Mp

Com.: This lemma is featured in a Masoretic list of *hapax legomena* that start with וּמ; see Frensdorff, *Ochlah*, §18, and Díaz-Esteban, *Sefer Oklah we-Oklah*, §19.

JUDGES 21:20

וַיְצַ֥ו אֶת־בְּנֵ֥י בִנְיָמִ֖ן לֵאמֹ֑ר לְכ֥וּ וַאֲרַבְתֶּ֖ם בַּכְּרָמִֽים׃

21:20   וַיְצַ֥ו

Read וַיְצַוּ   ויצוו ק   Mp

Com.: The *kǝṯîḇ* (ויצו), and the *qǝrê* (וַיְצַוּ) represent examples where the text, in accordance with older orthography, writes only one of two adjoining and identical vowel-letters; see Gordis, *The Biblical Text*, 96.

This lemma is featured in a Masoretic list of words where a ו which is not written is read; see Frensdorff, *Ochlah*, §119, and Díaz-Esteban, *Sefer Oklah we-Oklah*, §105.

21:20   וַאֲרַבְתֶּ֖ם

Unique   ל   Mp

JUDGES 21:21

וּרְאִיתֶ֞ם וְהִנֵּ֥ה אִם־יֵצְא֨וּ בְנוֹת־שִׁילוֹ֮ לָח֣וּל בַּמְּחֹלוֹת֒ וִיצָאתֶם֙ מִן־הַכְּרָמִ֔ים וַחֲטַפְתֶּ֥ם לָכֶ֛ם אִ֖ישׁ אִשְׁתּ֣וֹ מִבְּנ֣וֹת שִׁיל֑וֹ וַהֲלַכְתֶּ֖ם אֶ֥רֶץ בִּנְיָמִֽן׃

21:21   יֵצְא֨וּ

Fourteen times   יד   Mp

Com.: See **Josh 8:5**.

21:21   בִּמְחֹלוֹת

Unique   ל   Mp

1–3   **Judg 21:21**; 1 Sam 21:12; 29:5

Com.: The Mp heading here *of unique* is inexact since there are *three* occurrences of this lemma. The note more precisely should have read *unique in the book*.

Neither M^C nor M^A has a note on this lemma here.

21:21   וִיצָאתֶם

Twice   בׄ   Mp

Judg 21:21; Mal 3:20

וִיצָאתֶם *twice*   ויצאתם בׄ   Mm

Judg 21:21   מן הכרמים
Mal 3:20   ויצאתם ופשתם

Com.: The Masorah notes the *two* occurrences of this lemma with a ו consec., to distinguish them from its *two* occurrences without a ו (יְצָאתֶם) at Exod 13:3 and Deut 11:10.

21:21   וַחֲטַפְתֶּם

Unique   ל   Mp

21:21   שִׁילוֹ²

Three times plene   גׄ מל   Mp

Judg 21:21ᵃ; **21:21ᵇ**; **Jer 7:12** (בְּשִׁילוֹ)

Com.: The Mp heading here, and in M^C and M^A, and at Jer 7:12 of *three times plene* is inexact since there is another occurrence of this lemma at Gen 49:10. The note more precisely should have read *three times plene in the Prophets*.

The Masorah notes the *three* occurrences of this lemma written plene י, to distinguish them from its more numerous occurrences (8x) in various forms written defective י (שִׁלֹ); see directly above at **Judg 21:19**.

JUDGES 21:22

וְהָיָ֞ה כִּֽי־יָבֹ֨אוּ אֲבוֹתָ֤ם א֣וֹ אֲחֵיהֶם֙ לָרֹ֣וב ׀ אֵלֵ֔ינוּ וְאָמַ֣רְנוּ אֲלֵיהֶ֗ם חָנּ֤וּנוּ אוֹתָם֙ כִּ֣י לֹ֣א לָקַ֤חְנוּ אִישׁ֙ אִשְׁתּ֣וֹ בַּמִּלְחָמָ֔ה כִּ֣י לֹ֥א אַתֶּ֛ם נְתַתֶּ֥ם לָהֶ֖ם כָּעֵ֥ת תֶּאְשָֽׁמוּ׃ ס

21:22   לָרֹוב

Mp   לריב קר   Read לְרִיב

Mm   לריב ה׳   לְרִיב *five times*

1–5	Judg 21:22	והיה כי יבאו אבותם
	Amos 7:4	והנה קרא (לריב) [לרב] באש
	Isa 3:13	נצב לריב יהוה
	Job 9:3	אם יחפץ לריב עמו
	Prov 25:8	אל תצא לרב
	The last form is defective	בתרי חס׳

And *once* (וְלָרִיב): 2 Chr 19:8   וחד למשפט יהוה ולריב

Com.: The *kətîb* (לרוב), and the *qərê* (לְרִיב) are examples of *kətîb*/*qərê* variations where a ו in the middle of a word is read as a י; see Frensdorff, *Ochlah*, §81, Díaz-Esteban, *Sefer Oklah we-Oklah*, §72, and Gordis, *The Biblical Text*, 128.

In the Mm, the Masorah notes the *five* occurrences of this lemma with the def. prep. לְ, written plene and defective י, to distinguish them from its *two* occurrences with the indef. prep. לְ (לְרִיב) at Isa 34:8 and Isa 58:4.

This distinction is implied in the heading of the Mm at Isa 3:13, which specifically notes that these forms occur *five times with qameṣ* (under the לְ), thereby contrasting them with forms with another vowel under the לְ, which can only be a *šəwâ* (לְרִיב).

The Mm has an additional note that this lemma also occurs with a ו cj. (וְלָרִיב) at 2 Chr 19:8.

The Mm notes that the last entry in its list (Prov 25:8) is written defective י, but the second entry in the list at Amos 7:4 is also written defective י (לְרֹב) in both M^L and M.

21:22   חָנוּנוּ

Unique and plene   ל ומל   Mp

Com.: By noting that this lemma is *unique* and written plene וּ, the Masorah is also implying (correctly) that this lemma does not occur elsewhere written defective וּ.

21:22   אִישׁ אִשְׁתּוֹ

Three times   גֹ   Mp

1–2   Judg 21:21; **21:22**

Com.: The Mp heading here of *three times* is incorrect since there are only *two* occurrences of this lemma.

The Masorah notes the *two* occurrences of this lemma without a וּ cj., to distinguish them from its *two* occurrences with a cj. (אִישׁ וְאִשְׁתּוֹ) at Gen 7:2ᵃ and 7:2ᵇ.

Mᴬ correctly reads here *twice*, but Mᶜ has no note.

21:22   תֶּאְשָׁמוּ

Twice   בֹ   Mp

Judg 21:22; 2 Chr 19:10

JUDGES 21:23

וַיַּעֲשׂוּ־כֵן בְּנֵי בִנְיָמִן וַיִּשְׂאוּ נָשִׁים לְמִסְפָּרָם מִן־הַמְּחֹלְלוֹת אֲשֶׁר גָּזָלוּ וַיֵּלְכוּ וַיָּשׁוּבוּ אֶל־נַחֲלָתָם וַיִּבְנוּ אֶת־הֶעָרִים וַיֵּשְׁבוּ בָּהֶם׃

21:23   הַמְּחֹלְלוֹת

Unique   ל   Mp

21:23   וַיָּשׁוּבוּ

Six times plene in the Prophets   ו מל בנב   Mp

Com.: See **Judg 8:33**.

JUDGES 21:24

וַיִּתְהַלְּכֹוּ מִשָּׁם בְּנֵי־יִשְׂרָאֵל֙ בָּעֵ֣ת הַהִ֔יא אִ֥ישׁ לְשִׁבְטֹ֖ו וּלְמִשְׁפַּחְתֹּ֑ו וַיֵּצְא֤וּ מִשָּׁם֙ אִ֣ישׁ לְנַחֲלָתֹֽו׃

21:24   וַיִּתְהַלְּכֹוּ מִשָּׁם

Unique   ל   Mp

Com.: The Masorah notes the *sole* occurrence of וַיִּתְהַלְּכֹוּ with מִשָּׁם, to distinguish it from its *three* occurrences without מִשָּׁם.

21:24   וּלְמִשְׁפַּחְתֹּו

Unique   ל   Mp

The number of the verses in the book   סכום הפסוקים של ספר   Mf
is *six-hundred and eighteen*   שש מאות ושמונה עשר